THE GRACE OF LAW

A Study in Puritan Theology

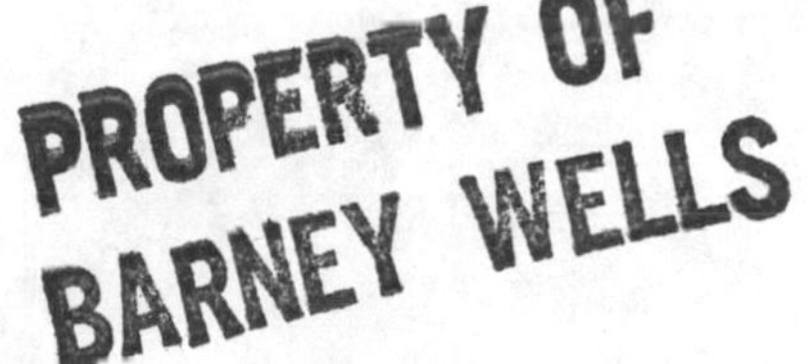

THE GRACE OF LAW

A Study in Puritan Theology

by

ERNEST F. KEVAN

BAKER BOOK HOUSE
Grand Rapids, Michigan

Paperback edition issued by
Baker Book House
1976

ISBN: 0-8010-5373-0

Reprinted in the
United States of America
with the permission of
The Carey Kingsgate Press Limited,
London, England

PHOTOLITHOPRINTED BY CUSHING - MALLOY, INC.
ANN ARBOR, MICHIGAN, UNITED STATES OF AMERICA
1976

This book is gratefully dedicated to

MY WIFE

without whose love and sacrifice the production of this book would not have been possible, and to the memory of

MY FATHER

who taught me so much theology.

CONTENTS

TABLE OF ABBREVIATIONS USED WITH PRIMARY SOURCES

Short titles as used in the footnotes are entered only when reference is made to more than two works by the same author and when the short title differs from the first words of the original title.

AMES, William:	
Epistles of Peter	*An Analyticall Exposition Of both the Epistles of the Apostle Peter.*
BALL, John:	
Covenant of Grace	*A Treatise of the Covenant of Grace: . . . clearly discovered.*
Grounds of Christian Religion	*A Short Treatise Containing all the Principal Grounds of Christian Religion.*
Of Faith	*A Treatise of Faith.*
BAXTER, Richard:	
Apology	*Richard Baxter's Apology . . . and an Admonition of Mr W. Eyre.*
Confession	*Rich: Baxter's Confesssion of his Faith, Especially concerning the Interest of Repentance and sincere Obedience to Christ, in our Justification and Salvation.*
Nonconformists Ministry	*An Apology for the Nonconformists Ministry.*
BOLTON, Robert:	
Afflicted Consciences	*Instructions for a Right Comforting Afflicted Consciences.*
Assise Sermons	*Two Sermons Preached at Northampton at two several Assises there.*
Comfortable Walking	*Some Generall Directions for a Comfortable Walking with God.*
True Happinesse	*A Discourse about the State of True Happinesse.*
BROOKS, Thomas:	
Glory of Christianity	*The Crown and Glory of Christianity.*
BURGESS, Anthony:	
Justification	*The True Doctrine of Justification.*

BURROUGHS, Jeremiah:	
Evil of Evils	*A Treatise of the Evil of Evils, or the Exceeding Sinfulness of Sin.*
BYFIELD, Richard:	
Sabbath	*The Doctrine of the Sabbath Vindicated.*
CHARNOCK, Stephen:	
Attributes	*Discourse on the existence and attributes of God.*
Conviction of Sin	*A Discourse of Conviction of Sin.*
Efficient of Regeneration	*A Discourse of the Efficient of Regeneration.*
Nature of Regeneration	*A Discourse of the Nature of Regeneration.*
CHAUNCY, Isaac:	
Fresh Antidote	*Alexipharmacon. A Fresh Antidote against Neonomian Bane and Poyson to the Protestant Religion.*
DENNE, Henry:	
Man of Sin Discovered	*Antichrist unmasked in two Treatises. . . . The second, The Man of Sinne discovered in Doctrine.*
DOWNAME, George:	
Duties	*An Abstract of the Duties Commanded . . . in the Law of God.*
Justification	*A Treatise of Justification.*
FLAVEL, John:	
Mental Errors	*Πλανηλογία, A Succinct and Seasonable Discourse of the Occasions . . . and Remedies of Mental Errors.*
Personal Reformation	*The Reasonableness of Personal Reformation and the Necessity of Conversion.*
GOODWIN, Thomas:	
Christian's Growth	*The Trial of a Christian's Growth.*
Ephesians	*Exposition of Ephesians.*
Glory of the Gospel	*A Discourse of the Glory of the Gospel.*
Justifying Faith	*The Objects and Acts of Justifying Faith.*
Mediator	*Of Christ the Mediator.*
Relapsing	*The Folly of Relapsing after Peace Spoken.*
GREENHAM, Richard:	
Sabboth	*A Treatise of the Sabboth.*

HOPKINS, Ezekiel:	
Conscience	*A Discourse of the Nature, Corruption and Renewing of the Conscience.*
Galatians	*Sermon on Galatians III. 10.*
John	*Sermon on John VII. 19.*
Lord's Prayer	*A Practical exposition on the Lord's Prayer.*
Ten Commandments	*Exposition of the Ten Commandments.*
MANTON, Thomas:	
Ephesians	*Sermon on Ephesians II. 10.*
James	*The Epistle of James.*
Lord's Prayer	*A Practical Exposition of the Lord's Prayer.*
Mark	*Sermon on Mark IX. 49.*
Psalms	*Sermon on Psalm XXXII. 1, 2.*
Thessalonians	*Sermons on the Second Chapter of the Second Epistle to the Thessalonians.*
OWEN, John:	
Dominion of Sin and Grace	*A Treatise of the Dominion of Sin and Grace.*
Gospel Vindicated	*Vindiciae Evangelicae: or the Mystery of the Gospel vindicated.*
Holy Spirit	*Πνευματολογία or, a discourse concerning the Holy Spirit.*
Indwelling Sin	*The Nature, Power, Deceit, and Prevalency of the Remainders of Indwelling Sin in Believers.*
Justification	*The Doctrine of Justification by Faith, through the imputation of the Righteousness of Christ.*
PERKINS, William:	
Of Conscience	*A Discourse of Conscience.*
Galatians	*A Commentarie, or Exposition upon the Five First Chapters of the Epistle to the Galatians.*
RUTHERFORD, Samuel:	
Triumph of Faith	*The Tryal and Triumph of Faith.*
SIBBES, Richard:	
Philippians	*Exposition of Philippians III.*
Precious Promises	*Yea and Amen: Or, Precious Promises.*

TAYLOR, Thomas:

Christian Practice	*A threefold Alphabet of Rules concerning Christian Practice.*

TRAILL, Robert:

Galatians	*Six Sermons on Important Subjects from Galatians II. 21.*
Justification Vindicated	*A Vindication of the Protestant Doctrine concerning Justification . . . from the unjust charge of Antinomianism.*
Throne of Grace	*Sermons concerning the Throne of Grace.*

FOREWORD

IN this age which seems to be without moral standards, and in which the words "right" and "wrong" have lost their absoluteness, the necessity for a return to a stable conception of Law is indisputable. This is recognized by educationalists, lawyers, politicians, and all who take a morally healthy view of the needs of mankind. The British Prime Minister, speaking at Brighton on the 14 October, 1961, referred to the need to rekindle at all levels of society "the old faith that makes a clear distinction between right and wrong".[1]

In common with the majority of contemporary Christian writers, J. Drewett perceives the present moral decay to be caused by the neglect of the Law of God. He begins his opening chapter in *The Ten Commandments in the 20th Century* by asking, "Are the commandments obsolete?" and he gives some of the reasons why many people answer this question in the affirmative. Two of these reasons, he says, come from outside the Church and can be traced to (*a*) the shift in ethical thought from the negative to the positive, and (*b*) the breakdown of belief in an objective moral Law. A third reason, and one which he regards as coming from within the Church, is found by him in the assumption of many Christian people that the "teaching of Jesus went so far beyond the Law of Moses that the Law is no longer binding upon Christians".[2]

It is at this place in the discussion that the teaching of the Puritans on the Law of God shows itself to be so appropriate to the modern situation. The Puritans stemmed the tide of moral indifference in their day by the use of the Ten Commandments, and it may well be that part of the answer to the modern dilemma is to be found by listening again to the voice of the Puritans and receiving the truth to which they bore testimony.[3]

The object of this work is to explore the Puritan teaching on the place which the Law of God must take in the life of a believer and to examine it for the contribution that it may make towards a true understanding of the Christian doctrine of sanctification.

After a delimitation of the area of inquiry, the Puritan material is analysed and presented under its main divisions. First, the Puritan recognition of the fact of Law is observed, in which it is shown that Law arises from the Creator-creature relation and is of the very essence of man's spiritual experience. This is followed by an exposition

1. Reported in *The Daily Telegraph*, 16 October, 1961.
2. Op. cit., 1941, pp. 9–12.
3. Cf. A. F. Mitchell and J. Struthers, *Minutes*, 1874, Introduction, p. lxvii.

of the relation of Law to sin and of the place which Law holds in the purposes of God's grace. The next chapter contains an examination of the Puritan teaching on the way in which Christ is the "end of the law", and by means of the important distinction between the ideas of "law" and "covenant" shows that there is no abrogation of the Law, either by the sin of man or by the grace of God. Attention is then drawn to the consistency of this truth with the continuance of moral obligation, and the sanction which is thereby given to the Christian practice of Law-keeping. Finally, the Puritans are shown to have defended their views against the charge of legalism by their doctrine of evangelical ability and spiritual freedom. Legalism is abhorrent to God and foreign to the Gospel, nevertheless only by a Divinely-given delight in the Law of God can sanctification be rescued from the realm of the merely subjective and emotional.

Critical discussion of the material presented has been conducted, in the main, by the use of arguments drawn from the Puritans themselves and in accordance with their own presuppositions. This has had the advantage of ensuring that the Puritan views have been seen in the light of their own times and without the distortion caused by the entry of anachronistic critical factors. Accompanying this contemporary discussion, there is a critical appraisal implicit in the analysis of the material itself, an analysis which shows that the Puritan arguments hold together in a coherent and consistent unity. In the conclusion the doctrine is assessed in the light of recent critical thought.

The title of this book may seem to require justification, but it is my hope that this has been sufficiently provided in the substance of the work.

I desire to record my thanks to the Rev. G. F. Nuttall, M.A., D.D., for the strength of his encouragement and for his guidance in the historical aspects of this study. I want also to acknowledge the helpfulness and courtesy received from the authorities of the Library of the British Museum and Dr Williams's Library, and particularly to pay tribute to the value of the fine collection of Puritan works in the Library of New College, London. I have much appreciated the privilege of access to these rare treasures.

To my wife, who typed the complete manuscript twice over in its preliminary stages, and to Miss J. Williamson, who did the final typing so perfectly, I express my very special gratitude.

This work has been approved by the University of London for the award of the Degree of Doctor of Philosophy.

ERNEST F. KEVAN.

London Bible College
1963

Introduction

THE PURITAN SCENE

Synopsis

A. THE PURITANS
- (i) *An ecclesiastical term*
- (ii) *A religious term*
- (iii) *Puritan preachers*

B. THE LAW OF GOD
- (i) *The authority of Scripture*
- (ii) *The moral Law*

C. ANTINOMIANISM
- (i) *Origin of Antinomianism*
- (ii) *Antinomian doctrine and practice*
- (iii) "*The chiefest Champions*" *of Antinomianism*

D. THE DEFENDERS OF PURITAN ORTHODOXY

E. CONTROVERSY
- (i) *Difficulties and prejudices*
- (ii) *The writings*

F. PERIOD UNDER REVIEW

G. THEOLOGICAL BACKGROUND
- (i) *Indebtedness to the Reformers*
- (ii) *Covenant Theology*
- (iii) *Anglican affinities*
- (iv) *British origin*
- (v) *Delimitations*

H. PATTERN OF THE INQUIRY

Introduction

THE PURITAN SCENE

It contains chiefly some friendly debates of some opinions, which have been maintained against the Law, wherein I have so endeavoured to hold up the Law, as not to intrench upon the liberties of Grace, and so to establish Grace, as not to make void the Law, nor to discharge beleevers of any dutie they owe to God or man.[1]

THIS is how Samuel Bolton describes his book, *The True Bounds of Christian Freedome*, and these words aptly express the constructive endeavours of the Puritans in their discussion of the place of the Law in Christian life. It is not entirely accidental that Samuel Bolton uses the words "bounds" in the title of his work, for when Anthony Burgess compares the Law and the Gospel he uses the same word and says, "It's one of the hardest taskes in all divinity, to give them their bounds, and then to cleare how the Apostle doth oppose them, and how not."[2]

A. THE PURITANS

Who were the Puritans? And what was a Puritan? Puritanism must be understood in two ways: first, as the endeavour to effect thoroughgoing reforms of ecclesiastical practice, and, secondly, as the attempt at a godly way of life.

(i) *An ecclesiastical term*

As an ecclesiastical term, it symbolizes the efforts of those who believed firmly in the maintenance of "one National Church in England", but who at the same time desired that Church "to be reformed after the model of Geneva".[3] The termini *a quo* and *ad quem* of this ecclesiastical movement have been the subject of historical discussion, but the period can be described as the century between the Acts of Uniformity, 1559, and 1662. It is better not to project the period either backwards or forwards, but to restrict it to that movement for Church reform whose "first great leader was Thomas Cartwright and whose last was Richard Baxter."[4] But, even within its

1. Samuel Bolton, *True Bounds*, 1645, The Epistle Dedicatory.
2. *Vindiciae Legis*, 1646, p. 5.
3. H. G. Wood, Article "Puritanism", 1918, *ERE*, X. 507; cf. T. Fuller, *Church History*, 1655, in *Works*, II. 474, 475.
4. H. G. Wood, ibid. Thomas Cartwright died in 1603, and Richard Baxter in 1691.

ecclesiastical connotation, the term is capable of a narrower and a wider meaning. J. B. Marsden, for example, interprets it narrowly, and contends that "Puritan" must be reserved exclusively for those within the Church,[5] and that it should not, in this early period at least, be given to the seceding minorities who became dissenters.[6] He does not carry the Puritans so far back as does H. G. Wood, but traces the beginning of what he calls "the doctrinal puritans" to about 1618, and describes them as the evangelical party in the Church of England who were against Laud's "high church" notions.[7] He holds that they disappeared in 1642, when the "church" disappeared, and argues that at that time the Puritans passed from the scene "and henceforth the history becomes that of nonconformists, not of the puritans properly so termed".[8] On this principle of definition, he likewise maintains that "the independents were not strictly puritans".[9] M. M. Knappen differs considerably from J. B. Marsden, and argues for the wider application of the term. He provides his readers with a diagram which shows a primary division of Puritans into Episcopalian Puritans (later, Low Church), Presbyterian and Independent (Congregational), and he follows this with a secondary division of the Independents into Non-Separatist[10] and Separatist.[11] This suffices for a glimpse at what a contemporary writer calls "my Ecclesiasticall puritan".[12]

(ii) *A religious term*

When the wider application of the term "Puritan" is accepted, and when the viewpoint of the late seventeenth century is reached, the term needs to be understood as including, not only those ministers who were eventually suspended, deprived, or ejected, but also many others who were theologically near them, both within and without the Anglican fold. At this stage, the idea of Puritanism overleaps the earlier ecclesiastical connotation and becomes religious.[13]

5. "Puritan Anglicans", J. D. Eusden, *Puritans, Lawyers, and Politics*, 1958, p. 13.
6. J. B. Marsden, *Early Puritans*, 1850, p. 54. Edward Dowden justifies the title of his book, *Puritan and Anglican*, 1900, by saying, "The Puritan writers with whom I deal are such as to render the title 'Puritan and Anglican' not inexact, although many of the Puritan party were loyal members of the Anglican Communion." Preface. See his discussion of the question, "Would an Anglican Bunyan have been possible?" op. cit., p. 232.
7. J. B. Marsden, *Early Puritans*, p. 325.
8. Op. cit., p. 385.
9. *Later Puritans*, 1852, p. 294.
10. Cf. J. D. Eusden, op. cit., p. 14.
11. M. M. Knappen, *Tudor Puritanism*, 1939, p. 493; and Preface, p. viii. See an excellent discussion by A. S. P. Woodhouse, in *Puritanism and Liberty*, 1938, Introduction, pp. 35–8; and F. J. Powicke, Article "Puritanism", 1904, *PD*, pp. 558, 559.
12. Anon. *Discourse concerning Puritans*, 1641, p. 11.
13. See J. D. Eusden, op. cit., p. 18, "We must look to theology ... and the attendant pattern of life."

This more general use of the word, says H. G. Wood, "cannot be ignored in any account of the subject",[14] for "after the failure of their ecclesiastical hopes . . . the Puritans did not cease to influence England".[15] Puritanism came to embody the ideal of a holy community, and was characterized by deep reverence for God and profound moral earnestness of life. "Puritanism was something more than a system of doctrine," says A. F. Mitchell, "It was above all . . . a life, a real, earnest, practical life."[16] It was not unassociated with the love of freedom, which was so prominent a feature of the seventeenth century,[17] but even this political and social aspect of Puritan testimony must be seen to spring from religious convictions.

(iii) *Puritan preachers*

Defeated in ecclesiastical politics, the Puritans became the theologians of the Christian life. As they were not allowed to reform the Church from without, they gave themselves to the ministry of reforming it from within. They reasoned that, if the Church was to be pure—if it was to contain within it only those who could show evidence of the life of God within them—then attention had to be given to the things which belonged to vital godliness. This was the stage at which the Puritan preachers emerged. They abandoned the political platform, mounted the pulpit, and undertook the task of creating a new understanding of spiritual things in a nation that had not fully awakened to the full implications of the Scriptural principles of the Reformation. United in this serious purpose of purifying the Church of God from within, they constituted a holy brotherhood, but this "brotherhood of spiritual preachers never . . . entered upon anything like formal corporate organization. It was at no time anything more than an association of ministers of the church united by personal ties and common purpose".[18] The Puritans dedicated their energies to the demands of the pulpit, and spared no pains in their preaching and writing, their writings being mostly the reproduction of their sermons, "or works of edification directly derived from sermons".[19] Puritanism cannot be understood apart from "the Puritan pulpit",[20] for its preachers did not give mere studies in doctrine, but laid "stress upon practical exegesis, or the application of the Scriptures to the Christian life", for which reason, "the great majority of their writings are upon themes comprehended by the term *Practical*

14. Op. cit., p. 507.
15. Op. cit., p. 512.
16. *Westminster Assembly*, 1883, pp. 6, 7.
17. Cf. W. Haller, *Rise of Puritanism*, 1938, p. 10.
18. W. Haller, *Rise of Puritanism*, p. 54.
19. W. Haller, op. cit., pp. 25, 36, 37.
20. W. Haller, op. cit., Preface, p. vii.

Divinity".[21] The Puritan preachers gathered round them congregations of earnest believers who desired to live in a manner well-pleasing to God. These believers—many of them obscure persons—"attempted a greater sobriety of life than was customary in Elizabethan England".[22] An anonymous author provides a picture of the godly behaviour of most of the Puritans when he says,

> The most ordinary badge of Puritans is their more religious and conscionable conversation, than that which is seene in other mens: and why this should make them odious or suspected of hypocrisie amongst honest and charitable men, I could never yet learne.[23]

He put the Puritans to the test, and found them zealous in godliness and without any trace of hypocrisy;[24] and, although not himself a Puritan[25] he expressed his indignation that "now nothing is so monstrous, which is not branded upon Puritans".[26]

Godliness always provokes resentment in those who do not desire it or whose lives thereby are condemned, and believers who endeavoured to live the godly life in the seventeenth century were contemptuously dubbed "Puritans". "The world is come to that wretched passe, and height of prophanenesse, that even honestie and sanctification, is many times odiously branded by the nick-name of Puritanisme."[27] If an ungodly man turns godly and begins to read the Scriptures and pray in his family, "in a word to turne Christian; Oh! then He is an arrant Puritan, a Precisian . . . an hypocrite, and all that naught is. . . . Hee was a good fellow, will they say, but hee is now quite gone: a proper man, and of good parts, but his Puritanisme hath mar'd al."[28]

21. C. A. Briggs, *Study of Theology*, 1916, II. 152.
22. H. G. Wood, op. cit., p. 507. See the delightful six-page pamphlet by John Geree on *The Character of an Old English Puritane*, 1646.
23. *Discourse concerning Puritans*, p. 53.
24. Op. cit., p. 7.
25. Op. cit., p. 2.
26. Op. cit., p. 2.
27. Robert Bolton, *True Happinesse*, 1611, p. 132, margin; cf. Richard Baxter's account of the abusive application of the name to his father. *Reliquiae Baxterianae*, 1696, Part I. pp. 2, 3.
28. Robert Bolton, *Afflicted Consciences*, 1631, p. 65. Robert Bolton resents the name, (*True Happinesse*, p. 132) but he himself had in his youth shared in the general contemptuous attitude to the name "Puritan"; B. Brook, *Lives*, 1813, II. 390. The term, having an early connection with the fanaticism of the Cathari, eventually came again to have that kind of connection, as is seen, for example, in the fact that by 1684 the word is used to stand for Antinomian perfectionists. (*Truths Victory*, 1684, p. 66) cf. John Ball, *Power of Godliness*, 1657, pp. 74–8; Robert Bolton, *Three-fold Treatise*, "Selfe-enriching Examination", 1634, p. 201; Samuel Rutherford, *Survey*, Part II. 1648, p. 30; Richard Baxter, *Reliquiae Baxterianae*, Part I. pp. 32, 33. On the origin of the name "Puritan", see M. M. Knappen, *Tudor Puritanism*, pp. 488–90.

B. THE LAW OF GOD

(i) *The authority of Scripture*

A fundamental principle of Puritanism was the recognition of the exclusive authority of Scripture for all things, a recognition which, in turn, drew attention to the significance of the Law of God. The ecclesiastical corruptions of the time led the Puritans to affirm that nothing should be tolerated in the Church which was not authorized by Holy Scripture.[29] When the Puritans declined to conform to the Elizabethan settlement or to acquiesce in other ecclesiastical compromises, they based their refusal solely on the Law they found in Scripture. This acknowledgment of the authority of the Law of God affected the attitude of the Puritans to the civil law. How far was the Christian obliged to obey the magistrate? What should the Christian do when the law of the land appeared to conflict with the Law of God? The Puritans affirmed that no king or magistrate could command their consciences, but they also concurred that it was normally lawful to obey human laws out of respect for those which are Divine—and for the same reason it was sometimes lawful to disobey them. But, as the masters of practical divinity, the major concern of the Puritans was that of the moral Law in its relation to the saving grace of God and the subsequent life of the believer.

(ii) *The moral Law*

The place occupied by the moral Law of God is observable in every department of theology, and particularly of Puritan theology. Sin is the transgression of Law, the death of Christ is the satisfaction of Law, justification is the verdict of Law,[30] and sanctification is the believer's fulfilment of the Law. It is in the realm of the doctrine of sanctification that the Puritan convictions about the Law assumed their special significance, and one of their most keenly debated questions was whether the Law still possessed commanding authority over the believer. The majority of the Puritans answered this question affirmatively, and it may, not unreasonably, be claimed that the

29. W. H. G. Thomas criticizes the Puritans for this, *Principles of Theology*, 1930, p. 284; and H. R. McAdoo charges them with "Bibliolatry", *Caroline Moral Theology*, 1949, p. 6. E. Dowden says, "The cardinal principle of Hooker's Puritan opponents was the sole and exclusive authority of Scripture", *Puritan and Anglican*, p. 81, and, despite the fact that this was essential Protestantism, it was precisely in this that they were "opponents". "For the Puritans", writes J. D. Eusden, "the Bible was the primary law book", op. cit., p. 120.

30. It was the view of the Puritans that the right preaching of the Gospel was dependent upon a true conception of the relation of the Law to the promise; but there was some division among them on the indiscriminate offer of salvation to men without reference to conviction of sin by the Law of God.

authority of Law as the principle of the life of the believer was central to the distinctively Puritan concept of Christian experience. "The true Puritan stood ever in the great Taskmaster's eye. He learned to fear God and found that he had nothing else to fear."[31]

C. ANTINOMIANISM

In the agitated thought-world of the seventeenth century there were many cross-currents of theological opinion; hence, it is not surprising to discover that the Puritan view of the Law of God met considerable challenge. The controversy that ensued gave rise to the use of party-names, and at this late stage it is impossible to conduct any discussion of the controversy without their use. (1) On the extreme right were those who maintained the necessity of Law-keeping to such a degree that they were regarded by some of their contemporaries as forsaking the Gospel altogether and reverting to a doctrine of salvation by good works. These teachers—found entirely outside of Puritanism—were occasionally called "Nomists", from their excessive adherence to Law. (2) On the extreme left were those who maintained that the believer was completely free from all obligation to the Law, and who held that any concession to legal duty was an infringement of free grace. These teachers—found within Puritanism, but associated more particularly with some of the smaller sects—were usually called "Antinomists", or "Antinomians", from their excessive repudiation of Law.[32] (3) Those who endeavoured to stand clear of both these extremes were—in a somewhat question-begging manner—occasionally described as the "orthodox", or more usually by the name "Puritans". The fact that the main body of Puritans occupied this central position may perhaps justify the reservation of the title to them in this present study.[33]

(i) *Origin of Antinomianism*

Antinomianism was the theological contrary to Puritanism in its

31. H. G. Wood, op. cit., p. 513.
32. Thomas Gataker says they were called "Antinomians or Antinomists" from "their opposition to the mandatory and obligatory power of the Law morall, or the Decalog", *God's Eye*, 1645, p. 2. Cf. Ephraim Pagitt, *Heresiography*, 1645, p. 88; Henry Burton, *Law and Gospel Reconciled*, 1631, The Epistle Dedicatory; and John Graile who, in sweet moderation, speaks of some "whom the Orthodox, not out of malice, but for distinction sake, and for the due desert of some of their Tenents do call Antinomians". *Conditions in the Covenant of Grace*, 1655, p. 25.
33. In the following pages, the exclusive use of the term Puritan to indicate the "orthodox" does not deny the historical right of the Antinomians also to be called Puritans. The distinction in the names, however, may be regarded as endorsed by Samuel Rutherford in such a sentence as "Antinomians shall wish to die Puritans", *Survey*, Part II. p. 30.

doctrine of the Law of God in Christian experience. Apart from its early appearance in New Testament times,[34] and in Valentinian Gnosticism, the formal rise of Antinomianism has usually been associated with Johannes Agricola,[35] sometimes called Islebius, an active leader in the Lutheran Reformation.[36] In his search for some effective principle by which to combat the doctrine of salvation by works, Agricola denied that the believer was in any way obliged to fulfil the moral Law. In the Disputation with Luther at Wittenberg (1537), Agricola is alleged to have said that a man was saved by faith alone, without regard to his moral character.[37] These views of Agricola were denounced by Luther[38] as a caricature of the Gospel, but in spite of this, the Antinomians made repeated appeal to Luther's writings and claimed his support for their opinions.[39] This claim, however, is based merely on certain ambiguities in Luther's expressions, and general misunderstanding of the Reformer's teaching.

So far as England is concerned, the occasion of Antinomianism has been found by most modern writers in the political, social and spiritual ferment of the times;[40] but Richard Baxter makes the rueful comment that, "Antinomianism rose among us from our obscure Preaching of Evangelical Grace, and insisting too much on tears and terrors."[41]

34. *Romans* vi. 1–2.
35. 1492–1566.
36. "The first man that appeared under the name of an Antinomian was Joannes Islebius Agricola a Schoole-master or Reader of divinity in Elsleben". Samuel Rutherford, *Survey*, Part I. p. 68.
37. J. M. Sterrett, Article "Antinomianism," 1908, *ERE*, I. 581, 582.
38. The origin of the name "Antinomian" is attributed to Luther. See S. Cave, *The Christian Way*, 1949, p. 122.
39. Neither Luther nor Melanchthon is entirely unambiguous on this subject. See J. M. Sterrett, op. cit., pp. 581, 582. On the one hand, Samuel Rutherford, in *Survey*, Part I, reproduces "A Treatise against Antinomians written in an Epistolary way, by D. Martin Luther, translated out of the high Dutch originall; containing the minde of Luther against Antinomians", and he spends eighty-three pages in the exposition of Luther's denial of Antinomian tenets, op. cit., pp. 69–163; while, on the other hand, J. Fletcher echoes the common allegations about Luther's "antinomian fits", *Fourth Check to Antinomianism*, in *Works*, 1772, II. 135, and attributes the "antinomianism" of the Synod of Dort to "what Luther's solifidian zeal had begun, and what Calvin's predestinarian mistakes had carried on." *An Equal Check to Pharisaism and Antinomianism*, Part I, in *Works*, 1774, II. 351. See, however, J. H. Blunt, Article "Antinomianism", *DDNT*, 1871, p. 31, where he attributes Antinomianism, not to Calvin's doctrine of predestination, but to his doctrine of imputed righteousness. On Luther's doctrine of the Law of God, see below, pp. 38–39.
40. A. F. Mitchell, *Westminster Assembly*, p. 343; S. W. Carruthers, *Everyday Work of the Westminster Assembly*, 1943, pp. 86–9; J. B. Marsden, *Early Puritans*, pp. 52, 53; and A. S. P. Woodhouse, *Puritanism and Liberty*, Introduction.
41. *Nonconformists Ministry*, 1681, p. 226.

(ii) *Antinomian doctrine and practice*

The main object of the moderate Antinomians was to glorify Christ; but, failing to understand the true relation between "law" and "grace", they extolled the latter at the expense of the former. The issue raised by the Antinomians had its origin in the wide separation which they made between the Old and the New Testaments. They were unable to see that the Old Covenant was truly a Covenant of Grace, though differently presented from the New Covenant, and that the position of believers under the Old and New Covenants was the same. In some ways, it appears that the Antinomians brought themselves into difficulty by thinking of "Law" as if it were an entity to be done away, and of "Grace" as an entity taking its place; but this hypostatizing of "Law" and "Grace" was false, for in salvation it is *God* acting in His Law and *God* acting in His grace. Another difficulty to the Antinomians was their inability to make a clear enough distinction between justification and sanctification. This is particularly true of John Eaton throughout almost the whole of *Honey-combe*.[42] Some of the questions which agitated their minds were whether the Covenant of Sinai was a covenant of works or of grace,[43] and whether justification was to be evidenced by sanctification.[44]

Although some writers, such as Thomas Edwards (*Gangraena*), Samuel Rutherford and Richard Baxter, wrote violently against the Antinomians, it is nevertheless only fair to say that most of the extravagances of behaviour, which they so rightly denounced, made their appearance not in England, but in New England. Robert Traill found the Antinomians strict in their church discipline and virtuous in their personal conduct[45] and, having "both opportunity and inclination to inquire", he says, "For all the noise of Antinomianism, I must declare, that I do not know . . . any one Antinomian minister or Christian in London, who is really such as their reproachers paint them out, or such as Luther and Calvin wrote against."[46] It cannot be denied, however, that many fanatical persons were found among the

42. See below, p. 26.
43. See below, Chapter III.
44. For a general account of the theological aspects of Antinomianism, see J. M. Sterrett, op. cit.; A. H. Newman, Article "Antinomianism and Antinomian Controversies", 1908, *S–H: E R K*, I. 196–201; J. H. Blunt, op. cit., pp. 30, 31.
45. *Justification Vindicated*, 1692, in *Works* I. 254. This is the verdict of Richard Baxter also, *Scripture Gospel Defended*, "Defence of Christ and Free Grace", 1690, p. 55, "far from wicked".
46. Op. cit., p. 281. E. Calamy's accusation of them as "Patrons of free vice under the mask of free grace" is grossly unfair. *Sermon before the Lords*, Christmas Day, 1644; qu. by C. E. Whiting, *English Puritanism*, 1931, p. 268, who seems too readily to accept the second-hand criticism of the Antinomians.

Antinomians,[47] and that Antinomians "Doctrinall" tended to become Antinomians "practicall".[48]

(iii) *"The chiefest Champions" of Antinomianism*

The leaders of the Antinomian party were named in a petition sent to the House of Commons by the Westminster Assembly on 10 August, 1643, when "the books complained of were Crisp's 'Christ Alone Exalted', Eaton's 'Honeycomb', 'The Dangerous Dish', 'The Doctrine and Conversation of John the Baptist', and 'Faith, a Sermon on Rev. iii. 18'. The individuals mentioned were Randall, Batt, Lancaster, Simpson, Haydon, Emerson, Erbury, Towne, and Penn."[49] Three of these, "Mr Randall, Mr Simpson, Mr Lancaster" are designated "three grand patrons and ring-leaders of this faction, what time they were convented before the worthy Committee of the honourable house of Commons in the Star-chamber".[50] Samuel Rutherford mentions "Ro Towne, who coldly refuteth Doctor Taylor", "M. Eaton in his Honey comb, and Saltmarsh of late falne off conformity to Antinomianisme, and Tob. Crisp, a godly man (as is thought) But Melancholious, who having builded much on qualifications and signes, fell to the other extremity of no signes of sanctification at all", and he adds the names of Henry Denne, William Dell and Paul Hobson.[51] One of the fascinating books of seventeenth century gossip is *Gangraena*, by Thomas Edwards, who declares that "the full Relation of the time-serving and Innovations of Denn, . . . Saltmarsh, . . . *cum multis aliis*, would make a new book".[52] With his customary contempt, Richard Baxter says, "It was formerly a very rare thing to meet with a man of Learning or considerable Judgement, of that way: What men had Dr Taylor to deal with? Dr Crisp, Eaton, Town, were the chiefest Champions since, whom Mr Burgess, Mr Geree, Mr Bedford have confuted. At last Den, Paul Hobson, Mr Saltmarsh took the Chair: The later strangely cryed up by many ignorant souls, and his weakness laid open by that Excellent, Learned, Reverend Mr Gataker."[53] Who were these men and what were they like?

47. Henry Burton sees that theological Antinomianism leads to political Antinomianism; and warns Charles I to take action against "these sonnes of Belial thus undermining the Kings Throne", *Law and Gospel Reconciled*, The Epistle Dedicatory.
48. Cf. John Sedgwick, *Antinomianisme Anatomized*, 1643, pp. 29f. Some of the evidence about the practical Antinomians, often called "Ranters", will be found in William Penn, Preface to George Fox's *Journal*, I. xxv; Samuel Rutherford, *Survey*, Part I. pp. 1–31; J. B. Marsden, *Later Puritans*, pp. 223, 224; and H. W. Schneider, *Puritan Mind*, 1931, p. 65.
49. S. W. Carruthers, *Everyday Work of the Westminster Assembly*, p. 86.
50. Thomas Gataker, *God's Eye*, To the Reader.
51. *Survey*, Part I. p. 193.
52. *Gangraena*, 1646, p. 75 (faulty pagination).
53. *Apology*, "Admonition of Mr William Eyre", 1654, Preface.

John Eaton[54] is described by Thomas Gataker as "the first founder of this faction among us",[55] and he speaks, later, of Antinomians as "those, who from one of the first Authours thereof are commonly called Eatonists."[56] Stephen Geree refers to him as "their fore-mentioned *Antesignanus* or Standard-bearer".[57]

> The first Antinomian among us (that I can hear of) was one Mr John Eaton who had been a Scholler of mine, and afterwards was Curate to Mr Wright, Parson of Catharine Colemā neare Algate, he was for his errors imprisoned in the Gate-house at Westminster. There is a booke set forth in his name, called the *Hony-comb of free Justification by Christ alone*, collected (as hee pretendeth) out of the meere authority of Scriptures, and common and unanimous consent of the faithfull Interpreters of Gods mysteries upon the same: the maine subject of which booke is to prove that God doth not, will not, nor cannot see any sin in any of his justified children.[58]

Clashing with the authorities, he suffered "much hurry" and "divers imprisonments".[59] He was deprived of his living at Wickham Market, Suffolk, in 1619, as "an incorrigible divulger of errors and false opinions", and his writings were forbidden to be published in his lifetime. In spite of this, one of his biographers can say, "Though he committed some mistakes, in his assertions about the doctrines of grace, he was, upon the whole, 'a pattern of faith, holiness, and cheerfulness in his sufferings, to future generations'."[60]

Tobias Crisp[61] was a moderate man, despite the fact that Antinomianism is sometimes called "Crispianism".[62] He is said to have begun his ministry "in the legal way", being himself "unblameable in his life and conversation"; but, later, having been brought to a knowledge of the doctrines of grace, he became exceedingly zealous in their propagation. One of his biographers states that his doctrine was "falsely charged with Antinomianism: though the innocency and harmlessness of his life, and his fervency in goodness, . . . was a manifest practical argument to confute the slanders of Satan, against the most holy faith which he preached".[63] Tobias Crisp had many detractors and many defenders, and those who defended him from

54. c. 1575–1641.
55. *God's Eye*, To the Reader.
56. *God's Eye*, p. 2.
57. *Plaine Confutation*, 1644, p. 5. Cf. A. Wood, Athenae Oxon, 1691, III, col. 21.
58. Ephraim Pagitt, *Heresiography*, p. 89.
59. John Eaton, *Honey-combe*, 1642, To the Reader.
60. B. Brook, *Lives*, II. 466.
61. 1600–1643.
62. E.g. the title of the anonymous book, *Crispianism Unmask'd*, 1693. J. Fletcher speaks of "Crispianity", *Fourth Check* in *Works*, II. 29.
63. J. Gill, "Memoirs of Tobias Crisp", in Tobias Crisp, *Works* (ed. Gill), 1832, I. vi.

the charge of Antinomianism pointed to his sermons on *Free-Grace the Teacher of Good Works,* and *The Use of the Law.*[64] Tobias Crisp's opinions so commended themselves to John Gill, two centuries later, that he edited them in 1832, adding footnotes and clearing Tobias Crisp from the accusations brought against him.[65] He was "altogether unblameable in his Conversation", and his "life was so innocent . . . that it seems to be set forth as a manifest practical argument" against the slander of those who would insinuate that his doctrine tended to licentiousness.[66] Despite all that can be said in favour of the orthodoxy of Tobias Crisp, his name has come down in history as "one of the champions of Antinomianism"[67] and it appears that Benjamin Brook is correct when he writes,

> Persons who have embraced sentiments which afterwards appear to them erroneous, often think they can never remove too far from them; and the more remote they go from their former opinions, the nearer they come to the truth. This was unhappily the case with Dr Crisp. His ideas of the grace of Christ had been exceedingly low, and he had imbibed sentiments which produced in him a legal and self-righteous spirit. Shocked at the recollection of his former views and conduct, he seems to have imagined that he could never go far enough from them.[68]

Robert Towne[69] is described by Oliver Heywood as "the famous Antinomian, who writ some books; he was the best scholar and soberest man of that judgment in the country, but something unsound in principles".[70] Like John Eaton and Tobias Crisp, he appears to have been a man of good character. He frequently repudiated the charge of being an Antinomian, and said in reply to Thomas Taylor, "If the Doctor himself had not been foulely guiltie of wresting and perverting our words and meaning . . . he had never numbred us amongst Antinomists, Abrogaters of the Law, Libertines", and he affirms, "We also do condemne and disclaim all that opinion and Sect."[71] Despite Oliver Heywood's praise of his scholarship, Robert

64. These are Sermon 3 (four sermons in one) and Sermon 9, which were added by Samuel Crisp to *Christ Alone Exalted* (1643) in 1690. Cf. Tobias Crisp, *Works*, IV. 25–74, 89–95.
65. B. Brook quotes Daniel Williams as saying that what is exceptionable in his writings "arises chiefly from unqualified expressions, rather than from the author's main design." *Lives*, II. 474.
66. Robert Lancaster, Preface to Tobias Crisp, *Christ Alone Exalted*, in *Works*, I.
67. *DNB*: cf. Isaac Ambrose, *Prima, Media, & Ultima*, "The Middle Things", 1650, p. 14, "Dr. Crisp our open adversary".
68. *Lives*, II. 473.
69. c. 1593–1663.
70. *Diaries*, 1630–1702, IV. 7.
71. *Assertion of Grace*, 1644, pp. 152, 153.

Towne showed himself to be confused in some of his statements, and unable to see the full implication of his own arguments.

John Saltmarsh,[72] from being a zealous advocate of episcopacy and conformity, became an eccentric champion of complete religious liberty; although "his controversial manner is gentle and dignified", being a spiritual writer rather than an eminent theologian.[73] Samuel Rutherford denounced him as a Familist who taught that "A Christian is not bound to the Law as a rule of his Christian walking", and "To act by vertue of, or in obedience to a command is a Law-Worke."[74] Benjamin Brook says more calmly that, "It appears from Mr Saltmarsh's writings, that he was strongly tinged with the principles of antinomianism."[75]

D. THE DEFENDERS OF PURITAN ORTHODOXY

The men who came forward as defenders of Puritan orthodoxy were as colourful personalities as those who opposed them. The list includes such outstanding persons as Thomas Gataker, Samuel Rutherford, and Richard Baxter,[76] together with others such as John Preston, Thomas Taylor, John Ball, John Sedgwick, Anthony Burgess, Edward Elton, and the anonymous author of *The Marrow*.

Thomas Gataker[77] stands out as a giant in the controversies of his time. His academic career was brilliant but short, and it is said that he refused to proceed to a D.D., one reason being that "like Cato the censor, he would rather have people ask why he had no statue than why he had one." His scholarship was vast, and he possessed an astonishing memory. He was a distinguished Hebrew and Greek scholar, "one of the first in Britain to write in defence of the opinion . . . that the Greek of the New Testament was of a different character from that of the classical authors."[78] He exercised a powerful ministry in Rotherhithe for forty-three years, and in 1643 was appointed to the Westminster Assembly, being elected in 1645 to the committee of seven, charged with the preparation of the first draft of the *Confession of Faith*. Thomas Gataker's views on justification, being different from those of many of the Puritans, had something in common with those of Richard Baxter; but, out of respect for the Westminster Assembly, he ordered that his work, *An Antidote*

72. Died 1647.
73. *DNB*, in loc.
74. Samuel Rutherford, *Survey*, Part I. pp. 172, 174.
75. B. Brook, *Lives*, III. 74 and D. Neal, *History of the Puritan*
76. Cf. C. A. Briggs, *Study of Theology*, II. 151–4.
77. 1574–1654.
78. A. F. Mitchell, *Westminster Assembly*, pp. 121, 122.

against Error Concerning Justification, should not be published during his life-time.[79]

Not less interesting than Thomas Gataker was Samuel Rutherford,[80] the staunch Presbyterian of Anwoth and St Andrews, Scotland, of which latter university he was made Principal in 1647. He was "a little fair man", but what he lacked in stature he made up in vigour. He had a brilliant intellect and was a powerful writer, and, "naturally of a hot and fiery temper", he was one of the most perfervid of Scotsmen. In controversy he was "bitter and scurrilous", and by his narrowness "he helped to destroy the presbyterianism which he loved so well." Violently opposed to episcopacy, he was equally antagonistic to independency. His work, *A Free Disputation against Pretended Liberty of Conscience,* has been described as "perhaps the most elaborate defence of persecution which has ever appeared in a protestant country."[81] His most notable contribution to the Antinomian controversy was entitled, *A Survey of the Spiritual Antichrist.* It was described by Richard Baxter as "one of the fullest . . . against the Errors of this Sect, and very usefull to the godly in these seducing times."[82] For his political activities he was cited before Parliament on a charge of treason, but death intervened.[83]

Richard Baxter[84] was a man by himself. He took a full share in the political and ecclesiastical controversies of his time, and he sided with Parliament against the King. His work has been variously estimated, according to the viewpoint from which the judgment is made, but the high quality of his ministry as a pastor of the flock cannot be gainsaid. By his immense labours in Kidderminster (1641–60), his name has become almost a symbol of pastoral faithfulness. Although not academically trained, Richard Baxter read voraciously and wrote voluminously, his works having all the marks of a trained mind. His individualism undoubtedly revealed itself in the theological position he adopted—an individualism which earned for his views the name "Baxterianism".[85] He held a Grotian[86] view of the work of Christ, and accepted many characteristically Arminian[87] ideas,

79. *DNB* and B. Brook, *Lives*, in loc.
80. 1600–61.
81. *DNB*, in loc.
82. *Apology*, "Admonition of Mr William Eyre", Postscript.
83. *DNB*, in loc.
84. 1615–91. "He formed no party but kept a position of his own." G. F. Nuttall, *Holy Spirit*, 1946, p. 169.
85. Cf. the title of the book by Thomas Edwards bearing that name, 1699.
86. *Scripture Gospel Defended*, "Breviate of Justification", 1690, The Preface. Cf. Richard Baxter, *Justification*, 1658, p. 264.
87. *Universal Redemption*, 1694, pp. 110 ff. 186 ff. K. R. Hagenbach says, "His theological system has been termed Baxterian, intermediate between Calvinism and Arminianism", *Christian Doctrines*, 1880, II. 464. Cf. J. I. Packer, "The Thought of Richard Baxter", 1954, pp. 256–70.

although it is probably better to describe him as Amyraldian.[88] One of his opponents, John Crandon, had no hesitation in thinking the worst, and spoke of the "Papists and Arminians, to whom Mr Br not without some fellowes, hath lately Apostatized."[89]

It is with Richard Baxter's views on the Law of God that the present study is particularly concerned, and his arguments are summarized in *Aphorismes*. So strong was his dislike of Antinomianism[90] that he fell into the opposite extreme of Neonomianism,[91] and thus exposed himself to the attacks of many of his orthodox friends. The Neonomianism of Richard Baxter is discussed below,[92] but it must be noticed here that it was this which distinctly separated him from the main stream of Puritan thought. For his own part, Richard Baxter professed to be completely unaware of any departure from the established doctrines. He said that his *Confession* was perused by James Ussher, who "altered not a word in it", and he added, "I got him and Mr Gataker to read it (and it was the last Work that Mr Gataker did in the World, as his Epistle and his Sons shew)."[93] Some of his arguments against Antinomianism were used by him for the support of his own peculiar ideas, but, abstracted from the misdirection he gave them, they are valuable in proof of the continuing use of the Law in the life of the believer.[94]

The anonymous author of *The Marrow* calls for the historian's notice, if only because of the controversy named after his book.[95] The book seems not at first to have attracted much attention, but only gradually to have emerged into public notice by almost fortuitous

88. In *Aphorismes*, 1649, Appendix, p. 164, Richard Baxter says, "The last week I have received Amiraldus ... who hath opened my very heart, almost in my owne words." He became Amyraldian in so far as he denied the "double decree" and asserted universal redemption. J. I. Packer rebuts "the charge that Baxter is vague and inconsistent", and he identifies his distinctive theology "as an improved amyraldism". Op. cit., abstract, p. (g), and pp. 459–62.
89. *Aphorisms Exorized*, 1654, The Epistle Dedicatory; cf. Part I. pp. 272–76. John Crandon obviously goes to excess in his dislike of Richard Baxter. The accusation of being a "Papist" is not to be understood in the literal sense of supposing Richard Baxter to have become a secret member of the Church of Rome (as Richard Baxter himself seems to think John Crandon means, *Reliquiae Baxterianae*, Part I. p. 110), but indicates the milieu of his thinking. Cf. John Owen, *Justification*, 1677, in *Works*, V. 137, 138.
90. D. M. McIntyre, "First Strictures", in *Evangelical Quarterly*, X. 1, January 1938, p. 68, calls him "the hammer of the Antinomians".
91. J. I. Packer says, "Antinomianism was the midwife which finally brought Baxter's system to birth", op. cit., p. 227. This is undoubtedly true, and Richard Baxter tells how he "narrowly escaped" Antinomianism. (*Aphorismes*, Appendix, p. 163).
92. See below pp. 204 ff.
93. *Scripture Gospel Defended*, "Defence of Christ and Free Grace", To the Reader.
94. *DNB*, and many other works.
95. See the comparatively recent discussion by D. M. McIntyre, op. cit.

circumstances. "I found it lying in my friends houses", says John Crandon.[96] Thomas Boston, who championed the book in Scotland, being troubled about the legalism of his preaching, says,

> As I was sitting one day in a house of Simprin, I espied above the window-head two little old books, which when I had taken down, I found entituled, the one *The Marrow of modern divinity*, the other *Christ's blood flowing freely to sinners*. . . . Finding them to point to the subject I was in particular concern about, I brought them both away. The latter, a book of Saltmarsh's, I relished not; and I think I returned it without reading it quite through. The other, being the first part only of the *Marrow*, I relished greatly; and having purchased it at length from the owner, kept it from that time to this day; and it is still to be found among my books.[97]

There can be no doubt about the influence of this work, but few Puritan writings were more misunderstood in later years than this one.[98]

E. CONTROVERSY

(i) *Difficulties and prejudices*

There was considerable misunderstanding and misrepresentation of the Antinomians by those who opposed them. This was caused partly by the "hearsay" reports of Antinomian teaching, which lost nothing in the telling,[99] although it is possible that some of the Antinomian preachers were less restrained in the pulpit than in their writings. The misunderstandings may also have been partly due to the uncertainties of meaning that were inherent in the discussion itself.[100]

96. *Aphorisms Exorized*, Part II. p. 154.
97. *A General Account of my Life*, 1730, pp. 150–52.
98. Richard Baxter ought to have recognized a friend in this book, but he opposed it and spoke of "*The Marrow of Modern Divinity*, which on pretence of Moderation is Antinomian or Libertine, and very injudicious and unsound". *Scripture Gospel Defended*, "Breviate of Justification", The Preface; cf. *Aphorismes*, p. 330, and Appendix, pp. 99–106.
99. For examples of this second-hand reporting, see Thomas Gataker, *God's Eye*, To the Reader, where such generalizations occur as, "one of them in the Pulpit", "averred by not a few, that then heard him", "delivered by him in private, and defended in publike". Robert Towne complains, "They are pleased to mistake the controverted points, and so to quarrel for what we never asserted. ... We decry duties, say they; are against Repentance; teach that the Law is of no use; would cast it out of the Church. But where do they read or finde these?" *Re-assertion*, 1654, Preface, and p. 47.
100. Isaac Chauncy, "But you call that Evangelical, which we call Legal." *Neonomianism Unmask'd*, 1692, Part I. p. 5; Richard Baxter, *End of Doctrinal Controversies*, 1691, pp. 17 f., and *Reliquiae Baxterianae*, Part I. p. 134, "separating the real from the verbal".

The exceptionable Antinomian statements about the perfection of believers were often little more than the indiscreet overflow of thought from their impassioned defence of free grace. As regards ill-considered expressions, J. B. Marsden makes an apt remark when he says of Tobias Crisp's works, "A person skilled in theology will perceive that many of his statements are capable of a sound interpretation. But they misled the ignorant and occasioned grievous errors."[101] This fair statement is true of many of the other Antinomian writers, although it cannot be denied that they did occasionally run to excess.

A further factor in discussions of this kind is that until a heresy arises the indefiniteness of expression of an earlier speaker or writer does not necessarily implicate him in that heresy, and the making of any such charge is an anachronism.[102] Many of Luther's words, for example, need to be construed in the light of Robert Traill's opinion that if men could foresee future controversies they would alter their speech.[103] A recollection of this difficulty may perhaps exonerate the Antinomians from the charge, which Thomas Gataker brings against them, of deliberately abusing the authority of Luther and Calvin.[104]

In accordance with the pattern of seventeenth century intolerance, measures were taken by the authorities to suppress Antinomianism. Thomas Gataker, in a speech in the Westminster Assembly, pressed for Parliamentary action against the Antinomians, and asked, "Is it not high time to require them to be suppressed?"[105] "Gangraena" Edwards declares for no toleration,[106] because it is too long since an example was made.[107] Demanding that magistrates should burn the books of the Antinomians, he exclaims, "O what a burnt-offering, a sweet smelling sacrifice would this be to God."[108] The Westminster Assembly concerned itself with Antinomianism as one of their first duties, and they presented a petition to the Commons who, in turn, and on the same day, appointed a committee to investigate this

101. *Later Puritans*, p. 227. J. Gill's edition of the *Works* of Tobias Crisp, was specially produced to indicate the possibilities of a "sound" interpretation of Tobias Crisp's language.
102. Isaac Chauncy, *Rejoynder*, 1693, p. 45.
103. *Justification Vindicated*, in *Works*, I. 262. Cf. Robert Towne, *Re-assertion*, p. 18, 19.
104. *God's Eye*, Preface. Against John Eaton: "He abuseth divers places of Luther, Calvin and other worthy Divines, who in all likelihood never once dreamed of this his fancy."
105. S. W. Carruthers, *Everyday Work of the Westminster Assembly*, p. 90.
106. *Gangraena*, p. 119.
107. Op. cit., p. 147.
108. Op. cit., p. 171. The demands of Thomas Edwards were adopted by the authorities, and some of the Antinomians were imprisoned and their books burned.

danger.[109] Keen debates were conducted in the Assembly at numerous sessions in January and February, 1645, on the Law of God and on Christian liberty.[110]

In addition to the public action that was taken against the Antinomians, there were many irresponsible accusations of heresy, joined with colourful language.[111] There was much point-scoring which did not materially advance the discussion.[112] Sometimes these pamphlets were marked by the lavish employment of abusive epithets, but as the majority of pamphleteers employed the same sort of weapons nobody seemed to be greatly disturbed.[113] It scarcely needs to be said that by those on the right the Puritans were called "Libertines", and by those on the left they were called "Legalists". Some of those who were embroiled in the controversies pleaded for a dropping of all such names, but nevertheless fell into the use of them. Their opponents retorted that this desire to be relieved of the name was due to a deceitful intention to avoid the implications of their views.[114] In the various heresiographies[115] of the time, the Antinomians were made to figure prominently.[116] Samuel Rutherford was the most vitriolic of all the opponents of Antinomianism and, unhappily, had no scruples about ignoring the distinction between moderate Antinomians and the fanatical extremists whom he denounced.[117] He put them all together with the Katharoi (called Puritans), who taught that regenerate men could not sin. On the title page of *A Survey of the Spiritual Antichrist*,

109. *Journal of the House of Commons*, 10 August, 1643, p. 201; cf. S. W. Carruthers, op. cit., p. 86.
110. A. F. Mitchell and J. Struthers, *Minutes*, pp. 177–211.
111. There is some humour in John Crandon who, having referred to Richard Baxter's way of deprecating the intelligence of his opponents, says, "Who can abstain from laughter, to see so great a Nimrod as Mr Baxter, hunting, with no lesse weapon then Hercules his Club, a nest of wrens to death?" *Aphorisms Exorized*, Part I, p. 263. Richard Baxter's description of John Crandon's work is equally interesting. He calls it a "dish adorned with the flowers of Billingsgate Rhetorick", *Apology*, "Admonition of Mr William Eyre", Postscript.
112. Robert Towne says to Anthony Burgess, "You are better skilled in tying knots, then in unloosing any", *Re-assertion*, p. 124.
113. Not all the writers were violent, and A. F. Mitchell points out that Thomas Gataker was notable for the "gentle spirit" of his share in the Antinomian controversy. *Westminster Assembly*, p. 122.
114. Thomas Gataker, *Antinomianism*, 1652, p. 34. Richard Baxter might have been inspired by this escape-motive when he said—albeit quite truly—that the "greatest enemy ... is mens studying onely names and words, instead of things". *Aphorismes*, To the Reader.
115. "The famous drag-nets of heresy", R. M. Jones, *Spiritual Reformers*, 1928, p. 254.
116. Thomas Edwards, *Gangraena*, p. 36, charges the Antinomians with one hundred and seventy-six errors, ranging from a denial of the Trinity to eating blackpuddings; Ephraim Pagitt, *Heresiography*; Thomas Welde, *Rise, reigne, and ruine*, 1644; Samuel Rutherford, *Survey*, Part I; Richard Baxter, *Scripture Gospel Defended*, "Defence of Christ and Free Grace", Chapter 2, entitled, "An Hundred of their Errours described".
117. "Not a very safe witness," says R. M. Jones, *Spiritual Reformers*, p. 87.

he associates the Antinomians with Familists, Libertines, Schwenckfeldians and Enthusiasts,[118] and in a subsequent chapter he provides the genealogy: "Libertines sprang from the Gnosticks, Familists from Libertines, Antinomians from both."[119]

(ii) *The writings*

It would be a mistake to dismiss this controversy as merely horse-play or an exhibition of bad feeling. The majority of the preachers and writers involved were men possessed by a deep moral earnestness and—rightly or wrongly—they saw important spiritual issues in jeopardy. Of the profound learning of the Puritans much has been said, and does not need to be told again, but this reminder of their immense erudition serves to check any false assumptions that the controversy about the Law of God was due to ignorant prejudice. Their work was marked by industrious[120] research into the writings of classical authors, and full use of the learning of the past. The pages of their writings were liberally interspersed with quotations in Hebrew, Greek and Latin, and contained grammatical discussions that turned on an intimate knowledge of these languages. The writers made frequent display of the syllogism, as they caught one another with its rules, and employed it for defence or attack. The systematic works of the Puritans were monumental. Their authors surveyed the evidence and marshalled the arguments with a precision that was minute and an order that was massive, leaving an impression on the modern reader of something majestic.[121]

Although the works of the Puritans were weighty with learning, they were not intended to be merely academic.[122] The Puritans were the custodians of a practical divinity;[123] they were the doctors of the Christian life. Their conviction of the continuing obligation of the moral Law of God meant that there were duties to fulfil, and also

118. A general term, used in the seventeenth century to denote fanatics, particularly those who claimed to be independent of the help of the Scriptures.

119. *Survey*, Part I. p. 163. The book is full of extravagant accusations which were applicable only to the extremists.

120. On their industry, see P. Miller, *New England Mind*, 1939, p. 21.

121. There is a valuable article on Puritan preaching and philosophical principles written by J. M'Cosh as an Introduction to the *Works* of Stephen Charnock, I. vii–xlviii.

122. B. B. Warfield says, "Puritan thought was almost entirely occupied with loving study of the work of the Holy Spirit, and found its highest expression in dogmatico-practical expositions of the several aspects of it." Introductory Note to A. Kuyper, *The Work of the Holy Spirit*, 1900, p. xxviii (1946 edition) cf. G. F. Nuttall, *Holy Spirit*, p. 7, who says that the Puritan interest is "experimental" and a "theologia pectoris".

123. The first sentence of William Ames in the *Marrow of Sacred Divinity*, 1641, reads, "Divinity is the doctrine of living to God", p. 1, and adds, "It is of it selfe manifest, that Divinity is practicall, and not a speculative discipline", p. 3. cf. Richard Baxter, *Confession*, 1655, p. 115.

that there were comforting evidences of godliness for which the child of God was entitled to look. The Puritans were not abstract theologians; they were preachers in a pastoral setting, and in their sermons these practical implications were made plain by the custom of indicating the many "Uses" of the doctrines they had established.[124]

The preaching of the Puritans was closely heeded by their congregations. Not everybody possessed the exegetical skill of the preachers, but the people were able to understand the arguments and to keep pace with the debate. Crowds came to hear the sermons and to discuss the issues raised. The flood of printed sermons bore witness to the controversies being followed, not merely by the intellectuals, but by the ordinary people. Occasionally, discussions were printed in dialogue form, and in nearly every instance at least one of the participants was described as an earnest enquirer, or by some title of similar meaning. This form of writing, although a literary device, was a witness to the fact that there were many such seeking minds among the people.[125]

The course of the controversy was partly reflected in the books that were written to answer the arguments of an opponent. Sometimes the work of the author under examination was taken to pieces almost sentence by sentence, being either quoted or misquoted, and then subjected to keen criticism. A broadside was fired by one writer, which received answering salvoes from another, and this occasionally continued through several rounds of reply and counter-reply. It would be tedious to set out all the inter-relations of the books involved, but the following are of particular interest. In answer to Thomas Taylor, *Regula Vitae* (1631), and to John Sedgwick, *Antinomianisme Anatomized* (1643), Robert Towne wrote *Assertion of Grace* (1644), which, being attacked by Anthony Burgess, *Vindiciae Legis* (1646), was defended by *A Re-Assertion* (1654). John Saltmarsh in *Free-Grace* (1645) allowed some remarks implicating Thomas Gataker in his Antinomian views, to which Thomas Gataker replied in, *A Mistake, or Misconstruction removed (whereby little difference is pretended to have been acknowledged between Antinomians and us)* (1646). This was answered by John Saltmarsh in *Reasons* (1646), which, in turn, was refuted by Thomas Gataker in *Shadows without Substance* (1646), and received a reply from John Saltmarsh in *Sparkles of Glory* (1647). Henry Denne's *Man of Sin Discovered* (1645) was answered by Thomas Bedford in *An Examination* (1646), and Richard Baxter's *Aphorismes* (1649) received a sharp retort from John Crandon in

124. "They do most excel in handling the Doctrines of the Gospel, who make it their work to joyn the Practical, and the Speculative together." Thomas Temple, To the Reader, in Simon Ford, *Spirit of Bondage and Adoption*, 1655.

125. This is borne out also by the enormous number of catechisms that appeared at this time. See A. F. Mitchell, *Catechisms*, 1886, Introduction, p. ix.

Aphorisms Exorized (1653)[126] and from William Eyre in *Free Justification* (1654). The latter was answered by John Graile in *Conditions in the Covenant of Grace* (1655) and by Benjamin Woodbridge's *Method of Grace* (1656).

The sermons of Tobias Crisp set in motion the longest chain of books carrying on their title page some such words as "Reply" or "Rejoynder to the Reply". His fourteen sermons *Christ Alone Exalted* made their appearance in 1643, and received an immediate answer from Stephen Geree in *A Plaine Confutation* (1643), and the reprinting of these sermons, at the end of the century, gave the signal for the renewal of the conflict. Richard Baxter started the attack by writing *Scripture Gospel Defended* (1690) and was supported by the author of *Crispianism Unmask'd* (1693), both of whom received a reply from Thomas Edwards, the former being answered in *Baxterianism Barefac'd* (1699), and the latter, by *A Short Review of Crispianism Unmask'd* (1693). At the same time Daniel Williams entered the conflict with *Gospel-Truth* (1692), and was answered by Robert Traill in *Justification Vindicated* (1692) and by Isaac Chauncy in *Neonomianism Unmask'd* (1692). Daniel Williams replied with *Defence of Gospel Truth* (1693), to which Isaac Chauncy gave his *Rejoynder* (1693) and *Fresh Antidote* (1700).

F. PERIOD UNDER REVIEW

It is not easy to decide the limits of discussion of a subject with, so to speak, premonitory rumblings and continuing echoes. There were events, however, which helped to mark out the period and which confined it very nearly to the precise boundaries of the seventeenth century. The opening year of that century saw the publication of the works of Richard Greenham, 1601, being followed two years later by the works of Richard Rogers, 1603. These two men are described by William Haller as "the first of the spiritual preachers to achieve full expression in writing",[127] and so may well be used to mark the beginning of the period for study. In 1691 Richard Baxter, one year before his death, published[128]—either with amazing optimism or

126. "Exorized" comes possibly from ἐξορίζω, meaning to banish or send over the frontier; "anthorized" comes possibly from ἀντι-ὁρίζω which underlies the English word "Anthorism", meaning a counter-definition, or a definition differing from that given by an opponent. The title might, therefore, be rendered, "expelled and contradicted".

127. *Rise of Puritanism*, p. 54 cf. p. 36, where he describes Richard Roger's *Seven Treatises*, 1603, as "the first important exposition of the code of behavior which expressed ... the Puritan conception of the spiritual and moral life. As such it inaugurated a literature the extent and influence of which in all departments of life can hardly be exaggerated." At this time also there appeared the great work of William Perkins, 1558–1602.

128. It was written some twenty years earlier.

with appalling egotism—*An End of Doctrinal Controversies*;[129] and this may be taken approximately as the event at which to terminate the survey.[130]

The writings which belonged to the second outbreak of the Antinomian controversy at the end of the century do not directly add much of theological value to the discussion, but are largely taken up with alternating attacks upon and vindications of Tobias Crisp and Richard Baxter, the two dominant figures of the controversy.[131] There is no doubt that the external history of the second outbreak of the controversy was precipitated by Samuel Crisp's republication of his father's sermons, and the addition of some new ones, in the winter of 1689–90. It thus came to have more of a "Crispian" character than the former Antinomian controversy.[132] After the death of Richard Baxter, Daniel Williams took up the quarrel with the Antinomians, and was answered by Isaac Chauncy, but many of the ministers of the time expressed interest in Isaac Chauncy's type of "Antinomianism" in preference to the "Baxterian half-way house to Arminianism", for, as Bishop Burnet told Edmund Calamy, "such as declared for the middle way, must at last, when pressed, fall into the Arminian scheme".[133] It is clear that at this stage the debate moved out to wider spheres than the place of the Law of God in the life of the believer and so went beyond the scope of the present study. From being Antinomian, or Neonomian, or "Baxterian", the controversy ultimately showed itself to be Arminian.[134]

The writings, therefore, which are taken as the authoritative sources for the present study of the Puritan doctrine of the Law of God in the life of the believer are those which emanated from the seventeenth-century preachers, and are bounded approximately by the authors mentioned above. In so far as the doctrine was a preached doctrine, and was one of immediate practical significance, only those

129. In 1664 Richard Baxter's self-confidence allowed him to write, "I must here record my Thanks to God for the Success of my Controversial Writings against the Antinomians." *Reliquiae Baxterianae*, Part I. p. 111.
130. Another way of describing this period is to regard it as extending from the beginning of the Puritan ascent to the Pulpit until the second outbreak of the Antinomian controversy.
131. The outbreak of controversy at the end of the seventeenth century deserves as much to be called Neonomian, or "Baxterian", as Antinomian. Robert Traill refers to the storm that broke at that time and says, "Some think, that the reprinting of Dr Crisp's book gave the first rise to it. But we must look farther back for its true spring" (*Justification Vindicated*, in *Works*, I. 252); and by this he means the "Arminianism" of Richard Baxter. Cf. Isaac Chauncy, *Neonomianism Unmask'd*, Part I. pp. 3, 10.
132. The Crispian controversy was touched off by the doubts whether these hitherto unpublished sermons were authentic. G. R. Cragg, *Puritanism in Persecution*, 1957, pp. 253, 254.
133. E. Calamy, *Historical Account*, 1731, I. 471.
134. See title page of Isaac Chauncy, *Neonomianism Unmask'd*.

writings which appeared in English, and for the guidance of the ordinary believer, are included. The name "Puritan" is taken to include those who, standing not merely for ecclesiastical reform, but also for a new spiritual earnestness of life, were either deprived of their benefices before 1662 or ejected from the ministry after that year, together with those whose sympathies were with the Puritans but who, for various worthy reasons, either did not take the step of separation or were not affected by the contemporary repressive legislation.[135] Writers who were not strictly within the boundaries described, but who nevertheless belonged to the Puritans by affinity of spirit, are indicated in footnotes.[136]

G. THEOLOGICAL BACKGROUND

(i) *Indebtedness to the Reformers*

The Puritans freely and constantly acknowledged their indebtedness to Luther and Calvin, and claimed no originality for their doctrines,[137] but this does not mean that Puritan theology was no more than a re-issue of continental thought.[138] It is nevertheless true that the teaching of the Reformers provided both the background and the material of their thinking, and all the writers of the period, Antinomian and Puritan alike, made it plain that to be able to enlist the support of Luther or Calvin gave them great satisfaction.[139]

So far as the doctrine of the Law of God in the life of the believer is concerned, the views of Luther and Calvin largely coincided.[140] It has been traditional in post-Reformation theology to speak of the three uses of the Law—*usus politicus,* to restrain sin; *usus pedagogus,* to lead to Christ, and *usus normativus,* to determine the believer's conduct. Lutherans and Calvinists concur in these three, but differ slightly in the stress they lay on the *usus normativus.* The Lutherans give but a very small place in their system to the *tertius usus legis,* and some doubt lingers as to whether Luther accepted it at all. H. H. Kramm, in a fairly recent study has no hesitation in saying that Luther did acknowledge it and writes, "I think it is clearly implied

135. This also refers to men like James Ussher, Edward Reynolds and others of the earlier decades, for whom the issue of nonconformity, or, ultimately, of separation did not exist.
136. Secondary sources for the present study do not abound, as most recent works on the Puritans are more concerned with polity, and only indirectly with doctrine.
137. Their writings show, however, that they themselves drank from the same fountain of inspiration—Augustine—as did the Reformers. See Perry Miller, *New England Mind,* pp. 4, 5.
138. See below, p. 42.
139. Perry Miller shows no hesitation in arguing for the fundamentally Calvinistic nature of Puritan doctrine. "Puritan Divinity", 1935, *Publications,* XXXII. pp. 247–54.
140. Cf. E. Brunner, *Divine Imperative,* 1937, pp. 99–101, 594.

in his writings and teaching that the Law has still some value for the believer. . . . I would say: it is like a compass, indicating the general direction of a journey, not like a detailed map prescribing certain roads."[141] There is at the same time, no question that Luther thought little of the strict requirements of the Law. H. H. Kramm points this out in Luther's opinions about divorce,[142] and explains Luther's famous *pecca fortiter* in the light of a non-rigid observance of the Law.[143] From a positive point of view, Luther acknowledged the third use when he taught that the Holy Spirit "makes heart, soul, body, works and manner of life new and writes God's commandments . . . on hearts of flesh according to 2 Corinthians iii."[144]

Calvin put much stress on the *usus normativus*. He described it as "the principal one, and which is more nearly connected with the proper end of it,"[145] and he made it the foundation of his doctrine of sanctification. He held that it was the office of the Law to remind believers of their duty, and thereby to excite them to the pursuit of holiness and integrity.[146] He considered that the principal use of the Law was to instruct believers in the way of spiritual life,[147] and emphasizes continually that respect must be paid by the believer to the sovereign authority of God.[148]

In making a comparison of the views of Luther and Calvin on this subject, J. S. Whale gives his judgment that "Whereas Luther distinguishes Law and Gospel and ever gives the pre-eminence to the latter, Calvin unites them; sometimes he comes near to transforming the Gospel into a new Law."[149]

There was a corresponding general agreement between Luther and Calvin on the saving significance of the Covenant of Grace, so closely related to the doctrine of the Law of God. The covenant idea lay at the foundation of their teaching about the application to sinners of the merits of the work of Christ; but W. Adams Brown shows that, in contradistinction to the theologians of the next century, Luther and Calvin did not bring God's dealings with Adam in Paradise under the covenant idea, nor did they know of any covenant between God and man, save the Covenant of Grace.[150]

141. *Theology of Martin Luther*, p. 61.
142. Op. cit., pp. 62, 63.
143. Op. cit., pp. 65, 66.
144. *Works of Martin Luther*, "On the Councils and the Churches", V. 267 f., quoted in H. T. Kerr, *A Compend of Luther's Theology*, 1943, p. 113.
145. *Inst.* 1559, II. vii. 12.
146. *Inst.* III. xix. 2. Cf. Louis Berkhof, *Reformed Dogmatics*, 1941, pp. 614, 615.
147. *Inst.* II. vii. 12.
148. "The law has sustained no diminution of its authority, but ought always to receive from us the same veneration and obedience." *Inst.* II. vii. 15.
149. *Protestant Tradition*, 1955, p. 164.
150. Article "Covenant Theology", 1911, *ERE*, IV. 216–24. The first specific treatise on the covenant appears to have been that of Bullinger, in 1534, who, likewise, perceived "only one covenant, the covenant of grace."

(ii) *Covenant Theology*

The important position which the Covenant of Grace held in Puritan theology has led to the common opinion that Puritanism was dominated by the Covenant Theology, but it might be nearer the truth to say that the Puritans were primarily influenced by the covenant idea in Scripture, and so became themselves partly responsible for the creation of Covenant Theology. W. Adams Brown considers it a mistake to think, as is often done, that this system of doctrine was imported from the Continent. It is true that Covenant Theology first made its appearance among the German Reformed theologians in the latter half of the sixteenth century, and was subsequently given "structural importance" as a method of theology by Cocceius,[151] who is "wrongly said to be its author"; but parallel with the movement in Germany there was another developing in England, of which the earliest expositors were William Perkins,[152] John Preston,[153] George Downame,[154] William Ames,[155] James Ussher,[156] and John Ball.[157] Through James Ussher, the doctrine of the covenants entered the *Irish Articles,* and so the *Confession of Faith.*[158] G. P. Fisher claims that the Covenant Theology "softened the rigor of Calvinistic teaching by setting up jural relations in the room of bare sovereignty",[159] and other writers make similar statements,[160] but affirmations of this kind reveal an inadequate estimate of the heart of Calvinism, which is far more than a "bare sovereignty".[161] The Puritans, on the whole, maintained their full Calvinistic convictions, and showed little, if any, sign of modification in their fundamental conceptions of the plan of salvation.[162]

151. 1603–69. For extensive quotations from Cocceius and his school, see H. Heppe, *Reformed Dogmatics,* 1861, Chapters XIII, XIV, XVI, XXII.
152. *Golden Chaine,* in *Works,* 1591, pp. 9, 26.
153. *New Covenant,* 1629. J. D. Eusden is a little uncertain of this influence and says that this work "contains Preston's so-called 'covenant' theology." *Puritans, Lawyers, and Politics,* p. 189.
154. *Covenant of Grace,* 1631.
155. *Marrow of Sacred Divinity,* 1641.
156. *Body of Divinitie,* 1645.
157. *Covenant of Grace,* 1645.
158. W. A. Brown, op. cit., pp. 216–24.
159. *History of Christian Doctrine,* 1896, p. 348.
160. C. Hill, *Puritanism and Revolution,* 1958, p. 246.
161. J. Orr, Article "Calvinism", 1910, *ERE,* III. 148.
162. See R. B. Perry, *Puritanism and Democracy,* 1944, p. 96, for an insight into the practical significance of the Covenant Theology for Puritanism; and J. D. Eusden, op. cit., pp. 19, 31. Perry Miller regards the concept of the Covenant as central and all-determining for Puritan doctrine and considers also that Cocceius did little more than build on the work of the English Puritans. He supplies a long list of Puritan writings on the Covenant. "Puritan Divinity", *Publications,* XXXII. pp. 258, 259.

(iii) *Anglican affinities*

The doctrinal affinities of Puritanism with Anglicanism are plain. There was what P. Miller and T. H. Johnson call "the vast substratum of agreement which actually underlay the disagreement between Puritans and Anglicans."

> Even while fighting bitterly against each other, the Puritans and Anglicans stood shoulder to shoulder against what they called "enthusiasm". The leaders of the Puritan movement were trained at the universities, they were men of learning and scholars; no less than the Anglicans did they demand that religion be interpreted by study and logical exposition; they were both resolute against all pretences to immediate revelation, against all ignorant men who claimed to receive personal instructions from God.[163]

There was "a mutual consent in doctrine" on the part of the Bishops and of the Puritans, and "much of what afterwards came to be named puritanic was then accepted and valued by almost all who favoured the principles of the Reformation."[164] A comparison of the *Articles of Religion* of the Church of England[165] with the *Confession of Faith* of the Assembly of Divines at Westminster[166] demonstrates this fundamental unity of outlook. There was an approximation of belief on such articles as the Doctrine of Scripture, the Trinity, Creation and Providence, the Person of Christ, the Fall of Man, Sin, Election and Predestination, Justification, and Sanctification.

This close doctrinal relation between Puritanism and Anglicanism persisted until the end of the reign of Elizabeth I,[167] but a gradual change became perceptible as Anglicanism, under Richard Hooker, drifted more to philosophy and history, Puritanism of the left moved away from dogma towards humanitarianism, and orthodox Puritanism became more Biblical and theological.[168]

Practical divinity—"the universal interest of the seventeenth century"[169]—which was the chief concern of the Puritans, received treatment also from the Carolines, but in a different manner. The moral theology of the Carolines differed from that of the Puritans, in that the Carolines were concerned to destroy the "legalism" of the Roman Catholic morality,[170] basing their arguments on an appeal to

163. P. Miller and T. H. Johnson: *The Puritans*, 1938, p. 10.
164. A. F. Mitchell, *Westminster Assembly*, p. 326.
165. 1562.
166. 1647.
167. J. B. Marsden, *Early Puritans*, p. 205.
168. A. S. P. Woodhouse, *Puritanism and Liberty*, Introduction, p. 39; cf. J. I. Packer, op. cit., pp. 99, 100.
169. H. R. McAdoo, *Caroline Moral Theology*, Preface, p. xi.
170. H. R. McAdoo, op. cit., p. 10, quotes the Roman Catholic writer T. Slater, *Cases of Conscience*, I. 36, that the object of moral theology "is to teach the priest how to distinguish what is sinful from what is lawful ... it is not intended for edification nor for the building up of character."

the patristic period, whereas the Puritans were occupied with the authority and sufficiency of Scripture for all moral conduct.

(iv) *British origin*

The theology of Puritanism was essentially British, as also was the genius of its practical outworking in the believer's life. In *Minutes* A. F. Mitchell and J. Struthers demonstrate this by showing how closely the *Confession of Faith* follows the *Irish Articles* of 1615.[171] In his opening pages of *Westminster Assembly*, A. F. Mitchell insists that the Puritanism of that Assembly "was no mere excrescence on the fair form of the Church of England", but "was in the English movement for the Reformation of the Mediaeval Church from its very origin".[172] In a later chapter he adds,

> It was long the received opinion that the Assembly's Confession was derived in a great measure from foreign sources, either Swiss or Dutch. The fact was overlooked that in Reynolds, Perkins, Whitaker, Carleton, Downame, the Abbots, Davenant, Overall, Prideaux, Ussher, Hall, Twisse, Ames, Ball, Featley, and Gataker, England for half a century had had a school of native theologians developing an Augustinian or moderately Calvinistic type of doctrine, without slavish dependence on the divines of any Continental school—a system perhaps quite as largely drawn from Augustine and other early western doctors, as from any of the Reformers.[173]

It is difficult to define Puritan doctrine in a single formula,[174] beyond saying that it was governed by a deep reverence for the glory of God and complete submission to the exclusive authority of Scripture. The Puritans regarded the Scripture as providing "a model or pattern for all life, social and national life as well as ecclesiastical, down to the smallest details of the individual's personal behaviour",[175] and it was because of this that even when the program of Church government was overthrown, Puritanism itself "continued uninterrupted to strengthen and extend its hold upon the English imagination."[176]

171. Op. cit., Introduction, pp. xlvi–xlix, lxv. Cf. A. F. Mitchell *Westminster Confession*, 1867, pp. 33–42, where he exhibits in detail the correspondence between these *Irish Articles* and the *Confession of Faith*.
172. Op. cit., pp. 1, 2.
173. Op. cit., p. 371; cf. pp. 377, 423.
174. A. S. P. Woodhouse, op. cit., Introduction, p. 37. Cf. R. B. Perry, *Puritanism and Democracy*, pp. 82–116, on "What did the Puritans believe?"
175. G. F. Nuttall, "Law and Liberty in Puritanism", in *Congregational Quarterly*, XXIX, 1, January, 1951, p. 21.
176. W. Haller, *Rise of Puritanism*, p. 18.

(v) *Delimitations*

The limits imposed by the particular aspects of the present study involve the omission of much closely-related material.

The first delimitation belongs to the Mosaic Law itself, commonly divided by the Puritans into the moral, the judicial and the ceremonial law respectively.[177] The judicial law, being the civil law of Israel, was regarded by most of the Puritans as no longer directly relevant to Christian life;[178] and the ceremonial law, concerned with the Levitical institutions of priesthood and sacrifice, was held to have been ended by the saving work of Christ. Attention is, accordingly, given not to the judicial and ceremonial aspects of the Law, but only to that which was commonly called the moral Law. The moral Law was understood by the Puritans to be stated fully in the Decalogue, and many voluminous expositions of the Ten Commandments came from their pens. The value of these works to the present inquiry is not so much in the substance of the expositions themselves, but in the underlying pre-supposition that the commandments are still obligatory.[179]

A second delimitation of the subject must exclude the political aspects of the Law, together with the problem of religious freedom. These impinge upon the consideration of the Law of God in the life of the Christian, but they occupy a sphere of their own.

A third delimitation relates to Antinomianism as a movement. Doctrinal Antinomianism rejected the necessity for repentance, repudiated "duty-faith", denied that there were any Gospel "conditions", offered the Gospel to "non-sensible" sinners, and taught the doctrine of eternal justification; all of which subjects are outside the scope of the present study.[180] Likewise, no attention can be given to the excesses of practical Antinomianism, as it appeared in the Ranters, as Familism and Libertinism, and in the excesses associated with its propagation in New England.

A fourth delimitation belongs to systematic theology generally; for the doctrine of the Law of God touches nearly every branch of it.

177. Anthony Burgess, *Spiritual Refining*, "Of Grace and Assurance", 1652, p. 559.
178. George Gillespie considers that some of the judicial laws of Moses are still to be implemented by magistrates in so far as they appoint the punishments of sins against the moral law. *Severity*, 1645, p. 6.
179. The Puritan works on the Sabbath are based on the assumption that all the commandments—and so the Fourth—are of moral obligation. Richard Greenham, *Sabboth*, 1599, in *Works*, pp. 158–201, and William Twisse, *Morality of the Fourth Commandment*, 1641.
180. The "Marrow" controversy in Scotland belongs to the discussion of Antinomianism as a movement, especially in so far as it enters a much wider area than the discussion of the Law and opens up many of the fundamental issues of the Calvinistic–Arminian conflict.

It is impossible, in the present study, to deal with subjects such as sin, judgment, atonement, forgiveness, reconciliation, and justification, for these, though closely impinging on the proposed inquiry, are properly outside of it.

H. PATTERN OF THE INQUIRY

The inquiry proceeds along the following lines.

(1) First, the Law of God as the expression of the Divine majesty is examined, together with the way in which God has put this Law within man as the medium of man's blessedness. This brings to light the Puritan view of the effects of the Fall on man's knowledge of the Law and his power to keep it.

(2) Inquiry is next made into the relation of Law and sin and the meaning of this for both the believer and the unbeliever.

(3) The Puritan contention that after the Fall God never entered into relation with sinful man solely on the basis of a Covenant of Works is next studied, together with the corollary that the Mosaic Covenant, though possessing its own distinctive place, was only a part of the Covenant of Grace.

(4) The significance of Christ as "the end of the Law" receives attention, especially showing the consistency between that fact and the truth that there is no abrogation of the Law. The Puritan arguments for the essential unity of the covenants are produced, together with their contention that the New Testament gives evidence of the use of the Law, not as a means of justification—for this it never was—but as the rule of Christian walking.

(5) The Puritan reasons for believing in the continuance of the moral Law, not merely in its matter, but in its mandatory form, are investigated, together with the Antinomian opinion that it is legalism to do good or to abstain from wrong merely because commanded.

(6) The Puritan conviction that evidence of justification must be sought in sanctification is demonstrated, together with the contention that the believer's sanctification is expressed in a life of evangelical obedience.

(7) It is shown that Puritanism stands for a view of Christian liberty which is consistent with the continued right of God to command the believer.

The work is concluded by an assessment of the Puritan doctrine in the light of recent critical studies.

Quotations from Puritan writers have been liberally and extensively made for three main reasons.

(i) Their books are not easily to be found, except in the large libraries, and most of them have long since gone out of publication.

(ii) This liberality of quotation is designed to prove that the views under discussion were not merely those of one or two well-known authors, but belonged to Puritanism generally.

(iii) In this way the Puritans are allowed to speak for themselves.

Chapter I

THE LAW OF GOD FOR MAN

Synopsis

A. GOD'S RIGHT TO COMMAND

(i) *The majesty of His Person*
(ii) *The absoluteness of His will*

B. THE LAW OF GOD IN THE HEART OF MAN

(i) *Its relation to man's reason*
(ii) *Its relation to man's conscience*
(iii) *Its relation to man's well-being*

C. THE PERFECTION OF THE LAW

(i) *A transcript of the holiness of God*
(ii) *Spiritual in its demands*
(iii) *An eternal Law*

D. THE LAW OF GOD AND THE FALL

(i) *An obscured knowledge of the Law*
(ii) *Moral perception not completely extinguished*
(iii) *Divine reasons for preserving some knowledge of the moral Law*
(iv) *Knowledge of the Law by the common grace of the Spirit*
(v) *The continuing testimony of conscience*
(vi) *Inability of man to keep the Law*

Chapter I

THE LAW OF GOD FOR MAN

IT was the common belief of the Puritans that when the Creator formed man He gave him

> a Law of Universal Obedience written in his heart, which by his Fall was much obliterated and defaced: Yet all Mankind have some Fragments of it remaining in their hearts; such as make the very Gentiles, who have not the written Law, inexcusable for their Transgressions.[1]

These words, written by Thomas Gouge, may well be regarded as an anticipation of what is to be discussed in this opening chapter.

The Puritans began their thinking on this subject, not with an abstract concept of "law", but with the experimental awareness of the exalted Lawgiver: behind the *lex* stood the Legislator. This thoroughly Biblical[2] approach was characteristic of the whole of their preaching and writing. To them, the Law must always be the Law of God, and all their doctrinal formulations were dominated by the recognition of God's overwhelming greatness. The study of the Puritan doctrine of the Law of God must begin, therefore, by an examination of the relation of God to the Law.

A. GOD'S RIGHT TO COMMAND

The Puritans could never insist too much on the fact that God was the Sovereign of all He had made, with the right to govern all things according to His will. This right to command resided in the majesty of His Person and was expressed in the absoluteness of His will.

(i) *The majesty of His Person*

The authority of God lies in His glorious Godhead and Creatorhood. God's personal majesty and His relation to His creatures give a quality of permanence to His Law which is inseparable from His personal glory.[3] This reveals a wide difference between human laws and Divine, for

> A man may breake the Princes Law, and not violate his Person;

1. Thomas Gouge, *Principles of Christian Religion*, 1645, pp. 190, 191.
2. "In the beginning God."
3. Stephen Charnock, *Attributes*, 1682, in *Works*, I. 192, 199.

> but not Gods: for God and his image in the Law, are so straitly united, as one cannot wrong the one, and not the other.[4]

Law is law, only if God be God,[5] and such is the connection between the Law of God and His personal majesty that even if there had been no Law revealed, to know God Himself would thereby cause man to know His requirements.[6]

God has the right to command, because He is the Source and End of all things. His sovereignty derives from the Creator-creature relation, and, since man was made in the moral image of God, "Moral Obedience immediately becomes due, from such a Creature to his Maker."

> He that said what we should Be, to him it certainly belongeth to say what we should Do.
> While Man is Gods Creature, 'tis impossible that he should not owe all possible Subjection and Obedience unto God his Maker. He must first cease to be a Creature, or God cease to be his rightfull and supream Governour, before this Obligation to obey God can cease.[7]

There is none greater than God, therefore all Law "is for Gods glory",[8] and man is to set this glory before him at all times, making sure that he is not aiming at it "with a squint eye".[9] To say that "God must be the end of all our actions"[10] means that the most indifferent action that can be conceived of shall nevertheless be done for God.[11]

> We must propound unto ourselves, in all the duties of a godly life, the will of God, and his glory, in yeelding obedience unto it, as that maine scope and end of all our actions; desiring chiefly . . . that wee may hallow and glorifie Gods Name, by doing his will.[12]

This being so, every departure from the Law of God is an affront to the glory of God, and no sin may ever be called small. The greatness of Adam's sin, as of every other transgression, must be measured, not by what it is in itself, "but by the offence it containeth against

4. Thomas Taylor, *Regula Vitae*, p. 233; cf. Jeremiah Burroughs, *Saints Treasury*, 1654, pp. 89, 90.
5. Anthony Burgess, *Justification*, 1655, Part II. p. 379; cf. John Barret, *Treatise of the Covenants*, 1675, p. 242.
6. William Ames, *Marrow of Sacred Divinity*, p. 219.
7. John Barret, *Treatise of the Covenants*, p. 16.
8. John Preston, *New Covenant*, p. 288.
9. Richard Greenham, *Good Workes*, in *Works*, p. 450.
10. Thomas Taylor, *Circumspect Walking*, 1631, p. 149.
11. Thomas Taylor, op. cit., p. 158.
12. John Downame, *Guide to Godlynesse*, 1622, p. 420; cf. pp. 13, 449.

Gods majestie";[13] and the sensitive believer will be "apprehensive of the Dishonour of God, by his sin".[14]

> Sin is the Practical-blasphemy of all the name of God. It is the Dare of his Justice, the Rape of his Mercy, the Jeer of his Patience, the Slight of his Power, the Contempt of his Love: It is every way contrary to God.[15]

Wide as were the divergences of opinion among the Puritans on some aspects of doctrine, there was no difference among them on this basic conviction, as the following paragraph from the Antinomian, John Eaton, shows.

> All sinne is the image of the Devill, and spirituall high treason against the highest spirituall Majesty; and so was horrible before the law was given: but after that God himselfe appeared in such fearefull Majesty, and gave a law forbidding the least sinne in such terrible thundering and lightening: now is the least sinne become double horrible.[16]

"We conflict immediately with God himselfe."[17] Sin "deposeth the Soveraignty of God. . . . 'Tis an Anti-will to Gods Will;"[18] it is "an affront to God's authority", "a despising of his commandments", "contempt of God himself" and "unsubjection to God".[19]

> Sin casts a soil of disgrace and debasement upon the honour which God hath, and goes about to despoil and rob him of it. . . . His sovereignty is slighted in every sin, and in it there is a contempt of his crown and dignity.[20]

It is "downright opposition to God and his Law"[21] in which "the whole authority of God, and therein God himself, is despised."[22] So deep is the antipathy of man to God, that William Strong feels justified in saying that the only reason men sin is because it is forbidden, and he graphically exposes the obduracy of the Pharisees "who did unlord the law, and take away the ruling power of it."[23]

There can be no question about the spiritual importance of this

13. William Perkins, *Golden Chaine*, in *Works*, p. 11.
14. Samuel Bolton, *Sin*, 1646, p. 2.
15. Samuel Bolton, op. cit., p. 25.
16. John Eaton, *Honey-combe*, p. 9.
17. Robert Bolton, *Afflicted Consciences*, p. 79.
18. Ralph Venning, *Sin, the Plague of Plagues*, 1669, pp. 11, 14.
19. Thomas Manton, *Hundred and Nineteenth Psalm*, 1681, I. 37, 179; cf. Thomas Manton, *Thessalonians*, 1679, in *Works*, III. 142.
20. Thomas Goodwin, *Mediator*, 1692, in *Works*, V. 93, 94.
21. John Owen, *Indwelling Sin*, 1668, in *Works*, VI. 182, 189.
22. John Owen, *Holy Spirit*, 1674, in *Works*, III. 610; cf. John Barret, *Treatise of the Covenants*, pp. 70, 71.
23. William Strong, *The Two Covenants*, 1678, pp. 40, 43, 45.

emphasis on the upliftedness of God and man's creaturely relation of dependence and submission to Him. The direction of attention to the personal majesty of God was in harmony with the theology of the Reformers and provided the basis which alone is sufficient for true spiritual worship and a right apprehension of God's saving acts. If religion is the life of man in relation to God, then any concepts which give a true representation of the majesty of God are valuable as a bulwark against the recurring insweeping tides of humanism which threaten to destroy religion. These humanistic influences were strong in the seventeenth century and are still operative today, hence the present revolt against them, in the interests of the upliftedness of God, creates a favourable situation for the re-examination of the Puritan concept of the majesty of God, with its corollary in the doctrine of the Law of God.

(ii) *The absoluteness of His will*

Law is the expression of will, and it is by making a law that God governs.[24] The moral Law, therefore, "is no other then the revealed Copy of Gods will touching mans dutie":[25] it is God's "will as notified".[26] In the absoluteness of His will, "it is God's prerogative to give a law to the conscience",[27] and "God's right is valid whether you will consent or not".[28] There is no necessity for God to explain Himself, and "sometimes God giveth no other account of his law, but this: 'I am the Lord'."[29] "It is of the very essence of a Duty, that it be commanded by God";[30] for man is to obey law as law, asking no questions.[31] The Ten Commandments, therefore, are given absolutely, "no Argument being brought to perswade or confirm the Equity of those Commands; but only the will of the Commander".[32] "Gods naked Command" is the all-sufficient reason for man's obedience.[33]

This unchallengeable authority of the command proceeds from "a sovereign lawgiver" who "hath absolute power to prescribe unto us

24. William Ames, *Marrow of Sacred Divinity*, pp. 44, 191, 193, 241, and *Conscience*, 1639, Book III. p. 56; Book V. pp. 166, 167.
25. John Sedgwick, *Antinomianisme Anatomized*, p. 8.
26. Richard Baxter, *Catholick Theologie*, 1675, Book I. Part 1. pp. 53 f.
27. Thomas Manton, *Hundred and Nineteenth Psalm*, I. 6.
28. Thomas Manton, op. cit., I. 309.
29. Thomas Manton, op. cit., III. 172; cf. Thomas Goodwin, *Mediator*, in *Works*, V. 85, 86, 131. Edward Elton, *Treatises*: "Complaint of a Sanctifyed Sinner", 1618, p. 158. *Gods Holy Minde*, "Matters Morall", 1625, p. 3.
30. Isaac Ambrose, *Prima, Media, & Ultima*, "The Middle Things", pp. 28, 38; cf. Samuel Rutherford, *Survey*, Part II. pp. 6, 7.
31. Stephen Charnock, *Attributes*, in *Works*, I. 192.
32. John Ball, *Grounds of Christian Religion*, 1629, p. 19 (unnumbered).
33. Francis Roberts, *God's Covenants*, 1657, p. 457; William Strong, *The Two Covenants*, 1678, p. 4. See J. D. Eusden's suggestion that authority revealed in the laws was also "hidden in the laws". *Puritans, Lawyers, and Politics*, p. 134.

what laws he pleaseth".[34] It is the absoluteness of the will of God in Law which constitutes its peculiarly obligatory nature.

> It doth not onely command things honest and to be done, but it doth tie men to yeeld obedience to it self for the Law-givers sake; hence it is called, *Lex a Ligando*: for if you destroy the Obligation of the Law you make void the Law.[35]

In distinction from natural or moral Law,[36] positive Law provides a conspicuous instance of the absoluteness of the Divine right to command. It is not necessarily connected with things that are essentially right or wrong, but is given independently.[37] The first appearance of positive Law is found in the prohibition given concerning "the tree which is in the midst of the garden".[38] This is called "a symbolicall precept, because the obedience unto it was a *symbolum* or outward testimony of our homage and service to God."[39] So far as man was concerned, "the thing forbidden was lawful in it self, and only sinful because forbidden, and forbidden, to prove and try his obedience."[40] In view of God's relation to man, the Puritans held that it was

> most reasonable also, that some positive commands should be superadded, that God's right of dominion and government over him as Creator might be more expressly asserted, and he might more fully apprehend his own obligation as a creature to do some things, because it was his Maker's will, as well as others, because they appeared to him in their own nature reasonable and fit to be done.[41]

34. John Owen, *Holy Spirit*, in *Works*, III. 610. Nathanael Culverwel writes, "obligation that's the very forme and essence of a Law; ... every Law *obligat in Nomine Dei*". The rational creature "as a creature has a superiour, to whose Providence and disposing it must be subject". *Light of Nature*, 1652, pp. 20, 30.
35. John Sedgwick. *Antinomianisme Anatomized*, p. 12.
36. To be discussed below, on p. 54.
37. Richard Hooker employs the category of "supernatural" duties, all of which he classes as "positive". John Keble points out that "Hooker opposes Positive to Natural, in regard of our ability or inability to *obtain the knowledge* of a law without express revelation: Butler ... opposes Positive to Moral, in regard of our ability or inability to *discern the reasonableness* of a law *made known* to us by revelation or otherwise." *Laws*, 1594, footnote to I. xv. 2.
38. Genesis iii. 3.
39. Anthony Burgess, *Vindiciae Legis*, p. 104; cf. Thomas Gouge, *Principles of Christian Religion*, p. 47.
40. John Barret, *Treatise of the Covenants*, p. 3. He points out that the positive Law which was added became obligatory by the Law of Nature which required that God should always be obeyed, op. cit., p. 35. Cf. Nehemiah Cox, *Of the Covenants*, 1681, p. 19.
41. John Howe, *Man's Creation*, 1660, in *Works*, I. 464. W. Adams Brown points out that Arminius considered that obedience to positive Law was "far inferior" to other obedience, but to Calvinists it was the "highest virtue". Article "Covenant Theology", *ERE*, IV. 217. Note, however, that this is not the only view of positive Law among the Puritans, for William Ames sees some evidence of God's grace here and considers that the additions of positive Law

Closely related to the Divine right to command—and to be noted in passing—is the place of sanctions. The Puritans believed that "a law implies a sanction; a sanction implies a judge, and a judgment-day."[42] Sanctions are imposed "that the Law may be the better obeyed",[43] and are of two kinds: penalty, and reward. Penalty belongs, not only to positive Law, as so explicitly stated by God in the giving of it, "but also to the Law of Nature, the Demerit of the Transgression of which Law, is known to man by the same Light as the Law it self is known to him."[44] Reward is deducible "from the natural Inclination of Men, to expect the Reward of future Blessedness, for their Obedience to the Law of God";[45] in other words, the Law is "ordain'd to life".[46]

The teaching of the Puritans about the majesty and absoluteness of God in His right to command has sometimes been misrepresented as a doctrine of Divine arbitrariness, but the Puritans would have denied this. To them the sovereignty of God is never abstract, but stands related to His moral perfections. It is the God who is known in Jesus Christ who has this right to command and whose grace and truth revealed in Christ are such as to forbid any questioning of His commands. To the Puritans, the Law of God did not make Him deistically remote but personally near.

B. THE LAW OF GOD IN THE HEART OF MAN

(i) *Its relation to man's reason*

"All the Commandements of God," says John Preston, "are grounded upon cleare reason, if we were able to finde it out,"[47] and

> if they were open to us, if wee did see the ground of them, we would see that there were so much reason for them, that if God, did not command them, you would see it best for you to practise them, you would see reason for it.[48]

The requirements of these commandments are such as are consonant with the true rational nature of all men everywhere,[49] "whereby things intrinsecally good are commanded, and intrinsecally evil

are because of man's weakness, and in order to provide him with "outward Symboles, and Sacraments", *Marrow of Sacred Divinity*, pp. 47, 48. Richard Greenham, likewise, thinks it is given for "an helpe to that which is morall". *Sabboth*, in *Works*, p. 162.

42. Thomas Manton, *Psalms*, 1678, in *Works*, II. 178.
43. Anthony Burgess, *Vindiciae Legis*, p. 61.
44. Nehemiah Cox, *Of the Covenants*, p. 20.
45. Nehemiah Cox, *Of the Covenants*, pp. 21, 22.
46. Ralph Venning, *Sin, the Plague of Plagues*, p. 5.
47. *New Covenant*, p. 32.
48. Op. cit., p. 64.
49. Samuel Bolton, *True Bounds*, p. 72.

are prohibited."[50] Nothing is contained in the Ten Commandments "which is not so rooted in right reason,[51] as it may also be taught by reason that is cleare, and not clouded and imprisoned; and be confirmed by humane reasonings."[52]

John Flavel opens his treatise on *The Reasonableness of Personal Reformation* with an exposition of the close relation between the rational and the moral.

> Reason exalts Man above all Earthly Beings. . . . Hereby he becomes not only capable of Moral Government by Humane Laws, . . . but also of Spiritual Government by Divine Laws . . . which no other Species of Creatures . . . have a subjective capacity for.
>
> Right Reason by the Law of Nature (as an home-born Judge) arbitrates and determines all things within its proper Province; . . . All Actions . . . are weighed at this Beam and Standard: None are exempted but matters of supernatural Revelation; and yet even these are not wholly and in every respect exempt from Right Reason. For though there be some Mysteries in Religion above the sphere and flight of Reason, yet nothing can be found in Religion that is unreasonable.
>
> And though these Mysteries be not of natural investigation, but of supernatural Revelation; yet Reason is convinced, nothing can be more reasonable, than that it takes its place at the feet of Faith.[53]

In John Flavel's judgment, the link between reason and morality was so strong that he could praise those "heathen" men "who yet by their single unassisted Reason arrived to an eminency in Moral Vertues"[54] and could daringly describe the sanctification of the believer as an act of God which but "snuffs and trims the Lamp of Reason.[55]

These extracts, from John Preston and others at the beginning of the period and from John Flavel at its end, are sufficient to exemplify

50. Anthony Burgess, *Justification*, Part II. p. 387; cf. *Vindiciae Legis*, p. 4.
51. To Cicero, "right reason" is "in agreement with Nature", (*De. Rep.*, III. xxii), but to the Puritans it is Divine reason.
52. Richard Byfield, *Sabbath*, 1631, p. 76. Lindsay Dewar and Cyril Hudson make the remark, "There is ... a problem of evil, but no problem of good." *Christian Morals*, 1945, p. 39.
53. John Flavel, *Personal Reformation*, 1691, pp. 1, 2; cf. Anthony Burgess, *Vindiciae Legis*, p. 73.
54. *Personal Reformation*, p. 9.
55. Op. cit., p. 3. This does not amount to a denial that sanctification is all the work of the Holy Spirit; for the Holy Spirit is given "to make sinners reasonable". Richard Baxter, *Unreasonableness of Infidelity*, 1655, Preface (pages unnumbered). J. I. Packer rightly remarks that fundamental to all Puritan thought is the view that "Grace elevates and perfects fallen reason, not merely by supplying information, but primarily by renovating the instrument." Op. cit., p. 57.

the Puritan conviction about the close relation between the Law of God and man's rational nature.

The Puritans regarded man as a rational being. By this they meant, not only that he was a participator in that Divine reason which is at the heart of the universe, but that he was unique, in that he alone of the inhabitants of the earth was aware of this Divine reason and of the obligation rightly to relate himself to it. This obligation of right relationship to Law—in distinction from the non-volitional aspects of conformity in the lower orders of being—gives rise to the concept of moral Law.[56] It likewise constitutes the Puritan definition of duty, for if reason be the distinguishing characteristic of man's mental life, then man's obedience to the Law of his nature is lifted above the level of the unconscious and instinctive, and emerges as moral behaviour. Moral Law belongs to the normative rather than to the descriptive, and so prescribes to man what is due from him to his Maker; that is to say, it declares his duty.

Because the moral Law is so closely bound up with the rational nature of which man is possessed,[57] it is sometimes spoken of as the Law of Nature; but the Law of Nature had a more theological meaning for the Puritans than it had for the Stoics, or even for Aquinas. In the judgment of the Puritans it derived from God's action in "making our Natures such as compared with objects, Duty shall result from this Nature so related."[58] Their use of this term, therefore, indicated not only life according to reason, but also man's creaturely obligation to render to God what is His due. Nevertheless, this creaturely obligation is fully in accordance with "the very *Natura rerum*",[59] and Ezekiel Hopkins can define the moral Law as a

System or Body of those Precepts which carry an universal and

56. The reservation of the term moral Law to express this particular aspect does not deny that the whole of God's sovereignty over the universe is a truly moral government; for all His actions are directed to moral ends. It would nevertheless be incorrect to say that all parts of the Divine creation are governed by the moral Law. God's government in all three realms of His creation—inanimate, animate, rational—is that of His sovereign will, but in the life of man, that government is effected through the reciprocal action of the human will.
57. David Clarkson, *Justification*, 1675, in *Works*, I. 282, points out that it is only because man is a rational creature that he is capable of being morally governed.
58. Richard Baxter, *Life of Faith*, 1670, p. 378. It is sometimes said that the Reformers "broke with Natural Law doctrine" (Lindsay Dewar and Cyril Hudson, op. cit., p. 43, n), but this seems to be falsely concluded from the Reformers' doctrine of depravity. Andrew Willet says, "In the lawe of nature, there are two principall things, first the understanding and judgement, in apprehending and conceiving these naturall principles touching our dutie: ... the other is in the will and affection, in giving assent and approbation unto" these things. *Hexapla: Romanes*, 1611, p. 119, cf. below, p. 75. It is because of the loss of the latter, more particularly, that the Reformers are wrongly regarded as having broken with "Natural Law doctrine".
59. Richard Baxter, *Catholick Theologie*, Book I. Part I. p. 110.

natural Equity in them, being so conformable to the Light of Reason, and the Dictates of every Man's Conscience, that as soon as ever they are declared and understood, we must needs subscribe to the Justice and Righteousness of them.[60]

The concept of the Law of Nature provides no difficulty so long as the following distinction is observed:

The Law of Nature, properly so called, is *in esse Objectivo*, that signification of God's Will concerning Man's Duty, which was discernible in the *Universa rerum Natura* in all God's Works; but principally in Mans own Nature, as related to God and all Persons, and Things about him.
But Improperly or Metonymically so called, the Law of Nature is *in esse subjectivo* the *Communes notitiae,* which Man had and was to have from the said Objective Law of Nature. But properly this is rather the Knowledge of the Law, than the Law it self. . . . Yet may it well be called God's Law written in the Heart, when we have the Knowledge and Love of his primary proper Law.[61]

This account of the relation between reason and the Law was, on the whole, common to all parties in the seventeenth century. It was fully expressed by Richard Hooker[62] and shows close affinity with the thought of Thomas Aquinas.[63] But although much of the thinking of the Puritans on this aspect of their subject was philosophical, it cannot be too firmly insisted upon that they were primarily not philosophers but theologians. This meant that at no time did they equate reason and Law in such a way as to regard the latter as a mere logical inference from the former.[64] They never wavered in their belief in the supreme authority and necessity of revelation, and they confidently assumed that the dictates of "right reason" received their full enunciation in the revelation of God's will contained in Scripture.

That which is said to be right reason, if absolute rectitude be looked after, it is not else-where to be sought for then where it is, that is, in the Scriptures: neither doth it differ from the will of God revealed for the direction of our life.[65]

They thought consistently of the moral Law as the promulgation of the preceptive[66] will of Him who was man's Creator and who had the

60. *Ten Commandments*, 1692, in *Works*, p. 59; cf. an excellent definition of natural Law by William Allen, *Christians Justification*, 1678, pp. 66, 67.
61. Richard Baxter, *End of Doctrinal Controversies*, pp. 113, 114.
62. *Laws*, Book I.
63. *Summa*, "Treatise on Law", QQ. XC–C. See P. Miller, "Puritan Divinity", *Publications*, XXXII. 267, 274.
64. Cf. Aquinas, op. cit., QQ. XC. 4 and XCI. 1.
65. William Ames, *Marrow of Sacred Divinity*, p. 199.
66. The Puritans distinguished the decretive from the preceptive will of God.

right to govern him, and it was this emphasis on the authoritative will of God and its promulgation in the form of commandment[67] which constituted one of the important differences between Puritan theology and the philosophical theories of the period.[68]

As a final paragraph to this section it must be added that these affirmations of the Puritans about the essential reasonableness of Law must not be understood to imply any belief in the present power of man's fallen and unaided reason to discover this moral Law. Their main purpose was not to prove or disprove anything about man's abilities—this they did elsewhere—but simply to insist that the moral Law bears a close relation to the rational nature with which man is endowed.

The Puritan doctrine of the Law of Nature needs to be scrutinized in the light of a re-awakened interest in the subject at the present time. There is a wide-spread desire to find some common ground on which "Christian men" and those "not living by Christian faith" can meet in a joint endeavour to solve the present-day social and

67. Nathanael Culverwel, who in some ways appears to stand both with the Puritans and the philosophers (see J. Tulloch, *Rational Theology*, 1874, II. pp. 141, 414, and F. J. Powicke, *Cambridge Platonists*, 1926, pp. 134, 148), goes all the way in identifying man's original knowledge of the Law with the light of reason. Reason and faith are not foreign to each other: "There is a twin-light springing from both, and they both spring from the same fountain of light." But he points out that this close relation between reason and Law is not such as to identify Law with the eternal ideas of the Divine mind. The rationality of moral actions "is indeed a sufficient foundation for a Law to build upon, but it is not the Law itself, nor a formal obligation". What reason perceives to be good or bad, this can make "a just foundation for a Law; but now before all this can rise up to the height and perfection of a Law: there must come a Command from some Superiour powers, from whence will spring a moral obligation also, and make up the formality of a Law. ... This Law of Nature ... becomes formally valid and vigorous by the minde and command of the Supreme Law-giver." The Law is, therefore, "publisht by Authority from heaven", and "Reason is the Printer". *Light of Nature*, pp. 2, 18, 29, 30, 42, 44, 59, 60.

68. That the Puritan doctrine of the moral Law did not go all the way with the philosophical concept of "natural law" can be seen in the contrast which Norman Wilde points out when he refers to the three ways in which moral Law has been conceived: theological, natural, and rational. He says, "Natural Law as a basis for morals may ... be described as an order of human nature, known to be such by the unaided reason of man, and recognized as binding without reference to the desires or pleasures ... of the sentient life. ... These rules are not imposed from without, but are the expression of his own nature and binding only as such. To be moral is to be truly a man and to be truly a man is to be truly a rational animal. The norms of reason are the moral laws."

Of the moral Law rationally conceived, he writes, "A moral law is ... a categorical imperative addressed by the reason to a being not naturally inclined to obedience. The motive to obedience is respect for the law itself whose authority we feel in our sense of moral obligation. ... The law, as grounded neither in the nature of God nor in its consequences for man, is thus absolute and the expression of a free reason which commands of itself alone." Article "Moral Law", 1915, *ERE*, VIII. 833-4.

international problems,[69] and this common ground is being sought in a revived concept of natural Law. In the course of the attempt to resuscitate this doctrine in its relation to man's moral life two opposing theories have emerged, which may be described as naturalistic and supernaturalistic respectively. The naturalistic theory teaches that all men are able to perceive this Law by the light of natural reason and do not need any specifically Biblical or Christian revelation. This theory has received its most recent answer in the form of a penetrating discussion by Jacques Ellul entitled, *The Theological Foundation of Law*. He points out that "law by itself, as an autonomous entity, does not exist in the Bible",[70] and he contends that the Stoic and Thomist and Rationalist arguments are insufficient to produce a Law at all.[71] In this contention he both supports and is supported by the Puritans.[72] Their doctrine stands in complete opposition to all naturalistic theories and has no affinities whatsoever with the utilitarian empiricism which seeks to secularize the concept. It is a strictly theological doctrine and perceives the essence of natural Law in the fact of its promulgation by God at the time of man's creation. This alone gives validity to the concept of natural Law and at the same time relates it to man's rational nature.

The supernaturalistic theory presents a totally different challenge to the Puritan doctrine and propounds the view that there is no genuine knowledge of the Law of God except by personal experience of the saving grace of Christ.[73] It is held that fallen man is totally unable to form any true idea of justice and goodness, and, therefore, that no such thing as natural Law exists.[74] This is as extreme in one direction as the naturalistic view is in another and is criticized by the Swedish scholar Gustaf Wingren, in his book, *Creation and Law*.[75] He challenges the adequacy of the "New Testament credal formulae" which form the basis of modern Barthian thinking. He argues that because of the historical position of these New Testament formulae and their necessarily Christological emphasis, they are not fully balanced theological statements. The result of this, he considers, is

69. A. R. Vidler and W. A. Whitehouse, *Natural Law*, 1946, pp. 16–18, 19; H. H. Schrey, H. H. Walz and W. A. Whitehouse, *Justice and Law*, 1955, pp. 20–43.
70. English trans., 1961, p. 45.
71. J. Ellul, op. cit., pp. 20–22.
72. Cf. the passages quoted above from Nathanael Culverwel.
73. In this insistence on the necessity of grace the supernaturalistic view gives full support to the Puritan doctrine.
74. J. Ellul, op. cit., p. 87 f. Cf. E. Brunner, *The Mediator*, English trans., 1934, p. 554. As is shown below, the Puritans were not unanimous, whether this knowledge was a remainder in man or whether it was the result of a new "inscription" of the Law within man; but they had no doubt about the reality of it.
75. 1961.

that the advocates of the supernaturalistic theory have underestimated the truth enshrined in the Trinitarian Creed and thereby disrupted the sequence of the Divine acts. Their thinking is dominated by a theological misdirection of the concept of the Lordship of Christ which issues in a dislocation of doctrine. Gustaf Wingren points out that this is due to the fundamental Barthian error of making human knowledge[76] of the Divine acts the organizing principle for the sequence of the acts themselves. Thus, because man's experience of God begins with Christ, God's earlier acts are of less significance, and the truths of Creation and Law are relegated to the background. This is a serious flaw in modern Barthian theology, and, when it is recognized, the supernaturalistic attack upon the Puritan doctrine of the Law of God is found to be much less damaging than at first appears. In contradistinction to the one-sidedness of the Barthian exposition, the Puritan doctrine is firmly set on a fully Biblical foundation, that is to say, on "the Bible in its wholeness."[77]

In their findings on natural Law, A. R. Vidler and W. A. Whitehouse come to a conclusion which is almost a re-statement of the Puritan doctrine,[78] but they indicate, nevertheless, that when the best attempt has been made to expound the Biblical concept of natural Law "important theological tensions still remain."[79] There can be no doubt that some of these tensions are due to the ambiguity which now attaches to the word "natural", and it might be better to speak of "primary" Law, rather than "natural". This would certainly be agreeable to the thought of the Puritans who, when they spoke of natural Law meant not a Law produced by nature (as the modern connotation seems to suggest), but a Law determinative of it. But perhaps it is too late in the day to suggest a new vocabulary.[80]

(ii) *Its relation to man's conscience*

It has been shown that man is such a being that not only does he stand in relation to the Law of Nature, but he has a moral awareness that he so stands. The Puritans, however, considered that there was more in this than the bare fact that man was created a self-conscious being. They held that, in addition to the possession of a rational nature, man was, from the very first, the recipient of a special revelation of the moral relation in which he stood to God. The demands of the moral Law were made known to him by an act of God over and

76. For all its appearances to the contrary, the Barthian position is fundamentally anthropocentric; see G. Wingren, op. cit., p. 12.
77. See G. Wingren, op. cit., p. 17. His contention is that the foundation of the doctrine must be the whole Bible and not uni-testamental.
78. *Natural Law*, p. 23; cf. Joseph Dalby, *Law of Nature*, 1943, p. 49.
79. Op. cit., p. 26.
80. Richard Baxter uses the word "primary" in *End of Doctrinal Controversies* p. 114.

above the gift of rationality.[81] The customary way in which the Puritans expressed this was to say that the Law of God was "written" in his heart.[82] Synonyms such as "engraven" and "imprinted" are also to be found in many places,[83] and occasionally this possession by man of the knowledge of the moral Law was described as "that inscription".[84] Other comparable expressions were sometimes used, such as from "pure nature",[85] "inbred and natural",[86] and "concreated with him".[87] These phrases, taken together, imply that the knowledge of the moral Law belonged to man at his beginning, but they also convey the idea that this knowledge was not a merely constitutional result, but was received by communication. Authority for this manner of speaking was usually found in Romans ii. 14, 15, where Paul writes of those who, although they never formally received the Ten Commandments at the hand of Moses, nevertheless "show the work of the law written in their hearts". This means, says Anthony Burgess, that they were "not without a Law ingrafted in their conscience, whereby they had common dictates about good and evil;"[88] indeed, as Paul at once points out in the immediately following clause, this inwritten Law is the very foundation of conscience.

It was recognized that there was a necessity to distinguish between this original endowment of man and that later work of grace in man's heart which was the subject of God's promise in Jeremiah xxxi. 33. For example, although Anthony Burgess makes direct use of Romans ii. 14, 15 to describe the way the moral Law was given to man at the first, he expresses a caution as follows:

> You must not, with Austine, compare this place with that gracious promise in Jeremy, of God writing his law in the hearts of his people. There is therefore a two-fold writing in the hearts of men; the first, of knowledge and judgement, whereby they apprehend what is good and bad: the second is in the will and affections, by giving a propensity and delight, with some measure of strength, to do this upon good grounds.[89]

81. Cf. Richard Hooker, *Laws*, I. xi. 1. Cf. John Ball, *Covenant of Grace*, p. 11.
82. See, for example, William Perkins, *Of Conscience*, 1596, in *Works*, p. 622; William Ames, *Marrow of Sacred Divinity*, p. 47; and a great many more.
83. William Ames, *Conscience*, Book V. p. 100; *The Marrow*, 1645, p. 20; Samuel Bolton, *True Bounds*, p.77.
84. Vavasor Powell, *Christ and Moses*, 1650, p. 184; cf. Nathanael Culverwel, *Light of Nature*, p. 29, "that sacred Manuscript".
85. Thomas Goodwin, *Of the Creatures*, 1682, in *Works*, VII. 44.
86. John Owen, *Indwelling Sin*, in *Works*, VI. 165.
87. Isaac Chauncy, *Rejoynder*, p. 31.
88. *Spiritual Refining*, "Of Grace and Assurance", p. 334.
89. *Vindiciae Legis*, p. 60; cf. *Spiritual Refining*, "Of Grace and Assurance", pp. 334, 335. See below, p. 225.

Thomas Goodwin, while not dissenting from his fellow-Puritans in the use of the word "written" to describe the original manner in which God gave man His Law, nevertheless denies that the passage in Romans has any reference to this.[90]

The Puritans believed that as the moral Law was given in this direct and intimate manner it was full and complete. "Adam heard as much in the garden, as Israel did at Sinai, but onely in fewer words and without thunder",[91] and "it's probable hee had written in his nature the substance of the Ten Commandments."[92] As Christ is the archetypal man, it might not be far from the truth to say that the form in which the Law was originally in the heart of man may be seen from the manner of its indwelling in Christ.[93]

The use of Romans ii. 14, 15 to substantiate the doctrine of an in-written Law of God in man's nature has not been without challenge. J. Ellul, for example, says, "It is the work, accomplished in compliance with the law, which is written upon their hearts. This text in no way affirms that the law is written upon man's heart, as it is wrongly asserted."[94] But this introduces a strange contradiction of ideas in which a man's activity is said to be passivity, and what a man actively performs he is said passively to have suffered. J. Ellul has the appearance of exegetical exactitude, because grammatically the word *γραπτόν* is construed with *τὸ ἔργον*, but what he has failed to see is that *ἔργον* in this place signifies a much larger idea than the actions themselves[95] and stands synecdochically for "the requirements of the law."[96] It seems to be bordering on the pedantic[97] to divert the meaning of these words into anything else than an intimation by Paul that the unregenerate man has some natural knowledge of what the Law requires.

(iii) *Its relation to man's well-being*

It is one of the brighter aspects of the doctrinal outlook of the Puritans that they regarded the Law, not as burdensome in its original purpose, but as the essence of man's delight. They vied with

90. See below, p. 72.
91. John Lightfoote, *Miscellanies*, 1629, pp. 182, 183. He proves his contention by enumerating the details of Adam's ten-fold breach of the Law.
92. Vavasor Powell, *Christ and Moses*, p. 186.
93. Thomas Goodwin, *Mediator*, in *Works*, V. p. 143.
94. Op. cit., p. 89.
95. Cf. *τὰ τοῦ νόμου*, in ver. 14.
96. This is how the words are rendered in R.S.V. and it is supported by H. Alford, J. Denney, F. Godet, J. A. Beet, W. Sanday and A. C. Headlam, C. Hodge and A. Gifford. The *N.E.B.*, in what at this place must be called a paraphrase rather than a translation, uses the same word that is employed by John Eaton, *Honey-combe*, p. 114, and renders the passage "they display the effect of the law inscribed on their hearts".
97. Perhaps J. Ellul needs to take to heart his own dictum about "absence of precision" and "theological insight", op. cit., p. 38.

one another in extolling the blessedness of man under God's gracious Law.

> As the flame lives in the oyle, or as the creature lives by its food; so a man lives by keeping the Commandements of God, that is, this spirituall life, this life of grace, it is maintained by doing the Commandements: whereas on the other side, every motion out of the wayes of Gods Commandements, and into sin, is like the motion of the fish out of the water, every motion is a motion to death.[98]

This conviction of the blessedness of the Law was based on the fact that all living beings have a "law" of some kind, and that only in living accordance with that law can their true life be found.[99] The Puritans were not aware of saying anything extravagant when they affirmed that obedience to the Law of Nature was Adam's highest joy and good.[100] They held that the Law was designed for the true well-being of man;[101] it was his "way of life",[102] and constituted his real liberty.[103]

> The fundamental Liberty of Conscience is, That the Laws that oblige it, are implanted in it for a nature, are fram'd into it, to be its very Constitution, are so adjusted, as to be its Excellency, and perfection: The Laws that bind it, are its Liberty.[104]

The Ten Commandments concern "humane nature it selfe", and "they all make so compleately to the profit of mankind in this life, that if these precepts were observed, men need not any other humane Lawes."[105]

> The Commandment . . . was given not only for Gods sake . . . but for Mans sake, that man might enjoy the good and benefit of his obedience, and find that in keeping the Commands of God there is great reward.[106]

98. John Preston, *Sermons*, "New Life", 1631, p. 53.
99. William Ames, *Conscience*, Book V. pp. 102, 107; cf. *The Marrow*, p. 146. Nathanael Culverwel, *Light of Nature*, pp. 29, 30, 46, says the possession of the Law is "such an happy privilege" that violation of it is "an injury to man's being". Cf. Thomas Aquinas, *Summa*, Q. XCII. 1, "make men good" and Richard Hooker, *Laws*, I. viii. 4, 9; ix. 1; xvi. 8, "mother of their peace and joy".
100. Anthony Burgess, *Vindiciae Legis*, p. 119.
101. Edward Elton, *Treatises*: "Complaint of a Sanctifyed Sinner", pp. 101, 103.
102. Richard Byfield, *Gospels Glory*, 1659, p. 107; cf. Thomas Wilson, *Romanes*, 1614, p. 238.
103. Edward Elton, *Treatises*: "Triumph of a True Christian", 1623, p. 50.
104. *Liberty of Conscience*, 1681, p. 2. This is anonymous.
105. Richard Byfield, *Sabbath*, p. 76.
106. Ralph Venning, *Sin, the Plague of Plagues*, p. 20.

When he answers the question, "Is the law death", Edward Reynolds recoils from such a thought by saying that to conceive of God publishing a Law that would destroy is impossible;[107] indeed, he thinks this to be so far from the truth that he adds, "the Law is of it selfe apt to carry unto Life and Righteousnesse."[108] Again, there is such blessedness in the commandments, that Thomas Manton departs from the usual word "obey", and, following the word in the Scripture, says they are to be "believed".[109] Man was originally made to delight in the Law,[110] and the delight of keeping the commandment is so great that "it is folly to sin against God at any time".[111] Further, not only is the Law "suited to the nature of man",[112] but it would not have "been agreeable to the goodness of God" to let man be without a Law.[113]

Richard Baxter finds it hard to keep silent on this subject, and in his *Aphorismes* he describes the Law of Nature in man as "wholly and only to his advantage".[114]

> God Commandeth us a Course of Duty or Right action to this end, that we may be Happy in his Love. . . . His very Law is a Gift and a great Benefit. Duty is the means to keep his first Gifts and to receive more. The very doing of the duty is a receiving of the Reward; the object of duty being felicitating. . . . Holiness is happiness, in a great part.[115]

In one of his later books, he adds, "It is a contradiction to be happy and unholy."[116]

C. THE PERFECTION OF THE LAW

(i) *A transcript of the holiness of God*

A Law emanating from the Divine reason, and given in so direct a manner by God Himself, and for so blessed an end, was held by the Puritans to be nothing less than the very transcript of the glory of God. Man has been made in God's image,[117] and so the moral Law written within him must be part of that very image itself.[118] But it

107. Edward Reynolds, *Three Treatises*: "Sinfulnesse of Sinne", 1631, p. 370.
108. Op. cit., p. 383.
109. *Hundred and Nineteenth Psalm*, II. 74; cf. p. 299 f.
110. Thomas Goodwin, *Work of the Holy Ghost*, 1703, in *Works*, VI. 402.
111. Thomas Goodwin, *Relapsing*, 1641, in *Works*, III. 414; cf. John Owen, *Gospel Vindicated*, 1655, in *Works*, XII. 565.
112. Stephen Charnock, *Attributes*, in *Works*, II. 27.
113. Op. cit., II. 312.
114. Richard Baxter, op. cit., p. 13.
115. Richard Baxter, *Catholick Theologie*, Book I. Part 1, pp. 53, 54.
116. Richard Baxter, *End of Doctrinal Controversies*, p. 205.
117. Genesis i. 27.
118. William Perkins, *Golden Chaine*, in *Works*, pp. 12, 13.

was not only because of this that the Puritans ascribed such glorious perfection to the Law. Their chief reason was the more theological one, that God could not be thought of as requiring from man anything less than that which accorded with the Divine character.

The evidence for this high view of the Law is abundant in the Puritan writings. The moral Law in man is a copy of the Divine nature, and what God wills in the moral Law is so "consonant to that eternall justice and goodness in himself", that any supposed abrogation of that Law would mean that God would "deny his own justice and goodnesse".[119] "To find fault with the Law, were to find fault with God",[120] for "the original draft is in God himself".[121] It is "the express idea, or representation of God's own image, even a beam of his own holiness".[122] God is the Being of essential perfection, "and from that Perfection all Laws in the world, that are just and good, have their Original; that is, Gods own Laws are the expressions of his holy perfect Will and Nature".[123] In the act by which the Law was conveyed to man, the Puritans perceived the ministry of Christ, and the Johannine concept of the *λόγος* seems to justify them in this. "The hand of him who was the 'Mighty Counsellor', did guide the pen that wrote it in Adam's heart at first", and "himself is the substantial image of God, and the *πρωτότυπον* of the law".[124] Expressions of this kind may be found throughout the Puritan writings.[125]

The Law is thus the glorious expression of the glory of God in so far as that glory is to be realized by the creatures whom He has made in His own image.

(ii) *Spiritual in its demands*

The spiritual nature of the demands of the Law of God is a corollary of its nature as the transcript of the holy character of God. The Law's demands are inward, touching motive and desire, and are not concerned solely with outward action.

> For such as God is that made the law, such is that lawe which hee made. It reacheth therefore to the inward parts of every man, and lyeth close upon his conscience. . . . It dooth especially differ from the lawes of men: for they doe tye the hand . . . but they meddle not with the heart. . . . Therefore all the obedience

119. Anthony Burgess, *Vindiciae Legis*, p. 4.
120. Ralph Venning, *Sin, the Plague of Plagues*, p. 3.
121. Thomas Manton, *Hundred and Nineteenth Psalm*, II. 308; cf. III. 213.
122. *The Marrow*, p. 146.
123. Richard Baxter, *Catholick Theologie*, Book II. p. 30.
124. Thomas Goodwin, *Mediator* in *Works*, V. 102. But see below, p. 72.
125. E.g. Samuel Bolton, *True Bounds*, p. 73; Edward Elton, *Treatises*: "Complaint of a Sanctifyed Sinner", p. 115; John Crandon, *Aphorisms Exorised*, Part I, p. 200.

> performed to God, must proceede from within, and come from the heart, else it shall bee no whit acceptable to him . . . Our obedience shall be spirituall, when it proceedeth from the soule, & is done to a good end, . . . with desire and purpose to shew our obedience to God.[126]

The spiritual demands of the Law make a penetrating distinction between precision of action and purity of heart.

> It may be demanded, whether the works of men unregenerate, (whereby they doe in some sort the same thing which the regenerate doe in their good works) be good works, or no:
> Ans. In such kind of works, we are to distinguish betweene the substance (as I may say) of the worke, and the fault of the person, wherewith it is defiled. . . . Now, every worke so far as it agreeth with Gods Law, is good. But for all that, there be some vices cleaving to them, which come, partly, from the person that doth them, partly, from the manner of doing, whereby such works are so defiled, that though in their owne nature, and in respect of others they be good, yet in respect of any spirituall obedience yielded by them unto God, they are not good.[127]

Unless, therefore, the heart be right, the endeavour to obey God's Law is nothing more than a display of legalism. The words "before me" in the First Commandment indicate a worship that is "inward and spiritual before God".[128] The Law is spiritual, "binding the Soul and Conscience",[129] and this is to be seen in the way "it forbids the sins of the spirit, not only externall sins; it forbids thy spirit pride, thy spirit envie; Even as God is the father of spirits, so is the Law, the law of spirits".[130] The very demand of the Law that all shall be done to the glory of God emphasizes its spirituality, "therefore we do refuse that distinction of a morall good, and theologicall, because every morall good ought to be theologicall".[131] Anthony Burgess takes this up again in his sermon on the "Rich Young Ruler", Matthew xix. 20, and observes,

> It is a very difficult thing to drive an unregenerate man out of this false sign of his good estate, viz. that he keeps the Commandements of God. This was the πρῶτον ψεῦδος. In this was the fundamentall miscarriage of this great man, that he had a confident

126. John Dod and Robert Cleaver, *Ten Commaundements*, 1603, pp. 8, 9; cf. *Confession of Faith*, XVI. 7.
127. William Ames, *Conscience*, Book III. p. 82.
128. James Durham, *Law Unsealed*, 1676, p. 18.
129. John Ball, *Grounds of Christian Religion*, p. 196.
130. Anthony Burgess, *Vindiciae Legis*, p. 7.
131. Op. cit., p. 59.

perswasion of his good estate, because he did no murder, he committed no Adultery, he bore no false witnesse against his neighbour. Now falsely judging this to be all the Law required, he concludeth that unlesse Christ hath some new and extraordinary way about this, these matters are so low and easie, that he observed them along while ago.[132]

The cause of such false self-estimates as this may be found in "an ignorance of the spirituall exactnesse and obligation of the Law,"[133] and a confusion of conscientiousness with sanctification.[134]

We may not think it enough to conform our selves to the Law of God in outward actions only. No, no; we must yeeld internal and spiritual obedience to the Law of God; the Law of God, in commanding outward good works, and in forbidding outward evil deeds, commands and forbids the very first motions and desires of those works, and therefore we must labour . . . in truth to yeeld obedience to the Law of God, not only in our bodies, but also in our hearts, souls and Spirits.[135]

The Puritans spoke with contempt of the superficial attitude of the man who professed himself satisfied with having attained an outward conformity to the Ten Commandments. In the dialogue of *The Marrow*, *Evangelista* rebukes the superficial ideas of *Nomologista* ("a Prattler of the Law") who thinks he has kept all the commandments because he has—in his own opinion—never committed any overt breach of them.

Alas! neighbour Nomologista, the commandments of God have a larger extent than it seems you are aware of . . . as though the Lord required no more but the bare external or actual performance of a duty, and as though He did forbid no more than the abstinence and gross acting of sin. The very same conceit of the law of God the Scribes and the Pharisees had, and therefore, it is no marvel though you imagine you keep all the Commandments even as they did.[136]

He points out that the inwardness of Law is particularly demonstrated in the Tenth Commandment.

I pray you take notice, and consider, that this tenth Commandment was given to be a rule and level, according to which we must

132. *Spiritual Refining*, "Of Grace and Assurance", p. 143.
133. Anthony Burgess, op. cit., p. 144.
134. Thomas Goodwin, *Work of the Holy Ghost*, in *Works*, VI. 245, 251; John Owen, *Holy Spirit*, in *Works*, III. 632.
135. Edward Elton, *Treatises*: "Complaint of a Sanctifyed Sinner", p. 136.
136. *The Marrow*, pp. 249, 250.

take and measure our inward obedience to all the other commandments contained in the second table of God's Law. . . For it is not said in this Commandment, Thou shalt not consent to lust, but Thou shalt not lust. It doth not only command the binding of lust, but it also forbiddeth the being of lust. Which being so who seeth not that in this Commandment is contained the perfect obedience to the whole Law?[137]

The Law must, therefore, be understood "in its spirituality";[138] and this provokes James Durham to write, not only of those in his day who were very ignorant of the letter of the Law, but of many more who had "but little insight in the spiritual meaning thereof".[139] He outlines ten rules for a right understanding of the commandments, in the fifth of which he says:

The Law is Spiritual, in that the obligation thereof reaches to the Spirit, and very inwards of the Heart, Affections & Thoughts, as well as to the outward Man; the love it requires, is love with all the Soul, Heart and Mind. Hence there is Heart-idolatry, Murder, and Adultery, as well as outward, therein condemned. . . . It is Spiritual, in respect of the manner; it requires, as to all outward duties, that they be done to a Spiritual End, from a Spiritual Principle, and in a Spiritual Way, opposite to the carnal way, to which the unrenewed heart of man is inclined.[140]

The spirituality of the Law makes demands on the believer which he is unable to fulfil. It calls for an "inward obedience" which can alone "come from that Spirit which is the author of the Law". This, therefore, must "warn us . . . to crave help of God, to strengthen us by his Spirit to give obedience to the Law in some measure of truth and sincerity".[141]

(iii) *An eternal Law*

A Law so related to the Divine reason, conveyed by so Divine an

137. *The Marrow*, pp. 314, 315. Arthur Dent, *Plaine Mans Pathway*, 1601, pp. 342 ff, causes *Theologus* to take *Asunetas* through the commandments a second time, expounding their inwardness, and this convinces *Asunetas* of his sin.
138. William Strong. *The Two Covenants*, p. 92. Puritan writers delight to quote from the works of Bishop Gervase Babington, 1550–1610, who expounds the Scripture in so "Puritan" a way. "Hath there never thought but good crept into that heart of yours? ... And what though you have never consented to it ... we see neverthelesse by this lawe of God that we are but gone. For here is condemned the verie entrance and beeing of anie vile conceit within us for any time, though upon some better wakening, we repell it, and abhorre it, and thrust it away without his act". *The Commaundements*, 1583, pp. 504, 505.
139. *Law Unsealed*, To the Christian Reader.
140. Op. cit., p. 8; cf. Obadiah Grew, *Sinner's Justification*, 1670, p. 43.
141. Thomas Wilson, *Romanes*, p. 220.

action, and embodying such Divine glory cannot pass away. It was the custom of the Puritans, therefore, to speak of the moral Law as eternal.

> Naturall Law, is the same, which usually is called the Eternall Law: but it is called Eternall, in relation to God, as it is from Eternity in Him; it is called Naturall, as it is ingraffed and imprinted in the Nature of man, by the God of Nature.[142]

The moral Law is the reflection of that "Law eternall, resident in the pure, glorious, infinite minde of God, which is that order which God before all ages hath set downe with himselfe, for himselfe to doe all things by."[143] Edward Elton presents an exposition of the Ten Commandments in a catechetical form, which at the fourth question proceeds as follows:

> *Quest.* How is the Morall Law eternall?
> *Ans.* Thus; it abideth for ever in this world and in the world to come, not in the manner of commanding (Thou shalt not Kill, or Lust, or the like;) but for the matter of it which is holinesse, love of God, and obedience to his will.[144]

Richard Baxter rejects the idea that the Law is eternal, and it is this which constitutes the fundamental difference between his teaching and that of most of his Puritan contemporaries. The general view was that the Law is the permanent expression of the eternal and unalterable requirements of God's holiness and justice, but Richard Baxter, proceeding on the hypothesis of the rectoral liberties of God, asserts that the Law is but a means to an end, and that God may change His Law providing the same end is attained. The theological implications of this have been well stated by J. I. Packer.

> The root difference between Baxter and orthodox Calvinism, from which all their other disagreements sprang and to which they can all be reduced, may here be pin-pointed. It concerned the idea of *law* . . .
>
> To orthodox Calvinism, the law of God is the permanent, unchanging expression of God's eternal and unchangeable holiness and justice. . . . God could not change this law, or set it aside, in His dealings with men, without denying Himself. When man sins, therefore, it is not God's nature to save him at the law's expense.

142. William Ames, *Conscience*, Book V. p. 100; cf. *Marrow of Sacred Divinity*, p. 42.
143. Robert Bolton, *Assise Sermons*, 1635, p. 7.
144. Edward Elton, *Gods Holy Minde*, "Matters Morall", p. 2. By "the manner of commanding" he means the negative form. Cf. Thomas Manton, *Hundred and Nineteenth Psalm*, II. 308; Nehemiah Cox, *Of the Covenants*, p. 18.

> Instead, He saves sinners by satisfying the law on their behalf. . . .
> Baxter's "political method" led him to a very different idea of God's law. To him, God's justice is merely a rectoral attribute . . . and His laws are no more than means to ends. . . . When man had fallen, and God purposed to glorify Himself by restoring him, He carried out His plan, not by *satisfying* the law, but by *changing* it. . . . Where orthodox Calvinism taught that Christ satisfied the law in the sinner's place, Baxter held that Christ satisfied the Lawgiver and so procured a change in the law. Here Baxter aligns himself with Arminian thought rather than with orthodox Calvinism.[145]

Richard Baxter contends that the Law must be defined merely in relation to God's rectoral authority. God's will is two-fold: as He is *dominus* His will is embodied in His decrees, and as He is *rector*, it is made known in His laws.

> Still keep in your minds a clear Distinction between Gods Rectoral or Legislative Will determining *de Debito, officii, premii,* & *poenae*: and his Will *de rerum existentia & Eventu* as such, determining *de facto* what shall be, and what not; Or between Gods Decrees and his Laws. And take heed of confounding these in any point of Theologie; much more in the whole frame.[146]

This distinction, he argues, "is of Greater and more Necessary use to us than any of the rest"; for "It is not the Will in it self that is a Law, nor doth any Immanent act oblige us, or constitute Duty: But it is Gods Will as signified. And therefore *Lex aeterna* is an improper speech."[147] It was his opinion that the confusion of God's purpose and God's Law led to serious misunderstandings about the Law,[148] and he was right in this opinion; but it is possible that Richard Baxter was more hampered by misunderstandings about this than those from whom he differed. His own confusion is seen in the *non sequitur* quoted above, for his conclusion is not to be found in the premises. The distinction between decree and Law can be recognized without making a denial of the eternity of the moral Law. Further, it by no means follows that, because the Law is said to be eternal, its requirements are thereby elevated to the status of a decree. God may decree His moral Law to be eternal without turning the moral response of man into a decree. Eternal demands are not to be equated with eternally-decreed events. The Puritans could concur with Richard Baxter in saying that "all sin is done against the Law or commanding Will of God, which determineth only of Duty, and

145. Op. cit., 303–5; cf. 458.
146. Richard Baxter, *Confession*, p. 290.
147. Richard Baxter, *Catholick Theologie*, Book I. Part 1, p. 52.
148. Richard Baxter, *Aphorismes*, pp. 38, 39.

not directly of Event";[149] but they firmly repudiated the inferences he drew from this.

D. THE LAW OF GOD AND THE FALL

The Puritans agreed that the effects of the Fall made themselves felt in two directions: in the dimming of knowledge and in the weakening of moral ability. They believed, however, that neither of these harmful results was complete or absolute, and that there was sufficient evidence to show that man still had some knowledge of the Law and that he still possessed a measure of ability.

(i) *An obscured knowledge of the Law*

The awareness of God's Law, which was so clear in the heart of man in his innocency, became dimmed through the Fall. It

> is in a manner wholly buryed by originall corruption, and almost totally overwhelmed by custome in sinning, as it were with some heape of evill lusts laid upon it; and because also the light of the understanding is involved, and obscured with manifold darknesse, so that neither those rules of honesty, which are within the booke of the mind, are fully and perfectly legible, nor can our understanding read anything therein, distinctly and plainly.[150]

This loss of the clear knowledge of God's Law was described as having been "razed out of man's heart by his fall",[151] or as "so obliterated and darkened, that it could not shew a man the least part of his wickednesse",[152] or "growne so dymme, and dark that in a manner it was deleated, and blotted out by the sinnes of men".[153] Man had become "blinded" to the true righteousness of God, for "the exactness of this righteousness of God never did any natural men know."[154] God's commandments needed re-writing,[155] for "not one of them is found remaining, since the fall, upon the heart of any naturall man compleat, full and faire, but singularly defaced, blotted and blurred like the limbes of an old worne picture".[156]

> The Light of Reason was at first the bright Lamp or Candle of the Lord, till Sin, like a Thief melted it down to a Snuff; whereby

149. Richard Baxter, *Catholick Theologie*, Book II. p. 37.
150. William Ames, *Conscience*, Book II. p. 2.
151. *The Marrow*, p. 146.
152. Anthony Burgess, *Vindiciae Legis*, p. 9; William Allen, *The Covenants*, 1673, p. 57.
153. Vavasor Powell, *Christ and Moses*, p. 187.
154. Robert Traill, *Galatians*, 1696, in *Works*, IV. 174; Thomas Goodwin, *Unregenerate Man's Guiltiness*, 1692, in *Works*, X. 154–73, 257.
155. Francis Roberts, *God's Covenants*, p. 1394.
156. Richard Byfield, *Sabbath*, p. 76; cf. William Ames, *Conscience*, Book V, p. 108.

> (comparatively speaking) it is become a poor glimmering Light in the best of men, and almost quite extinguished in some men.[157]

In a characteristically striking phrase, John Flavel speaks of sin prevailing "to the very Unmanning of Men".[158]

(ii) *Moral perception not completely extinguished*

Although such expressions as "razed out" and "obliterated" are so strong, it would be a mistake to construe them absolutely, for the Puritan writers make it plain that fallen man is not altogether without some knowledge of the Law of God.[159] Their statements must be understood in a sense relative to the perfect knowledge of the Law in its purity and glory.

William Perkins draws attention to this continuing knowledge when he says, "The remnant of God's image is certaine notions concerning good and evill: as, that there is a God",[160] though he quickly adds that "even these notions, they are both generall and corrupt, and have none other use, but to bereave men of all excuse before God's judgment seat." In *The Marrow, Evangelista* tells *Nomologista* that although the Commandments were obscured by the Fall, "yet some impressions and reliques thereof still remained."[161] In the same volume in which he speaks of the Law as "obliterated", Anthony Burgess also gives a characteristic list of the evidences which the Puritans found in proof of the fact that the Law of nature is still in man in some measure,[162] and remarks,

> This light of Nature may be considered . . . as it's a relict or remnant of the image of God: . . . It is true, this light of Nature, comparatively to that of faith, is but as a glow-worme to the Sun; yet some light and irradiation it hath, . . . which the Apostle calleth (Rom. i) Truth; he vouchsafeth that name to it, They detain the truth in unrighteousnesse.[163]

It may well be that the best that can be said of this remaining knowledge is to speak of it as "this moon-light or glimmering of Nature";[164] but this at least implies that the knowledge of the moral Law is not

157. John Flavel, *Personal Reformation*, p. 3.
158. Ibid. Cf. Richard Baxter, *Directions and Perswasions*, 1658, p. 115, "Sinne hath unmanned us".
159. Thomas Aquinas teaches this, and so, too, does John Calvin, though he does not define its extent, *Inst*. II. ii. 22.
160. *Golden Chaine*, in *Works*, p. 12.
161. *The Marrow*, p. 51; cf. Vavasor Powell, *Christ and Moses*, p. 187.
162. *Vindiciae Legis*, pp. 62–65.
163. Op. cit., p. 67, 68.
164. Ibid.

altogether effaced, even between Adam and Moses.[165] John Eaton, although he differed from his fellow-Puritans on so many other things, concurred with them here, and speaks of that "glymmering knowledge" of the Law, by which man still comes to an awareness of sin.[166] John Saltmarsh, similarly, affirms that

> They that are yet in their carnall or unregenerate state, have certain convictions against sin, from the law of their natural conscience, which is strong enough to reprove, but not to reform or change into a new creature: . . . because they commit it against some inward law or beam of natural glory and excellency which is in the soul.[167]

The continuance of some point of moral contact between God and man was undoubtedly one of the basic concepts of Puritan thinking.

(iii) *Divine reasons for preserving some knowledge of the moral Law*

The Puritans saw many reasons why God did not allow the knowledge of the moral Law to disappear entirely. The most obvious is the one drawn from Romans i. 20, namely, that it was God's intention to leave sinful man "inexcusable".[168] A brighter reason which some of them found is that God sustained the knowledge of the moral Law in the minds of the unregenerate so "that there might be a ground of conversion".[169] Anthony Burgess puts forward the view that some continuance of the Law of God in fallen men

> is absolutely necessary . . . as a passive qualification of the subject for faith; for, there cannot be faith in a stone, or in a beast. . . . Therefore Reason, or the light of Nature, makes man in a passive capacity fit for grace; although he hath no active ability for it.[170]

This statement is exposed to attack from two directions, and Anthony Burgess defends himself against both. On the one hand, he refutes those who argue that men are so fallen that they are no more than "stockes, and stones, or beasts"; and, on the other, he rejects the opinion of those who contend that men have an inherently active power "to convert or turn to God". The Puritan view is that in man

165. Francis Roberts, *God's Covenants*, p. 684; Cf. Nathanael Culverwel, "Because the eye of Reason is weakened, will they therefore pluck it out immediately? ... The Candle of the Lord do's not shine so clearly as it was wont, must it therefore be extinguisht presently?" *Light of Nature*, p. 3.
166. John Eaton, *Honey-combe*, p. 8.
167. *Free-Grace*, pp. 5, 6.
168. Anthony Burgess, *Vindiciae Legis*, p. 70.
169. Anthony Burgess, *Spiritual Refining*, "Of Grace and Assurance", p. 337.
170. Anthony Burgess, *Vindiciae Legis*, p. 72.

there is a "passive capacity of grace", though man has no power to convert himself.[171]

(iv) *Knowledge of the Law by the common grace of the Spirit*

Some Puritans asked whether it was correct to speak of "remains" and "relicts" of the knowledge of the Law of God in fallen man, or to think of such knowledge as "continued". They questioned the accuracy of this language, and taught that whatever knowledge fallen man now had of the moral Law of God was to be attributed to a new act of grace on God's part. William Strong, for example, argues that "no man has by nature the Law of God in his heart",[172] and, as for the Law written in the heart, Romans ii. 14–15,

> the writer is Christ, and the ink is the Spirit, and the table is the heart; . . . We do not read that the Law is said to be written in Adams heart, only God created man righteous; but writing notes rather an act from an extrinsecal hand. And therefore I should rather conceive those practic notions, Rom. 2. 15 to be written in man by the common work of the Spirit of Christ, than to be left in him after the fall, not the dross of the old Adam, but the foundation of the new.[173]

Thomas Goodwin, too, feels strongly on this subject, and while he readily grants that the unregenerate man is not without some knowledge of the Law of God, he strenuously denies that this knowledge is the result of any residue of goodness in him.

> In the 3d of John, 'That which is born of the flesh is flesh'; that is, all that is derived to man by virtue of his birth is possessed and filled with nothing but flesh and corruption, . . . so that if those sparks of literal light (as I choose with the Scriptures to call it) be more than flesh, as is objected, and will easily be granted, then I affirm that they are not derived, as raked up in the ashes of our nature, and so by birth, but struck in by some external hand. . . . That phrase, Rom. ii. 14, proves the same thing, where this light is said to be written in men's hearts, for writing is *opus artificis, non naturae*, a work of art, not of nature. These characters are written, not born with us; we by nature have but *abrasas tabulas*, tables in which everything is razed out; it is the new work of some second hand hath took the pains to write them there.[174]

171. Op. cit., pp. 94, 95; Richard Baxter, God "moveth not a man as a beast or stone", *Christian Directory*, 1673, p. 593.
172. *The Two Covenants*, p. 103.
173. William Strong, *The Two Covenants*, p. 103.
174. Thomas Goodwin, *Unregenerate Man's Guiltiness*, in *Works*, X. 101; *Of the Creatures*, in *Works*, VII. 44–47.

John Edwards, in his *Truth and Error*, answers this objection and understands Romans ii. 14, 15 to teach that

> The Gentiles do by Nature (i.e. by virtue of this Light in their Minds) the things contained in the Law, viz. the Moral Law: and on that score may be said to be a Law unto themselves. . . . It is evident to any unprejudiced Person, that the Law written in the Heart is to be understood here of that Law which is implanted in their Natures, and originally imprinted in their Hearts from their birth. It is manifest from the Context that the Apostle's meaning is, that the same Truths and Duties which are commanded by the Moral Law or Decalogue, are primitively engraven on their Consciences.[175]

It is possible that the disagreement is more apparent than real, and that while William Strong and Thomas Goodwin were anxious to deny continuity of cause, John Edwards was concerned to affirm identity of substance. The former were anxious that no credit should accrue to the unregenerate man for the knowledge of God's Law, while the latter was concerned to identify the Law that is in unregenerate man with the primitive Law under which he was created. In a number of places, provided the fact of some knowledge of the Law is recognized, the question whether it be by purely natural "remains" or by some supernatural act of God is left open. Individual writers are not always consistent with themselves. For example, in one passage the author of *The Marrow* refers it to "reliques",[176] and in another he attributes it to "visions and revelations."[177] Even Thomas Goodwin refers to "natural light left even in corrupt nature."[178]

The Puritans saw evidence of fallen man's awareness of the Law of God in many directions, but most clearly in the testimony of conscience.

(v) *The continuing testimony of conscience*

The Law of God persists in man's conscience, which is "like the eye of a keeper, reserved in man, partly to reproove, partly to represse the unbridled course of his affections, Roman 2. 15".[179] Even the unenlightened conscience in fallen man indicates some awareness of the moral Law; "for every naturall man is a Justiciary".[180] The Law is

175. John Edwards, *Truth and Error*, 1701, pp. 31, 32.
176. Op. cit., p. 51.
177. Op. cit., p. 146.
178. *Of the Creatures*, in *Works*, VII. 44.
179. William Perkins, *Golden Chaine*, in *Works*, p. 13.
180. Thomas Taylor, *Progresse of Saints*, 1630, p. 105.

> written and engraven in every mans conscience: so that let wicked men strive, and labour, and doe what they can to make themselves Atheists, yet . . . they cannot blot out Gods writing. These lawes sticke imprinted in their hearts and soules, so firmly, that they cannot be removed. For as Paul saith, God hath not left himselfe without witnesse; but in every mans bosome, and every ones nature, hath planted so much of his law, as will serve to leave them without excuse, and to condemne them.[181]

There are honest pagans who suffer "the instigations of naturall conscience", and "the torture of a troubled Conscience".[182] The unregenerate man clings to any "old rags of righteousness"[183] that he can find. The heathen are "a law unto themselves",[184] in that "their inward conscience, is in stead of a Law".[185]

Conscience belongs not to the affections or the will, but to the understanding, in proof of which a long argument is conducted by William Perkins in *Discourse of Conscience*,[186] and an elaborate syllogism is produced by William Ames.[187] The verdicts of conscience are influenced by the light that it has, and so a distinction has to be drawn between the "naturall" conscience and an "inlightened" conscience,[188] although this is a difference, not in kind, but only in degree. Whatever the degrees of enlightenment may be, conscience makes itself felt, and Samuel Rutherford provides the following catechism.

> *Q*. Quhat is the conscience?
> *A*. It is the judging pairt of the soull under God, teaching and counselling good and comforting us quhen we doe it . . . and forbidding ill and tormenting us after wee have committed ill.
> *Q*. Quhat ar the lights that directeth conscience?
> *A*. The law of nature in manes heart and the light of the Word ar the two candles that God hes lighted to lett it see to walk.
> *Q*. Quhat are the proper works of conscience?
> *A*. It works ether upon the law as ane litle God, or upon our deeds as a witnes, or it applyeth the law to our deeds as a judge.[189]

It is this power of conscience as it "applyeth the law to our deeds", that gives rise to the vast casuistical literature of the period.

181. John Dod and Robert Cleaver, *Ten Commaundements*, p. 4.
182. Robert Bolton, *Afflicted Consciences*, pp. 70, 79, 83.
183. Thomas Goodwin, *Unregenerate Man's Guiltiness*, in *Works*, X. 394.
184. Romans ii. 14.
185. Thomas Wilson, *Romanes*, p. 70.
186. *Of Conscience*, in *Works*, p. 619 ff.
187. *Conscience*, Book I. pp. 1–5.
188. Op. cit., Book I. p. 5.
189. *Catechisme*, reproduced by A. F. Mitchell, *Catechisms*, p. 165.

(vi) *Inability of man to keep the Law*

The Puritans never conceived of man's knowledge of the Law as standing alone: he was "made capable of . . . obedience".[190] Created as a moral being, man was

> intire and perfect, made after the Image of God in Righteousnesse and true holinesse, furnished not only with a reasonable soule and faculties beseeming, but with divine qualities breathed from the whole Trinity, . . . inabling and fitting him to obey the will of God intirely, willingly, exactly.[191]

When God made man he "created in him a holy nature",[192] "which Uprightness or Rectitude of Nature did consist in the perfect Harmony of his Soul, with that Law of God which he was made under".[193] With the Law written in his heart, man had also "power to fulfil it",[194] for if there had been no original ability, there would have been no condemnation.

This ability, however, did not remain after the Fall, for with the dimming of the knowledge of the Law there came an incapacity to perform it. The Fall influenced not only the understanding, but also "the will and affections."[195] Having been endued with an original moral ability, Adam sinned away that power for himself and for his posterity.[196]

> No man of brains denyeth that man hath a will that's Naturally free; . . . But it is not free from evil Dispositions. It is Habitually averse to God. . . . It is enslaved by a sinful byas. . . . You have not this Spiritual Moral Free-will, which is but your right Inclination. . . . If you had a will that were freed from wicked Inclinations, I had no need to write such Books as this.[197]

The degree of depravity caused by sin is such that the corrupted natural light becomes "a desperate enemy to what is good . . . I Corinthians 2. 14."[198] Such is the moral landslide, that the unregenerate man opposes what he at the same time knows to be right, and man's fallen reason does not even accept "the first principles of religion."[199]

190. David Clarkson, *Justification*, in *Works*, I. 282.
191. John Ball, *Covenant of Grace*, p. 11.
192. William Strong, *The Two Covenants*, p. 3.
193. Nehemiah Cox, *Of the Covenants*, p. 18; John Barret, *Treatise of the Covenants*, pp. 8, 9.
194. *Confession of Faith*, IV. 2; James Ussher, *Body of Divinitie*, p. 124.
195. Andrew Willet, *Hexapla: Romanes*, p. 119.
196. Anthony Burgess, *Vindiciae Legis*, p. 130; Jeremiah Burroughs, *Saints Treasury*, p. 94.
197. Richard Baxter, *Call to the Unconverted*, 1658, Preface (pages unnumbered).
198. Anthony Burgess, *Vindiciae Legis*, p. 70.
199. Thomas Goodwin, *Unregenerate Man's Guiltiness*, in *Works*, X. 184, 185, 225.

Serious as is this loss of ability, however, it is not lost entirely. As there are corrupted remnants of knowledge of the moral Law, so also are there corrupted remnants of conformity to it, though these remnants of conformity cannot be regarded as completely well-pleasing to God. The Gentiles "do by nature the things contained in the law",[200] but this does not mean that they truly fulfil the Law, but only that they sometimes act according to the Law and so reveal that the Law has left its mark on them.[201] They are actions "which shew the work of the law written in their hearts";[202] but when these actions are examined they are found to be in accordance with the Law only after an outward manner. Nevertheless, this outward morality, although falling short of the Divine requirement, is not disparaged by Paul.[203] The remainders of moral ability—poor shadows of the original strength though they are—derive from the remainders of moral knowledge which reveal themselves in the accusing and excusing conscience of the unregenerate man.

> In the will those remainders appeare by a certaine inclination unto good knowen in that manner: which although it be vanishing, and dead, yet it is found in all in some measure: whence also it is that at least the shaddowes of vertues, are allowed and embraced of all.[204]

Thomas Goodwin has no hesitation in saying that unregenerate men even keep the Law, and corresponding to the "sparks of truth" that are still in the mind of fallen man "there are also inclinations, dispositions, stamps, impressions upon the will to some good, conformable to the law".[205] Man is, no doubt, a spiritual ruin, but as with all ruins, the remains give a hint of what was previously glorious.

The definition of the effects of the Fall on man's knowledge of the Law is one of the most keenly discussed problems of present-day theology. Does fallen man possess any continuing knowledge of the Law of God? The answer to this question cannot be given independently of the view that is held about natural Law. Belief in a continuing[206] knowledge and belief in natural Law stand or fall together. Without the latter the former would have no content; and without the former the latter would have no relevance. The same evidence that is available in support of the doctrine of natural Law is equally applicable to that of the continued knowledge of it, and

200. Romans ii. 14.
201. Andrew Willet, *Hexapla: Romanes*, pp. 116, 117.
202. Romans ii. 15.
203. Obadiah Grew, *Sinner's Justification*, pp. 41, 42.
204. William Ames, *Marrow of Sacred Divinity*, p. 63.
205. *Unregenerate Man's Guiltiness*, in *Works*, X. 95, 96.
206. Or specially recovered knowledge, as William Strong and Thomas Goodwin would understand it.

C. H. Dodd gathers this evidence from both the Old Testament and the New.[207] In doing this he provides the reply to the charge of J. Ellul that the doctrine of a continuing knowledge of the Law of God is built "upon one single text".[208] The Puritan doctrine of man's continuing knowledge of the Law seems to emerge from the present controversies unscathed. It is temperately stated; it takes full cognisance of the serious effects of the Fall without lapsing into the extravagances of neo-Calvinism; and presents a picture of man which is true both to Scripture and experience.

The purpose of this opening chapter has been to introduce the material and to outline the basic assumptions upon which Puritan thought about the place of Law in the Christian life was built. Upon these main presuppositions there was general agreement, and it has been possible to quote, side by side, men who belonged, not only to widely different periods of the seventeenth century, but also to the different theological parties of the time. These writers were well-nigh unanimous about the nature of the Law, the knowledge of it by man, the glory that shines from it, the spiritual demands made by it, and the relation of it to man's well-being. No one of them questioned the sanctions that belong to Law, nor the right of God to command, which lies behind them. The Puritans conceived of positive Law as the touch-stone by which man's acknowledgment of this right is tested, and they did not enter upon profitless enquiries about the origin of right as an abstract notion. They perceived that since God's Law is the immediate expression of His perfections, then whether "what God willed was right" or "what was right God willed" was irrelevant, for they must merge into one and the same thing. The particular importance of positive Law will appear later when the question comes to be considered whether a Christian should make conscience about the keeping of the Law. For the present, it seems that a correct understanding of the purpose of positive Law has already provided the answer. The requirements of the Law may or may not make an immediate appeal to the believer's sense of the fitness of things, but positive Law lays stress on the doing of right, not merely because it is intrinsically good, or coincides with the understanding, but from the simple motive of worshipping God in utter obedience—an obedience which has in it both the sublimity of faith and the humility of creaturely subjection.

207. *Natural Law in the Bible*, 1946. He finds material in Genesis, in Job, in the concept of the Logos in the Fourth Gospel, and more particularly in Matthew vii. 11; Mark x. 1–9; Romans i. 19–21, ii. 14–15, xii. 17, xiii. 6; I Corinthians xi. 1–16; and I Peter ii. 12, iii. 16. Cf. a good discussion on "St Paul's Conception of Law" by M. F. Wiles in *The Churchman*, LXIX. 3 and 4, September and December, 1955, and A. R. Vidler, *Christ's Strange Work*, 1944, pp. 20–34.

208. J. Ellul, op. cit., p. 62.

Chapter II

THE LAW AND SIN

Synopsis

A. SIN AS LAW-BREAKING

(i) *Restraint of Law*
(ii) *Provocation of Law*
(iii) *Condemnation of Law*

B. THE CONVICTING POWER OF THE LAW

(i) *The Law as a mirror*
(ii) *The Law to be preached*
(iii) *"The Spirit of bondage"*
(iv) *No Gospel without the Law*

C. SIN IN THE BELIEVER

(i) *Indwelling corruption*
(ii) *Justification and sanctification*
(iii) *Knowing sin and seeing sin*

D. MAKING CONSCIENCE OF SIN

(i) *Sin still sin*
(ii) *Sin more than disease*
(iii) *Confession of sin*

Chapter II

THE LAW AND SIN

THIS chapter is occupied with a discussion of the relation of Law and sin. In their views of this the Puritans of all parties were in the main stream of Protestant thought, namely, that Law and sin are correlatives, in the Biblical sense that where there is no Law there is no sin.[1] The inquiry takes note of the fact that as Law is definitive of sin, it therefore condemns it and convicts the sinner of his guilt, but at the same time has the paradoxical effect of provoking sin. These things being so, the believer has to acknowledge the indwelling of sin in his own life, to recognize it as sin, and humbly to confess it. The survey of the Puritan thought on these subjects exposes some of the seventeenth century misunderstandings about justification, and shows the value of the work of the Law both as a preparation of the sinner for justification, and as a faithful monitor to the believer in his confession and prayer.

A. SIN AS LAW-BREAKING

In the course of an argument which is aimed by him at a different conclusion[2] from that of his contemporaries, John Saltmarsh rightly affirms that no trouble for sin can arise in the soul but "from the obligement of the Law" and the satisfaction it demands.[3] This is because sin is Law-breaking. It is "a deviation from the Law of God",[4] or "Disconformity to the Law".[5] Vavasor Powell, with an apology for the seeming violence of what he is about to say, says that "The Law gives (if I may so tearme it) a being unto sin; and therefore is called the strength of sinne".[6] The Puritans affirmed that "sin supposeth a Law in being", and that therefore "the Law is against sin before 'tis committed".[7] It is by the majestic demands of the Law of God

1. Romans vi. 15; v. 13.
2. See below, p. 169.
3. *Free-Grace*, p. 44.
4. William Ames, *Marrow of Sacred Divinity*, p. 58.
5. Richard Baxter, *Catholick Theologie*, Book I. Part 1, p. 86; cf. Edward Reynolds, *Three Treatises*: "Sinfulnesse of Sinne", pp. 370, 371; Thomas Goodwin, *Aggravation of Sin*, 1637, in *Works*, IV. 157, 158.
6. *Christ and Moses*, p. 188.
7. Ralph Venning, *Sin, the Plague of Plagues*, pp. 7, 98, 166, 167; Andrew Willet, *Hexapla: Romanes*, p. 208.

that men are brought "to see the rebellions of their hearts to be sin".[8]

The sinfulness of sin is the more revealed by the entry of the commandment, for

> The Law entring upon sinne doth make the fault thereof so greatly to abound, Rom. v. 20. that sinne is made out of measure sinnefull by the Commandement.[9]

If the heinousness of the guilt of man's sin is thus revealed, much more is it true that the terrible defilement of sin can be seen only

> with respect unto the holiness of God as expressed in the law. . . . Original sin is the habitual inconformity of our natures unto the holiness of God expressed in the law of creation. Actual sin is our inconformity to God and his holiness expressed in the particular commands of the law. The nature of all sin, therefore, consists in its enmity, its inconformity to the rule.[10]

This common Puritan view of the nature of sin found expression in the Answer to Question 24 in *The Larger Catechism* of the Westminster Assembly:

> Sin is any want of conformity unto, or transgression of, any law of God, given as a rule to the reasonable creature.

These corollaries follow from the definitive relation which the Law bears to sin.

(i) *Restraint of Law*

As the expression of the will of the Lawgiver, the first purpose of the Law is, positively, to secure right-doing, and, negatively, to restrain wrong-doing. Anthony Burgess, for example, has no doubt that the Law is "to restrain and limit sin", and "to excite and quicken" believers "against all sinne and corruption".[11] This was the opinion among the Puritans generally.[12]

(ii) *Provocation of Law*

But such is the corruption of the human heart by sin that the Law which is intended to restrain sin has also the opposite effect of pro-

8. Edward Elton, *Treatises*, "Triumph of a True Christian", p. 178. In "Complaint of a Sanctifyed Sinner", pp. 77–81, 131, he affirms that it is the commandment that shews sin to be sinful.
9. John Eaton, *Honey-combe*, p. 9.
10. John Owen, *Holy Spirit*, in *Works*, III. 427; Thomas Manton, *James*, 1651, in *Works*, IV. 210, argues that it is the Law that makes sin in the believer.
11. *Vindiciae Legis*, pp. 8, 9.
12. Cf. Vavasor Powell, *Christ and Moses*, p. 190; William Strong, *The Two Covenants*, p. 96; Ezekiel Hopkins, *John*, 1701, in *Works*, p. 240.

voking it. The apostle Paul had pointed out this anomaly from the beginning, and the Puritans recognized the fact that "the use of the Lawe in unregenerate persons is . . . accidentarily to effect and augment sinne, by reason of the flesh",[13] and

> Such is our bondage to the Law, that instead of mortifying any of our sinnes, it rather stirres them up: . . . it doth stir up lust (though accidentally) and makes our sin out of measure sinfull.[14]

Vavasor Powell puts the truth rather quaintly when he describes the power of the Law to "unkennell sins and make them take hold upon a mans soule".[15] The Puritans were careful to point out that the power of the Law to irritate sin is only "accidentall to the Spirituall Law,"[16] and in the unregenerate it "doth by accident make these lusts swell higher."[17] This accidental effect of the Law, however, is due to the sinful lusts of the human heart. At the presence of the Law "Lust grows mad".[18]

> Now, whereas thou sawest that so soon as the first began to sweep, the dust did so fly about . . . that thou wast almost choaked therewith. This is to shew thee, that the Law, instead of cleansing the heart (by its working) from sin, doth revive . . . and increase it in the soul".[19]

Law—in the unregenerate—has no other fruit but to enrage and increase sin in man. "Chains put not a fierceness into a beast, but yet it does outwardly draw forth that fury that was in its nature."[20] The Law is thus the cause of sin, not *per se* but *per accidens*.[21] There is therefore no blemish in the Law itself, for "the Law is holy as well when it does by accident enrage sin, as when by it self it discovers it".[22]

(iii) *Condemnation of Law*

Because sin is law-breaking, the Law must condemn it, and the documents of the Westminster Assembly are clear on this.

> Every sin, both original and actual, being a transgression of the righteous law of God, and contrary thereunto, doth, in its own

13. William Perkins, *Golden Chaine*, in *Works*, p. 72.
14. Jeremiah Burroughs, *Saints Treasury*, p. 95.
15. *Christ and Moses*, p. 190.
16. Samuel Rutherford, *Survey*, Part II. p. 94.
17. Thomas Goodwin, *Unregenerate Man's Guiltiness*, in *Works*, X. 64.
18. Ralph Venning, *Sin, the Plague of Plagues*, p. 169.
19. John Bunyan, *Pilgrim's Progress*, 1678, p. 21.
20. William Strong, *The Two Covenants*, pp. 41, 42.
21. William Strong, ibid.
22. William Strong, op. cit., p. 39.

nature, bring guilt upon the sinner, whereby he is bound over to the wrath of God, and curse of the law, and so made subject to death, with all miseries spiritual, temporal, and eternal.[23]

William Perkins contends that the use of the Law in unregenerate persons is "to denounce eternal damnation".[24] The broken commandment becomes an instrument of death,[25] because "the Law of God can only damn all sinners",[26] and make "death a doore to hell".[27]

The Law cannot contradict it self, having already pronounced a peremptory sentence of death upon the sinner, 'tis impossible the Law should ever give repentance unto Life.[28]

"That Man that overtook you," said *Christian* to *Faithful*, "was Moses, he spareth none, neither knoweth he how to shew mercy to those that transgress his Law."[29] Even Richard Baxter finds it impossible not to affirm that God, having spoken threats, cannot now pardon "absolutely".[30]

The Puritans were particularly sensitive to the fact that this condemnatory aspect of the Law was only accidental to it.[31] The inability of the Law "to light us to heaven" is "not through its own, but our deficiency".[32] They accepted the full significance of the words of Paul that the Law "was weak through the flesh",[33] and taught that Law cannot give righteousness, not because of any fault in the Law, but because of the weakness of the sinner, Romans viii. 3.[34] The difference between Law in itself and Law as it is experienced arises from the sin of man. It is sin which makes the Law to be contrary to the promise, and condemnation is accidental to the purpose of the Law as it is to the Gospel.[35]

23. *Confession of Faith*, VI. 6.
24. *Golden Chaine*, in *Works*, p. 72; *Galatians*, 1604, p. 347, The law is "the ministerie of death". Samuel Rutherford, *Covenant of Life*, 1655, p. 7, remarks that under the Law of Nature the heathen "beleeve that sin deserves wrath".
25. Edward Elton, *Treatises*: "Complaint of a Sanctifyed Sinner", p. 113.
26. Robert Traill, *Justification Vindicated*, in *Works*, I. 277.
27. Thomas Taylor, *Regula Vitae*, p. 9.
28. Thomas Cole, *Repentance*, 1689, p. 93.
29. John Bunyan, *Pilgrim's Progress*, p. 93.
30. *Aphorismes*, p. 18.
31. See above, p. 81.
32. Thomas Adams, *Sacrifice of Thankfulness*, 1616, in *Works*, I. 119.
33. Romans viii. 3. See *The Marrow*, p. 30; Ralph Venning, *Sin, the Plague of Plagues*, p. 172; Edward Elton, *Treatises*: "Triumph of a True Christian", p. 33.
34. Richard Byfield, *Gospels Glory*, p. 8.
35. Edward Reynolds, *Three Treatises*: "Sinfulnesse of Sinne", pp. 371, 383, 385.

B. THE CONVICTING POWER OF THE LAW

"By the law is the knowledge of sin":[36] that is to say, it brings conviction of its guilt.[37] The Law pierces the conscience when men have sinned, and it is in this way that it is said to make sin abound[38]. Its designed effect is "not that men may sin more", but that they may "see their sin more."[39] George Downame uses a familiar seventeenth century metaphor when he says, "The law by reason of our transgression is an enemy unto us", and this is to be seen in "the bondage wherein the morall law did hold us".[40] Men must learn, through the Law, what that bondage is into which sin brings them.[41] Evidence for this belief among the Puritans can be produced almost indefinitely,[42] but it may be summed up in the careful words of Edward Elton

> Without the true knowledge of the Law, the corruption of nature lies hid, and as it were dead . . . Men are ready to soothe up themselves; and to think well of themselves. . . . Being ignorant of the Law of God, . . . they blesse themselves, and think they are well and in very good case; and when they are in the worst case of all, they think themselves in the best. . . . The Law of God . . . shewes men their sins, and it makes men see and feel themselves as dead men, and in a most wretched case, by reason of their sins.[43]

(i) *The Law as a mirror*

One of the favourite Puritan ways of stating this truth about the Law of God was to liken it to a glass or mirror.[44] Robert Bolton speaks of "the cleare Cristall of Gods pure Law, which can discover unto thee the least spot that ever stained so much as any one of thy thoughts",[45] and in *Helps to Humiliation* he says,

> Be acquainted with all the wayes thou canst possible to anatomize thy sinne. . . . Be perfect in the Law of God, and look thy selfe in

36. Romans iii. 20.
37. Stephen Charnock, *Conviction of Sin*, 1684, in *Works*, IV. 183; John Owen, *Mortification*, 1656, in *Works*, VI. 57, 58.
38. Romans v. 20.
39. Ralph Venning, *Sin, the Plague of Plagues*, p. 173.
40. *Covenant of Grace*, p. 49.
41. Thomas Goodwin, *Work of the Holy Ghost*, in *Works*, VI. 261, 262.
42. John Preston, Richard Sibbes, Jeremiah Burroughs, Anthony Burgess, Stephen Geree, William Allen, Thomas Manton, Thomas Brooks, David Clarkson, Robert Traill, and *The Marrow*.
43. *Treatises*: "Complaint of a Sanctifyed Sinner", pp. 86, 89, 95.
44. This was found in Luther and Calvin.
45. *Comfortable Walking*, 1625, p. 342.

> the pure Christall glasse thereof; be throughly catechised in the Commandements.[46]

So few men know what they do when they sin against God, that they need "the bright glass of the Law wherein we may see the evil of sin".[47] The Law was given to reveal transgressions "as a Reprover and corrector of sinne . . . not onely to discover sin, but to make it appeare exceeding sinfull".[48]

There must be awareness of, and repentance for, particular sins, and this needs the Law; for unless the commandments are particularized, there is no conviction. Richard Greenham asks,

> How shall wee come to the right sight of our sinnes, and a sound perswasion of the greatnes of them?
> By the spirit of God leading us into the true understanding of the law, and a due examination of ourselves thereby.[49]

Men show a great disinclination to descend to particulars, and

> For want of light in Gods Law, they looke upon their sinnes, as we doe upon the Starres . . . see onely the great ones . . . here one, and there one.[50]

Conscience applies God's Law in conviction of sin,[51] and sinners should, therefore, detail their sins under the various commandments, and so perceive them specifically as breaches of those commandments.[52] Accordingly, Samuel Bolton says that sin may be seen in

> The Glass of the Law. A Glass which discovers sin in all its Dimensions. . . . Search into the Law, and thou shalt discover Thousands of sins which fall under Any One Law of God. Oh! here is A Glass! . . . You can have No Magnifying Glass, to greaten sin above the Greatness of it.[53]

46. Op. cit., 1631, pp. 6, 14.
47. Jeremiah Burroughs, *Evil of Evils*, 1654, pp. 80, 124; Richard Sibbes, *Church's Complaint*, 1639, in *Works*, VI. 185.
48. Samuel Bolton, *True Bounds*, pp. 119, 121.
49. *Short Catechisme*, in *Works*, p. 212.
50. Robert Bolton, *Afflicted Consciences*, pp. 102, 215, 218, 221. In his *Assise Sermons*, 1629, pp. 80–83, he contrasts the natural Puritan and the commandments, the moral Puritan and the commandments, the superstitious Puritan and the commandments, and the Pharisaical Puritan and the commandments, dealing at the same time with what he calls the "unwarrantable opinionist".
51. William Ames, *Conscience*, Book I. p. 35 and see pp. 26, 28, 38–43. Cf. Richard Hooker, *Laws*, I. xii. 2.
52. Cf. William Ames, *Conscience*, Book II. p. 8 and Isaac Ambrose, *Prima, Media, & Ultima*, "The First Things", 1650, Appendix, p. 20, and Henry Scudder, *Daily Walke*, 1628, p. 88, who says that if a man cannot remember he should "get some Catalogue or Table wherein the same are set downe".
53. *Sin*, pp. 27–29.

This concept of the Law as a mirror is used also by men like John Eaton, who says,

> yet to sharpen thy stomack unto Free Justification, and because the Paschall Lambe must bee eaten with sowre herbs, give me leave to give thee a glimse of this pure glasse of the Law, that thou maist see some few spots of thy soule leprosie, in the spirituall breach of all Gods Commandements.[54]

(ii) *The Law to be preached*

The majority of the Puritans placed much stress on the preaching of the Law to bring men to an awareness of sin. William Perkins knew that true repentance was the result of Gospel grace, but he opposed those who for this reason would despise the preaching of the Law in this respect.[55] When Richard Greenham gave *A sweete comfort for an afflicted Conscience* he did not see "why it should not be very convenient, first to lay open the righteousnes of the law, that men may see their sinnes", for "we may urge more fearfully the use of the law to a man, as being the stronger vessell".[56] Even the Antinomian John Eaton requires that ministers shall

> preach the Law . . . as killingly as we can: or else . . . it doth make but hypocrites; for the more killingly the Law is preached, the more truly it is preached.[57]

Anthony Burgess agrees with him and declares that the exhibition of "the pure, strict and exact obligation of the Law" makes "all thy deformities" to appear, and so "in this sense it is good to be a legal Preacher, and a legal hearer often".[58] He considers that this legal preaching is "the great work that the Ministers of God have to do in their Congregations in these times".[59] "Men must come to the knowledge of sin in themselves, by the Law", and this is no "easie matter", but

> It is the preaching of the Law of God . . . that will . . . discover to them their hidden and secret sins; never was any brought to a sight of his sinnes, . . . but only by the preaching of the Law of God.[60]

54. *Honey-combe*, p. 11; *Dangerous Dead Faith*, 1642, p. 89.
55. *Two Treatises*, 1593, in *Works*, p. 540.
56. Op. cit., in *Works*, p. 140. Apparently a man can stand more than a woman!
57. *Honey-combe*, p. 124.
58. *Justification*, 1648, Part I. p. 299.
59. *Spiritual Refining*, "Of Grace and Assurance", p. 143; cf. op. cit., "Of Sinne", 1654, pp. 142, 184, 253, 254.
60. Edward Elton, *Treatises*: "Complaint of a Sanctifyed Sinner", pp. 69, 72, 76; cf. "Triumph of a True Christian", p. 175; Simon Ford, *Spirit of Bondage and Adoption*, pp. 34, 47.

Giles Firmin regretted that "of late years this kind of preaching is laid by". He knew that "some Ministers" could be "imprudent in their preaching of the Law", but held that "the Principle it self" still remained, "that the preaching of the Law is necessary to make men know their sins. . . . Men may be convinced of Sin without the Gospel, but not without the Law."[61] The Law is to be preached that "as a Map discovers rocks and quicksands that men may avoid them; and Physick books, poisons, to warn men of them",[62] so it may lead men to salvation. Richard Byfield cites the Pauline statement[63] that the Law is a killing letter, and points out that the apostle does not say, "a dead letter", for "no part of the Word of God is a dead letter; for then it could not be of such power as to be a killing letter".[64]

John Flavel has two sermons on "The great Usefulness of the Law . . . in order to the application of Christ" in which he says, "The Law of God hath a Soul-wounding an Heart-cutting Efficacy" and until the soul "be wounded for Sin, it will never be converted from Sin, and brought effectually to Jesus Christ."[65] Therefore, "we are fain to make it the greatest of our business to preach the law, and come with that great hammer to break your bones in pieces first, that we may then preach the Gospel".[66]

(iii) "*The Spirit of bondage*"

In the work of conviction of sin, the Law does not possess this power of itself, "without it be applyed by the Spirit",[67] for He "who hath lashed and whipped the conscience" is none other than God the Holy Spirit.[68] Robert Bolton accounts for the trembling of sinners under the Law by recognizing "the Spirit of God in the Law",[69] and John Eaton, from the other side of the theological controversy, likewise attributes the discovery of sin to the work of the Holy Spirit.

> Thus the holy Ghost shewes us our sins, whereby they begin to see their Leprosie to bee very foule, and their miserie most fearefull for one sinne, much more for many sinnes: . . . this is the holy Ghosts, and not the light of natures, first shewing us our sinnes.[70]

61. *Real Christian*, 1670, pp. 51–53.
62. Simon Ford, *Spirit of Bondage and Adoption*, p. 35.
63. II Corinthians iii. 6, 7.
64. *Gospels Glory*, p. 34.
65. *Method of Grace*, 1681, pp. 221, 224.
66. Thomas Goodwin, *Reconciliation*, 1651, in *Works*, V. 512.
67. Vavasor Powell, *Christ and Moses*, p. 189.
68. Thomas Goodwin, *Child of Light*, 1636, in *Works*, III. 282.
69. *Afflicted Consciences*, p. 147.
70. *Honey-combe*, p. 159.

Tobias Crisp is in agreement with this opinion, and says that the Law may be a looking glass, but the sinner does not see his filthiness till grace gives him eyes.[71]

The work of the Holy Spirit in bringing conviction of sin by the Law, was understood by the Puritans to be the meaning of Paul's remarkable phrase, "the spirit of bondage".[72] The "Antecedent" to the Spirit of sonship

> is the Spirit of bondage, for that of necessitie must go before, so that if thou never hadst the Spirit of bondage, certainely thou has not yet received the spirit of the Sonne. . . . Except the spirit of bondage put an edge upon the Law, put a Sword into hand of the Law, to pricke the heart, to wound the heart, . . . You may heare the Law, and the threatnings and curses applyed to you tenne thousand times over, and yet no feare bee bred in you, except the spirit of bondage joyne with it, that makes it effectuall.[73]

The Puritans found no embarrassment in saying that "the Spirit of bondage must be first set on worke, to shew us our spirituall misery, to humble us to prepare for Christ",[74] or that "the Spirit must first become a Spirit of bondage and fear";[75] nor did they ever resort to any expedients to "explain" what might at first appear so strange. Because the Holy Spirit convicts of sin He is called "the Spirit of bondage", Romans viii. 15. "It was no other but the Spirit of God, discovering unto, and setting upon the heart of a man or woman, that bondage that they be in under the Law."[76] Edward Elton says that "the Spirit of bondage" is the work of the Holy Spirit in relation to the holy Law and human sin, bringing the sinner into bondage,[77] and even Robert Towne remarks, "For as the Spirit useth and worketh by the Law, so its called the Spirit of bondage".[78] God's working of faith brings "a discovery of sin, which the Lord makes by the law and by the Spirit, Rom. vii. 7. . . . This is the work of the spirit of bondage."[79] The Spirit of Bondage is not man's

71. *Christ Alone Exalted,* in *Works,* I. 24; II. 239.
72. Romans viii. 15.
73. John Preston, *New Covenant,* p. 394; cf. *Breastplate of Faith and Love,* "Of Faith", 1630, pp. 160, 161.
74. Robert Bolton, *Afflicted Consciences,* p. 337.
75. Richard Sibbes, *Witness of Salvation,* 1629, in *Works,* VII. 371.
76. Jeremiah Burroughs, *Evil of Evils,* p. 409; *Saints Treasury,* p. 97; cf. also Francis Roberts, *God's Covenants,* pp. 937, 964, 965; Andrew Willet, *Hexapla: Romanes,* p. 358; Stephen Charnock, *Conviction of Sin,* in *Works,* IV. 173; Richard Byfield, *Gospels Glory,* p. 245; Thomas Hooker, *Soules Preparation,* 1632, p. 124.
77. *Treatises*: "Triumph of a True Christian", p. 172.
78. *Assertion of Grace,* p. 147.
79. David Clarkson, *Of Faith,* 1696, in *Works,* I. 78, 80; Thomas Goodwin, *Child of Light,* in *Works,* III. 243.

natural or fallen spirit, which would be described as properly his own, but it is

> a Spirit received (as a gift of grace) from God; and that this can be no other then the Holy Spirit of God. He it is that creates trouble in the hearts of Gods Elect in order to conversion, as well as peace after it.[80]

This bondage is no "unholy" bondage: it is "not a bondage to sin, but a bondage for sin: and a bondage, that is the beginning of liberty from sin."[81]

The interpretation of the phrase "spirit of bondage" as referring to the Holy Spirit is an extremely unusual idea at the present time. Such New Testament scholars as Beet, Dodd, Gifford, Meyer, Moffatt, Murray, and Sanday and Headlam treat the word "spirit" as a common noun in the sense of a "slavish spirit". Other scholars, however, understand the word as a proper noun, and among these are Alford, Godet and C. Hodge, who perceive in the phrase a reference to the Holy Spirit but understand Paul to be denying that the Holy Spirit is the cause of fear. This is the meaning indicated by the *New English Bible* in the initial capital letter given to "Spirit" combined with the paraphrase, "The Spirit you have received is not a spirit of slavery leading you back into a life of fear". Calvin refers to a "twofold spirit", received from the Law and Gospel respectively, both of which he describes as being "given". His editor understands his meaning to be that the "spirit of bondage" is the Holy Spirit "the effect of whose administration was bondage".[82] Bengel, followed by Wesley, admits some effects of the Holy Spirit's work in this "fear", even though the Spirit is not primarily a "Spirit of bondage", and he regards this "bondage" as a kind of accidental effect. Burkitt, likewise, suggests that the bondage and fear are the result of the Holy Spirit's work, but that Paul's meaning is that for the true believer who has been brought into the freedom of Christ the Holy Spirit "never again becomes a spirit of bondage to the same soul".

No such division or uncertainty of opinion exists among the Puritan scholars, however, and they are unanimous in their view that the apostle here refers to the convicting work of the Holy Spirit. The evidence from the Puritan writings has been sufficiently indicated above, but it can be supplemented almost indefinitely. The only place where there seems to be even the faintest suggestion of deviation is

80. Simon Ford, *Spirit of Bondage and Adoption*, p. 7; "the same Spirit of God, who lays on them those fetters, in his due time knocks them off again", op. cit., p. 182.
81. Op. cit., p. 7.
82. Calvin, *Romans*, 1539, (1948 edn.) footnote to p. 296.

found in Tobias Crisp, *Christ Alone Exalted,* where he says, with some possible echoes of Calvin, that in the words of the apostle

> you have two spirits set in opposition; the spirit of fear and bondage, and the spirit of adoption. The Spirit of bondage is nothing else but a spirit that speaks from such Principles as always lead unto bondage: The true meaning is this, so long as men have no other spirit speaking in them but from the principle of their own righteousness, so long they have no other spirit but such as leads to bondage.[83]

Tobias Crisp does not differ from the common Puritan opinion here, but is only less definite in his form of expression. He indicates that while a man is dominated by "Principles" of mere Law-keeping, he will find the Holy Spirit none other than a "Spirit of bondage".

It must be admitted that there are ambiguities in the passage and that they are not altogether unlike the difficulties found in the similar uncertainty attaching to the word πνεῦμα in Romans i. 4. This is one of those instances where a theological insight penetrates farther than merely grammatical exegesis. The Puritans saw the theological truth which was the corrollary both of the convicting function of God's Law and of the impossibility of the Law to do this effectively without the activity of the Holy Spirit. The moderns are right descriptively and as to the experience involved, but the Puritans were right in finding their way to the ultimate cause. It might be possible to combine both of these aspects of the truth by saying that the Roman believers had gone past the stage when the Holy Spirit had to be to them a spirit of bondage.

(iv) *No Gospel without the Law*

There was keen discussion among the Puritans about the place of Law in conversion, and the "conditions" of the Gospel.[84] Their general view was that, if it be true that the Gospel is rightly preached without any conditions, then neither Jesus nor the apostles ever preached the Gospel. The apostolic preaching of the Gospel was not a bare preaching of Jesus, without any demand for repentance. Antecedently to faith, it is presupposed that there has been the work of the Law in the conviction of sin, and the order, relation and use of the Law and the Gospel evince this.[85]

83. Op. cit., in *Works,* II. 470.
84. It will go beyond the scope of the present work to pursue the "Marrow" controversy which, in effect, was a difference of judgment about the necessity of preaching the Law as part of the Gospel, and the requirement of the condition of repentance before the offer of the Gospel should be made.
85. John Owen, *Justification,* in *Works,* V. 74, 75.

The Antinomians sometimes spoke differently,[86] and it is here that the name given to them seems to have some justification. John Saltmarsh, for example, maintains that the Gospel promises belong to sinners as sinners, not as repenting sinners.[87] In his opposition to the Antinomian view, Thomas Gataker alludes to the alleged reasoning of a woman who said, "God will save sinners; I am a sinner; God will save me". He contends that it is "sporting with a poor wounded conscience" to say this, for the troubled soul could equally well reply, "God will damn sinners; But I am a sinner; Therefore God will damn mee." It is the presence or absence of repentance that makes the difference.[88] Against Thomas Gataker's statement that "we require of those that desire pardon of sin . . . repentance, and humiliation, and sorrow for sin, and prayer for pardon",[89] John Saltmarsh contends that this "would work God down into his old and former way of revealing himself as under the Law".[90] Henry Denne caricatures repentance as washing away sin with tears,[91] and in his *Conference,* he has no answer to give the Sick Man who asks, "Can you shew me any reason why I should beleeve this, rather than Judas?" than to retort, "You must not looke at reason".[92]

The issue which these contrary opinions raise is whether the promises of the Gospel apply to sinners as such, or only to "sensible" sinners. The Antinomians stood for the former, with the denial that the Law has any part in the conversion of sinners,[93] basing their objections on the argument that fallen man needs, not merely the light that the Law gives, but new life. This statement, of course, is correct, but it is insufficient for dismissing the Law as useless. To argue against the Law because it is powerless without the Spirit, is to argue similarly against the Gospel, for that, too, is powerless without the Spirit.[94]

On the whole, the Puritans regarded conviction of sin as the

86. George Fox rebukes the Antinomians on this very point by saying, "You ... never came thorough the Prophets, nor Moses house". George Fox and James Nailor, *A Word from the Lord*, 1654, p. 13.
87. *Free-Grace*, pp. 191, 192.
88. *Shadows without Substance*, pp. 57, 58; *Antinomianism*, p. 26.
89. *A Mistake*, p. 36.
90. *Free-Grace*, p. 169; John Eaton, *Honey-combe*, p. 84, says of Christ that "his Sermons, for the most part, runne all upon the perfect doctrine and works of the Law."
91. *Man of Sin Discovered*, pp. 25–28.
92. *Conference*, 1643, p. 33.
93. Robert Towne, *Assertion of Grace*, p. 163.
94. Cf. Samuel Rutherford, *Triumph of Faith*, 1645, p. 105. Not all the Antinomians stand solidly on this. Tobias Crisp is more restrained, and, although his sermon on John vi. 37 is marked by unguarded expressions, John Gill defends him thus: "It should be observed, that all before spoken, is said to such who are deemed sensible of their rebellion and vileness; and also under some temptations that Christ will not receive them, being so very sinful." Tobias Crisp, *Works*, (ed. Gill), I. 223.

necessary pre-requisite for the enjoyment of Divine forgiveness, and Robert Bolton writes scornfully of the "cruell mercies of unskilfull Dawbers",[95] who "serve Satans craft in this kinde", and who injure the souls of men by offering comfort too easily and too soon.[96] He exclaims, "How pestilent is the Art of Spirituall Dawbing. . . . When mercy, Christ, the promises, salvation, heaven, and all are applied hand over head, and falsely appropriated to unhumbled sinners."[97] When he enters upon the task of giving "Instructions for a Right Comforting" of the troubled sinner, he describes his purpose as follows:

> I first desire to . . . rectifie some ordinary aberrations about spirituall Cures. Which fall out, when the Physitian of the Soule . . . applies unseasonably the Cordials of the Gospell, and comforts of Mercy. . . . Were it not absurd in Surgery, to powre a most soveraigne Balsam of exquisite composition, and inestimable price upon a sound part? It is farre more unseemely and senselesse, and of an infinitely more pestilent consequence in any Ministeriall passages, to profer the bloud of Christ, and promises of life to an unwounded conscience, as belonging unto it, as yet.[98]

He contends that all who have ever set themselves "to save Soules, have followed the same course; to wit, First, to wound by the Law, and then to heale by the Gospell."[99] In support of this view, he mentions a large number of teachers of "Orthodox Antiquity",[100] and "Perkins that great Light of our Church"[101] who says,

> First of all a man must have knowledge of foure things, namely of the law of God, of sinne against the lawe, of the guilt of sinne, and of the judgement of God against sinne, which is the eternall wrath of God.[102]

Robert Bolton warns against a misunderstanding of these preparatory experiences.

> Wee must therefore by no meanes conceive of the fore-named preparative humiliations and precedent workes of the Law and

95. *Afflicted Consciences*, p. 134.
96. Op. cit., p. 151; cf. Simon Ford, *Spirit of Bondage and Adoption*, p. 27, "there is danger lest wee snatch comfort before it is fit for us, or wee for it."
97. Op. cit., pp. 159, 165. John Saltmarsh does not like this, and complains that "many Preachers, like some Chirurgions who keep their Patients from healing too soone, that they may make the cure the more admired, doe accordingly keepe ... soules with their wounds open." *Free-Grace*, p. 37.
98. Op. cit., pp. 134, 135.
99. Op. cit., p. 135.
100. Op. cit., p. 139.
101. Op. cit., p. 142.
102. William Perkins, *Two Treatises*, in *Works*, p. 541.

Gospell, as of any meritorious qualifications to draw on Christ (for he is given most freely) but as of needfull predispositions, to drive us unto Christ.[103]

Further, no special degree of legal terrors is called for.

We doe not prescribe precisely just such a measure and quantitie . . . But sure wee are, a man must have so much, and in that measure, as to bring Him [*sic*] to Christ. It must make him Weary of all his sinnes, and of Satans bondage wholy: . . . that hee may heartily thirst for mercy.[104]

These cautions, however, do not minimize the necessity of this preparatory Law-work, and "the Spirituall Physition" must not apply comfort "too soone".[105] Too many have damaged the souls of men by

stifelling the very first stirrings of Legall remorse, by healing the wounds of their conscience with sweet words, before they be searcht, and sounded to the bottome.[106]

Robert Bolton was not alone, however, in his anxiety about the "short cut" Gospel. Richard Greenham "would mislike them that would not abide to tarrie the Lords leisure, but they must needes be helped at once".[107]

In Puritan thinking, the sharp needle[108] of the Law, as it pricks the conscience, was found to be attached to the scarlet thread of the Gospel.[109] "The application of the Law doth ordinarily go before", in order that a man may be prepared to receive the promises;[110] and thus

being schooled by the law, by which the Holy Ghost worketh in us the legall faith which is a preparative to the Evangelicall, we become fitt auditours of the Gospell, by which the Holy Spirit worketh in us the grace of justifying faith.[111]

Ane Catachisme conteining The Soume of Christian Religion, by Mr Samuell Rutherfurd, asks,

Q. Then ther goeth no preparatione befor Godis effectuall calling?

103. Op. cit., p. 175.
104. Op. cit., pp. 268, 269; cf. Simon Ford, *Spirit of Bondage and Adoption*, p. 65, "some stay longer".
105. Op. cit., p. 275.
106. Op. cit., p. 324; cf. Ralph Venning, *Sin, the Plague of Plagues*, p. 174; John Rogers, *Doctrine of Faith*, 1627, p. 97.
107. *Grave Counsels*, in *Works*, p. 5.
108. Anthony Burgess, *Spiritual Refining*, "Of Grace and Assurance", p. 29.
109. William Perkins, *Galatians*, p. 246, "As the needle goes before, and draws in the thrid".
110. William Ames, *Marrow of Sacred Divinity*, p. 111.
111. George Downame, *Covenant of Grace*, p. 88.

A. Yes, God casteth us downe with the terrours of the Law, making us see our miserable estait.[112]

and "the Lord soe disposes upon the working of the law, that in it, by contraries as it were, he drawes lif out of death."[113]

C. SIN IN THE BELIEVER

No discussion of the Puritan view of the relation of Law and sin can be complete without a consideration of the Antinomian controversy on the subject of sin in the believer. Has the Law any relation to the believer such as would cause his shortcomings to be regarded as sin?

(i) *Indwelling corruption*

Although there is no condemnation to those who are in Christ Jesus, there is nevertheless much sin still attaching to them. This sin consists in a remaining pollution of the life and in the actions which spring from it.

> The new creature, or new worke of grace, can never be fully fashioned in this life. . . . For although the new birth is universall, and of the whole man: yet is it not entier, perfect, pure.[114]

Richard Greenham's imaginative pen enables him to write,

> the body of sinne and wicked motions and affections shall never be out of us as long as we live, for they are almost continually boyling and walloping [*sic*] in us, foming out such filthie froth and stinking savour into our mindes.[115]

"Sinne although it doe not raigne in the saints, yet doth remayne, and dwell in them"[116] in the form of what the Puritans repeatedly called sinful dross, because "the whole man and the very conscience is onely in part[117] regenerate, and therefore in some part remaines still corrupt."[118] The reason why the godly cannot keep the Law perfectly is to be traced to indwelling sin.

> Rom. 7. 19. Gal. 5. 17 do strongly confirm, that because of the innate corruption still abiding in us, we are not able to do anything so perfectly as the Law requireth: in the most holy men there are

112. Op. cit., cap. 19, quoted by A. F. Mitchell, *Catechisms*, p. 201.
113. Catechism "by Mr. Thomas Wyllie", quoted by A. F. Mitchell, op. cit., p. 247.
114. Arthur Dent, *Plaine Mans Pathway*, p. 15.
115. *Faith, Justification, and Feeling*, in *Works*, p. 307.
116. John Preston, *Law out lawed*, 1631, p. 10.
117. i.e., it is not entire and perfect.
118. William Perkins, *Of Conscience*, in *Works*, 659; cf. William Ames, *Marrow of Sacred Divinity*, pp. 59, 128, 337.

... defects ... and affections contrarily withstanding the obligation of the Law.[119]

This "innate corruption" within believers is not merely passive, "it is also stirring in them, and lusting, and rebelling against the Spirit, and against that grace that is in them".[120] It remains in the believer "according to its Physicall and reall indwelling: ... it dwelleth in him, having the compleat essence and being of sin",[121] and the "corrupt principles of carnal reason"[122] remain "unpurged out".[123] Christ's justification does not take away sin as a fact, or a sinful fact, or a fact deserving of punishment.[124]

Similar statements about man's corruption were made by the Antinomians. John Eaton, for example, concedes that the Church "hath some sin in the imperfections of her Sanctification that the Devill seeth; and every one of us in our consciences doe feele it";[125] and Tobias Crisp affirms, "A Person that is a Believer ... doth nothing but Sin, his Soul is a Mint of Sin".[126] Robert Towne repudiates the charge that he ever denied that sin and pollution should not be in the flesh,[127] while John Saltmarsh affirms, not only that the sinful nature remains, but also that the Law is still able, at least, to "tell" the believer he sins.[128]

Along with these admissions of sin in the heart of the believer, there are Antinomian statements to the effect that God sees no sin in the believer. How do such contradictory statements arise? The answer to this question has to be found by means of an enquiry into the seventeenth century understanding of the doctrines of justification and sanctification.

(ii) *Justification and sanctification*

The difficulties of the subject arise partly from the inherited pre-Reformation view that, etymologically, the word "justify" means to "make" righteous,[129] and partly from the fact that at certain periods in the history of Christian doctrine the word "sanctification" has been employed as an inclusive term to cover all the experiences of the grace

119. Anthony Burgess, *Spiritual Refining*, "Of Grace and Assurance", p. 63; cf. Edward Elton, *Treatises*: "Complaint of a Sanctifyed Sinner", pp. 161, 163.
120. Edward Elton, *Treatises*: "Complaint of a Sanctifyed Sinner", p. 174.
121. Samuel Rutherford, *Triumph of Faith*, p. 171. "Physical" does not connote any materialistic idea, but indicates the grip of sin on man's nature.
122. Thomas Goodwin, *Child of Light*, in *Works*, III. 254.
123. Thomas Goodwin, *Christian's Growth*, 1641, in *Works*, III. 448.
124. Richard Baxter, *Aphorismes*, p. 206.
125. *Honey-combe*, pp. 38, 39.
126. *Christ Alone Exalted*, in *Works*, I. 8.
127. *Assertion of Grace*, p. 40.
128. *Free-Grace*, pp. 59, 128; cf. Henry Denne, *Man of Sin Discovered*, p. 12.
129. For a 17th century discussion, see George Downame, *Justification*, 1633, p. 50.

of God, and thus sometimes to mean regeneration or justification.[130] In accurate theological definition, however, the terms justification and sanctification are kept apart, as standing for two distinct, though complementary, acts of Divine grace. Justification is understood, forensically, to indicate the act of God in declaring the sinner to be free from all legal charge, on account of the satisfaction made by Christ on his behalf; and sanctification is that act of God by which the believer's life is transformed more and more after a godly pattern. The Westminster *Larger Catechism* explains the distinction as follows:

> *Q.* Wherein do justification and sanctification differ?
> *A.* Although sanctification be inseparably joined with justification, yet they differ, in that God in justification imputeth the righteousness of Christ; in sanctification his Spirit infuseth grace, and enableth to the exercise thereof; in the former, sin is pardoned; in the other, it is subdued.[131]

When the Antinomians expounded the doctrine of justification, they repeatedly took pains to deny that justification is based on the personal inherent righteousness of the believer, and so it is clear that a forensic verdict of this kind carries with it no indication of the moral and spiritual condition of the one justified.

If this extremely important distinction is firmly held, there is no difficulty in disentangling the doctrinal confusion caused by the Antinomian statements about Christian perfection. Put succinctly, they erroneously used the categories of justification when speaking of sanctification, and consequently ascribed qualities of perfection to the latter which belong only to the former.[132]

Much of what the Antinomians wrote can be taken in an orthodox sense. Tobias Crisp, for example, can be cleared of most of the charges brought against him, as, when he says,

> You have no sooner received him, but you are instantly justified by him; and in this Justification, you are discharged from all the faults that may be laid to your charge.[133]

Replying to the question whether a believer must be reckoned to be a sinner, while he still commits sin, he answers,

> I am far from imagining any Believer is freed from acts of Sin, he is freed only from the charge of Sin; that is, from being a subject

130. Richard Baxter traces this use to Augustine. To the Reader, in William Allen, *The Covenants*. There is also some warrant in I Peter i. 2 for this inclusive use.
131. Op. cit., 1647, Question 77; cf. James Ussher, *Body of Divinitie*, pp. 193, 202; George Downame, *Justification*, pp. 76–81.
132. Richard Baxter commits the opposite error, and uses the language of sanctification to expound the doctrine of justification, and, as a result, takes away from justification that perfection which truly belongs to it.
133. *Christ Alone Exalted*, in *Works*, I. 5.

to be charged with Sin . . . God doth no longer stand offended nor displeased with him, when he hath once received Christ. . . . I have not said, God is not offended with the sins that Believers commit; but God stands not offended with the persons of Believers, for the sins committed by them.[134]

Tobias Crisp was fortunate in having two most able defenders, Isaac Chauncy at the end of the seventeenth century, and John Gill in the early nineteenth century. Isaac Chauncy composed a dialogue between *Neonomian* and *Antinomian*,[135] in which most of the arguments of *Antinomian* are paraphrases of Tobias Crisp, and are shown to be about justification.[136] John Gill provides footnotes in his edition of *The Complete Works of Tobias Crisp* in which he argues that "the Doctor" is concerned with "condemnation", "the eye of justice", "acceptance with God", and sin "in its penal aspects".[137] Robert Towne labours to make clear that when he says that God does not see sin in believers it is "with respect to the Law".

I can looke upon myselfe, my actions, yea, into my Conscience, and see my sinnes remaine; but looke into the Records of Heaven and Gods Justice, and since the bloudshed of Christ, I finde there nothing against me.[138]

The phrase, "God is not displeased with the sins of the justified", is spoken in terms of the person's acceptance in Christ.[139] These explanations are those also of John Saltmarsh who, in many pages of *Free-Grace,* likewise affirms that it is only in connection with justification that God sees no sin in the believer,[140] and Henry Denne says that

The called of God (even the most upright of them) have sin in the flesh, . . . but they have no sin . . . in the conscience: for the true faith of God's elect, and sin in the conscience, can no more stand together, then light and darknesse.[141]

134. Op. cit., I. 10, 15, 16.
135. Isaac Chauncy takes the risk of appearing in the part of *Antinomian.*
136. *Neonomianism Unmask'd*, Part I. pp. 14, 15; Part II. pp. 67, 68; Part III. pp. 4, 13, 14, 36.
137. Tobias Crisp, *Works*, (ed. Gill), I. 5, 8, 13, 15; II. 119.
138. *Assertion of Grace*, p. 97.
139. Op. cit., p. 106.
140. Op. cit., pp. 129 f., 143–5.
141. *Man of Sin Discovered*, p. 12; cf. pp. 13, 14, 32. By no "sin in the conscience" he means no remaining guilt of unpardoned sin: he does not mean no awareness of sinfulness in the life. It is justification, not sanctification, of which he writes. Thomas Boston defends the author of *The Marrow* in this way against the charge of Antinomianism when he explains that the author's reference to the believer having "no conscience of sins" is in relation to "everlasting condemnation". *The Marrow,* Thomas Boston's Notes, 1818, p. 255, quoted from Samuel Rutherford.

Perhaps the least deserving of the protection of this *apologia* is John Eaton, yet even some of his statements are capable of an orthodox interpretation. He explains that the absence of sin from the believer is to be understood "not simply, but in the sight of God; . . . because their iniquitie is (though mystically above reason, sence and feeling) yet truely put out from before God".[142] To objections based on James iii. 2 and 1 John i. 8, which are objections against perfect sanctification, John Eaton replies, "Is not God able to abolish those sins that we feel daily dwelling in us, out of his own sight; although he doth not abolish them out of our sight?"[143] and he retorts to those who contend that God still sees sin in believers:

> But how comes God to see them in us, after hee hath covered them out of his own sight? These Objectors answer, By looking under the covering. But I would gladly know of them, wherefore did God cover them out of his sight, if hee peepe under the covering to see them againe? Or, I would know of them, whether God so cover our sinnes out of his owne sight, as men cover things with a net, that lye as naked to view as they did before they were covered?[144]

An illustration which sometimes does duty here is that of the colour given to water through a red glass, and it is used to explain how all the elect are perfectly righteous in God's sight.[145]

The foregoing passages from the Antinomian authors reveal undeniably that they were writing about justification; but, unhappily, they did not stop there. They allowed themselves to be swept away into enthusiastic but erroneous deductions. From the forensic language of justification, they made inferences about the spiritual condition of those who are justified; from the premise of the believer's perfect standing, they drew the conclusion of the believer's perfect state.

John Eaton, for example, finds it only a short step to affirm that believers are without spot of any kind: "neither the matter, nor the forme of sin, nor any part thereof remaines":[146] and he expounds Ephesians v. 25–27 as meaning "not having now at this present time (as the Greek and Latine Participle of the present time doth signifie) one spot or wrinkle of sinne."[147] Just as every man born of Adam has been "made a true and reall sinner", so the second Adam

> truly endues, with his own righteousnesse, all that come of him, that every little Infant before it hath done or thought any evill, being justified, is not barely counted, but truly made righteous.[148]

142. *Honey-combe*, p. 36.
143. Op. cit., p. 48; cf. pp. 87, 88.
144. Op. cit., p. 57.
145. John Eaton, *Honey-combe*, pp. 273–5.
146. Op. cit., p. 32.
147. Op. cit., p. 30.
148. Op. cit., p. 293.

John Eaton says that by imputed righteousness "all our works . . . are made perfectly holy", and this includes bad deeds, as well as good.[149] When it is asked, "How then are all these sorts of actions in Gods children, made perfectly holy and righteous in the sight of God?" he replies, "By the perfection of Justification." It is this which "presents all their works and holy walking, to bee perfectly holy and righteous in the sight of God freely, and by this meanes are made continually acceptable and pleasing in the sight of God".[150] "All our works are thereby justified as well as we",[151] and "all the thoughts, words, and deeds of Gods Justified children", are "excellent in the sight of God."[152] This was true of Abraham, even when he lied,[153] for "the wedding-garment of Christs perfect righteousnesse" makes

> All our works of unjust, just before God, that is perfectly holy and righteous, from all spot of sin, in the sight of God . . . all our sanctified actions, which by their imperfection are in themselves foule and filthy, are by free Justification made . . . perfectly holy and righteous, . . . Christ's righteousnesse, justifying both our persons and works.[154]

Tobias Crisp concurs in John Eaton's interpretation of Ephesians v. 25, 27[155] and maintains that the transference of sin to Christ means that "Thou ceasest to be a Transgressor. . . . Christ Himself is not so compleatly righteous, but we are as righteous as He was."[156] Robert Towne holds that to be made a new creature is to be "made personally, perfectly, and everlastingly righteous".[157]

149. Op. cit., p. 321; and pp. 76–78.
150. Op. cit., pp. 322, 323.
151. Op. cit., p. 325.
152. Op. cit., p. 79.
153. Ibid.
154. *Abraham's Steps of Faith*, 1642, pp. 174–176; cf. *Dangerous Dead Faith*, p. 83. Thomas Gataker quotes John Eaton, that even if a believer did all that David did regarding Bathsheba and Uriah, "God would not so much as once so see it, as to take any notice at all ... or be at all angry." *God's Eye*, To the Reader. He tells, further, of John Eaton "covering the hour-glasse that he preacheth by in publik, an other the Bible that he collateth by in private; and affirming withall, that God no more seeth any sin in any justified persons, then the auditory then present saw, either the Glass the one, or the Book the other; and consequently, that he taketh not notice of it, nor is at all displeased with them, fall they never so foully, or live they never so loosly", Op. cit., p. 2.
155. *Christ Alone Exalted*, in *Works*, I. 7.
156. Op. cit., II. 270. Quoted by Thomas Bedford, *An Examination*, p. 59, and defended by Isaac Chauncy in *Neonomianism Unmask'd*, Part II. pp. 83 ff.
157. *Assertion of Grace*, p. 9. Samuel Rutherford understands him to mean that "a justified person cannot sinne, ... and if so, the way of Grace is a wanton merry way; the justified are freed from the Law, and from any danger of sinning." *Triumph of Faith*, p. 24. He complains that "Antinomians have not to this day explained in their writings, whether the justified can sin or no; but in practise they say they may, lye, whore, sweare, cousen; God seeth no such sinnes in them." *Survey*, Part I. p. 3. Henry Burton refers to some who hold

These inferences about sanctification from the facts of justification betray a confusion of the two concepts. John Eaton, for example, makes the orthodox statement that the righteousness of believers, when thought of as imputed, is to be called justification, and when regarded as inherent, is to be called sanctification.[158] But this is difficult to reconcile with his statement that sanctification is the second part of justification,[159] for what is imputed may not be described as imparted, and it is insufficient to speak of what is imparted as if it were only imputed. The author of *Truths Victory* has ground for his complaint that whereas Papists, Socinians, Quakers and others affirm Christian perfection of an inherent kind, the Antinomians maintain it by imputation: there being no inherent holiness in us nor required of us.[160] The Papists made sanctification into justification, and the Antinomians made justification into sanctification. John Eaton is inconsistent also in his illustrations about looking under the cover, and the appearance of colour in the water in a coloured glass. He admits[161] that the object under the cover is still there, although covered, and the water is still colourless, although seen through red glass, and yet he wants it to be understood that there is no sin left in the believer. William Woodward interjects the caution, "Let none from hence infer, that they are as righteous as Christ, and are infinitely perfect as Christ."[162] Edward Elton puts his finger on the spot when he says that by imputation the believer is as righteous as Christ, but not "in the same manner",[163] for it was confusion over the "manner" which was the crux of the Antinomian controversy in this respect.[164]

The root of the Antinomian fallacy was in the concept of the justification of the believer's works, but nowhere in Scripture are the works of a sinful man said to be justified. It is morally impossible to

---

that a man may live altogether without all sin; for all his sins of unjust are made just, and that I John iv. 17 means that "there is noe difference betweene our state here and in heaven, but onely in our ... apprehension." *Law and Gospel Reconciled*, pp. 16, 36. Thomas Gataker quotes Giles Randall as saying, "It is as possible for Christ himself to sin, as for a child of God to sin." *God's Eye*, To the Reader.

158. *Honey-combe*, p. 310.
159. Op. cit., pp. 22, 51, 253.
160. Op. cit., 1684, p. 90.
161. *Honey-combe*, pp. 273–275.
162. *Lord our Righteousness*, 1696, p. 48.
163. *Treatises*: "Triumph of a True Christian", pp. 51, 52; John Owen, *Communion with God*, 1657, in *Works*, II. 164; and see a good discussion in Samuel Rolle, *Justification Justified*, 1674, pp. 13, 14.
164. Two other aspects deserve a note: (1) The Antinomian conception that sanctification can be perfect towards God while imperfect "to manward", Robert Towne, *Assertion of Grace*, p. 77, John Saltmarsh, *Free-Grace*, pp. 129–54; (2) The confusion between sanctification and glorification, John Eaton, *Honey-combe*, p. 30, Tobias Crisp, *Christ Alone Exalted*, in *Works*, I. 7.

justify sinful works; God cannot call evil good, or make unjust works just. Sin can never be anything but sin. It is the person who is justified, as to his standing in the Law of God, but not his deeds. Justification opens the way to sanctification, but it is not itself sanctification.[165]

As masters of practical divinity, the Puritans always had a pastoral application to make.

> Now usually when you mourne for sinne, you thinke there is a crack in your justification. . . . Whereas wee should look on justification as a thing entire in the hands of Christ, that wee have nothing to doe in.[166]

The reason for spiritual depression was

> because in some sort, even to this day, you mix sanctification with justification. . . . Could you leave your justification alone in the hands of Jesus Christ, and look on it (as I said) as cash in the cupboard, not to be touched; . . . then would your hearts break and shatter to pieces, when you have done the least evill against God; then you would know what true sorrow, and what true repentance is, and not before. . . . What greater Mysterie then for me being a just and righteous man through Christ, yet to be so sinfull, that I can say there is none more sinfull. . . . A Christian knowes this, and he knowes how it is so.[167]

(iii) *Knowing sin and seeing sin*

The Antinomians made repeated appeal to two passages of Scripture, namely, Numbers xxiii. 21 and Jeremiah l. 20. The crucial sentences are, "He hath not beheld iniquity in Jacob, neither hath he seen perverseness in Israel", and "the iniquity of Israel shall be sought for, and there shall be none; and the sins of Judah, and they shall not be found."

It was agreed by all that there was a difference between knowing and seeing, and, therefore, though God knows all the sins of His people, it is at the same time true that He removes them out of His sight. But this distinction was put to a rather sophistical use by John Eaton who, on the basis that an object has to be present to be seen but not to be known,[168] proceeds to argue that the sins of believers are "abolished".[169] Nothing is left in the believer but "the feeling of sin",[170] although this obliteration of sin from before God does not

165. Cf. Henry Burton, *Law and Gospel Reconciled*, p. 16. For later stages of the controversy see Isaac Chauncy, *Neonomianism Unmask'd*, Part III. p. 13 ff.
166. Walter Cradock, *Gospel Holinesse*, "Priviledge and Practice of the Saints", 1651, pp. 234, 235.
167. Ibid.
168. *Honey-combe*, pp. 61 and 67–70.
169. Op. cit., p. 158.
170. Op. cit., p. 26.

mean that the believer will not still see his sin, for God has power not to see, what he leaves the believer still able to see.[171]

The discussion of this subject is conducted best by the Puritans themselves, and Thomas Taylor replies to John Eaton that to "see" means to know (1) simply, and (2) respectively, that is with a purpose to act. In this way God does not see the sins of believers, but this does not mean they are not present. The fact that God records the sins of the elect, many years after they are pardoned, refutes the idea that God does not see in the simple sense of seeing.[172] Thomas Gataker maintains

> The common interpretation of Num. xxiii. 21 is impossible. (1) Because God plagued and chastened his people for their sins. (2) The aim of Balaam was to bring the people into disfavour with God.[173]

Anthony Burgess considers that the passage in Jeremiah refers to a judicial inquiry, and that it is only in that sense that it may be said that God does not find sin in His people. Forgiveness removes the guilt of sin, but the nature of sin still remains.[174] He further maintains that the covering of sin relates only to condemnation, and that it was in this way that David's sin was covered, while it was still open to God's fatherly chastisements. Further, covering relates only to sins that are past and confessed, not to new sins until they be confessed.[175] God does see sin and is offended by it in believers. God is not made to "peep" under the covering again. Cover is a metaphor and signifies not that God cannot see them at all but that he will not notice them in judgment.[176]

D. MAKING CONSCIENCE OF SIN

One of the assumptions underlying the Antinomian denial of sin in the believer is that the believer so passes out of the orbit of Law that whatever imperfections still cleave to him are no longer strictly to be called sins. The Puritans rejected this opinion outright, and held that not only is the indwelling corruption truly of the nature of sin, but that it manifests itself in actions which are themselves nothing

171. Op. cit., p. 61.
172. *Regula Vitae*, p. 88 f.; cf. Richard Allen, *Antidote against Heresy*, 1648, p. 83; William Woodward, *Lord our Righteousness*, pp. 45–51.
173. *God's Eye*, p. 17. He makes the suggestion that Numbers xxiii. 21 means that God cannot endure seeing any evil done against his people.
174. *Justification*, Part I. pp. 22, 44–52.
175. Op. cit., Part I. p. 241.
176. Op. cit., Part I. pp. 51, 53. Cf. James Ussher, *Body of Divinitie*, p. 159; Francis Roberts, *God's Covenants*, p. 1475; John Crandon, *Aphorisms Exorized* Part I, p. 243.

other than breaches of the holy Law of God. Believers who sin in this way are boldly described by Robert Bolton as "relapsed Christians".[177]

(i) *Sin still sin*

When the Puritans spoke about "making conscience of" any action, they meant the measuring of it against the moral Law.

> The Question is not, Whether the sin of the justified person shall be charged upon him to endanger his salvation, but Whether the act be sin in him or not.[178]

Anthony Burgess had no doubt about the answer.

> The sinnes of godly men cease not to be sins, though they are justified. We may not say, that in Cain killing of another is murder, but in David it is not.[179]

It was therefore "no less sinful"[180] for the believer to act "against the law"[181] than ever it was, and because sin is so evil "the People of God" must "be afraid of everie sin" and "be Consciencious to Gods Authoritie in small things".[182] What the Antinomians called sins in the "conversation" are no different from sins in the "conscience", for all alike

> are against the Law of God, and must be sinnes in the conscience, else they are against no Law of God, which make the sinnes of the justified and their doing golden graces.[183]

"The sins of the Saints" need to be corrected "as sins",[184] for, although believers have no condemnation, yet

> the sinnes of those that walk after the Spirit are sinnes, they are transgressions of Gods holy Commandments. . . . That their sinnes condemn them not, is not from any lesse desert. I John i. 8–10.[185]

Thomas Goodwin believes that "a regenerate man is . . . guilty of more known sins than an unregenerate man".[186] He holds that the more knowledge there is the greater is the sin.[187] The sins of the

177. *Afflicted Consciences*, p. 141.
178. Thomas Bedford, *An Examination*, p. 14.
179. *Justification*, Part I, pp. 78, 79.
180. James Durham, *Law Unsealed*, p. 3.
181. Jeremiah Burroughs, *Saints Treasury*, p. 104.
182. Jeremiah Burroughs, *Evil of Evils*, p. 448, 449.
183. Samuel Rutherford, *Survey*, Part II. p. 17.
184. Samuel Rutherford, *Triumph of Faith*, p. 24.
185. Richard Byfield, *Gospels Glory*, p. 321.
186. *Aggravation of Sin*, in *Works*, IV. 169.
187. Op. cit., p. 185.

believer are not only against light and knowledge, they are also sins "against mercy".[188]

(ii) *Sin more than disease*

The Antinomians liked to speak of their shortcomings as a disease or infirmity.[189] Although there is some truth in calling sin a "disease" this is a completely insufficient account of it, for if sin is construed in terms of mere disease there is a deficiency in the concept, which contradicts the heinousness of it in the sight of God. So far are the failures of believers from being mere infirmities, that the author of *The Marrow* insists that the breaking of the Law by a Christian is even worse than the same action by an unbeliever,[190] and Thomas Cole declares,

> I look upon it as a great Error, to hold that all sins committed in a state of Grace are sins of Infirmity. . . . An Infirmity in the true Notion of it, is the deficiency of a good Action, . . . but when we do that which is materially Evil in its own nature, and forbidden by God, this is more than an Infirmity: . . . 'tis not a weak action, but a wicked one.[191]

(iii) *Confession of sin*

What is to be the believer's attitude to the sin that he finds within himself? If his imperfections are not properly sins, and God takes no notice of them, he will not need to be concerned about them; but if they are displeasing to God, then he will grieve over them and confess them.

Among the Antinomians there was the fairly general opinion that believers should not give themselves any care at all about their shortcomings. John Eaton was emphatic that the justified believer has no need to grieve over his imperfections; but when confronted by Christ's teaching about prayer for forgiveness, he defended his position by saying that the believer continues daily to ask forgiveness from God for three reasons: first, because the more grace a man has the more he feels the imperfections of his sanctification; secondly, because by

188. Op. cit., p. 188; cf. John Owen, *Justification*, in *Works*, V. 145; *Mortification*, in *Works*, VI. 51; and his entire treatise on *Indwelling Sin*, in *Works*, VI.
189. Robert Towne, for example, says, "Thus whilst God useth as a tender father the rod or physick, the cause hath not properly with him the nature of sinne, which is an offence to divine justice; but it is now considered as a disease troubling his childe." *Assertion of Grace*, p. 113. It is a little surprising to find in Thomas Manton that "Great sins may be infirmities, as Lot's incest; David's adultery; when they are not done with full consent of soul", *Hundred and Nineteenth Psalm*, I. 27.
190. Op. cit., p. 154; cf. John Preston, *Law out lawed*, p. 7.
191. *Repentance*, pp. 119, 120. Cf. Isaac Chauncy, *Neonomianism Unmask'd*, Part II. p. 63.

daily praying for this glorious justifying forgiveness he will grow to greater assurance; and thirdly, because by daily praying for this benefit the believer will come not only to possess forgiveness, but also to enjoy it.[192] Robert Towne finds an illustration for his argument in the instance of a released debtor who is told to mourn over his debts no longer.[193] John Saltmarsh continues in the same vein, "No believer ought to pray for pardon of sin, being a righteous person, at once in Christ and wholly pardoned", and he then adds the half-truth, "We beleeve, repent, love, and obey . . . not that we may be saved, but because we are saved".[194] Christians are not to be troubled for any sins in them, nor to imagine that God is displeased with them, or that any afflictions do befall them for their sins, or that they shall ever be called to any account for them.[195]

"Hearsay" was active on this subject, and reported the Antinomians as teaching that "neither our omissions, nor commisions should grieve us",[196] and "You cannot sin in saying what you will, or sinning you need not be sorry for the same."[197] Thomas Welde refers to their error that "a man must take no notice of his sin, nor of his repentance for his sin",[198] and Thomas Edwards remarks how pleasing to the flesh it is to accept the idea that God loves men "as well sinning as praying".[199] Thomas Gataker hears tell of "Mr. Randall" who said "a child of God need not, nay ought not to ask pardon for sin: and that it is no lesse then blasphemy for him so to do."[200]

In contradistinction to the foregoing views there was the opinion that believers must not only confess their sins, but must grieve over them, and seek pardon for them.

> When once that blessed Fountaine of Soule-saving bloud is opened upon thy Soule, in the side of the Sonne of God, by the hand of Faith for sinne and for uncleannesse; then also must a Counter-spring, as it were, of repentant teares be opened in thine humbled heart, which must not be dried up untill thy dying day.[201]

192. *Honey-combe*, pp. 147, 154–7.
193. *Assertion of Grace*, p. 13.
194. *Sparkles of Glory*, p. 192.
195. John Saltmarsh, *Free-Grace*, pp. 173, 174.
196. Thomas Taylor, *Regula Vitae*, Preface.
197. John Sedgwick, *Antinomianisme Anatomized*, p. 3.
198. *Rise, reigne, and ruine*, p. 12, and see also the anonymous *Truths Victory*, p. 67 and Daniel Williams, on Tobias Crisp and others, in *Gospel-Truth*, pp. 170, 174.
199. *Gangraena*, p. 135.
200. *God's Eye*, Preface. One of the alleged reasons for denying the necessity to pray for forgiveness is found in a misapplication of the doctrine of eternal justification, and the failure to distinguish between God's immanent and transient actions. Cf. Tobias Crisp, *Christ Alone Exalted*, in *Works*, II. 306, 363, 364; John Flavel, *Mental Errors*, 1691, p. 320.
201. Robert Bolton, *Afflicted Consciences*, p. 288.

It is never needless, even when assured of the answer.

> Though wee know our sinnes pardoned, yet must wee pray for pardon. . . . Though God in heaven have by an eternall sentence blotted out the sinnes of the beleever in the first act of his conversion, and this sentence can never bee blotted out, yet we may and must pray for pardon of sinne; namely, that this sentence of pardon may be pronounced in our owne consciences.[202]

There must be renewed repentance for renewed sins,[203] and a confession by the believer of his "unworthiness", together with an unburdening of conscience.[204] "How should a man recover a relapse?" asks John Ball; and he gives the answer,

> By a speedy consideration of what he hath done, renewing his repentance with sorrow and shame, bewailing his sinne before God, reforming his life, and laying hold upon the promise of mercy.[205]

Believers are to pray "forgive us our sins",

> For notwithstanding our assurance of forgiveness, if the eye be taken off Christ never so little, the remembrance of former sinnes will disquiet afresh . . . We ask the continuance of his grace, . . . and God who continueth his mercy towards us, willeth that we should ask it daily by hearty supplication. We ask the manifestation of it. . . . We desire that God would keep us from security, hardness of heart and impenitency.[206]

Tobias Crisp does not stand with the extremists among his usual friends on this subject, for he says, "There is . . . more Joy in the Mourning of a Believer, than in all the Mirth of a Wicked Man."[207] He contends that this is no denial of Christ's work of complete satisfaction for sin, and asks,

> May not a Person come and acknowledge his Fault to his Prince, after he hath received his Pardon under the hand of his Prince, when he is brought from the place of Execution? Nay, may not he acknowledge it with Melting and extream Bitterness of Spirit, because he knoweth he hath a Pardon? . . . I say, that when Christ doth reveal himself to your Spirits, you shall find your Hearts more wrought upon, with sweet Meltings, and Relentings of Heart,

202. Thomas Taylor, *Regula Vitae*, pp. 113, 114; cf. Tobias Crisp, *Christ Alone Exalted*, in *Works*, II. 369, where he distinguishes between forgiveness in heaven and in the conscience, Isaac Chauncy, *Neonomianism Unmask'd*, Part III. p. 17.
203. William Ames, *Conscience*, Book II, p. 22.
204. William Ames, *Conscience*, Book IV. p. 34; cf. *Marrow of Sacred Divinity*, p. 129.
205. *Catechism*, 1642, p. 41.
206. John Ball, *Power of Godliness*, p. 465.
207. *Christ Alone Exalted*, in *Works*, I. 52.

and breakings of Spirit, when you see your Sins pardoned, than in the most despairing condition you can be in.[208]

Anthony Burgess goes so far as to say that believers must "bewail unknown sinnes";[209] "so that you may suppose a Believer to be damned, if you suppose him not to repent".[210] The Lord's Prayer is offered that we may be preserved in a state of justification. As we renew sin daily so we need a daily pardon although we pray for assurance and the sense of pardon, this is not all we pray for. We pray for the pardon itself.[211] Samuel Rutherford maintains the rightness of the believer's confession of sin and affirms that the

> justified beleever is to confesse his sins . . . though they be pardoned. . . . I am to be secure and to enjoy a sound Peace, . . . But yet am I to be disquieted, . . . to sorrow that such a Ghuest as sin lodgeth in me. . . . A perplexed conscience is lawfully consistent with a justified sinners condition.[212]

"So long as sin continues, there is need of a continuing intercession",[213] and the saints must "continually keep alive upon their hearts a sense of the guilt and evil of sin".[214]

Richard Baxter denies the completeness of a sinner's justification by faith, and on this ground calls for the continued repentance and faith of the believer;[215] but very few Puritans concur in his extreme views, and he stands nearly alone. Thomas Cole once more summarizes what is important in this discussion.

> The visible neglect of Repentance in the Professors of this age, has brought a reproach upon the doctrine of faith, and caused it to be evil spoken of, that faith that does not sanctifie, will never justifie, and without Repentance there can be no Sanctification: not that we make Repentance any Meritorious Cause of Pardon, or that it is to be rested in as any satisfaction for sin, only we affirm that justifying faith alwayes works Repentance. . . . We should repent as often as there is new matter for Repentance.[216]

208. Op. cit., p. 215.
209. *Spiritual Refining*, "Of Sinne", p. 193.
210. *Justification*, Part I. p. 90.
211. Op. cit., Part I. pp. 122–4; cf. John Ball, *Of Faith*, 1630, pp. 102–104; *The Marrow*, p. 192; Edward Elton, *Gods Holy Minde*, "Prayer", 1624, p. 78.
212. *Triumph of Faith*, pp. 143, 193.
213. Thomas Goodwin, *Christ Set Forth*, 1642, in *Works*, IV. 65.
214. John Owen, *Communion with God*, in *Works*, II. 193.
215. *Aphorismes*, pp. 196 ff. 226–33; *End of Doctrinal Controversies*, p. 255.
216. *Repentance*, pp. 117, 121; cf. also pp. 85, 92, 95. The Puritans made an important distinction between "legal" and "evangelical" repentance. Cf. William Perkins, *Galatians*, p. 246; Stephen Charnock, *Conviction of Sin*, in *Works*, IV. 199 ff; Edward Elton, *Treatises*: "Complaint of a Sanctifyed Sinner", pp. 96–98; David Clarkson, *Of Faith*, in *Works*, I. 133, 134; Robert Bolton, *Afflicted Consciences*, p. 324.

The Puritans took a serious view of sin, and this was derived from its relation to Law. Sin, to the Puritan, was not a psychological maladjustment to life; it was wilful rebellion against the commandments of God; it was not merely man's faulty behaviour, but deep-seated corruption of the man himself. Sin is no less sin because it is committed by a believer; and the Christian experience that begins with the cry, "God be merciful to me a sinner",[217] must be continued by the prayer, "Cleanse thou me from secret faults."[218]

217. Luke xviii. 13.
218. Psalm xix. 12.

Chapter III

THE PLACE OF LAW IN THE PURPOSE OF GOD

Synopsis

A. USE OF THE WORD "LAW" IN SCRIPTURE

B. THE LAW OF MAN'S CREATION

C. LAW AND THE COVENANTS OF GOD

(i) *Nature of the Mosaic Covenant*
(ii) *Relation of the Mosaic Law to the Law of man's creation*
(iii) *Mosaic Law not for justification*

D. LAW AS A MEANS OF GRACE

(i) *The continuity of the Covenant of Grace*
(ii) *Mosaic Covenant consistent with grace*
(iii) *The expression of grace in the Law*
(iv) *Law as an instrument of grace*

E. THE DISTINCTIVE PLACE OF LAW

(i) *Obscurity of its revelation*
(ii) *Rigour of its ministry*

F. OPPOSITION BETWEEN LAW AND GOSPEL

(i) *The historic abuse of the Law*
(ii) *No absolute opposition*

Chapter III

THE PLACE OF LAW IN THE PURPOSE OF GOD

THE object of this chapter is to exhibit the ways in which the Puritans understood the Mosaic Law and its place in God's purpose of grace for mankind, for

> The Mystery of the Gospel cannot be throughly apprehended by us, without some good understanding of the Oeconomy of the Law, yea, and also of the State of things before the Law.[1]

First, the twofold use of the word "law"—sometimes as that which is solely preceptive, and sometimes as covenant—is distinguished, and then an examination is made of the Puritan view of the relation of the Law to the different forms and administrations of the Covenant of Grace, showing that the Law itself is an instrument of grace. Then it is necessary to inquire into Paul's deprecatory language about the Law, and the appearance of opposition of the Law and the Gospel.

A. USE OF THE WORD "LAW" IN SCRIPTURE

The Puritans accepted the distinctions between moral, ceremonial and judicial laws which have been observed already,[2] and also the commonly understood meanings that arise from the history of such terms as *tôrâh*, *nomos* and *lex*.[3] In the light of this general agreement about the laws of the Old Testament, and in view of his own special concern, Anthony Burgess does not think it is required of him to "say much about Lawes in generall" because "many have written large Volumes, especially the School-men, and it cannot be denyed but

1. Nehemiah Cox, *Of the Covenants*, p. 3.
2. See above p. 43; cf. Edward Elton, *Treatises*, "Mystery of Godliness Opened", 1653, p. 27; Anthony Burgess, *Vindiciae Legis*, p. 147; Francis Roberts, *God's Covenants*, p. 661. Some recent writers repudiate this distinction, at least so far as to say that it is non-Biblical. M. F. Wiles allows himself to say that he does not believe it is possible to find "any trace" of it in the writings of Paul, and he quotes Kirsopp Lake as his authority ("St Paul's Conception of Law", *The Churchman*, LXIX. 3, p. 148), but the Puritan Paul Baynes considers that Paul makes this distinction in Ephesians ii. 15 (*Ephesians*, 1643, p. 293). Cf. Patrick Fairbairn, *Law in Scripture*, 1868, pp. 82–146. He and many others understand the distinction to be implicit in Christ's attitude to the ceremonial aspects of the Law. Op. cit., pp. 216 f.
3. Anthony Burgess, *Vindiciae Legis*, p. 11, Francis Roberts, *God's Covenants*, pp. 656, 657.

that good rationall matter is delivered by them". It is, therefore, not necessary to "examine the Etymology of the words that signifie a Law".[4] But there is still one important feature of the use of the word "law" in Scripture which needs careful study, namely, the distinction between the Law, in the narrow sense of the Divine requirements of man, and the Law in the wider sense of the whole Mosaic order of things. "More strictly and properly the Law signifieth the Covenant of workes, which is also called the Law of workes, Rom. 3. 27"; but "more largely *Thorah* the Law signifieth the whole doctrine of the old Testament. . . . In this large sense the Evangelicall promises made in the old testament are contained in the Law, though properly belonging to the Gospell".[5] Put briefly, the Law can be considered as it is an "abstracted Rule of righteousness", or as comprehending "the whole Doctrine and Administration of the Sinai-Covenant".[6] This double way of thinking about the Law is present even within the Decalogue, where the concept of "law" can be understood, either in the narrow sense of the mandatory part alone, or in the larger sense that covers the preface and the promises.[7] The relation between the narrower and the wider connotation of the word "law" was put in various ways. The author of *The Marrow*, for example, says, "the law of the Ten Commandments was the matter of the Covenant of works",[8] and John Preston reverses the subject and predicate and refers to "the Covenant that is expressed by Moses in the Morall Law".[9]

The above differences, as these examples show, were not ignored by the Puritans, but in the enthusiasm of preaching, or in the heat of controversy, they occasionally forgot to define their terms, hence, their discussion of the place of the Law of God in Christian experience is sometimes difficult to follow. The author of *The Marrow* provides an instance of this when he exults in quoting Luther's rhetorical exclamation, "I will be bold to bid Moses with his tables . . . be gone";[10] but neither Luther nor he takes the trouble to explain what he means.[11]

B. THE LAW OF MAN'S CREATION

What was "the State of things before the Law"? It was the uniform conviction of the Puritans that, on the basis of the moral Law im-

4. Op. cit., p. 60.
5. George Downame, *Justification*, p. 465.
6. Francis Roberts, *God's Covenants*, pp. 773, 774.
7. Anthony Burgess, *Vindiciae Legis*, p. 147.
8. Op. cit., p. 18.
9. John Preston, *New Covenant*, p. 317.
10. Op. cit., p. 142.
11. Thomas Boston's note on p. 212 (1818 edn.) explains it in the sense of the Covenant of Works. Cf. John Barret, *Treatise of the Covenants*, p. 78.

planted by nature within man, God engaged Himself to man in what has come to be known as a Covenant of Works.[12] The concept of a Covenant of Works was relatively new, being no part of the theological formulation of Calvin and those who laboured with him.[13] The Reformers never went beyond the belief in one covenant, namely, the Covenant of Grace.[14] The idea of the Covenant of Works was introduced into British theology by William Perkins and others at the beginning of the seventeenth century,[15] and was intended to serve as a kind of bridge linking revealed theology to natural theology. Not all the Puritans, however, were satisfied about the title "Covenant of Works", and some preferred to call it a "Covenant of Innocency",[16] "a Covenant of Friendship",[17] "of Bounty and Goodness",[18] "a Covenant of Creation",[19] or "a Covenant of Nature".[20]

It was mostly admitted that the existence of this Covenant with Adam was nowhere explicitly stated in Scripture,[21] and therefore it was to be accepted by inference, albeit a necessary and true inference.[22] "The Covenant of Works made with Adam in innocency, is more darkly spoken of than the Covenant of Grace", says John Barret, and he finds the reason for this in the fact that the "first Covenant was soon broken, on man's part", and so he can now "claim no priviledge or benefit by it".[23]

In this respect it is, as if it had never been. . . . Therefore the

12. William Perkins, *Golden Chaine*, in *Works*, p. 26, cf. p. 9. William Ames, *Marrow of Sacred Divinity*, pp. 45–48 where the idea, if not the word, is expounded; John Preston, *New Covenant*, p. 317; Henry Burton, *Law and Gospel Reconciled*, p. 26; Jeremiah Burroughs, *Gospel-Conversation*, 1648, p. 42; James Durham, *Law Unsealed*, p. 3; *The Marrow*, p. 17; John Sedgwick, *Antinomianisme Anatomized*, p. 9; Thomas Gouge, *Principles of Christian Religion*, p. 46; John Flavel, *Vindiciae Legis & Foederis*, 1690, p. 32; Samuel Slater, *Two Covenants*, 1644 (pages unnumbered).
13. For the distinction which Calvin allows, see *Inst*. II. ix. 4.
14. Cf. Bullinger, *De Testamento seu Foedere Dei Unico et Aeterno*, 1534.
15. See above, pp. 39, 40.
16. Richard Baxter, *Catholick Theologie*, Book I. Part 2, p. 1. But this is because he conceived of the Covenant of Grace as also a Covenant of Works.
17. William Strong, *The Two Covenants*, p. 2; Anthony Burgess, *Vindiciae Legis*, p. 124.
18. John Ball, *Covenant of Grace*, p. 7; Nehemiah Cox, *Of the Covenants*, p. 29.
19. Nehemiah Cox, *Of the Covenants*, pp. 24, 29, 44.
20. Thomas Goodwin, *Mediator*, in *Works*, V. 82.
21. Cf. Charles Hodge, *Systematic Theology*, 1871, II, 117. Neither of the theological terms "Covenant of Works" or "Covenant of Grace" is found in Scripture in precisely this form, but there is no doubt about the substance of the latter being present.
22. John Ball, *Covenant of Grace*, p. 6; Francis Roberts, *God's Covenants*, p. 14; Thomas Brooks, *Paradise Opened*, 1675, in *Works*, V. 293; John Flavel, *Vindiciae Legis & Foederis*, Prolegomena; Anthony Burgess, *Vindiciae Legis*, p. 123; Thomas Blake, *Covenant of God*, 1653, p. 8.
23. *Treatise of the Covenants*, p. 2.

promissory part of that first Covenant is not mentioned here . . . but only implyed.[24]

Thomas Goodwin was uncomfortable with the covenant idea, and preferred to speak of the "Law of Creation" indicating man's "estate of pure nature by creation-law",[25] and aiming at man's obedience.[26] John Owen writes in the same way of man's "immediate relation" to his Creator,[27] and Richard Baxter makes the observation that Natural Law

> as it is in Nature, it is a meer Law; and not properly a Covenant. Yea to Adam in his perfection, the forme of the Covenant was known by superadded Revelation, and not written naturally in his heart.[28]

He reasons, therefore, that the "Divine Instrument" for man's duty "is called a Law in one respect, and a Covenant in another".[29]

Nearly all the Puritans concurred in the view that whatever good Adam would have received by his obedience was of grace;[30] and some even hold "the Covenant with Adam, wherein works were injoyned, to be a Covenant of Grace . . . and thereupon divide the Covenant of Grace into the Covenant of Works, and the Covenant of Faith".[31] Thomas Blake considers that although for distinction's sake one covenant is called the Covenant of Works and the other the Covenant of Grace,

> the fountain and first rise of either, was the free grace and favour of God. For howsoever the first Covenant was on condition of obedience, and engaged to the reward of Works, yet it was of Grace that God made any such promise of reward to any work of man.[32]

There was no real merit involved in Adam's relation to God, although because of the covenant it would have been "in justice"[33] that God would have rewarded him. As an eternal rule,[34] however, the moral Law is laid upon man by his Maker: it is obligatory on all men from

24. Ibid.
25. *Of the Creatures*, in *Works*, VII. 22; John Owen, *Justification*, in *Works*, V. 275.
26. *Mediator*, in *Works*, V. 86.
27. *Justification*, in *Works*, V. 44.
28. *Aphorismes*, p. 14.
29. *End of Doctrinal Controversies*, p. 99 (pages disarranged).
30. Thomas Goodwin, *Mediator*, in *Works*, V. 82; *Of the Creatures*, in *Works*, VII. 25; John Owen, *Justification*, in *Works*, V. 277; Anthony Burgess, *Vindiciae Legis*, pp. 123, 129; John Ball, *Covenant of Grace*, pp. 7, 9; Francis Roberts, *God's Covenants*, p. 17.
31. John Graile, *Conditions in the Covenant of Grace*, p. 26.
32. *Covenant of God*, pp. 8, 9.
33. John Ball, *Covenant of Grace*, p. 10; cf. Ezekiel Hopkins, *True Happiness*, 1701, in *Works*, p. 382.
34. Samuel Bolton, *Sin*, p. 34.

the first, exacting perfect obedience,[35] and is for this reason sometimes called "the Law of works".[36] This Law includes not "the least Iota of pardoning Mercy",[37] and to fail in obedience is to fail with no hope of recovery.

C. LAW AND THE COVENANTS OF GOD

(i) *Nature of the Mosaic Covenant*

There have been many attempts to expound the covenants of God, and, in particular, to find a place for the Mosaic Covenant within God's saving purposes for mankind. The outward appearance of the Mosaic Covenant, however, seems not at first sight to be compatible with such saving purposes, and the demands of the Law, with the severity attaching to them, approximate more to the likeness of a Covenant of Works. This semblance of a Covenant of Works receives some support from the passages of Scripture in which the Law and Gospel are compared or even contrasted, and, conspicuously in the Prologue to the Fourth Gospel, where Moses and Christ are represented as the opposite poles of revelation. There is, without doubt, a great difference between the manifestation of God in Christ and that earlier manifestation by Moses,[38] although it is possible falsely to magnify this difference. It is not surprising, therefore, to find a wide variety of thought among the Puritans about the exact nature of the Mosaic Covenant.

An outline of the ways in which the Mosaic Covenant was regarded by the Puritans is provided by Anthony Burgess in *Vindiciae Legis*.

> In expressing this Covenant there is difference among the Learned: some make the Law a Covenant of works, and upon that ground that it is abrogated: others call it a subservient covenant to the covenant of grace, and make it only occasionally, as it were, introduced, to put more luster and splendour upon grace: Others call it a mixt covenant of works and grace; but that is hardly to be understood as possible, much lesse as true. I therefore think that opinion true . . . that the Law given by Moses was a Covenant of grace.[39]

It is not possible to make an accurate classification of the Puritans on the basis of their views about the Mosaic Covenant, because many of them held several of the different views in varying combinations. On the whole, however, they can be divided into two groups on this

35. Samuel Crooke, *True Blessednesse*, 1613, p. 33.
36. Francis Roberts, *God's Covenants*, p. 743.
37. Nehemiah Cox, *Of the Covenants*, p. 29; John Ball, *Covenant of Grace*, p. 11.
38. See II Corinthians iii. 6–18 and Hebrews ix and x.
39. Op. cit., p. 213.

subject; those who regarded the Mosaic Covenant as a Covenant of Works, and those who regarded it as a Covenant of Grace.

William Pemble was among those who regarded the Mosaic Covenant as a Covenant of Works, and spoke of the Covenant of Works in two administrations, first with Adam, and secondly in "the renuing thereof with the Israelites at Mount Sinai."[40] John Preston had no hesitation in equating it with the Covenant of Works, whose terms were by Moses "written in Tables of stone, and presented" to the people.[41] The kind of difficulties which were felt by the Puritans are seen in the following extract from *The Marrow*.

> The Lord saw it needful that there should be a new edition and publication of the covenant of works . . . That they, by looking upon this covenant, might be put in mind what was their duty of old, when they were in Adam's loins, and what was their duty still, if they would stand to that covenant, and so go the old and natural way to work.[42]

The Covenant of Works renewed at Sinai was "added" to the Covenant of Grace, yet not

> by way of ingrediency, as a part of the covenant of grace, as if that covenant had been incomplete without the covenant of works. . . . It was added by way of subserviency and attendance, the better to advance and make effectual the covenant of grace; so that although the same covenant that was made with Adam was renewed on mount Sinai, yet I say still, it was not for the same purpose.[43]

There does not seem to be any doubt that the author thinks the Mosaic Covenant to be so subservient to the Covenant of Grace that whatever features of the Covenant of Works it might appear to possess are of no consequence. The convicting use of the Law was indicated by the terrifying accompaniments of Sinai, and this was the purpose of all the severities attaching to the Mosaic Covenant,[44] but when the Law as a Covenant of Works had driven the Israelites to Christ, then it was to be abolished to them in that respect,[45] and its covenant frame was to be dissolved.[46] Vavasor Powell speaks of the Covenant of Grace as in being before the Covenant of Works, and this implies

40. *Vindiciae Fidei*, 1625, p. 138.
41. *New Covenant*, p. 318.
42. Op. cit., p. 52.
43. *The Marrow*, pp. 54, 55; cf. his view that there were two covenants at Sinai, op. cit., pp. 47 and 70 and Thomas Boston's note on p. 67 (1818 edn.). Cf. Nehemiah Cox, *Of the Covenants*, pp. 104–109.
44. *The Marrow*, pp. 66, 71.
45. II Corinthians iii. 13.
46. Op. cit., pp. 77, 78.

that the Mosaic was understood by him to be a Covenant of Works.[47] He describes the Ten Commandments as a Covenant of Works, and considers Moses to have been but a typical mediator of the Covenant of Grace, his own Covenant being properly that of Works.[48] After enumerating the five ways in which the Mosaic Covenant has been understood he writes, "Yet as they differ one from another, so shall I differ somewhat from them all",[49] and then affirms that the Law is "doubtlesse a pure Covenant of works to some men (but not to all)".[50] But the sense in which it is a Covenant of Works has rightly to be understood, for "upon this hinge chiefly doth the dore (of entrance into the right understanding of the Law and Gospell) and whole weight of the Controversie concerning this Subject hang".[51] He concludes, therefore, that "its a Covenant of works occasionally, and accidentally, & only to those that are not related to . . . the Covenant of grace".[52] In the judgment of the Antinomians the Mosaic Covenant and the Covenant of Grace are so completely contrary[53] that the Mosaic can be described in no other way than as a Covenant of Works. John Saltmarsh thinks of it in this manner and affirms that the Sinaitic Covenant is a legal covenant, and that in it God's love was to be had "in the way of purchase by duty, and doing".[54]

On the other side of the discussion there is James Ussher who gives as the reason for obedience to the Decalogue, that "it proceedeth from him who is not only the Lord our Maker, but also our God and Saviour",[55] thus placing the Law in the category of God's gracious relations with men. John Ball thinks that to make the Old and New Testaments respectively into a Covenant of Works and a Covenant of Grace is to be untrue to their contents, and to oppose them not merely in degree, but in substance and in kind. He says,

> Neither can it be proved, that ever God made the Covenant of works with the creature fallen: but whensoever the Scripture speakes of Gods entring into Covenant with man fallen . . . it must be understood of the Covenant of Grace.[56]

Henry Burton understands the characteristics of the first and second Covenants to be those of works and grace respectively, and adds that the differences between them "will plainely shew, that the Law given under Christ the Redeemer in Mount Sina, was not that first

47. *Christ and Moses*, p. 2.
48. Op. cit., p. 26.
49. Op. cit., p. 200.
50. Op. cit., p. 202.
51. Op. cit., p. 206.
52. Op. cit., pp. 206, 207.
53. John Sedgwick, *Antinomianisme Anatomized*, p. 29.
54. *Free-Grace*, p. 167.
55. James Ussher's form of Q. 44 in *The Shorter Catechism*, quoted in A. F. Mitchell, *Catechisms*, p. 17.
56. *Covenant of Grace*, pp. 93, 95.

Covenant of workes".[57] Thomas Blake cannot allow it to be true that the Jews were ever under the Law as a Covenant of Works,[58] and he insists that the Law of Moses is the Covenant of Grace. He alludes to some who deny this identity of the Mosaic Covenant and the Covenant of Grace, and who try to find a middle way by calling the former a "mixt" covenant; but he regards this as laying the Mosaic Covenant too low, "not vouchsafing it the honour of a Gospel-Covenant, or at the best a mixt Gospel".[59] As is to be expected, William Strong, who considers even the Covenant made with Adam before the Fall as one of grace, regards the Mosaic Covenant in the same way, and calls it the "Covenant of Mercy".[60] Francis Roberts likewise maintains that after the Fall of man all God's covenants were in grace. In his immense work[61] on *God's Covenants* he sets out these Covenants diagrammatically.[62]

God's COVENANT is twofold

1. *A Covenant of Works,* in the first Adam, before the Fall.

2. *A Covenant of faith,* in the second Adam, after the Fall; comprehending.

1. *The Covenants of Promise,* under the Old Testament. (1) With Adam. (2) With Noah. (3) With Abraham. (4) With Israel in Mount Sinai. (5) With David. (6) With the Jews about their return from Babylon.

2. *The Covenant of Performance,* or the New Covenant under the New Testament.

Samuel Rutherford is of the same mind as Francis Roberts, and says that, "The Law as pressed upon Israel was not a Covenant of Works. . . . It was the Covenant made with Abraham, which was a Covenant of Grace."[63]

All these expositions of the Law as truly a part of the Covenant of

57. *Law and Gospel Reconciled,* p. 28.
58. *Covenant of God,* pp. 48, 49.
59. Op. cit., pp. 157 f., 189; John Crandon, *Aphorisms Exorized,* Part I. pp. 102, 103; and John Flavel, *Vindiciae Legis & Foederis,* p. 33.
60. *The Two Covenants,* p. 2.
61. Of 1721 pages.
62. Op. cit., p. 16, cf. pp. 177, 739 f.
63. *Covenant of Life,* p. 60.

Grace are in line with the earlier Protestant theologians who minimized the difference between the Old Testament and the New, and regarded the Law of Moses and the Gospel of Christ "as different forms of the one covenant of grace."[64]

These differences of interpretation are discouraging, but on closer examination they are discovered to be more apparent than real. So many concessions are made by one group of writers to the opinions of those who differ from them, that, in the end, the cumulative weight of the concessions comes to constitute the major part of the evidence, and the Puritan opinion reveals itself to be much more deeply united than at first appears. The outcome of the Puritan debate was that, on the whole, it was agreed that the Mosaic Covenant was a form of the Covenant of Grace; and this view was embodied in the *Confession of Faith.*[65]

(ii) *Relation of the Mosaic Law to the Law of man's creation*

It is necessary to determine the significance of the Mosaic Covenant, not only in relation to the concept of a Covenant of Works, but also in relation to that original Law implanted in man at his creation. It was commonly held among the Puritans that the Law enshrined in the Mosaic Covenant was identical with the Law of Nature. "The Patriarkes knew the morall law of God".[66]

> He that should think this Law was not in the Church of God before Moses his administration of it, should greatly erre. . . . And when we say, the Law was, before Moses, I do not meane only, that it was written in the hearts of men, but it was publikely preached in the ministry that the Church did then enjoy, as appeareth by Noah's preaching. . . . So that we may say, the Decalogue is Adams, and Abrahams, and Noahs, and Christs, and the Apostles, as well as of Moses.[67]

The Mosaic Law is "conform and answerable to the Law of Nature written in Adam's heart at his Creation".[68] John Flavel takes it as generally understood that "the very matter of the Law of Nature" is found in the Ten Commandments,[69] and Richard Baxter likewise

64. W. Adams Brown, Article "Covenant Theology", *ERE*, IV. 218.
65. Op. cit., VII. 5, 6.
66. Richard Greenham, *Sabboth*, in *Works*, p. 162; but cf. William Ames, *Conscience*, Book V. p. 107.
67. Anthony Burgess, *Vindiciae Legis*, p. 150. See his reasons for regarding the Moral Law as greater than Natural Law, pp. 148, 149.
68. Francis Roberts, *God's Covenants*, p. 663 and 686 where he gives similar reasons to those of Anthony Burgess for believing in the superiority of the Moral Law. Cf. John Sedgwick, *Antinomianisme Anatomized*, p. 14; "virtually one and the same", though not for the same purpose. See below, p. 118.
69. *Vindiciae Legis & Foederis, Prolegomena*, and cf. p. 118.

teaches that the Mosaic Law contains the "preceptive and directive part of the Law of Nature".[70] William Ames anticipates a question at this stage and writes,

> But it may bee objected, that if the Morall were the same with the Law of Nature, it had no need to bee promulgated either by voyce or writing for it would have beene writ in the hearts of all men by Nature.[71]

The answer to this is found in the Puritan belief that the Law of Nature was so "expunged"[72] that the special revelation of the moral Law became necessary in order to renew fallen man in the knowledge of it.[73] Men of all points of view concurred in this opinion. John Saltmarsh, says that "man having fallen . . . hath the first law of righteousness presented to him in a new ministration of letter by Moses",[74] and Tobias Crisp that "God published the Law anew, because . . . it began to be so obliterated".[75]

(iii) *Mosaic Law not for justification*

All the Puritans were agreed, that, into whatever category the Mosaic Law had to be put, it was not given by God as a means of justification. The Law, coming 430 years after the promise, "cannot disannul" it[76] and, therefore, is completely misunderstood if it is thought to be a system of merit.[77] The Law was never a covenant of life;[78] for "the Law given to Adam, and the Law received by Moses, are not one and the same".[79]

> The Law differs from it selfe, in that use which it had before, and which it hath since the Fall. . . . It was given to Adam for this end, to bring himselfe to Life. . . . But unto Man fallen, although the Band of Obedience doe remaine: yet the End thereof (viz.). Justification and Life by it, is now abolished by the promise.[80]

The giving of the Law at Sinai is no more to be understood as a way of earning salvation, than the Lord's words[81] to the rich young ruler

70. *Catholick Theologie*, Book I. Part 2, p. 35.
71. *Conscience*, Book V. pp. 107, 108.
72. Francis Roberts, *God's Covenants*, p. 714; Ezekiel Hopkins, *Ten Commandments*, in *Works*, pp. 53, 54. See Chapter I above.
73. Samuel Bolton, *True Bounds*, p. 116.
74. *Sparkles of Glory*, p. 57.
75. *Christ Alone Exalted*, in *Works*, IV. 91.
76. Galatians iii. 17.
77. John Preston, *New Covenant*, p. 363.
78. Jeremiah Burroughs, *Gospel-Conversation*, p. 47.
79. John Sedgwick, *Antinomianisme Anatomized*, p. 14.
80. William Pemble, *Vindiciae Fidei*, p. 140.
81. Matthew xix. 16–22.

are to be so understood.[82] Henry Burton denies the possibility that the Mosaic Covenant could provide a way of justification by works, and he conducts a study of the Covenant of Works in order to show how different it was from the Sinaitic Covenant.[83] For the same reason, Anthony Burgess is at pains to demonstrate the opposition of the law of works to the law of faith, and to show that the Mosaic Law was never a "law of works", in the sense of prescribing works for justification.[84]

> Its true in the Old Testament, the People were under tutors and bondage; but that was in regard of the carnall commandement of Ceremonies. . . . But Servile obedience through apprehension of legall terrors, was never commanded in the spirituall Law of God to the Jews, more then to us. The Jews were not justified by the works of the Law more then we.[85]

There is no hope of winning God's favour by Law-keeping.[86] Such an aim is not only beyond the reach of man, but reveals a failure to grasp the implications of the Fall. This opinion is unambiguously expressed by such men as Tobias Crisp,[87] Thomas Gataker,[88] Francis Roberts,[89] James Durham,[90] Edwards Reynolds,[91] and John Owen.[92]

D. LAW AS A MEANS OF GRACE

The Puritans understood that the Covenant of Grace began in the Garden of Eden, and that Genesis iii. 15 is the first statement of it. It was "delivered to our first parents",[93] immediately upon the Fall.[94] "From Genesis iii. 15 onwards the Redeemed of the Lord were . . . brought into a new-Relation to God in . . . Christ".[95] They

82. Cf. William Strong, *The Two Covenants*, pp. 23–28; John Flavel, *Vindiciae Legis & Foederis*, Prolegomena; Samuel Bolton, *True Bounds*, pp. 159, 160.
83. *Law and Gospel Reconciled*, p. 27.
84. *Vindiciae Legis*, p. 238.
85. Samuel Rutherford, *Triumph of Faith*, p. 107.
86. Cf. Vavasor Powell, *Christ and Moses*, p. 206.
87. *Christ Alone Exalted*, in *Works*, IV. 89 ff.
88. *Antinomianism*, pp. 6, 7.
89. *God's Covenants*, pp. 679, 744.
90. *Law Unsealed*, p. 3.
91. *Three Treatises*: "Sinfulnesse of Sinne", p. 377.
92. *Dominion of Sin and Grace*, 1688, in *Works*, VII. 543.
93. William Perkins, *The Creede*, 1595, in *Works*, p. 184.
94. John Ball, *Covenant of Grace*, pp. 16, 36, 41, 42; John Preston, *New Covenant*, p. 351; Samuel Crooke, *True Blessednesse*, p. 33; James Ussher, *Body of Divinitie*, p. 158; Nicholas Byfield, *Patterne*, 1618, p. 179; Francis Roberts, *God's Covenants*, p. 61; Vavasor Powell, *Christ and Moses*, p. 21; John Barret *Treatise of the Covenants*, p. 298; Samuel Slater, *Two Covenants*.
95. Nehemiah Cox, *Of the Covenants*, p. 47.

were accepted "upon Terms of Faith . . . by the Covenant of Grace".[96] This covenant, made with Adam, was truly the *Protevangelion*, "the first opening of the Grace of God in Christ to Fallen Man".[97]

(i) *The continuity of the Covenant of Grace*

The continuity of the Covenant throughout the centuries was affirmed again and again by the Puritan writers. It is "one in substance", though more fully formulated to Abraham and, subsequently, "distinguished into the olde and newe testament."[98] "By the Covenant of Grace we understand in one word, the Gospell, i.e. the gratious appointment of God to bring man to Salvation by Jesus Christ", which, throughout the course of history, has been "diversely ordered".[99] Tobias Crisp deviates from the usual terminology when he speaks of two Covenants of grace, both founded on promises, one Covenant being good, the other better.[100] This deviation of expression in Tobias Crisp requires that some attention be given to the terminology of the historical or dispensational periods of the Covenants of God. Discrepancy appears occasionally in the designation of the Covenants as first and second, old and new; but usually the Puritans employ the term "first" to indicate the Covenant originally made with Adam, and the term "second" for the Covenant of Grace which immediately followed the Fall. The adjective "old" refers to that part of the Covenant of Grace that belonged to the times of the history of Israel (including its Abrahamic and Mosaic forms), and "new" indicates that part which was promised in Jeremiah and which came to realization in the times of the Gospel.[101] John Crandon maintains that the expression "new covenant", Jeremiah xxxi. 31–33, makes a comparison, not with the Covenant of Works, but with the Mosaic Covenant. The Old Covenant is called old, not in opposition to the Covenant of Grace as made in Genesis, but in opposition to the Covenant of Grace as it is in the Gospel. They are called "old" and

96. Ibid.
97. John Flavel, *Vindiciae Legis & Foederis*, p. 33; cf. Richard Baxter, *Catholick Theologie*, Book I. Part 2, p. 31; *End of Doctrinal Controversies*, p. 126 f.
98. William Perkins, *Golden Chaine*, in *Works*, p. 73; cf. Andrew Willet, *Hexapla: Romanes*, p. 177 and John Ball, *Covenant of Grace*, pp. 24–27.
99. William Pemble, *Vindiciae Fidei*, p. 136; Ezekiel Rogers, *Chief Grounds*, quoted in A. F. Mitchell, *Catechisms*, p. 58.
100. *Christ Alone Exalted*, in *Works*, II. 241 f. John Gill inserts a footnote. "Notwithstanding all the worthy Doctor has said, these don't appear to be two covenants essentially distinct; since he himself owns, that Christ is the subject-matter of both, and remission of sins is in them both." Tobias Crisp, *Works* (ed. Gill), I. 251.
101. Some of the indefiniteness in sorting out the nomenclature can be seen in William Perkins, *Golden Chaine*, in *Works*, p. 73; John Preston, *New Covenant*, p. 317; Henry Burton, *Law and Gospel Reconciled*, p. 26; Francis Roberts, *God's Covenants*, p. 1263; Thomas Brooks, *Paradise Opened*, in *Works* V. 296; Richard Baxter, *End of Doctrinal Controversies*, p. 140.

"new", not because they differed in substance, but on account of their different ways of administration. The Church of Israel and the Church of Christ are both under the same Covenant of Grace in substance. They are distinguished as being first under a legal, then under an evangelical administration. The Old Covenant speaks of Christ to come; the New Covenant of Christ already come.[102] A bold attempt at an exposition of the difficult sentence, "God is one", in Galatians iii. 20, is made by Samuel Bolton, who says that this means that God is the same in His grace as in His laws.[103] In all the covenants since the Fall, there is the same Christ, the same faith, and the same recovery of sinners;[104] and the newness of the New Covenant is "Not in Substance, but in Circumstance; Not in Essence, but in Accidents; Not in Inward Constitution, but in Outward Administration."[105]

> That place in Heb. 8. 8, 10 taken out of Jer. 31. 31, 32, 33 which speaketh of a new & old covenant, is thus to be understood; not of two Covenants differing in substance; not of the two Covenants, the Covenant of workes, and the Covenant of Grace; but of one and the same Covenant of Grace distinguished in their different manner of Administration; . . . Here . . . we see that a proof out of the old Testament is as much Gospel if rightly applied, as any in the New-Testament.[106]

William Ames,[107] Vavasor Powell,[108] William Allen,[109] and John Barret,[110] speak to the same purpose, and William Strong sums up their views when he affirms that there are three eras of the Covenant of Grace, and that "though there be some difference in circumstances . . . yet it is for substance the same from the fall unto the worlds end."[111]

(ii) *Mosaic Covenant consistent with grace*

From these generally agreed views about God's ways with fallen

102. *Aphorisms Exorized*, Part I. pp. 108, 109.
103. *True Bounds*, p. 132; cf. Edward Reynolds who says that God is one and the same in both covenants and has the same purpose of grace in both law and gospel. *Three Treatises*; "Sinfulnesse of Sinne", pp. 380–82.
104. Francis Roberts, *God's Covenants*, Introduction.
105. Op. cit., p. 1255; cf. James Durham, *Law Unsealed*, p. 10; Samuel Slater, *Two Covenants*.
106. Richard Byfield, *Temple-defilers*, 1645, pp. 38, 39.
107. *Marrow of Sacred Divinity*, p. 170.
108. *Christ and Moses*, pp. 21, 31.
109. *The Covenants*, pp. 3–5.
110. *Treatise of the Covenants*, pp. 298, 326, 330, 331.
111. *The Two Covenants*, pp. 65, 66. Cf. Samuel Slater who says that the New Covenant is so named "in respect of that difference, which is between the gracious administrations under the Old Testament, and those now under the New." *Two Covenants*.

man, the Puritans clearly saw how inconceivable it was to suppose that the Mosaic Covenant could be a cancellation of grace or a reversion to a basis of salvation by works. They contended, therefore, that the Mosaic Covenant could not possibly be inconsistent with grace. Because of its rigorous form, the Mosaic Covenant was recognized as occupying a distinctive place of its own;[112] but, in view of its integral relation to the Covenant of Grace, this rigorous form must be interpreted as subservient to the ends of grace. The Puritans freely acknowledged the difference of the Mosaic Covenant from the Covenant that followed it, but no admissions of this kind were allowed to detract from the truth that there was perfect harmony between them. John Sedgwick delights to say that the doctrine of Law and the doctrine of grace are "sweetly co-ordinate",[113] and even Tobias Crisp is able to admit that Law and Gospel can stand consistently with each other.[114] "How vain a thing it is, to advance grace and Christ oppositely to the Law: nay, they that destroy one, destroy also the other."[115] So harmonious are they, that

> there was no end or use for which the law was given, but might consist with Grace. . . . we preach the law, not in opposition, but subordination to the Gospel.[116]

The Law "is diverse but not adverse; subordinate, not contradictory to the New Testament",[117] and "you must know that the difference is not essentiall, . . . but accidentall".[118] So "sweetly the Law and Gospel do agree in one",[119] that it is unthinkable that the Law should disannul the promise.[120] Samuel Rutherford cannot insist too firmly that Law and Gospel are not contrary,[121] and this is the truth that Richard Byfield so vividly expresses in the title of his book, *The Gospels Glory, without prejudice to the Law.*

> The Law for righteousnesse, and Christ for righteousnesse, do stand in direct opposition; yet the Law is not against the Gospel: the Law drives to Christ alone; the Law is fulfill'd, when Christ is received, the Law comes in that the offers of Christ might be

112. See below, pp. 126 f.
113. *Antinomianisme Anatomized*, p. 8.
114. *Christ Alone Exalted*, in *Works*, IV. 89–95, on "The use of the Law". John Flavel is quick to pick up this admission, *Mental Errors*, pp. 196, 197.
115. Anthony Burgess, *Vindiciae Legis*, pp. 16, 153, 232–3, 251.
116. Samuel Bolton, *True Bounds*, pp. 76, 102.
117. Francis Roberts, *God's Covenants*, p. 744
118. Anthony Burgess, op. cit., p. 251.
119. Francis Roberts, op. cit., p. 778.
120. Francis Roberts takes Paul's remark, in Galatians iii. 12, that "the law is not of faith" to refer, not to the Mosaic Law, but to the Adamic, op. cit., p. 767.
121. *Survey*, Part II. p. 119.

esteemed, which else a proud sinner would wholly neglect or pervert, and never understand aright.[122]

The Puritans found much significance in the fact that the tables of stone were placed "in the ark".[123]

> The booke of the Law was placed betweene the Cherubims, and upon the Mercy-seat, to tell us under the Gospel; that every Law comes now to the Saints from the Mercy-seat.[124]

This fact supplies John Flavel with one of his reasons in proof of the consistency between the old and new Covenants.

> The Sinai Covenant was neither repugnant to the New Covenant in its scope and aim . . . nor yet set up as co-ordinate with it, . . . and accordingly we find both Tables of the law put into the Ark, Heb. 9. 4, which shows their Consistency and Subordination with, and to the method of Salvation by Christ in the New Covenant.[125]

(iii) *The expression of grace in the Law*

The consistency of the Law with grace led many of the Puritans to make the stronger affirmation that the Mosaic Law was an expression of the Covenant of Grace. One of their proofs that it was the Covenant of Grace is found in the Preface to the Decalogue.[126] James Durham points to the difference between the Law taken by itself, and the Law in the context of its promulgation, and says that the Preface to the Decalogue indicates that obedience is to be in the channel of the Covenant, that is o say, "having God for our God".[127] The Covenant at Sinai is but the working out of the Covenant with Abraham, both in its promises and its requirements. At Sinai there was a formal betrothal between God and His people, and the Passover sacrament was the sign of grace.[128] "There were mercifull and Evangelicall intentions" in the Mosaic Law.[129] These are clear from the way God introduces Himself, the pardon of sin that is offered, the faith that is accepted, the sacrifice and blood that are provided, and the continuity of the Covenant with Abraham and Isaac, as shown in

122. Richard Byfield, op. cit., p. 107.
123. *The Marrow*, p. 67.
124. Samuel Bolton, *True Bounds*, pp. 52, 53.
125. *Vindiciae Legis & Foederis*, p. 35; cf. John Barret, *Treatise of the Covenants*, pp. 113, 115, 116.
126. John Ball, *Covenant of Grace*, pp. 102–107; Henry Burton, *Law and Gospel Reconciled*, pp. 24, 25; Samuel Crooke, *True Blessednesse*, p. 88; Edward Elton, *Gods Holy Minde*, "Matters Morall", p. 3.
127. *Law Unsealed*, p. 10.
128. John Ball, *Covenant of Grace*, pp. 108, 109, 122, 132, 142.
129. John Sedgwick, *Antinomianisme Anatomized*, p. 14.

Deuteronomy vii. 12 and Galatians iii. 17, 18.[130] The Decalogue is an evangelical publication, expressing "Gods singular favour, love, compassion and goodness",[131] so that it may truly be said that "the Sinai-Law was Israels Gospel".[132] Jeremiah Burroughs,[133] James Ussher,[134] John Owen,[135] John Barret,[136] and many others, all perceive the grace that is in the Law. Edward Reynolds brings an unusual argument when he says that evidence that God will do more for His mercy than for His wrath is seen in the fact that in order to be merciful He will republish the Law. He would not have done this for His judgments, "but would have left men unto that reigne of sin & death which was in the world betweene Adam and Moses."[137] John Flavel, similarly, adds a fresh thought when he asks, "If the Law were intended by God to be an Adam's Covenant to them . . . where then is the Privilege of Gods Israel above other nations?"[138]

The Antinomians were unable to perceive any grace in the giving of the Law, and Robert Towne, in reply to Anthony Burgess who tries to press him to see God's goodness in it, denies that the Law was "in a proper and strict sense given for Evangelical purposes".[139]

(iv) *Law as an instrument of grace*

All that expresses grace is necessarily instrumental to it, and so the Puritans taught that the intention of God in giving the Mosaic Covenant was that it should be subservient to that Covenant of Grace of which it was but a part. It is never to be forgotten that the Law was "added" to the promise, and that the old Covenant looked forward to a "new" and a "better" Covenant, and so subserved that which was greater than itself. "The Lord had a farther design to lay aside the transient Law-dispensation and to set up Christ".[140] William Twisse answers the final question of his "third Catechisme" by saying that the Law is "To drive us unto Christ".[141] Law is subordinated to promise;[142] it is to be a "schoolmaster",[143] leading

130. Anthony Burgess, *Vindiciae Legis*, pp. 151, 213, 234–6; cf. Thomas Blake, *Covenant of God*, pp. 165–7.
131. Francis Roberts, *God's Covenants*, p. 678 and his marginal reference to Deuteronomy vii. 6–9.
132. Francis Roberts, *God's Covenants*, p. 788.
133. *Gospel-Conversation*, p. 47.
134. *Body of Divinitie*, p. 212.
135. *Dominion of Sin and Grace*, in *Works*, VII. 542.
136. *Treatise of the Covenants*, p. 310.
137. *Three Treatises*: "Sinfulnesse of Sinne", p. 374.
138. *Mental Errors*, pp. 204, 205, where he lists a large number of authorities.
139. *Re-assertion*, p. 76.
140. Samuel Rutherford, *Covenant of Life*, p. 14.
141. *Christian Doctrine*, 1632, p. 41. Cf. also Samuel Slater, *Two Covenants*, "to indeare the promise of Grace to the heires thereof".
142. Samuel Bolton, *True Bounds*, pp. 116, 117.
143. Francis Roberts, *God's Covenants*, p. 157.

to Christ;[144] it is designed "to be subservient"[145] and stands as "an Appendix".[146] The Law was brought in "that it might be as Hagar to Sarah; a handmaid to further the ends of the Gospel".[147] The relation between Law and Gospel is mutual, however, and each serves the other. "The law leading to Christ serves the gospel, and the gospel serves the law by fulfilling it".[148]

This subservient aim of the Law means that the Law is nothing less than the Divinely-appointed instrument of grace. "God doth use the Law instrumentally, for to quicken up grace, & increase it in us".[149]

> Evangelical allurements (on which by some the whole of the work is laid) can never (I suppose) work on the soul without Law-convictions. . . . And to say the Gospel discovers sin as well as the Law, taking the Gospel in opposition to the morall precepts (as here it must be taken), is the greatest absurdity.[150]

The Law is thus a schoolmaster, not only dispensationally to the Jews, but also experimentally to all men to lead them to Christ.[151] Edward Reynolds maintains that when the Law is preached "as subordinated to Christ and his Gospel" it is "neither sinne nor death";[152] and he understands the phrase "till the seed", Galatians iii. 19, to mean that the Law was instituted for evangelical purposes. Its design was to stir up an expectation of Christ, "the Seed", and to be an instrument of conviction till the "seed", the company of believers, be completed: and, therefore, so long as there are yet any to come to Christ, the Law will drive them to Him.[153]

> I may say of the Law, as it's said of Christ, had there not been some souls that Christ did intend to life, he had never come into the world; so had there not been a seed unto whom the Law was to be a servant, the Lord had never given the Law, never renewed it, . . . but had it not been for the seed, the Law had never been added as a handmaid to the Gospel: . . . It is a high act of Grace, and one of the greatest priviledges that Believers have by Christ, that the Law is a servant to the Gospel.[154]

144. James Durham, *Law Unsealed*, To the Christian Reader.
145. William Allen, *The Covenants*, pp. 6, 55.
146. John Flavel, *Vindiciae Legis & Foederis*, Prolegomena.
147. William Strong, *The Two Covenants*, p. 29 and see p. 88.
148. Robert Traill, *Galatians*, in *Works*, IV. 199.
149. Anthony Burgess, *Vindiciae Legis*, p. 183.
150. Thomas Blake, *Covenant of God*, p. 95.
151. Vavasor Powell, *Christ and Moses*, pp. 191–198.
152. *Three Treatises*: "Sinfulnesse of Sinne", p. 370. See above, pp. 61, 62.
153. Op. cit., p. 379. Tobias Crisp acknowledges this subservient intention when he explains "the seed", in Galatians iii. 19, of the aggregate of believers who are "in Christ". *Christ Alone Exalted*, in *Works*, IV. 93.
154. William Strong, *The Two Covenants*, p. 109.

The Law, therefore, must be looked at with "Gospel-Spectacles".[155]

The preaching of the Law as an instrument of grace was challenged by the Antinomians, and was disparagingly described by them as "legal preaching", and it is in reply to this that John Flavel asks,

> If then I preach the Law to the very same Evangelical Uses and Purposes for which God added it to the Promise, do I therein make an ill use of the Law?[156]

E. THE DISTINCTIVE PLACE OF LAW

One of the contrasts so easily observed when comparing the Mosaic Covenant with that of the Gospel is the difference of clarity in the revelation of God's grace. Indeed, John Barret considers that the very obscurity of the Old Covenant served to create expectations which were to be realized only in the New.[157]

(i) *Obscurity of its revelation*

John Preston lists "six differences betweene the Old and New Testament",[158] the fifth of which reads, "In the New Testament there is a more cleere perspicuous knowledge of things, there are better promises, a larger infusion of the spirit."[159] The Old Covenant "was in obscure and dark expressions",[160] and any "faultiness" in it was not that it was opposite, but that it was dim.[161] The Law is the Covenant of Grace "very obscurely", nevertheless the Law and the Gospel are the same, "differing only as the acorne while it is in the huske, and the oke when it's branched out into a tall tree".[162] The phrase, "before faith came",[163] is an expression of comparison, and must not be understood to mean more than before faith came to be revealed "so fully and clearly".[164] Thomas Goodwin's comment on Paul's words in 2 Corinthians iii. 10 is that, "though he attributeth a glory to the law, yet in comparison of the gospel he makes it no glory",[165] and Richard Baxter speaks of two editions of the "Law of

155. Francis Roberts, *God's Covenants*, p. 789.
156. *Vindiciae Legis & Foederis*, p. 25. The Puritan view of the gracious purpose of the Law was clearly taught both by Luther (on Galatians iii. 21) and Calvin (*Inst.* II. vii.)
157. *Treatise of the Covenants*, p. 326.
158. *New Covenant*, p. 326.
159. Op. cit., p. 328.
160. Richard Sibbes, *Excellency of the Gospel*, 1639, in *Works*, IV. 204.
161. John Ball, *Covenant of Grace*, p. 118, cf. John Crandon, *Aphorisms Exorized*, Part I. p. 109.
162. Anthony Burgess, *Vindiciae Legis*, p. 232.
163. Galatians iii. 23.
164. Francis Roberts, *God's Covenants*, pp. 768, 769.
165. *Glory of the Gospel*, 1703, in *Works*, IV. 315.

Grace", saying that the revelation of grace "is far clearer in the second Edition than in the first".[166]

The Antinomians agreed here with the orthodox. John Eaton, for example, says that "these glorious things, were vailed; yea and greatly obscured, and darkned",[167] and John Saltmarsh concurs that "God was very sparing in that time of the discoveries of himselfe in Christ."[168]

(ii) *Rigour of its ministry*

The rigour of the Mosaic Law gives it a distinct place in the Divine Covenant of Grace, but the precise definition of this place occasioned no little trouble to the Puritans. Those who regarded the Mosaic Covenant as a Covenant of Works were able easily to recognize the unique place it occupied. Thus, Richard Sibbes has no hesitation in saying,

> The covenant of works is taught to shew us our failing . . . Why was the covenant of works added in the wilderness afterwards? It was . . . to increase the sense of transgression, that we by the law might see what we should do, and what we have not done, and that we are by that come under a curse.[169]

The rigour of the Law can easily be accounted for when the Law is thought of as the Covenant of Works, but it is less easy to do so when it is not so regarded. Further, it is impossible to place the Puritans in two simple groups on this subject, because of the inter-relation of their ideas.

William Ames endeavours to define the particular place of the Mosaic Law by drawing attention to the differences of administration of the Covenant of Grace in the times before and after Christ. He says that in the former times, "there was some representation of the Covenant of workes"; but the freedom experienced under the New Testament can be said to consist in the fact that "the government of the Law, or mixing of the covenant of workes, which did hold the ancient people in a certaine bondage, is now taken away".[170] John Ball finds his answer to the problem by regarding the Law as part of the Covenant of Grace, but "in a manner fitting to the state of that people, time and condition of the Church".[171] Samuel Bolton boldly

166. *End of Doctrinal Controversies*, p. 140; cf. p. 134.
167. *Honey-combe*, p. 98.
168. *Free-Grace*, p. 166.
169. *Faithful Covenanter*, 1640, in *Works*, VI. 5.
170. *Marrow of Sacred Divinity*, pp. 175, 176.
171. *Covenant of Grace*, p. 102.

acknowledges the rigorous and legalistic aspects of the Covenant and says,

> I grant that in the externall view of them . . . the Law and Gospel doe seeme to stand upon opposite termes, but yet these opposite termes on which the Law seemes to stand, had its subservient ends to Christ and Grace.[172]

Although the Mosaic Covenant is not different in species or kind from the Covenant of Grace, it is nevertheless "distinct".[173] It is a Covenant of Grace for substance, but propounded in rigorous terms, and "dispensed in an altogether unusual way of Majesty, Glory, Terrour, Rigour, Servitude, and Bondage".[174] Under the Old Covenant with the Israelites there was "a harder pressing of the Law on them",[175] and their observances "looked much like a Covenant of works".[176] Tobias Crisp, who approximates to the orthodox view in many things, contrasts Law and Gospel as Covenant of Grace weak and the Covenant of Grace strong, and speaks about grace being "dispensed in the Mosaic way",[177] and when John Saltmarsh allows himself to concede the presence of grace in the Old Testament he, too, says that it was preached "in a rough and hairy garment, or, more Legally".[178]

The object of this rigorous Law-work is to function as a pedagogue, "by stripes and correction".[179] "Here's the true use of the Morall Law, since the fall of Man: . . . to prove him to be unjust and worthy of death",[180] and to show the sinner's "owne unrighteousnes & insufficiency" and cause him to "fly to Christ".[181] The Law is to teach man his need,[182] indicting him by "a sharp ministry",[183] leaving him "broken by law" and reduced to "humiliation".[184] It was for this end that believers were to feel the hardness of the Law as it "comes roughly upon them";[185] God having given that Law as "a means to beat man out of himself".[186]

The Antinomian writers concur in this general opinion about the

172. *True Bounds*, p. 156.
173. Francis Roberts, *God's Covenants*, p. 18.
174. Op. cit., pp. 753, 754; Vavasor Powell, *Christ and Moses*, p. 203; Richard Byfield, *Gospels Glory*, pp. 17, 115.
175. Samuel Rutherford, *Survey*, Part II. pp. 15, 119.
176. Simon Ford, *Spirit of Bondage and Adoption*, p. 35.
177. *Christ Alone Exalted*, in *Works*, II. 247.
178. *Reasons*, "Shadows Flying Away", p. 3.
179. William Perkins, *Galatians*, pp. 285–90.
180. William Pemble, *Vindiciae Fidei*, p. 141.
181. John Dod and Robert Cleaver, *Ten Commaundements*, p. 374.
182. John Preston, *New Covenant*, p. 385.
183. John Preston, *Breastplate of Faith and Love*, "Of Faith", p. 134.
184. John Preston, *Breastplate of Faith and Love*, "Of Love", 1630, pp. 12, 13.
185. Jeremiah Burroughs, *Saints Treasury*, p. 93.
186. John Sedgwick, *Antinomianisme Anatomized*, p. 14.

severities of the Law. John Eaton says that God's purpose in the Law was "to shew that nothing pleased him, but that perfect righteousnesse revealed in his Law".[187] He teaches that "the School-master of the Law, that held the Church of the Jewes . . . is also a School-master to drive with lashes of crosses and afflictions the unconverted Gentiles also unto Christ",[188] and therefore must be preached to the ungodly.

The ministry of the Law to sinners is "to Seal up Condemnation, by convincing all of sin";[189] and so, although the Covenant administered by Moses is the Covenant of Grace, yet that function is especially ascribed to him

> which consisted in teaching what the true righteousness of works was, and what rewards or punishments attend upon the observers or breakers of the Law. Upon which account Moses is compared with Christ; The Law was given by Moses: but Grace and Truth came by Jesus Christ.[190]

God set up the Law for the Israelites "as a Covenant of Grace with Evangelical offers of Grace to bring them to Christ"; but at the same time, he "kept it in the form of a Covenant of Works, that it might be the more effectual to drive men to Christ".[191]

> The Lords intention in giving the Law was double, unto the carnal Jews to set forth to them the old Covenant which they had broken; and yet unto the believing Jews it did darkly shadow and set forth unto them the Covenant of Grace made with Christ . . . and therefore it was delivered after a sort in the form of a Covenant of Works. . . . It was to the carnal Jews plainly a Covenant of Works, not in Gods intention, but by their own corruption. . . . Now if the Lord will not give it as a Covenant, why does he not propound it as a rule, and lay down the precepts without any such terms of a Covenant, . . . when he did never intend to deliver it as a Covenant, in which men should attain life by doing, but by believing? Thus the Lord did, that the terms of the first Covenant might be promulgated to the World, and that they that did still desire to be under the Law, might not plead ignorance of the terms that God required in the Law.[192]

187. *Honey-combe*, p. 100.
188. Op. cit., p. 122; cf. Henry Denne, *Man of Sin Discovered*, pp. 5, 6.
189. Francis Roberts, *God's Covenants*, p. 157.
190. Francis Roberts, op. cit., p. 775, cf. pp. 776, 788, 891 f.
191. William Strong, *The Two Covenants*, p. 23.
192. William Strong, *The Two Covenants*, pp. 88, 89; cf. Thomas Goodwin, *Of the Creatures*, in *Works*, VII. 36; Thomas Brooks, *Paradise Opened*, in *Works*, V. 287; John Barret, *Treatise of the Covenants*, p. 323.

It was thus God's purpose towards men in the times of the Old Covenant "by such a dreadful representation of the severe and impracticable terms of the first Covenant . . . to convince them of the impossibility of legal righteousness", and "to drive them to Christ".[193]

In the light of all the foregoing, therefore, it may be concluded that the Puritan opinion about the place of the Law in the Covenant of Grace is that its rigorous demands provide that rough surface which the "Spirit of bondage" can use to prepare the heart for the reception of grace and liberty.

F. OPPOSITION BETWEEN LAW AND GOSPEL

(i) *The historic abuse of the Law*

The Old Testament provides an almost continuous commentary on the inability of the Israelites rightly to understand the revelation that was given to them. They misconceived the Divine purpose of the sacrifices, and so abused them.[194] This was true also about the Law of Moses; for as they construed the ceremonial Law in terms of an *ex opere operato* principle, so they interpreted the moral Law in terms of a Covenant of Works. William Perkins takes up the clause, "ye that desire to be under the law",[195] and explains it as the ignorance of the Galatians "in mistaking and misconceiving the true scope of the law", adding the comment that it was precisely this which "was to the Jewes as a vaile before their eies in the reading of the lawe, 2 Cor. 3. 14."[196] The shining face of Moses is thought by the author of *The Marrow* to symbolize the Law rightly understood.

> And yet . . . the blind leaders of the blind . . . used it not as a pedagogue to Christ, but. . . . turned the whole law into a covenant of works to be done for justification. . . . The difference between the Jews' covenant of grace and ours was chiefly of their own making. They should have been driven to Christ by the law; but they expected life in obedience to it, and this was their great error.[197]

Samuel Rutherford marks this false use of the Law by the Jews, and in a severe chapter which he heads, *Antinomians ignorant of Jewish Law-service, and of Gospel-obedience,* he charges the Antinomians with the same error.

193. John Flavel, *Vindiciae Legis & Foederis*, Prolegomena, and p. 25; William Allen, *The Covenants*, p. 56; John Crandon, *Aphorisms Exorized*, Part I. p. 109. William Eyre, *Free Justification*, p. 45; Edward Reynolds, *Three Treatises*: "Sinfulnesse of Sinne", pp. 368, 371, 384, 385; Thomas Cole, *Repentance*, pp. 85–95.
194. Cf. Isaiah i. 11–15.
195. Galatians iv. 21.
196. *Galatians*, p. 344.
197. Op. cit., pp. 78, 79, 80; cf. Francis Roberts, *God's Covenants*, p. 787.

> I perceive, Antinomians miserably mistaken, in confounding the error of the Jewes, and the state of the Jewish Church. . . . It was the error and sin of men, not the state of the Church in its non-age, under Tutors, nor the dispensation of God, that The Jews followed after the law of righteousnesse, but obtained not the law of righteousnesse. . . . It was never lawfull for the Jewes to dreame they could get, or earne Gods free love, and undeserved grace, by fasting and praying, and other acts of obedience.[198]

God's intention in the Mosaic Law "was fatally mistaken by the Jews . . . and was . . . notoriously perverted to a quite contrary end to that which God promulged it for".[199] By separating the law from faith, they made law a cause of death and put it into apparent opposition to Christ.[200]

(ii) *No absolute opposition*

This perverted use of the moral Law by the Jews and the Judaizing section in the Galatian churches explains the strong language of Paul in his opposition to the Law. Paul's words that seem to be so derogatory to the Law are written only because the Law had been abused by separation from the Gospel, for the contrariety of the Law to the Covenant of Grace "is not in themselves, but in the ignorance, pride and hardnesse of heart of them, who . . . did pervert the right end of the Law".[201] Paul's reference to the covenants in Galatians iv creates a problem at first sight, for he seems to suggest that Sinai was merely a Covenant of Works, but Henry Burton offers the solution that Paul is speaking of the Law only in the killing sense given to it by the carnal Jews, for Sinai and Sion are opposite only as the unbelieving heart makes them opposite.[202] Anthony Burgess believes that Paul had the Jewish abuse of the Law especially in mind in 1 Timothy i. 8, 9, "the law is good, if a man use it lawfully". The Jews opposed the Law to Christ, and "this was the Jewes fundamentall errour, and under this notion doth the Apostle argue against it in his Epistles to the Romans and Galatians".[203] When he

198. Samuel Rutherford, *Survey*, Part II. 70. But the Antinomians are not the only ones to pervert the Law in this direction, for Richard Baxter does the same thing. He says that the Jews perverted the Mosaic Covenant of Grace into a Covenant of Works, *Catholick Theologie*, Book I. Part 2, p. 36, and *End of Doctrinal Controversies*, pp. 137, 139; but he himself also teaches that the believer is justified, not only on account of Christ's doing, but also on his own performance of that which is determined by a "new Rule", *Catholick Theologie*, Book I. Part 2, p. 22. See below, Chapter VI.
199. John Flavel, *Vindiciae Legis & Foederis*, p. 35.
200. John Ball, *Covenant of Grace*, pp. 115, 116; cf. William Strong, *The Two Covenants*, p. 29.
201. John Ball, op. cit., p. 121.
202. *Law and Gospel Reconciled*, pp. 26, 27.
203. *Vindiciae Legis*, pp. 19, 20.

comes to discuss Romans vi. 14, 15, "Ye are not under the law", Anthony Burgess asks his hearers to think first of all "in what sense the Apostle argueth against the Law". He agrees that the "principall thing in question" had to do with that part of the Law which belonged to the priestly ceremonies, and then adds:

> Yet the Apostle, to set forth the fulnesse of grace, and Christ, doth extend his arguments . . . to the Morall Law: for the Jewes did generally think, that the knowledge and observation of the Morall Law without Christ, was enough for their peace and comfort. That the Apostle argueth against the Law in their abused sense of it, is plain, because when he speaks of it in it's own nature, he commends it, and extols it.[204]

He maintains that in such passages as Romans x. 1–3, Galatians iii. 18, Romans iv. 14, Paul is not speaking against the Law in an absolute manner, but only against the perverted Law as mishandled by the Jews.[205] Paul's words are against the Law "in the oldnesse of the Letter",[206] that is to say, in a manner "such as may come from men as yet in their old corruption";[207] for the opposition between Law and Gospel is entirely of men's "owne making".[208]

Francis Roberts enters upon a discussion of Paul's words that appear to be derogatory to the Law of God. Expounding 2 Corinthians iii. 6–7, he writes,

> These expressions . . . touching Moses Ministration of the Law, are not to be taken absolutely; as if it had been absolutely and in it self the Ministration of death and Condemnation. For Scripture elsewhere stiles it, λόγια ζῶντα, Lively Oracles; Or (as some Copies) λόγον ζῶντα, a lively word, or living word; that is An enlivening word, giving life. But understand them respectively and accidentally, in respect of this errour and mistake of the carnal and ignorant Jews.[209]

He illustrates this accidental significance of the Law by a corresponding accidental use of the Gospel which, although it be "called The Ministration of the Spirit, . . . because it is such absolutely and in itself; yet accidentally upon occasion of mans abuse and Corruptions, it is The Savour of death unto death".[210] James Durham draws the distinction between the Law as God gave it and the Law as the carnal

204. Op. cit., p. 224.
205. Op. cit., p. 237.
206. Edward Elton, *Treatises*: "Complaint of a Sanctifyed Sinner", p. 62.
207. Ibid.
208. Samuel Bolton, *True Bounds*, pp. 160, 161.
209. *God's Covenants*, p. 741. Cf. a good summary in Charles Hodge: *Systematic Theology*, II. 375, 376.
210. Op. cit., p. 742.

mind abused it,[211] and he contends that Paul is speaking by accommodation to the situation when he speaks of Sinai gendering to bondage, for it was Sinai as the Jews had made it. Similar arguments are found in Vavasor Powell,[212] Edward Reynolds,[213] and Ezekiel Hopkins.[214] John Owen maintains that in Romans vi. 14, 15 Paul does not dismiss the Law from the life of the believer, but grapples with it in its mistaken and perverted use. He understands the expression "under the law" to be indicative of "contendings against sin . . . from legal principles and motives",[215] this being a wrong use of the Law. John Flavel holds the same view of the meaning of Paul's apparently derogatory statements about the Law, and argues that the distinction between God's intention in the Law and man's abuse of the Law must be clearly kept in mind.

> The Law in both these Senses is excellently described, Gal. 4. in that Allegory of Hagar and Sarah, the figures of the two Covenants. Hagar in her first and proper Station, was but a serviceable Hand-maid to Sarah, as the Law is a Schoolmaster to Christ; but when Hagar the Hand-maid is taken into Sarah's Bed, and brings forth Children, that aspire to the Inheritance, then saith the Scripture, Cast out the bond-woman, with her son. So it is here; take the Law in its primary use, as God designed it, as a School-master, or Hand-maid to Christ and the promise; so it is consistent with them, and excellently subservient to them; but if we marry this Hand-maid, and espouse it as a Covenant of Works, then are we bound to it for life, Rom. 7. and must have nothing to do with Christ. . . . This fatal mistake of the Use and Intent of the Law, is the ground of those seeming Contradictions in Paul's Epistles. Sometimes he magnifies the Law, when he speaks of it according to Gods end and purpose in its Promulgation, Rom. 7. 12, 14, 16, but as it was fatally mistaken by the Jews, and set in opposition to Christ; so he thunders against it, calls it a ministration of Death and Condemnation, . . . and by this distinction, whatsoever seems repugnant in Paul's Epistles, may be sweetly reconciled; and 'tis a distinction of his own making, 1 Tim. 1, 8. We know that the Law is good, if we use it lawfully. There is a good and an evil use of the Law.[216]

From all the foregoing it is clear that the doctrine of the Law of

211. *Law Unsealed*, p. 4.
212. *Christ and Moses*, pp. 202–203.
213. *Three Treatises*: "Sinfulnesse of Sinne", p. 385.
214. *Galatians*, 1701, in *Works*, p. 250.
215. *Mortification*, in *Works*, VI. 47.
216. *Vindiciae Legis & Foederis*, Prolegomena, and pp. 36, 37; cf. John Barret, *Treatise of the Covenants*, pp. 339, 343. William Lillie, *Law of Christ*, 1956, p. 21 points out that similar words of Jesus are corrections, not of the Law as such, but of Jewish misuse of it.

God must be integrated into the entire system of Christian theology. Law and grace belong together, and are the same under the Old Covenant and the New. In these beliefs the Puritans were true followers of the Reformers; for Luther and Melanchthon recognized no difference in principle between God's dealings with His people under the old dispensation and under the new,[217] and Calvin devoted many pages of the *Institutes* to the exposition of the continuity of the purpose of Divine grace in the Old and New Testaments.[218] It is a fair summary to say with H. G. Wood that "the Puritans were more impressed with the unity of the Bible than with the difference between Law and Gospel".[219] The moral Law thus comes into its own and enters upon its essential fulfilment in the grace manifested in Christ.

217. W. Adams Brown, Article "Covenant Theology", *ERE*, IV. 220.
218. *Inst.* II. vii. and ix.
219. Article, "Puritanism", *ERE*, X. 512.

Chapter IV

THE END OF THE LAW

Synopsis

A. THE END AS FULFILMENT

B. THE PASSIVE AND ACTIVE OBEDIENCE OF CHRIST
   (i) *Passive obedience*
   (ii) *Active obedience*

C. IMPUTED RIGHTEOUSNESS

D. ANTINOMIAN DOCTRINE OF ABROGATION

E. LAW IN ITS COMMANDING AND COVENANTING ASPECTS
   (i) *Distinguishable and separable*
   (ii) *The Law in covenant form*

F. LAW NOT ABROGATED BY THE FALL

G. LAW NOT ABROGATED BY GRACE

H. IDENTITY OF THE MOSAIC LAW AND THE LAW OF CHRIST

I. RELATION OF BELIEVERS TO THE LAW
   (i) "*Dead to the law*" *and* "*not under the law*"
   (ii) "*The law of sin and death*" *and the bondage of the Law*
   (iii) "*That being dead wherein we were held*"

Chapter IV

THE END OF THE LAW

THE place of the Law of God in the Divine purposes having been surveyed, it now becomes necessary to inquire what impact on the Law, if any, was made by the work of Christ. This chapter, therefore, examines how the Puritans related the work of Christ to the Law, and, in particular, in what ways they thought Christ could be said to be the end of the Law.

Many questions arise, such as whether the work of Christ can be regarded as a fulfilment of the Law; whether such fulfilment includes the whole obedience of Christ, the active as well as the passive; whether the active obedience of Christ is imputed to the believer; and, if so, what this means for Him in His relation to the Law. The investigation of this last question calls, first, for a distinction between the Law as command, and the Law as covenant, and then yields the answer that the Antinomians held that the Law was abrogated, the Baxterians, that the Law was modified, and the Puritans, that the Law was established.

A. THE END AS FULFILMENT

The apostle Paul strikingly declares that "Christ is the end of the law for righteousness to every one that believeth".[1] But what does he mean by this? The asking of this question immediately uncovers a double problem, namely, that of finding out what Law it is to which the apostle refers, and what he means by the word "end".

It is easy to suggest that it is the ceremonial Law which the apostle has in mind. But this would not be pertinent to his argument; he is speaking of the kind of Law that was thought to produce righteousness, "which must be the Morall Law only".[2]

If it be accepted that the reference is to the moral Law, the remaining question has to do with the meaning of the word "end". Here an important divergence appears, for not all the Puritans understood the word τέλος in the same way. The Antinomians understood it to mean termination, or abolition, and they had no hesitation in affirming that Christ brought the demands of the moral Law to an end. Those who thought that the apostle was here referring to the

1. Romans x. 4.
2. Anthony Burgess, *Vindiciae Legis*, pp. 265 f.

ceremonial Law,[3] likewise understood the word "end" as meaning termination, and so also did those who defined the Law in terms of a Covenant of Works.[4]

With characteristic thoroughness Anthony Burgess writes:

> By reason of the different use of the word τέλος, there are different conjectures; some make it no more than *extremitas*, or *terminus*; because the ceremoniall Law ended in Christ: Others make it *finis complementi*, the fulness of the Law is Christ: Others adde, *finis intentionis*, or *scopi* to it; so that by these the meaning is, The Law did intend Christ in all its ceremonialls and moralls, that, as there was not the least ceremony, which did not lead to Christ; so not the least *iota* or *apex* in the morall Law, but it did also aime at him.[5]

What his own conviction is can be judged from his concluding lecture in *Vindiciae Legis*, to which he gives the title, *To teach the abrogation of the Law, offensive to God*. He borrows the language of Augustine—*finis interficiens* and *finis perficiens*—and finds the latter more consonant with Paul's obvious reference to the moral Law in Romans x. 4. He approves also of a further distinction, made by Thomas Aquinas, that such an end is two-fold: it is either that to which a thing naturally inclines of itself, or it is that for which a thing is appointed by the one who brings it into being. The end of the Law to which naturally it inclines is eternal life, to be obtained by a perfect righteousness in man; but the appointed end, which God the Law-giver made in the promulgation of it, was the Lord Jesus Christ, so that whatever the Law commanded, promised, or threatened, was for the purpose of stirring up the covenant people to seek Christ.[6] Anthony Burgess, therefore, believes the meaning of the word "end" in this passage to be, not that of termination, but of realization or fulfilment.[7]

> 'Tis a mistake to think, that Christ was *finis interficiens*, and not *perficiens*; the end of the law abolishing it, not accomplishing it: for he established the law, and the law had its great end in him.[8]

"Christ is the end of the Law to a Believer, as soon as a man is brought

3. Cf. Ezekiel Hopkins, *Ten Commandments*, in *Works*, p. 59; Richard Baxter, *Scripture Gospel Defended*, p. 63.
4. Cf. *The Marrow*, pp. 67, 68; Francis Roberts, *God's Covenants*, p. 181; Thomas Manton, *James*, in *Works*, IV. 219; William Strong, *The Two Covenants*, p. 2.
5. Anthony Burgess, *Vindiciae Legis*, p. 7.
6. Op. cit., pp. 266, 267.
7. Cf. Thomas Taylor, *Regula Vitae*, p. 170; Richard Allen, *Antidote against Heresy*, p. 84; Joseph Caryl, *Nature of Love*, 1673, pp. 8, 9; Francis Roberts, *God's Covenants*, p. 731; Ezekiel Hopkins, *Ten Commandments*, in *Works*, p. 59; John Ball, *Covenant of Grace*, p. 109.
8. William Woodward, *Lord our Righteousness*, p. 52.

to a full close with Christ",[9] and is thus the realization of the end of the Law in both the senses proposed by Thomas Aquinas: the "appointed" end comprehends the "natural". The object of the Law is thus fully realized, first as to its natural inclination in the perfect righteousness of Christ, and then as to its appointed end in the salvation of sinners.

The discussion among the Puritans about the meaning of Paul's words in Romans x. 4 is but one chapter in an expository debate that has continued for many centuries. The crux of the problem contained in this expression—to put it in the simple words with which A. R. Vidler has summed up the voluminous discussion—is that "'end' may mean either that at which something is aimed (an aim) or the point at which it terminates (a full stop)",[10] and a study of the work of the commentators reveals that they fall approximately into two groups distinguished by these meanings.[11]

"End" is understood in the sense of "terminus" by J. A. Beet—the principle of law "has been displaced";[12] J. Denney—"law as a means of attaining righteousness has ceased";[13] C. H. Dodd—"an end to law" as a "way of righteousness";[14] A. E. Garvie—"not fulfilment, but termination";[15] E. H. Gifford—as a means of justification law is "at an end in Christ";[16] C. Hodge—to be understood "metonymically for he who terminates";[17] H. A. W. Meyer—the termination of the "validity of the law" as a means of righteousness;[18] A. Nygren—the "end to law as a way of salvation";[19] and W. Sanday and A. C. Headlam—"Law as a method or principle of righteousness had been done away with in Christ."[20] In a way that appears to be oblivious of a possible alternative meaning the *New English Bible* fastens an interpretation on the sentence by rendering it "Christ ends the law".[21]

The idea of the "end" of the Law as its "aim" is held by H. Alford

9. Simon Ford, *Spirit of Bondage and Adoption*, p. 64.
10. *Christ's Strange Work*, p. 63.
11. Limitations of space do not allow a full discussion of all the relevant New Testament expressions bearing on this subject, nor even for an adequate examination of the passage under review, but because a true understanding of these words is crucial to the Puritan position a brief survey of its interpretation is made.
12. J. A. Beet, *Romans*, 1887, p. 301.
13. J. Denney, *Romans*, 1917, p. 669.
14. C. H. Dodd, *Romans*, 1932, p. 165.
15. A. E. Garvie, *Romans*, 1910, p. 229.
16. E. H. Gifford, *Romans*, 1886, p. 183.
17. C. Hodge, *Romans*, 1864, pp. 333–5.
18. H. A. W. Meyer, *Romans*, 1874, II. 172–4.
19. A. Nygren, *Romans*, Eng. trans. 1952, p. 379.
20. W. Sanday and A. C. Headlam, *Romans*, 1895, pp. 283–5.
21. A number of these writers acknowledge that there is also a subsidiary purposive connotation in the word, and so the division is not hard and fast.

—"the object at which the law aimed";[22] C. K. Barrett—the key to the meaning is found in the words "by realizing righteousness";[23] K. Barth—the end of the law stands for "its sense and meaning";[24] J. A. Bengel—"the life which the law points out but cannot give";[25] W. Burkitt—"Christ is the end of the law, inasmuch as he is to a believer what the law would have been to him if he could have perfectly kept it";[26] J. Calvin—"The word completion, seems not to me unsuitable in this place";[27] F. Godet—"bestowing righteousness and life, which the law points out, but cannot give";[28] M. Stuart—"accomplishes the object";[29] J. Wesley—"the scope and aim" of the law in leading men to justification.[30] A. R. Vidler himself understands the meaning to be "aim".[31]

Sometimes the concept of "fulfilment" is understood to belong to the meaning of the word. J. A. Bengel goes so far as to say that τέλος and πλήρωμα are synonymous, though F. Godet and W. Sanday and A. C. Headlam categorically affirm that τέλος never means τελείωσις. It is nevertheless not difficult to move from the idea of realization of aim to that of fulfilment. W. Burkitt adds the thought of "accomplishment", so, too, does H. Alford when he remarks that this is "a sense included in the general meaning, but not especially treated here". C. Hodge makes a similar concession with the rider that the idea of "fulfilment" is "scriptural, but not consistent with the meaning of the word", though he goes on to say that the "end" is achieved by Christ "by fulfilling its demands" and "it is because Christ is the fulfiller of the law, that he is the end of it".[32]

The interpreters who understand the word to mean "aim", or even "fulfilment", find their guidance in the more extended context of Scripture. They avoid the error of ignoring the immediate context, but at the same time are not imprisoned by it. As is so often true, the broader basis of theological understanding comprehends the divergences of exegesis and leads to a more unified conclusion. The lexicographer is not contradicted, he is merely left behind, as was seen in the discussion of the meaning of the phrase "the spirit of bondage". The idea of "aim" is drawn from that of pedagogue in Galatians iii. 24 and the phrase "end of the commandment" in

22. H. Alford, *Greek Testament*, 1865, p. 417.
23. C. K. Barrett, *Romans*, 1957, pp. 197, 198.
24. K. Barth, *Romans*, Eng. trans. 1933, pp. 374–6.
25. J. A. Bengel, *Gnomon*, Eng. trans. 1857, III. 139, 140.
26. W. Burkitt, *New Testament*, II (d. 1703), 90.
27. J. Calvin, *Romans*, Eng. trans. 1947 reprint, p. 383.
28. F. Godet, *Romans*, Eng. trans. 1892, II. 195, 196.
29. M. Stuart, *Romans*, 1865, pp. 455–7.
30. J. Wesley, *New Testament*, 1754, on Romans x. 4.
31. *Christ's Strange Work*, p. 63.
32. The citations in this paragraph are found in the sources already mentioned.

1 Timothy i. 5. It is not altogether unassociated with the meaning of such passages as Luke xxii. 37, where both the noun and the verb are found, 1 Corinthians x. 11, and 1 Peter i. 9. In spite of the appearance of tautology it would not be without meaning to say that "end" must be understood "teleologically", or "eschatologically" in so far as eschatology is consummation and fulfilment.[33]

This exegetical examination of the passage leaves the Puritan arguments where they were. Their system of doctrine was big enough to absorb into itself the views of those who understood "the end of the law" to be its terminus or cessation, when the Law is considered to be a means of obtaining righteousness.[34] They agreed firmly with the Antinomians in this respect, although not in the Antinomian assertion that the moral demands of the Law were terminated. It is possible that some of the Puritans were occasionally a little neglectful of the immediate context of the words in Romans x. 4,[35] but they were much more concerned with the great outlines of Christian doctrine, and they painted on a wide theological canvas. In this theological context the arguments of the Puritans seem to receive full support from all those commentators who interpret the phrase as indicative of the aim or design of the Law.

B. THE PASSIVE AND ACTIVE OBEDIENCE OF CHRIST

The "law" being the Moral Law, and the "end" being understood as the purpose for which it is given, it has to be asked in what way Christ's fulfilment of the Law was expounded by the Puritans. This, they said, was by His obedience, first in a life well-pleasing to the Father, and, secondly, in the giving up of Himself to death: these two aspects of His obedience they described as active and passive, respectively.

(i) *Passive obedience*

The passive obedience of Christ has always held first place in the Christian doctrine of salvation, and this was so with the Puritans. In their *Larger Catechism*, Christ is said to have "felt and borne the weight of God's wrath".[36] This enduring of the wrath of God was

33. Cf. also A. T. Robertson, *Word Pictures in the New Testament*, 1931, IV. 387, 388.
34. They held, as has been shown above, that the Sinaitic Law never was such a means, and so the concept of termination refers only to the Adamic Law as a "Covenant of Works".
35. But it should be observed that Anthony Burgess considers *finis perficiens* to be the preferable meaning of the word, chiefly because it is consonant with Paul's use of it in this place.
36. Op. cit., Answer to Q. 49.

directly related to the Law,[37] and, on this account, believers are freed from "the rigour and exaction of the law" for justification.[38] This deliverance is "because the law as a Covenant of works hath executed upon them in Christ all its penalty for all their sins".[39]

Richard Baxter is an exception to the Puritan belief in this respect and denies that Christ's sufferings were a proper execution of the threatening of the Law upon man.[40] He adopts a Grotian view of Law and punishment,[41] and asserts that it was not "all the punishments" of the elect that Christ bore, but rather that His suffering made "full sufficiency to those Ends for which it was designed".[42] He argues that the work of Christ must not be thought of in the category of a human obedience, but in His office of mediator.[43] No Puritan doubted that there was some sort of mediatorial law under which Christ was sent to be the Saviour of the elect,[44] but that this mediatorial law provided the formal cause of Christ's suffering they strenuously denied.[45]

(ii) *Active obedience*

The Puritans did not stop short at the passive obedience of Christ, however, but attached great, if not equal, importance to His active obedience. This was because they held it to be axiomatic that the sinner owed God a double debt; the homage of obedience and satisfaction for disobedience.

> It may be demaunded, what is that thing in Christ, by and for which, we are justified. I answer, the Obedience of Christ, Rom. 5. 19. And it stands in two things, his Passion in life and death, and his Fulfilling of the law joyned therewith. . . . The obedience of his passion stands before God as a satisfaction for the breach of the law. . . . By the second Obedience in fulfilling the lawe, the sonne of God performed for us, all things contained therein, that we might have right to life everlasting, and that according to the tenour of the lawe, Levit. 18. 5.[46]

37. Galatians iii. 13.
38. George Downame, *Covenant of Grace*, pp. 49, 50.
39. John Crandon, *Aphorisms Exorized*, Part I. p. 87; cf. John Barret, *Treatise of the Covenants*, p. 52; Walter Cradock, *Gospel-Holinesse*, "Priviledge and Practice of the Saints", p. 249.
40. Richard Baxter, *Aphorismes*, pp. 25, 26; Isaac Chauncy, *Fresh Antidote*, p. 61.
41. Op. cit., pp. 18–35, 42, 52, 56.
42. *Catholick Theologie*, Book I. Part 2, pp. 39, 59, 63, 69, 78; cf. *Aphorismes*, p. 37; *End of Doctrinal Controversies*, pp. 121, 122.
43. *Aphorismes*, p. 57.
44. Cf. John Owen, *Communion with God*, in *Works*, II. 158.
45. Cf. Robert Traill, *The Lord's Prayer*, 1705, in *Works*, II. 181.
46. William Perkins, *Galatians*, pp. 237, 317, 318.

John Dod and Robert Cleaver, therefore, speak of Christ "doing the whole law, whereby hee purchased righteousnesse for us. Galatians 4. 4–5, Romans 8. 3, 4",[47] and Richard Rogers, in his *Seven Treatises*, expounds the saving work of Christ on the same pattern.

> The onely sufficient remedie for the saving of man, is to satisfie Gods justice, which by sinne is violated: without which satisfaction, the wrath of God cannot be appeased. . . . Now then Gods justice is satisfied only by these two meanes: First, by suffering the punishment due to sinne, which is the curse of God; and the perfect keeping of the law, without which there can be no deliverance from sinne and condemnation.[48]

God was so "set upon His Law, that when Christ did undertake for mankind, if Christ had not satisfied every part of the Law that was required, if there had been one jot of the Law unfulfilled, al man-kind must have perished."[49] Christ offered His fulfilment of the Law for sinners, "that whatsoever the Law requireth to justification might bee fulfilled in it".[50] Anthony Burgess explains that by the obedience of Christ "is not meant onely Christs death, but his active conformity to the Law of God",[51] for

> If the end of humane laws be to make good and honest men, much rather is the end of the Morall Law appointed by God himself. . . . Christ therefore, that the Law may have its end, he taketh our nature upon him, that the righteousness of the Law might be fulfilled in us.[52]

There is a full discussion of the subject by Thomas Goodwin, in which he affirms that Christ has both recovered the glory of the Law, and fully met its claims.[53] Citations in the same strain can be multiplied almost indefinitely, some of which are to be found in Andrew Willet,[54] Edward Elton,[55] Thomas Wilson,[56] Samuel Rolle,[57] Stephen Charnock,[58] John Owen[59] and many others. Thomas Gouge states

47. *Catechism*, 1604, p. 8.
48. Op. cit., p. 7.
49. Jeremiah Burroughs, *Gospel-Conversation*, p. 78.
50. George Downame, *Justification*, p. 29.
51. *Justification*, Part II. p. 119; cf. *Vindiciae Legis*, p. 210.
52. *Vindiciae Legis*, p. 270.
53. *Mediator*, in *Works*, V. 102, 125, 180 f., 188, 337 f.
54. *Hexapla: Romanes*, p. 282.
55. *Treatises*: "Complaint of a Sanctifyed Sinner", p. 104.
56. *Romanes*, p. 252.
57. *Justification Justified*, pp. 13, 14.
58. *Attributes*, in *Works*, II. 62.
59. *Communion with God*, in *Works*, II. 156 f.

the Puritan view concisely when he refers the believer's justification to Christ's "whole obedience", which includes

> His active obedience, which consisted in submitting himself to the Law of God, and fulfilling the same. And his passive Obedience, which compriseth under it all his sufferings, even from his Birth to his Death.[60]

C. IMPUTED RIGHTEOUSNESS

It was the view of the Puritans that the manner in which the benefits of Christ's obedience were conveyed to the believer was by imputation; but the question arose whether this imputation included Christ's active, as well as His passive, obedience. All were agreed about the latter, but there was some difference among them about the former. They had no doubt that righteousness was imputed to believers through Christ, but whether it was formally the righteousness of Christ that was so imputed was a "great dispute amongst the Orthodox".[61]

The Antinomians held fervently to the doctrine of the imputation of Christ's righteousness. "Justification is, when we . . . are by the power of Gods imputation, so cloathed with the wedding garment of Christs owne perfect righteousnesse."[62] John Eaton taught that Christ's active righteousness was the wedding garment of free justification by virtue of which Christ became the end and the fulfilment of the Law to the believer. In this view he was supported by all the other Antinomian writers.

The doctrine of the imputed righteousness of Christ, however, was by no means the monopoly of the Antinomians: it was the belief of most of the Puritans. William Perkins, for example, states it thus:

> Justification standes in . . . the imputation of Christ his righteousnes; which is an . . . action of God whereby he accounteth and esteemeth that righteousnes which is in Christ, as the righteousnes of that sinner which beleeveth in him.[63]

"The imputation of Christs righteousnesse is the formall cause of

60. *Principles of Christian Religion*, p. 114.
61. Anthony Burgess, *Justification*, Part II. p. 122a (page enumeration confused).
62. John Eaton, *Honey-combe*, p. 7. Although John Eaton denies that the righteousness is an inherent one, he nevertheless contends that the elect are "not barely counted, but truly made righteous".
63. *Reformed Catholike*, 1598, in *Works*, p. 680; in *Golden Chaine*, in *Works*, p. 87, he has a diagram of imputation. See also Edward Elton, *Treatises*: "Triumph of a True Christian", pp. 48 f.; James Ussher, *Body of Divinitie*, p. 71; Francis Roberts, *God's Covenants*, pp. 87, 588, 589.

justification;"[64] and this imputation is both necessary and implied, since the believer has no righteousness of his own, Romans v. 12, 17, 18.[65] Further, "if the paiment of the punishment of the Law, be all the righteousnesse Christ hath purchased for us, then we had a more noble and perfect righteousness in Adam".[66]

Thomas Goodwin expounds Romans viii. 4 as teaching Christ's fulfilment of the Law "in us"; and he devotes considerable space to the exposition of the imputation of Christ's active obedience.[67] In his work on *Justification by Faith*, John Owen gives 113 pages to the truth of "free justification through the imputed righteousness of Christ",[68] and, rejecting the notion of a second justification, he says that there "is but one, and is at once completed".[69] When David Clarkson teaches the imputation of the passive and the active righteousness of Christ, he remarks that the latter is "not of so great importance as the former, nor the denial of it of so dangerous consequences".[70] Nevertheless, he holds it to be a truth "of some moment to the honour of Christ and comfort of believers",[71] and says, "I fain would know how that which is neither in us nor performed by us can be ours otherwise than by imputation".[72] Imputation of righteousness to the believer is the same in its manner as imputation of sin to Christ.

Richard Baxter pours scorn on this doctrine. He acknowledges the doctrine of justification by imputation, but denies that this is by the direct imputation of Christ's active righteousness.

> It is abusive subtilty to divide Christ's Performance into little Parcels, and then say, This Parcel is imputed to me for this use, and that for that use, and by one he merited this, and by the other that . . . When . . . it was only the entire performance that was the Condition of the Benefits.[73]

The most he admits is that the active righteousness of Christ has some contribution to make to the believer's justification,[74] and that

64. George Downame, *Justification*, p. 39.
65. Anthony Burgess, *Justification*, Part II. pp. 297, 298.
66. Anthony Burgess, op. cit., Part II. p. 455; see also *Vindiciae Legis*, p. 271, and Thomas Taylor, *Regula Vitae*, p. 9.
67. Thomas Goodwin, *Mediator*, in *Works*, V. 181, 182, 338, 339, 341–7; cf. *Justifying Faith*, 1697, in *Works*, VIII. 133 ff.; Thomas Jacomb, *Romans*, 1672, p. 348; Thomas Brooks, *Golden Key*, 1675, in *Works*, V. 73; *Glory of Christianity*, 1662, in *Works*, IV. 45.
68. *Justification*, in *Works*, V. 53, 162–275; cf. *Communion with God*, in *Works*, II. 159, 162, 164.
69. Op. cit., p. 137.
70. *Justification*, in *Works*, I. 290.
71. Ibid.
72. Op. cit., I. 321; cf. William Woodward, *Lord our Righteousness*, p. 13.
73. *End of Doctrinal Controversies*, p. 125.
74. *Aphorismes*, pp. 44–50, 226.

the works of Christ are "the meritorious Cause" of the believer's justification.[75] One of his reasons for rejecting the commonly-received Puritan doctrine is found in his peculiar view of the mediatorial work of Christ. He teaches that Christ rendered "Perfect Obedience to the Law of Innocency", which obedience, he says, "exempteth us".[76] Richard Baxter's antipathy to the doctrine of imputed righteousness was partly provoked by his fear of Antinomianism, and his assumption that "an imputed holiness takes away any need for a real one",[77] but the doctrine under review is not that of imputed "holiness", but imputed "righteousness". Puritans, such as William Twisse and Thomas Gataker, did not hold the doctrine of the imputed righteousness of Christ, but this was for reasons other than the Grotian-neonomianism of Richard Baxter.[78]

D. ANTINOMIAN DOCTRINE OF ABROGATION

The inevitable question when an endeavour is made to understand the significance of Christ as "the end of the Law" is that stated by Francis Roberts.

> Whether the Law of God given by Moses on Mount Sinai to Israel, be abrogated to us now under the New Testament or no? And how far it concerns or obligeth us, if not abrogated?[79]

This demands an answer, he says, because of "the Antinomian errour, endeavouring totally to abolish the Law given by Moses on Mount Sinai, as of no use at all, for Matter or Form, to Christians now under the New Testament"; but it is nevertheless "a Knotty and difficult Question: and learned men have rendered it the more intricate, by their cross disputes about it".[80]

The Puritans frequently accused the Antinomians of abrogating the Law. Thomas Taylor, for example, lists "Twelve Antinomian Errors", the first of which is that "Christ came to abolish the Morall Law",[81] and, therefore, that as creatures believers are under moral

75. *End of Doctrinal Controversies*, pp. 240–54.
76. *Scripture Gospel Defended*, "Breviate of Justification", pp. 8, 22.
77. J. I. Packer, op. cit., p. 280.
78. In the final draft of Chapter XI of the *Confession of Faith*, the Assembly agreed to omit the word "whole" before "obedience" in Section i, in deference to William Twisse and Thomas Gataker. A. F. Mitchell, *Westminster Assembly*, pp. 149–56. The doctrine of the imputation of the righteousness of Christ was rejected also by those who adhered to the Arminian system, their main objection being that it is a legalistic conception. See John Goodwin, *Imputatio Fidei*, 1642, Part I. p. 69 ff.
79. *God's Covenants*, p. 689.
80. Op. cit., p. 689.
81. *Regula Vitae*, pp. 65, 70; cf. Thomas Welde, *Rise, reigne, and ruine*, p. 1.

Law, but as Christians they are only bound to do what Christ bids.[82] Anthony Burgess charges Tobias Crisp with indulging in a decrying of the Law,[83] and remarks that it is the assertion that the Law is abrogated which gives Antinomianism its name.[84] Richard Byfield affirms that the Antinomians "over-throw the Law Morall" and "hold that Christ came to abolish it".[85]

Reason has been found, earlier,[86] for observing that many of the charges made against the Antinomians appear to be based on hearsay from sermons or reports of their sayings. It is more than probable that some of the radicals among them may have spoken as they are reported, but an examination of the deliberate writings of the Antinomian authors does not yield the same amount of colourful evidence as their opponents found themselves able to discover. Without doubt, the Antinomians made strong statements to the effect that the Law was abrogated, but it is clear that, here and there, they qualified their assertions in ways that can be interpreted in a less unorthodox manner. Perhaps, too, it is easier for a twentieth century reader to perceive this, than it was for those engaged in the controversies of the seventeenth.

What do the Antinomians say in their books? John Eaton, upon whose head so much orthodox wrath descended, says in the *Honeycombe*,

> The Law . . . failing in works, terrifieth the conscience, . . therefore let us not suffer the Law in any case to beare rule in our conscience; . . . let the godly learn therefore, that the Law and Christ are two contrary things, . . . when Christ is present, the Law may in no case rule, but must depart out of the conscience.[87]

Tobias Crisp holds that Christ is the end, not only of the curse of the Law, but also of the life of the Law,[88] and that a believer has no more to do with the Law of Moses than an Englishman has with the "Laws of Turky", though he at the same time admits that the Law is not "absolutely abolished", but only in its curses.[89] Robert Towne speaks with a double voice, when he says,

> I am of that mind, that the whole Law is in as full force and power as ever it was . . . Matt. 5. 19. But yet that beleevers

82. Op. cit., pp. 183–91.
83. Cf. Tobias Crisp, *Christ Alone Exalted*, in *Works*, I. 119, alluded to by Anthony Burgess, *Vindiciae Legis*, p. 15.
84. Op. cit., p. 208; cf. Thomas Gataker, *God's Eye*, p. 97.
85. Richard Byfield, *Temple Defilers*, p. 20; cf. *Epistle Dedicatory*.
86. See above, p. 31.
87. Op. cit., p. 449.
88. *Christ Alone Exalted*, in *Works*, I. 154.
89. Op. cit., I. 123, and note his concession in IV. 93.

> should be under it, its to me full of danger, and contrarie to all Scripture.[90]

He dislikes being charged with affirming the abrogation of the Law, and in his *Re-assertion* he says that the Law is "inviolable and for ever".[91] He refers this only to unbelievers, however, for his main contention is that if believers are not under the Law in its damnatory aspect, they cannot be under it in the mandatory.[92] John Saltmarsh makes a curious collocation of "Satan, sin, sinfull flesh, and the Law",[93] as if all were in the same category and were equally abolished by Christ.[94]

E. LAW IN ITS COMMANDING AND COVENANTING ASPECTS

The inquiry into the subject of the abrogation of the Law calls, first, for the separation of the two ideas of commandment and covenant.

(i) *Distinguishable and separable*

There can be commandment without covenant, and there can be covenant without commandment; and there can also be a close relation between them. The important thing to understand, however, is that they are not only distinguishable, but separable.

In their discussion of the abrogation of the Law the Puritans were not always careful to be sure that they were talking about the same thing. One writer would be thinking of the Law as a covenant and would contend that it was abolished, while another, thinking of the Law in terms of commandment, would write a book against his brother insisting that the Law could never be abolished. There is no doubt that much of the seventeenth century controversy on this subject was vitiated by a misunderstanding among the protagonists in their use of terms. Ambiguities lurked everywhere, and in consequence much unfair judgment was given.

Happily, the Puritans themselves drew attention to the necessity of observing the distinction between commandment and covenant; and they had this in mind when they distinguished "substance" from "promulgation". Thomas Taylor thinks in this way when he says

90. *Assertion of Grace*, p. 33.
91. *Re-assertion*, pp. 95, 139.
92. *Assertion of Grace*, p. 32.
93. *Free-Grace*, p. 140; the 1792 edn. puts it, "the world, the flesh, the devil, and the law", p. 154.
94. Cf. G. Huehns, *Antinomianism*, 1951, pp. 37–54 and J. Buchanan, *Justification*, 1867, pp. 158, 159.

that the Law is to be understood, first, in the substance of it, and secondly, in the circumstances of it, and that the believer is "under the Law" in the first sense, but not in the second.[95] John Ball distinguishes the functions of the Law in its different dispensations. In the Covenant of Works, he says, it is itself a covenant, and as such is abolished; but in the Covenant of Grace, it is an unchangeable rule of life, and so is as lasting as the grace itself. The rule is one, but the covenants differ.[96] The author of *The Marrow* argues that the commandments of the moral Law can be regarded as either the matter of the law of works, or the matter of the law of Christ; and by "matter of" he means according as they have their place in one or the other, thus distinguishing the covenant aspect from the preceptive.[97] It is not without significance that *Nomista* and *Antinomista*, in the dialogue, are both corrected by the one principle of making this necessary distinction.[98] Thomas Bedford likewise insists that the moral Law must be distinguished in its Substance (Duties) and Circumstance (Covenant).[99]

(ii) *The Law in covenant form*

The distinction between the Law as a command and as a covenant becomes important when the question is asked about the continuance of the Law as a Covenant of Works. The Puritans had no doubt about the answer so far as the believer was concerned. Samuel Bolton states the normal Puritan position—with a justifiable little grumble of his own—when he writes:

> We are freed from the Morall law. First, as a Covenant say our Divines. It would save a great deale of trouble to say we are freed from the law, as a condition upon the obedience whereof we expected life. But take it in those words, we are freed from the law as a covenant.[100]

When the Puritan view about the relation to the Covenant of Works of those who remain unbelievers is examined, the solution is not so simple. Different opinions emerged, and some Puritans maintained the continuance of the Covenant of Works for those who were not believers. Richard Sibbes, for example, acknowledges that "the covenant of works was disannulled by our sins", but at the same time thinks of the Mosaic Covenant as a renewal of the Covenant of Works

95. Cf. *Regula Vitae*, p. 19.
96. *Covenant of Grace*, p. 15; see above, pp. 118, 119.
97. Op. cit., pp. 13–15.
98. Op. cit., pp. 196, 197.
99. Thomas Bedford, *An Examination*, pp. 10–12.
100. *True Bounds*, p. 21. Unless the context intimates otherwise, the Puritan assertion that believers are "freed from the Law as a Covenant" may usually be taken in the sense of a Covenant of Works. It is from the tyranny of law-keeping for the purpose of justification that Christ delivers His people.

for a subordinate purpose.[101] It is this subordinate purpose that the author of *The Marrow* has in mind when he says that the Law as a Covenant of Works is useful to unbelievers, and when he adds the curious comment that although obedience cannot procure heaven it might secure the easiest place in hell.[102] With the same meaning William Strong writes,

> To all those who are in the first Adam, the first Covenant stands in force to this day. . . . Every unregenerate man is under the Law as a Covenant of works.[103]

The quotations given above reveal a failure carefully to separate the ideas of command and covenant, and it is likely that the writers do not really mean the Covenant as such, but only the Law which underlies it.

Other Puritans declared that the Covenant of Works was abolished for all men, but they asserted this on fundamentally different grounds. Richard Baxter, who at first thought that the Covenant of Works was still in force,[104] changed his mind, though even in the *Aphorismes* he reveals that he was not quite sure of himself.[105] His formal withdrawal of the statement about the continuance of the Covenant of Works is found in *Confession*, where he says there is no "continuation of the whole Covenant, Promise and all",[106] and in *Catholick Theologie* he says that the Law is laid aside as a "Covenant".[107] His reason for the abolition of the Covenant of Works arises from the humanistic philosophy which defines responsibility in terms of ability,[108] and therefore regards man as no longer "a capable subject" of such a covenant.

When the Puritans declared that the Covenant of Works was abolished, they spoke from the Godward aspect, rather than the human, and laid stress on the fact that the best works of fallen man could never repair the breach of the covenant, or satisfy the demands of God contained within it. Nehemiah Cox writes about the impossibility "that this Covenant now broken should be renewed . . . for the same Ends",[109] and John Flavel that "this Covenant of Works being once broken, can nevermore be available to the Justification and Salvation of any Fallen Man."[110]

101. Richard Sibbes, *Faithful Covenanter*, in *Works*, VI. 5.
102. Op. cit., pp. 68, 70, 335.
103. *The Two Covenants*, pp. 2, 38; cf. Thomas Brooks, *Paradise Opened*, in *Works*, V. 303, John Barret, *Treatise of the Covenants*, pp. 76, 78.
104. *Aphorismes*, p. 78.
105. Op. cit., p. 283.
106. *Confession*, p. 106.
107. Op. cit., Book I. Part 2, p. 21.
108. *End of Doctrinal Controversies*, p. 120; see below, p. 151.
109. *Of the Covenants*, p. 36. Cf. John Owen, *Principles*, 1645, in *Works*, I. 476, footnote.
110. *Vindiciae Legis & Foederis*, p. 32; cf. Francis Roberts, *God's Covenants*, p. 68.

The consideration of the relation of believers to the Law in the Mosaic Covenant brings another set of problems, because of the shades of Puritan opinion about the nature of the Covenant itself.[111] By most of the Puritans, the Mosaic Covenant was held to be part of the Covenant of Grace; and within this whole the Mosaic portion was called the "Old Covenant", in view of its replacement by the "New Covenant" of the Gospel era. In so far as the New Covenant had taken the place of the Old, they held that it was true to say that the Law as a Covenant was abrogated.[112]

F. LAW NOT ABROGATED BY THE FALL

The ending of the Law in its covenant aspect leaves the Law still to be considered as a commanding rule.

It was the generally accepted Puritan view that the Law was not abrogated by the Fall. "Is not right right? Is not the Law the Law!"[113] The Puritans held tenaciously to the fundamental principle that moral inability did not cancel obligation. The Law is "a rule of our duty, not of our strength".[114] Man had the responsibility of keeping himself morally able, and he is to blame for what he has allowed himself to become.[115]

Anthony Burgess repudiates the idea that human inability negates the Law. He takes notice of the objection of those who say that, man now being unable to obey, it is mockery for God to command him, and that it would be as if a blind man were commanded to see, and meets this by pointing out that there are three ways in which a thing may be said to be impossible. There is simple impossibility, there is natural impossibility, and there is moral impossibility, in which things having no simple or natural impossibility attaching to them sometimes become morally impossible through man's fault. It is no mockery for a man to be commanded to do something which through his own fault he has made himself unable to do. It is, therefore, irrelevant to bring into the argument such an impossibility as commanding blind men to see; the impossibility under discussion is a moral one, and the impossibility to fulfil the commandment is an impossibility

111. See Chapter III above.
112. William Hinde, *Office and Use of the Morall Law*, 1622, p. 16, says, "Luther speakes only of the abolishing of certain uses of the Law, as, for righteousnesse, justification, life and salvation, for terrifying, accusing, condemning those that are justified by faith in Christ Jesus".
113. Richard Sibbes, *Precious Promises*, 1638, in *Works*, IV. 117.
114. Thomas Blake, *Covenant of God*, p. 107.
115. See Nathanael Culverwel, *Light of Nature*, p. 21, in which he insists that "the want of his will is not enough to enervate and invalidate a Law when 'tis made; all Lawes would then be abrogated every moment."

which man has brought upon himself.[116] The objection would be valid "if God had given a Law which Men never had strength to performe," but the situation is the opposite of this, and "Adam had strength sufficient to fulfill it. . . . Nevertheless though Strength to obey be lost: yet the obligation to Obedience remaines. We are no more discharged of our duties, because we have no strength to doe it: then a debter is quitted of his Bands because he wants money to make payment."[117] The sophistry about "impossibility" is repudiated by James Ussher,[118] and the indignation of John Ball can be felt as he writes,

> It is altogether undecent . . . that that which provoketh the execution, should procure the abrogation of his Lawes, that that should supplant and undermine the Law, for the alone preventing whereof the Law was before established.[119]

John Barret says equally incisively that such a view is "as if a man could satisfie and discharge a Bond by forfeiture. As if a subject by breaking the Law, could make himself lawless"; and he regards it as altogether unreasonable to think that God would "take Man's failing in his duty, as a ground of excusing him from his duty."[120]

It was the conviction of the Puritans that the authority of God was bound up with the continuance of the moral Law. "God hath not lost his right, though man hath lost his power; their impotency doth not dissolve their obligation".[121] Men are born necessarily under the obligation to obey their Creator. "The Law of Creation binds, when the Covenant of Creation is broken; tho' the Transgression of Man hath forfeited his Interest in the one, yet it cannot dissolve the Obligation of the other."[122]

With the writings of Richard Baxter, the discussion of the abrogation of the Law becomes exceedingly confused. He imagines that he has solved his own problem, and the problems of everybody else, when he withdraws his aphorism about the continuance of the Covenant of Works, and when he affirms in *Catholick Theologie* that though the Law is abolished as a "covenant", yet "the Precept as a Rule of Life continues"[123] and "undoubtedly is still in force."[124]

These words sound straightforward enough, but, unfortunately,

116. Anthony Burgess, *Vindiciae Legis*, pp. 15, 96, 97; and Edward Elton, *Gods Holy Minde*, "Matters Morall", p. 380.
117. William Pemble, *Vindiciae Fidei*, pp. 91, 92.
118. *Body of Divinitie*, pp. 124, 125; cf. Andrew Willet, *Hexapla: Romanes*, p. 139.
119. *Covenant of Grace*, p. 289.
120. *Treatise of the Covenants*, pp. 76, 77; cf. p. 125.
121. Thomas Manton, *Lord's Prayer*, 1684, in *Works*, I. 143; cf. Thomas Goodwin, *Work of the Holy Ghost*, in *Works*, VI. 233.
122. Nehemiah Cox, *Of The Covenants*, p. 44.
123. Richard Baxter, op. cit., Book I. Part 2, p. 21.
124. Op. cit., Book I. Part 2, pp. 35, 67 and Book I. Part 3, pp. 4, 5.

they cannot be taken at their face value, for in the same context he writes,

> These Precepts bind us not now in so full a sort as they did Adam, even to obedience; Though the Law be as perfect: Because there is some *Dispositio Recipientis* necessary to the effecting an Obligation upon us: And where any Natural Impossibility hath befaln us, though by sin, it will make some alteration in the obligation.[125]

Hidden in these words there lies the ultimate ambiguity of Richard Baxter's position. In something of an aside, he says, "though the Law be as perfect", and yet his main purpose in this paragraph is to prove that there is "some alteration in the obligation." If the obligation be not of "so full a sort" as it was, then the Law cannot be "as perfect" as it was, and the demands of the Law have been lowered to the level of the changed *Dispositio Recipientis* in man. By reducing the Law in this manner, he has virtually abolished it. In the *End of Doctrinal Controversies* he says

> It is not to be supposed, that the very preceptive part of the Law of Innocency is now in force to us, as it was to Adam: For it bound him to be perfectly innocent in Act and Dispositions. But to a Man that has lost his Innocency . . . it is not to be supposed, that the Law saith, Thou shalt be innocent: For that were to command not only a Moral, but a Physical absolute impossibility, as saying, Thou shalt not have sinned.[126]

This "Law of Innocency", however, is a "man of straw", which Richard Baxter puts up in order to knock down. He imagines it to be an absurdity that a "Law of Innocency" should say to a guilty man "be innocent", or that it should require "that existent sin should not be existent."[127] But no one has ever uttered such an absurdity, and he has merely demolished an imaginary foe.

In so far as, by "the Law of Innocency", he means the Covenant of Works, he affirms no more than is found in the writings of all the other Puritans. But the fact is that Richard Baxter's argument about the Law of Innocency becomes, in effect, an abrogation of the moral Law, for he destroys not merely the idea of the continuance of the Law as a Covenant, but also its "very preceptive part." A page or two later he teaches the abrogation of the Law of Nature in its primary sense.

> The Law of Nature is now the Law of lapsed redeemed Nature, and not of innocent Nature. And it obligeth us for the future to

125. Op. cit., Book I. Part 2, p. 29.
126. Richard Baxter, op. cit., p. 150.
127. *Catholick Theologie*, Book I. Part 2, p. 61.

> as much perfection of Duty, as we are naturally capable of performing at that time.[128]

Here are two forms of the "Law of Nature", the earlier of which is abolished, and the later one takes its place.

In *Scripture Gospel Defended*, Richard Baxter makes the orthodox statement that "we are not under the . . . Law of Moses as such", meaning the Law of Moses in the Covenant sense, and then he melodramatically adds, "If this be Antinomianism, I am an Antinomian that have written so much against them."[129] This, however, is nothing less than theatrical, for Richard Baxter knew that no one considered that opinion to be Antinomian, but he also knew that it was his modification of the Law of Nature that drove some of his contemporaries to speak of him in that way.[130] John Crandon, for example, says,

> Mr Br. . . . denies Christ to require under the Gospel, the perfect holiness and righteousness which the Law commandeth, and Consequently that it is not either our duty to perform it, or our sinn to fail in it. . . . If this be not Antinomianism then Islebius himself hath been unjustly Charged with it.[131]

Walter Marshal, a writer of different temperament from John Crandon, likewise considers Richard Baxter's doctrine to be "ranked among the worst Antinomian Errors."[132] Paradoxical as it may seem, there is an affinity between Antinomianism and Neonomianism,[133] and Richard Baxter comes strangely near to Antinomianism in his own scheme. All this seems to make the open and naive Antinomianism of those who are generally so named a much less unpleasant error than the hidden and subtle form of it which is found in its alleged opponent. It is not difficult, however, to sympathize with the

128. *End of Doctrinal Controversies*, p. 151.
129. Op. cit., "Breviate of Justification", p. 70.
130. Cf. Thomas Edwards, *Baxterianism Barefac'd*, p. 2.
131. *Aphorisms Exorized*, Epistle Dedicatory, cf. Part I, p. 277. On this charge of Antinomianism Isaac Chauncy says, "One that Asserts the Old Law is abolished, and therein is a superlative Antinomian, but pleads for a New Law, and Justification by the Works of it, and therein is a Neonomian", *Neonomianism Unmask'd*, Part I, Epistle Dedicatory, and cf. p. 3. In *Rejoynder* he says to Daniel Williams, "I treated you under the Appellation of a Neonomian (which is an Antinomian in the truest Sense)", op. cit., p. 21.
132. *Sanctification*, 1692, p. 125, cf. p. 23.
133. Robert Towne, for example, deduces that the Gospel is "a new Law" from the fact that it is "called a New Covenant." (*Assertion of Grace*, p. 151). Tobias Crisp makes a similar inference when he speaks of the absurdity of telling a man to take England on his shoulders to the West Indies, and thus puts obedience to the moral Law, as Richard Baxter does, in the category of the naturally impossible. (*Christ Alone Exalted*, in *Works*, I. 119).

feelings of Thomas Blake when he says, "It is a wearisome thing to rake further in this puddle."[134]

Needless to say, Richard Baxter's view of a new Law with altered obligations was rejected by most of his contemporaries.[135] They insisted that the Law still demanded perfect righteousness, and that no change in human ability could have the slightest effect on moral obligation.

G. LAW NOT ABROGATED BY GRACE

If the Law is not abrogated by man's failure, neither is it abrogated by his recovery; God's grace cannot destroy God's Law.

> The Law of God, although in respect of the faithfull it bee as it were abrogated, both in respect of the power of justifying which it had in the state of integrity, and in respect of the condemning power which it had in the state of sinne: yet it hath force and vigor, in respect of power to direct, and some power also it doth retaine of condemning, because it reproves, and condemnes sinne in the faithfull themselves, although it cannot wholy condemne the faithfull themselves, who are not under the Law, but under Grace.[136]

As it was humanism, and subsequently Richard Baxter, that provoked the Puritans to declare that the Law was not abrogated by the Fall, so it was the Antinomian extolling of "free grace" that made it necessary for them to affirm with equal intensity that the Law was not abrogated by the Gospel.

> There is many that make a great noise about Evangelical truths . . . and they think that this doth wholly take away their obedience to the Law of God, and that it must not be so much as a rule of life. Certainly there is nothing holds forth the excellency of the Law more then the knowledge of Jesus Christ . . . being subjected to the Law, . . . But we never reade that this subjection to the Law was to make voide our obedience to it.[137]

The Antinomian view was that "the Law-giver, in the Gospel, gives up all his authority as Law-giver, to command beleevers".[138] With his usual inability to penetrate to the heart of the distinctions

134. *Covenant of God*, p. 57.
135. The attempts of Daniel Williams to defend Richard Baxter against the charges of Isaac Chauncy are not particularly successful, and do little more than repeat Richard Baxter's own arguments. Cf. Isaac Chauncy, *Neonomianism Unmask'd*, and Daniel Williams, *Gospel-Truth*, and *Defence of Gospel Truth*.
136. William Ames, *Marrow of Sacred Divinity*, p. 194.
137. Jeremiah Burroughs, *Gospel-Conversation*, p. 79.
138. Samuel Rutherford, *Survey*, Part II. p. 121.

involved, Robert Towne says to Thomas Taylor, "You say, Christ was the end of Morall Law because he obeyed the Law . . . And what Christ performed for us we are freed from, now you are with us, that is, Christ hath freed us from subjection to the Morall Law."[139] Anthony Burgess refutes the argument[140] that the Law cannot be a law unless it be a cursing law, by asking what kind of Law that was which was given to the holy angels and to Adam in his innocency,[141] and he reasons with considerable force that if the Law be abrogated to believers under the New Covenant then it must also have been abrogated to believers under the Old.[142] He holds that when God afflicts a godly man He

> doth so farre use the Law as an instrument to make him sensible of his sinne: and therefore this is a sure Argument, that the Law is not abolished as to all uses to the Believer.[143]

In contradiction to the Antinomian assertions, John Sedgwick declares that the Law is valid to believers "in its Mandatory part".[144] He gives ten reasons why "the Doctrine of Faith doth not make void the doctrine and duty of the Morall Law" and follows these with a list of twelve ways in which the moral Law is strengthened by the doctrine of faith.[145] God never abdicates His throne, even in grace, and "when God became a Saviour to the Elect of mankind, he did not cease to be a Sovereign".[146] There is no suggestion anywhere in the New Testament that the Law has lost its validity in the slightest degree, nor is there even a hint of its repeal. "Christ hath expunged no part of it".[147]

> That it is not repealed, I shall shew, and that it is not capable of any repeal. If it be repealed, then either by Christ at his coming in the flesh, or else by his Apostles by commission from him after the Spirit was given; But neither Christ in person, nor the Apostles by any Commission from him did repeal it; but instead of a repeal, did put a new sanction upon it.[148]

139. *Assertion of Grace*, p. 140.
140. Put forward by Robert Towne, op. cit., pp. 30, 31.
141. *Vindiciae Legis*, p. 6.
142. Op. cit., p. 215. The Antinomian rejoinder to this, that there is a difference between believers in the Old Testament and in the New, will not stand; for if they were in Christ in God's sight—as their arguments about no sin in the believer require—then Christ is the same for all.
143. *Justification*, Part I. p. 31, cf. an unusual argument employed by Edward Reynolds, *Three Treatises*: "Sinfulnesse of Sinne", p. 368.
144. *Antinomianisme Anatomized*, p. 12.
145. Op. cit., pp. 13–24.
146. Thomas Blake, *Covenant of God*, p. 47.
147. John Crandon, *Aphorisms Exorized*, Part I. p. 214; cf. Epistle Dedicatory.
148. Thomas Blake, *Covenant of God*, p. 49; cf. pp. 55, 56.

Samuel Bolton infers from Galatians iii. 17 that the coming of the Law "four hundred and thirty years after" is proof that the Law abides as a rule,[149] and

> Against that opinion which holds forth the abrogation of the law, and saith that we are freed from the obedience of it; I shall lay downe, and endeavour to make good . . . That the law for the substance of it (for we speake not of the circumstances and accessories to it) doth remain as a rule of walking to the people of God.[150]

Samuel Rutherford rejects the Antinomian argument that the mandatory and damnatory aspects of the Law are inseparable, and confesses,

> Because Christ hath died for me, therefore Ile keep that same Law of God I was under before, only now I fear not actuall condemnation which is accidentall to the Law.[151]

A searching question is put by Thomas Manton, when he asks,

> If the law might be disannulled as to new creatures, then why doth the Spirit of God write it with such legible characters in their hearts? . . . Now that which the Spirit engraves upon the heart, would Christ come to deface and abolish?[152]

Nothing can "annihilate the commanding authority of the law",[153] for "though God laid aside his Wrath through Christ, yet he will not lay down his Authority".[154]

The Puritans were convinced that no change in dispensation could in any wise involve the abrogation of the Law, and that since "covenant" was but an accident of "law",[155] the moral Law was stedfast whatever the covenants might be. "The Saints are bound to the Law under the danger of committing sin", and "they are as strictly bound to obedience in their own persons, under the second Covenant, as they were under the first".[156]

The concise summary of the Puritan conviction about the continuing authority of the law of God is provided in the Westminster *Confession of Faith.*

149. *True Bounds*, p. 46.
150. Op. cit., p. 76, and cf. pp. 77–79; James Ussher, *Body of Divinitie*, p. 159; Francis Roberts, *God's Covenants*, pp. 862, 1052, and Thomas Manton, *Hundred and Nineteenth Psalm*, II. 502.
151. *Triumph of Faith*, p. 196.
152. *Hundred and Nineteenth Psalm*, I. 5; and see the same question in Francis Roberts, *God's Covenants*, pp. 1392, 1393.
153. John Owen, *Justification*, in *Works*, V. 146 and cf. *Holy Spirit* in *Works*, III. 609; *Principles*, in *Works*, I. 476.
154. Thomas Gouge, *Principles of Christian Religion*, p. 192; Samuel Rutherford, *Survey*, Part II. p. 122.
155. Samuel Rutherford, *Survey*, Part II. p. 8.
156. William Strong, *The Two Covenants*, pp. 106, 164; cf. John Barret, *Treatise of the Covenants*, p. 20.

> The moral law doth for ever bind all, . . . and that not only in regard of the matter contained in it, but also in respect of the authority of God, the Creator, who gave it. Neither doth Christ in the gospel any way dissolve, but much strengthen this obligation.[157]

H. IDENTITY OF THE MOSAIC LAW AND THE LAW OF CHRIST

The Law which is obligatory on the believer is the same in substance as the Law of Moses. This is implicit in the foregoing discussion, but, because of ambiguities that made their appearance in the midst of the Antinomian controversy, the Puritans deemed it necessary to emphasize this. William Perkins says that the Law was cleansed by Christ from the glosses of the Pharisees, and, "it beeing defaced . . . by originall sinne," the Law was "renued againe in the hearts of beleevers".[158] Thomas Taylor reasons to the same effect,[159] and concludes,

> Wee must conceive the Law in the substance of it, the image of God written in the heart of Adam, in innocency, and by the finger of the same spirit written in the hearts of all the elect.[160]

It is the same Law of Moses which is now written in the affections of the heart, and "administred in the hand of Christ."[161] "The Morall law belongeth to us Christians",[162] and the Gospel which is the rule by which believers walk, "implies in it all the substantiall Precepts of the Law: so in that respect we are bound to the Law."[163] In *The Marrow, Nomista* asks for a definition of the Law of Christ, and receives the following answer from *Evangelista*.

> The law of Christ in regard of substance and matter, is all one with the law of works. . . . Which matter is scattered through the whole Bible, and summed up in the Decalogue, or Ten Commandments. . . . So that evangelical grace directs a man to no other obedience than that whereof the law of the Ten Commandments is to be the rule.[164]

157. Op. cit., XIX. 5. "I take that to be very sound", says John Barret, *Treatise of the Covenants*, p. 17.
158. *Galatians*, pp. 419, 420.
159. *Regula Vitae*, pp. 40–43.
160. Thomas Taylor, *Regula Vitae*, pp. 232, 233; cf. William Ames, *Marrow of Sacred Divinity*, pp. 193, 194; Richard Sibbes, *Bruised Reed*, 1630, in *Works*, I. 59.
161. John Ball, *Covenant of Grace*, p. 118.
162. George Gillespie, *Severity*, p. 7.
163. Walter Cradock, *Divine Drops Distilled*, 1650, p. 161.
164. Op. cit., p. 144; cf. Thomas Gataker, Preface to Edward Elton, *Gods Holy Minde*.

Christ gave no new laws, but expounded and cleared the old, as a painter who works over an old picture and recovers its glory.[165] The Law of Moses is newly-minted "as a Gold-smith doth with old coyne" as "The New Commandement and Law of Christ"[166] so much so, that "every beleever . . . is answerable to the obedience of the whole Law."[167] The obedience of the believer "is the same very obedience commanded in the Law,"[168] and his instruction in holiness is that "which the Spirit borroweth from the ten Commandements delivered by Moses".[169] The moral Law was "adopted and taken in as a part of the gospel by Christ",[170] that "there is no sin prohibited in the Gospel which is not a breach of some Precept in the Decalogue".[171]

I. RELATION OF BELIEVERS TO THE LAW

(i) "*Dead to the law*" *and* "*not under the law*"

The understanding of the relation of the believer to the Law is closely bound up with the interpretation of such phrases as "dead to the law",[172] and "not under the law".[173] The general view among the Puritans was that these expressions were almost synonymous, and that they meant that the believer was free from the Law as a Covenant of Works.[174] Walter Cradock teaches that the words in Galatians ii. 19 and Romans vii. 4 mean:

> I am dead to the law, as it is a Covenant of works, the law hath no more to doe with me then the Lawes of men have to doe with a man that is in debt when he is dead, when he is dead he is free from it. . . . The meaning is not as though the substance and matter of law were not eternall; . . . but the law as it is . . . a Covenant of works . . . is perfectly fulfilled by Christ, and we are dead to it.[175]

The believer is dead to the Law in the sense that he is "never more looking for righteousnesse and justification of life that way",[176] and

165. Anthony Burgess, *Vindiciae Legis*, p. 177.
166. Vavasor Powell, *Christ and Moses*, p. 240.
167. Thomas Taylor, *Regula Vitae*, p. 10.
168. Samuel Rutherford, *Survey*, Part II. p. 7; cf. Walter Marshall, *Sanctification*, p. 107.
169. Samuel Rutherford, *Survey*, Part II. p. 117.
170. Thomas Manton, *James*, in *Works*, IV. 163.
171. Richard Baxter, *Aphorismes*, pp. 147–9, 156.
172. Romans vii. 4; Galatians ii. 19.
173. Romans vi. 14, 15.
174. Cf. William Perkins, *Galatians*, p. 245; Thomas Taylor, *Regula Vitae*, pp. 2, 23.
175. Walter Cradock, *Gospel Holinesse*, "Priviledge and Practice of the Saints", p. 218.
176. Richard Byfield, *Gospels Glory*, p. 36.

no longer expects "by duties to get Christ and God's favour".[177] This is the view also of Richard Sibbes,[178] Jeremiah Burroughs,[179] Thomas Adams,[180] and, indeed, of all the other Puritan writers. The opinions of later commentators show no appreciable variation from this view, and many of them give the meaning in almost the same terms as the Puritans.

These phrases were certainly taken by the Puritans to apply to the sphere of justification, but they insisted that they were not to be understood in any manner that would be detrimental to the continuing authority of the Law.

> Wee are dead to the Law . . . in regard of the terrour and rigour of it; as a woman is from the threats and rigour of a dead husband: but the Apostle saith not, that the Law is dead either in respect of the direction of it, or our obedience to those directions.[181]

Francis Roberts points out that the apostle's words cannot mean that believers are not under the rule of the Law, for that would not prove the thing in hand, namely, that sin shall not have dominion. He thinks, therefore, that the words mean that believers are not under the terror of the Law.[182] Anthony Burgess likewise considers that the reference is not to the Law *per se*, but to the provocative power of the Law as it stirs up the desire to sin, as in Romans vii. 8, and suggests that the phrase, "under the Law", implies more properly "under sin".[183]

(ii) *"The law of sin and death" and the bondage of the Law*

Most Puritan writers regard the phrase "the law of sin and death"[184] as a metaphorical expression indicating the imperious mastery that sin acquires in the life of fallen man. "This is the title that he gives unto the powerful and effectual remainder of indwelling sin even in believers".[185] Andrew Willet considers "the lawe of sinne" to be "the corruption of nature",[186] and Edward Elton regards the word "Law" as "put . . . Metaphorically, to signifie the corruption of nature, and not that barely, but the power, and force and strength of it".[187] Thomas Jacomb likewise understands the word "Law" to be a meta-

177. Thomas Goodwin, *Christian's Growth*, in *Works*, III. 472.
178. *Hidden Life*, 1639, in *Works*, V. 205.
179. *Saints Treasury*, p. 100.
180. *Fatal Banquet*, 1614, in *Works*, I. 229.
181. Thomas Taylor, *Regula Vitae*, p. 172, on Romans vii. 4–6.
182. *God's Covenants*, p. 729.
183. *Vindiciae Legis*, pp. 227, 228; and note his comment on p. 212 that the change is not in the Law but in the believer towards it.
184. Romans vii. 23, 25; viii. 2.
185. John Owen, *Indwelling Sin*, in *Works*, VI. 163–9.
186. *Hexapla: Romanes*, p. 331.
187. *Treatises*: "Complaint of a Sanctifyed Sinner", pp. 193, 196.

phor for the way in which sin "assumes a strange kind of authority" over the sinner.[188]

But not all the Puritans interpret the phrase in this way, and there are some who hold that what Paul here calls "the law of sin and death" is the Law of God, and that the apostle describes it in this manner, not in respect of what it is in itself, for it is "holy",[189] but in respect of what it has become in the experience of sinful men. Thomas Jacomb draws attention to this other view when he says that a large number of the older expositors considered "the law of sin" to be the Mosaic Law, "because it discovered sin, irritated sin, made sin to be sin".[190] Edward Elton seems to hold both views, or else not to make himself clear, for he not only regards the phrase as standing for the "corruption of nature", but, when expounding Romans vii. 10–13 and rightly following the apostle's thought, he argues that through the wickedness of man's heart, which turns every good thing to its opposite use, God's holy commandment thus becomes the cause of both sin and death in the same way as the Gospel becomes "the savour of death unto death".[191] Thomas Manton approaches the subject a little differently and says that the Law is described in this manner "because it convinceth of sin, and bindeth over to death".[192] In his exposition of the Law as "the ministration of death",[193] John Preston says "this ariseth not from hence, that the Law of God is a cruell deadly Law: (for the Law is good) but it ariseth from the weaknesse and the infirmity of the flesh".[194] Walter Cradock affirms that "There is so great affinity and nearness between walking legally, and walking sinfully that they are promiscuously in Scripture taken one for another. . . . Sin, and the law are (as it were) of so near a kin, that the law makes sin more sinfull, and the more a man strives to keep the law, the more he sins".[195]

If this second view contains any element of truth, it demonstrates the profound relation that exists between the Law of God and the sin of man, and at the same time it provides an insight into the nature of that freedom with which Christ sets free.[196]

188. *Romans*, p. 109.
189. Romans vii. 12.
190. *Romans*, p. 102.
191. Op. cit., pp. 130, 131.
192. *Hundred and Nineteenth Psalm*, I. 301.
193. II Corinthians iii. 7.
194. *New Covenant*, p. 319.
195. *Gospel-Holinesse*, "Priviledge and Practice of the Saints", p. 265.
196. There is a harshness about this expression—though not more so than in "the ministration of death"—which compels some commentators to repudiate the idea that it could possibly refer to the Law of God, but this reference should not be dismissed solely for that reason. It is defended, for example, by J. A. Bengel, (*Gnomon*, III. 98) J. Forbes, (*Romans*, 1868, pp. 275, 304, 305) R. Haldane, with special reference also to Romans vii. 5 and 1 Corinthians xv. 56, (*Romans*, 1835, pp. 317, 318), C. Hodge, (*Romans*, 1864, p. 249), B. Jowett, (*Romans*, 1859, II. 251) and more recently by C. K. Barrett who says

The "bondage of the Law"—an expression which the Puritans frequently used—needs to be understood in the same way as the Biblical phrase just examined. The freedom of the Gospel was often spoken of by the Puritans as deliverance from "the bondage of the Law",[197] but this was to speak metonymically, by substituting "law" for "sin". Strictly, there is no bondage in the Law;[198] the bondage is either that of sin and corruption which, in turn, derive their strength from the Law,[199] or it arises from an abuse of the Law.[200] When the Puritans exulted in deliverance from the Law, they meant first of all that they were made free from sin's condemnation,[201] and so the curse of the Law having been removed they were brought out from under sin's bondage.

(iii) "*That being dead wherein we were held*"

There was considerable difference of understanding among the Puritans about the interpretation of the apostle's words in Romans vii. 6, "that being dead wherein we were held," particularly in their connection with verses 2 and 3. Some of the Puritans took Paul's analogy to mean that the "Law" was the "husband", and that the Law was now dead. Robert Towne speaks of "the Law our former husband",[202] and says, "The law is dead to us. . . . The Law and Christ are set in opposition, as two husbands to one wife successively.[203] The author of *The Marrow* expounds Romans vii. 1 by changing "he" to "it", and reads, "the law hath dominion over a man as long as it liveth". He therefore concludes from verse 6 that the Law is "dead",[204] and, borrowing from Richard Greenham, he says, "O Law! be it known unto thee that I am now married unto Christ".[205]

Some writers were led into a mixture of interpretations—partly justified by the multiple use which the apostle makes of his analogy—

"Sin has taken possession of the law ('the law of sin', v. 23), and made out of it a subtle perversion of law", and that by the "law of sin and death" is meant "the law of Moses, seized and perverted by sin and consequently leading to death". (*Romans*, pp. 151, 155). Some further discussion of this subject can be found in E. F. Kevan, *The Evangelical Doctrine of Law*, 1955, pp. 22–25.

197. E.g. William Ames, *Marrow of Sacred Divinity*, p. 123.
198. Psalm xix. 8; cxix. 47, 96; Romans vii. 22.
199. Romans vii. 8, 13; 1 Corinthians xv. 56.
200. Galatians v. 1.
201. William Perkins, *Galatians*, p. 320.
202. *Assertion of Grace*, p. 118.
203. Op. cit., pp. 141, 142.
204. Op. cit., pp. 107, 139, 151.
205. Op. cit., p. 141; cf. Samuel Bolton, *True Bounds*, p. 26; Thomas Goodwin, *Work of the Holy Ghost*, in *Works*, VI. 257, 258; Robert Traill, *Galatians*, in *Works*, IV. 229, 230.

and spoke of both the Law and the believer being "dead". Vavasor Powell was one of these and says,

> Believers are dead to, and free from the law as it is a Husband. . . . If you be believers, and married to Christ, the law hath no more power over you, then a dead husband hath over his relict and liveing wife.[206]

William Woodward writes with the same uncertainty of meaning when he regards the Law as "the husband", but adds that Paul "doth not say the law as a Husband is dead, 'tis not dead to this day as a rule; mark that, but we are dead to the law."[207]

John Flavel introduces a cautious observation when he sees the husband as the abused Law,[208] and so prepares the way for the views of others that the former "husband" of Romans vii is not the Law, but sin. Thomas Blake bridges the gap between these interpretations, and writes:

> The power which the Law loseth, is that which corruption gave it, which is irritation and condemnation; corruption never gave command to the Law, and the death of corruption through the Spirit can never exempt the soul from obedience, or take the power of command from it. Let it be granted that the Law is the husband here mentioned, the similitude is this. That as the Law through our corruption was fruitful in mans nature to the bringing forth of sin and condemnation; So Christ by the Spirit is to be fruitful in our nature to bring forth works of grace to salvation, and so the death of the Law is meerly in respect of irritation or enflaming to sin, and binding over to condemnation, not in respect of command.[209]

Samuel Rutherford stands in this mediating position when he explains the "husband" to be "the Law, as given to the siner".[210] The argument of Thomas Blake and the Law-for-the-sinner concept of Samuel Rutherford move in the direction of the latter's main exposition, namely, that the "husband" is sin itself.

Anthony Burgess teaches that the "husband" is sin,[211] so also do Francis Roberts[212] and William Strong.[213] John Preston interprets the passage as meaning:

206. *Christ and Moses*, p. 233; see Thomas Blake, on Vavasor Powell in *Covenant of God*, p. 51.
207. *Lord our Righteousness*, p. 84.
208. *Vindiciae Legis & Foederis*, Prolegomena.
209. Thomas Blake, *Covenant of God*, pp. 53, 54.
210. *Triumph of Faith*, p. 196.
211. *Vindiciae Legis*, p. 228.
212. *God's Covenants*, p. 730.
213. *The Two Covenants*, p. 19.

> We were married to sinne, and it had dominion and command over us, as the husband over the wife, but now it is dead, and there is a divorce betweene us, and now wee are married to Christ and hee commands us, and wee obey.[214]

Edward Elton warns against overpressing the details of the analogy, and he says the difficulties will be removed

> if we consider the drift and purpose of the Apostle, which is this, to shew that death sets a man free from the Law of God . . . as death sets a wife free from the Law of Marriage . . . whether it be by the death of the wife; or by the death of the husband it skils not.[215]

He says, however, that the words, "that being dead", are

> rather put down absolutely, as if the reading were thus, "that thing being dead". And if any demand what is then meant by that thing? I answer in a word, that sin, that corruption, that is in us by nature . . . Which did strongly, forcibly, and as a tyrant hold us in bondage under the Law.[216]

Andrew Willet may best summarize and conclude the Puritan discussion of this complicated passage. After having surveyed the many opinions that have been expressed, he gives his own view as follows:

> Now that the law is not as the husband, but sinne, the Apostle evidently sheweth, v. 5. "When we were in the flesh the motions of sinne which were by the law had force in our members to bring forth fruit unto death . . ."[217]

He then refers to the double similitude in verse 4, and says that the apostle

> joyntly applyeth the two similitudes before alleadged: the one, that the lawe hath no dominion over one, but while he liveth, v. 1, the other that the woman is bound to the man, but while he liveth: in the application, he putteth both together: to answear to the first, he saith we are mortified to the lawe, and so it hath no more power over us: and touching the second, he saith, that beeing dead, wherein we were holden, namely, sinne, v. 5, we should be now for an other husband.[218]

One of the superficial causes of the Puritan difficulty was the false

214. John Preston, *Law out lawed*, p. 2.
215. *Treatises*: "Complaint of a Sanctifyed Sinner", p. 10
216. Op. cit., p. 52.
217. *Hexapla: Romanes*, p. 316.
218. Andrew Willet, *Hexapla: Romanes*, p. 317.

reading, ἀποθανόντος instead of ἀποθανόντες, followed by the translators of the A.V. and which appears subsequently in the *Textus Receptus*. But the Puritans were not unaware of this textual weakness, and it must not be thought that when some of them wrote of the Law as "dead" they were building their argument on verse 6 alone. Their chief problem lay in the analogy itself and confronted them in the ambiguity of the death not only of the "husband" but also of the "wife".

Among later expositors there are but few who understand Paul to mean that the Law is "dead",[219] and the generally recognized interpretation follows the line suggested by the R.V. and now in the *New English Bible*.[220] It is thus the "old man, which is corrupt according to the deceitful lusts"[221] in which the believers are considered to have died, and this is in keeping with Paul's teaching in such passages as Romans vi. 2–11; vii. 4; Galatians ii. 19, 20; vi. 14.[222]

From the evidence surveyed in this chapter it is impossible to avoid the conclusion that the Puritans, when rightly discerning the mandatory aspects of the Law of God, affirmed with well-nigh one voice that the eternal Law of God was incapable of being terminated in time. The true end of the Law is, therefore, to be found in its perfect realization in the work of Christ and through that work in the obedience of regenerate sinners.

219. F. Godet says, "the idea of the abolition of the law is foreign to this passage". *Romans*, II. 12.
220. See Alford, Barrett, Barth, Beet, Denney, Forbes, Garvie, Gifford, Hodge, Jowett, and Sanday and Headlam.
221. Ephesians iv. 22.
222. J. A. Bengel does not concern himself unduly with the niceties of the analogy and writes, "When either party dies, the other is considered to be dead", *Gnomon*, III. 86, 87, and J. Murray similarly contends that it is arbitrary to construct a rigid allegory. *Romans*, 1959, I. 241, 242; cf. C. H. Dodd, *Romans*, p. 101 and C. K. Barrett, *Romans*, p. 138.

Chapter V

THE CONTINUANCE OF MORAL OBLIGATION

Synopsis

A. ANTINOMIAN REJECTION OF COMMANDMENT
- (i) *"No Moses now"*
- (ii) *The Puritan reply*

B. THE HUMAN OBLIGATION TO OBEY
- (i) *Its basis in man's creaturely relation to God*
- (ii) *Obligation increased by grace*
- (iii) *The holy fear of God*

C. UNALTERED DEMANDS OF THE LAW
- (i) *No licence to sin*
- (ii) *Universal obedience*

D. OBEDIENCE TO LAW AS LAW

E. LAW "IN THE HANDS OF CHRIST"
- (i) *Christ as Lawgiver*
- (ii) *"In the law to Christ"*
- (iii) *An abused concept*

F. THREATENINGS AND PROMISES OF REWARD
- (i) *Threatenings*
- (ii) *Promises of reward*
- (iii) *Rewards of grace*

G. CHASTISEMENT
- (i) *Antinomian denial of chastisement*
- (ii) *Chastisement related to sin*
- (iii) *No vindicatory element in chastisement*

Chapter V

THE CONTINUANCE OF MORAL OBLIGATION

It has been established that the Puritans held that the work of Christ as "the end of the Law" does not mean that the Law is abolished, and, more particularly, that the experience of the grace of God in no way detracts from the authority and permanence of the Law of God.

The purpose of this chapter is to trace the ways in which the Puritans worked out the implications of this in terms of Christian experience. The unalterable fact of human obligation is first recognized, together with the undiminished demands of the Law of God. It is then shown that these demands are to be acknowledged, not merely in their intrinsic goodness, but in their form as authoritative commands, and that, so far from an action losing moral value when performed because commanded, it is only when an action is performed in this manner that it possesses the quality of true goodness. This commanding Law is "in the hand of Christ"; nevertheless, sanctions are attached to it, and chastisements follow upon the believer's breach of it.

A. ANTINOMIAN REJECTION OF COMMANDMENT

There is possibly no part of the discussion of the place of the Law in the life of the believer where Antinomians were more "antinomian" than at this place. They were mostly willing to concede the eternity of the matter of the Law, but they held that to serve God because of commandment to do so was legalistic and unspiritual.

(i) "*No Moses now*"

On the basis of the view that the Law was abrogated,[1] John Eaton complains of those who "turne Christ into Moses, and Moses into Christ".[2] Robert Towne rejects the distinction between the "Raigne" of Law and the "Rule" of Law,[3] and although he readily agrees that "the Spirit . . . doth ever guide and bring forth fruits of holinesse

1. See Chapter IV.
2. *Honey-combe*, p. 381; John Sedgwick quotes them as saying, "Away with Moses, Out of doors with Moses, we beleevers can no longer abide his voice". (*Antinomianisme Anatomized*, p. 4).
3. *Assertion of Grace*, pp. 1, 2.

and righteousnesse according to the Law",[4] he cannot accept the active and authoritative aspect of the Law. He displays his complete intermixing of opposite concepts when he asks the lame question, "What if it be affirmed that even in true sanctification the Law of works is a meer passive thing, as the Kings high way which a Christian freely walketh in?"[5] Later on he adds the petulant remark, "If the Spirit be free, why will you controll and rule it by the Law, whereas the nature of the Spirit is freely to conform the heart and life to the outward rule of the law and without the help of the law."[6] The utmost that he seems willing to acknowledge in this respect is that the Law "ministreth occasion"[7] to do the things that are right, but ten years later in the *Re-assertion,* he becomes bolder and asserts, "To faith, or in the state or things of faith, there is no obligation, nor use of the law."[8]

As so often, Robert Towne speaks with two voices. He rejects the idea of walking by the rule of the Law and charges Thomas Taylor with an unwillingness to "trust a beleever to walke without his Keeper; as if he judged no otherwise of him then of a malefactor of Newgate."[9] But when statements of this kind expose him to the charge of Antinomianism, he replies, "I never deny the Law to be an eternall and inviolable Rule of Righteousnesse: but yet affirme that its the Grace of the Gospel, which effectually and truely conformeth us thereunto", and retorts again to Thomas Taylor by saying, "I am perswaded that neither you nor any your confederates dare say that ever they heard one of an indifferent judgment and understanding . . . simply to deny the use of the Morall Law to true beleevers."[10] He holds that "the Law is useful" to the believer, "for if I love God and my Neighbour, I can testifie it onely by the workes of the Law",[11] and when asked by Thomas Taylor, "What is the law of Christ, but the commandment of Christ enjoyning the love of our brethren?" he replies, "Its his law for the expression of our love; but not to beget the inward affection of it."[12]

There is something exasperating about this kind of argument—these cross-questions and crooked-answers. It shows how confused Robert Towne is, and at the same time reveals the problem he makes for himself as he confounds the requirements of duty with the power to fulfil them.

John Saltmarsh dislikes those who say "that duties are to be done

4. Op. cit., p. 9.
5. Op. cit., p. 10.
6. Op. cit., p. 138.
7. Op. cit., p. 170.
8. *Re-assertion*, p. 118.
9. Robert Towne, *Assertion of Grace*, p. 5, and *Re-assertion*, p. 5.
10. *Assertion of Grace*, pp. 6, 37.
11. Op. cit., p. 147.
12. Op. cit., p. 149.

because commanded",[13] and in *Free-Grace* he reveals his contempt for those whose Gospel preaching is "over-much heated by the Law, and conditions and qualifications",[14] and who hold the believer in poverty of spirit by keeping him "both under Grace and the Law at the same time".[15] He says that to urge believers to "Repent . . . and walk according to the law of God" is a legal way of bringing comfort to a soul,[16] and that the preachers who do this give "rather somthing of the Law then the Gospel",[17] for "nothing but the taking in of the Law . . . can trouble the peace and quiet of any soul."[18] "The Gospel is . . . a perfect law of life and righteousnesse . . . and therefore I wonder at any that should contend for the ministery of the Law or ten Commandments under Moses."[19] The believer is now under grace, and there is "no Moses now".[20] It can do no other than bring the believer into bondage if he does things "meerly as commanded from the power of an outward commandment or precept in the Word", and such a relation to the Law produces "but a legal, or at best but a mixt obedience and service of something a finer hypocrisie".[21]

Most of the expressions used by John Saltmarsh are capable of being sympathetically understood when the Law, or "Moses", is thought of as a Covenant, but it is clear that at the root of these Antinomian controversies there lies the inability of many to keep the distinction between the Law as commandment and the Law as Covenant.

(ii) *The Puritan reply*

The Puritans did not fail to see the drift of Antinomian thought, and they wrote against it in no uncertain terms.[22] John Sedgwick considers the Antinomian war-cries of Free Grace, Christ's Righteousness, and Gospel Liberty, to be "Baits and Snares . . . to cast down Obedience, to keep Christians from their dutie to God", and he deplores the "Law-destroying, and Dutie-casting-down course"

13. John Saltmarsh, *Sparkles of Glory*, p. 242; cf. pp. 193, 194.
14. John Saltmarsh, *Free-Grace*, An Occasionall Word.
15. Op. cit., To the Reader.
16. Op. cit., p. 27.
17. Op. cit., p. 37.
18. Op. cit., p. 44.
19. Op. cit., p. 146; cf. *Sparkles of Glory*, pp. 240, 243, 246. It is this kind of statement that justifies Henry Burton in saying "our Adversary shutts out the law quite, as out of date to a true beleever, and of no use at all, not so much as to be a rule of life." *Law and Gospel Reconciled*, p. 21.
20. John Saltmarsh, op. cit., p. 160. Cf. Thomas Watson, *A Body of Divinity*, 1692, p. 2.
21. John Saltmarsh, *Free-Grace*, pp. 179, 180.
22. Cf. Thomas Taylor, *Regula Vitae*, Preface; Thomas Welde, *Rise, reigne, and ruine*, p. 1; Thomas Edwards, *Gangraena*, p. 25; Henry Burton, *Law and Gospel Reconciled*, pp. 22, 69; Thomas Bedford, *An Examination*, p. 9; Samuel Rutherford, *Survey*, Part I. p. 151.

of the Antinomians.[23] James Durham affirms that this rejection of the principle of obligation is itself a breach of the First Commandment,[24] and Thomas Gataker defends the principle of obligation by reference to the word, ὄφειλει in 1 John ii. 6, and the occurrence of the same verb in Romans viii. 12.[25]

> To deny the Morall Law to be of any more use to believers, or to be so much as a rule of conversation, or that they owe obedience unto it in poynt of duety and conscience: this strikes at the very root, and cutts in sunder the knot, not onely of christian charity, but even of all civill society.[26]

The issue involved in this controversy is put plainly by Anthony Burgess in *Vindiciae Legis* when he says,

> The question is not, whether the things of the Law be done, . . . but, Whether, when these things are done, they are done by a godly man, admonished, instructed, and commanded by the Law of God.[27]

The possibility of such a question, however, is based on "the Antinomian distinction of the Law abolished as a Law, but still abiding in respect of the matter of it".[28] To Robert Towne's protest that "the law in the matter of it so farre as I know was never denied to be the rule, according to which a beleever is to walk and live",[29] Anthony Burgess replies, "To say the matter of the Law bindeth, but yet not as a Law, is a meere contradiction; for what is a Law, but such an object held forth by the command and will of a superiour?"[30] By way of defence, Robert Towne makes the assertion:

> If you apply and urge these or any other never so earnestly with all your motives, and meanes fetcht from the Law, you can never hereby make me to keep them inwardly. . . . The law sanctifieth not therefore, nor giveth any heart or ability in truth to perform what it requireth.[31]

But no one ever claimed that the Law could do this, nor is it a valid denial of the authority of the Law to say that it affords no aid. Samuel

23. *Antinomianisme Anatomized*, To the Reader; cf. Richard Allen, *Antidote against Heresy*, p. 84.
24. *Law Unsealed*, p. 25.
25. *Antinomianism*, pp. 14, 15.
26. Henry Burton, *Law and Gospel Reconciled*, Epistle Dedicatory; cf. Robert Bolton, *Three-fold Treatise*, "Saints Guide", 1634, p. 87.
27. Op. cit., pp. 51, 277.
28. Anthony Burgess, *Vindiciae Legis*, p. 214.
29. *Assertion of Grace*, p. 170.
30. *Vindiciae Legis*, pp. 214, 215.
31. *Assertion of Grace*, p. 38, 170.

Rutherford gives a direct and uncompromising reply to the Antinomian denial.

> The Law is yet to be preached, as tying us to personall obedience, whatever Antinomians[32] say on the contrary. . . . Antinomians judge that by the Gospel, Christ hath done all for us, which is most true in the kinde of a meritorious and deserving cause, satisfying justice, but they doe loose us from all personal duties, or doing ourselves, or in our own persons, so as we should be obliged to doe, except we would sinne. We thinke the same Law-obligation, but running in a Gospel-channel of Free-grace, should act us now as if we were under a covenant of works, but not as if the one were Law-debt, and the other wages that we sweat for, and commeth by Law-debt; Antinomians make all duties a matter of courtesie.[33]

He points out that the Antinomians[34] "contend for a Christian liberty wherewith Christ hath made us free, and we contend for the same, but the question is, wherein the liberty consisteth, it concerneth us much, that we take not licence for liberty",[35] and in reply to Robert Towne's assertion that the Gospel persuades rather than commands he makes the rejoinder, "But say we, it both commands, (as the Law doth) and with a more strong obligation of the constraining love of Christ, beside the authority of the Lawgiver, and also perswadeth".[36]

Some of the orthodox writers probe deeper than the theoretical discussion of this subject, and Ezekiel Hopkins, for example, speaks with penetrating insight, of "a company of flush Notionists, who are very willing to shake off the Yoke from their Necks; and to deliver themselves rather from the Conscience, than from the Power of Sin.[37] John Bunyan tells of his conversations with the "Ranters" who condemned him "as legal and dark", pretending that in their perfection they "could do what they would and not sin", but exclaims, "Oh! These temptations were suitable to my flesh."[38] Richard Baxter dismisses whatever evidence of virtue the Antinomians produce with the scornful remark, "But how conscionably soever they live, it is no thanks to their ungodly unchristian Doctrine",[39] and, fairly or unfairly, he writes

> Truly I finde as farre as I can discern, that most of the prophane people in every Parish where yet I have liv'd, are Antinomians;

32. See Robert Towne, *Assertion of Grace*, p. 31.
33. *Survey*, Part II. pp. 28, 29.
34. See Robert Towne, *Assertion of Grace*, p. 26.
35. Samuel Rutherford, *Survey*, Part II. p. 93.
36. Op. cit., p. 122.
37. *John*, in *Works*, p. 239.
38. *Grace Abounding*, 1666, p. 21.
39. *Scripture Gospel Defended*, "Defence of Christ and Free Grace", To the Reader.

> They are born and bred such; and it is the very natural Religion of men, that have but the advantage to believe traditionally in Christ: I mean, their corrupt nature carrieth them without any teaching to make this use of Christ and the Gospel. And almost all the successe of my Labours which hath so much comforted me, hath been in bringing men from natural Antinomianism or Libertinism, to true Repentance and saving Faith in Christ.[40]

There was, without doubt, considerable misunderstanding between the Antinomians and their opponents, and a tendency among the orthodox unjustly to impute wrong motives to the Antinomians. Any endeavour for freedom, in whatever sphere, is accused at some time or other with anarchic or unworthy motives, and it has to run the risk of this. In this present instance the Antinomians suffered as much through the excessive fervour of their friends—the "Ranters"—as they did from their opponents. The Antinomians were in error, however, and the Puritan exposure of their mistaken inferences must be regarded as necessary in the interests of true godliness.

B. THE HUMAN OBLIGATION TO OBEY

The human obligation to obey is implicit in the Divine right to command, but the Puritans did not leave it tacitly there. They taught that man "is bound to acknowledge Divine Sovereignty, together with his own subjection.[41]

(i) *Its basis in man's creaturely relation to God*

> An Obligation to obey our Creator, is a Natural resultancy from our Condition, as we are Creatures. . . . If Gods Commands, as they are his Commands, do not constitute and determine Man's duty, and lay a necessary tye upon man to Obedience, then God hath lost his Authority over man.[42]

Man, therefore, is subject to the Law "by nature",[43] for the moral Law "bindes the consciences of all men at all times, even of blind and ignorant persons, that neither knowe the most of it nor care to knowe it."[44] "To binde (in this morall sense) is to have such an authority, as the Conscience ought to submit it selfe unto."[45] The duty of obedience is based on "a law, whose obligation arises from our very nature and being, and is founded in the relation between God and

40. Richard Baxter, *Apology*, "Admonition of Mr William Eyre", Preface.
41. John Ball, *Power of Godliness*, p. 1.
42. John Barret, *Treatise of the Covenants*, pp. 16, 19.
43. Edward Reynolds, *Three Treatises*: "Sinfulnesse of Sinne", p. 368.
44. William Perkins, *Of Conscience*, in *Works*, p. 622.
45. William Ames, *Conscience*, Book I. p. 6, cf. Book V. pp. 166–7.

man. . . . To deny perfect obedience to be due from man is to deny him to be man."[46] Whatever incapacities may have come about through the entry of sin into human life, man's "obligation to God is . . . indelible",[47] and the Decalogue obliges "all Christians, to the worlds end."[48] "The thing properly willed by God in a Law, is but the *debitum*, the duty of the subject to do what is commanded",[49] yet it must not be thought that the obedience rendered by man is something that God "hath any neede of."[50] Isaac Ambrose yields to a play on words by defining "duty" as "mans tye to that which is due."[51]

> Moral obligation is nothing short of a strict subjection. Our obedience towards God, although in respect of readinesse of mind it ought to be the obedience of sons: yet in respect of that strict obligation to subjection, it is the obedience of servants.[52]

One of the clearest evidences of the obligatory nature of the Law is found in fallen man's resentment against it: sinful man resists the Law because, by its holy obligations, the Law first resists him, for "without the law sin is dead."[53] Conversely, because by man's sinful nature he "would not be under command",[54] the best evidence of the believer's restored relation to God is obedience.[55]

The challenge to God's sovereignty contained in man's fall must be matched in his restoration by the renewed recognition of that sovereignty, for it is "the authority of God" which constitutes "the formal object of our obedience, or the reason why we observe the things he hath commanded.[56]

(ii) *Obligation increased by grace*

"Howsoever we are freed from the curse . . . of the law; yet we are not freed from the obedience of the law morall."[57] The believer is committed to an "inward and sound obedience due to Gods law",[58]

46. David Clarkson, *Justification*, in *Works*, I. 297; *The Lord Rules over all*, 1696, in *Works*, II. 487; Richard Baxter, *End of Doctrinal Controversies*, p. 298. See above Chapter I.
47. Stephen Charnock, *Efficient of Regeneration*, 1683, in *Works*, III. 225; cf. Anthony Burgess, *Vindiciae Legis*, pp. 61, 64.
48. Samuel Rutherford, *Survey*, Part II. pp. 5–7.
49. Richard Baxter, *Catholick Theologie*, Book I. Part I. p. 77.
50. John Preston, *New Covenant*, p. 103.
51. *Prima, Media, & Ultima*, "The Middle Things", p. 15, cf. p. 38.
52. William Ames, *Marrow of Sacred Divinity*, pp. 191, 195, 196.
53. Romans vii. 8. Cf. Edward Elton, *Treatises*: "Complaint of a Sanctifyed Sinner", pp. 78, 84, 85.
54. Thomas Manton, *Thessalonians*, in *Works*, III. 142; cf. Stephen Charnock, *Man's Enmity to God*, 1699, in *Works*, V. 472.
55. Cf. George Hughes, *Dry Rod Blooming*, 1644, p. 103.
56. Stephen Charnock, *Attributes*, in *Works*, II. 491; cf. 427–33.
57. George Downame, *Covenant of Grace*, p. 66.
58. William Perkins, *Golden Chaine*, in *Works*, p. 14.

and, having believed, he "must goe yet further, and enter into a practise of the doctrine of the Gospell as wel as of the precepts of the morall lawe; knowing that the gospell doeth as well bind conscience as the law, and if it be not obeied will as well condemne."[59] The Law "doth tye even Christians and Believers now, as well as of old."[60] "Christians are bound to serve God",[61] and, having the Law of God in their hearts, "they make conscience of internal obedience" and of external obedience too.[62] They recognize that although they are not under the reign of the Law, they are still under the rule of it.[63] "It is the doctrine of the Scripture", says Richard Rogers, "that all the commaundements of God be had in account of us, and conscience made of one as well as of another."[64] "Our freedome and deliverance from the rigour and curse of the Law, binds us strongly to the service of God",[65] hence the mandatory part of the Law is to be preached "as it doth teach beleevers their duties."[66] Sanctifying grace is as a law that rules,[67] and "Gospel-duties" are called for because the Law itself is part of the Gospel and never was anything but a Covenant of Grace.[68] The obligations of the believer towards the Law of God are part of the terms of that saving Covenant.

Thomas Bedford deals with objections based on Paul's statement that "the law is not made for a righteous man",[69] and says that although it does not condemn the law-abiding man, it is still of use to instruct him, as it was to Adam in Paradise.[70] Christ's full submission to the Law does not "take us away from obeying the Will of God, which was Christs meat and drink to do."[71] A saving relation to Christ increases obligation to Christ, and the Covenant vow, renewed continually at the Lord's Supper, acknowledges that "we are bound to the strictest duties."[72] In his strong opposition to Antinomianism, Samuel Rutherford writes,

59. William Perkins, *Of Conscience*, in *Works*, p. 625; John Dod and Robert Cleaver, *Ten Commaundements*, p. 7.
60. James Durham, *Law Unsealed*, pp. 2, 3, 5; cf. Thomas Blake, *Covenant of God*, pp. 50, 51.
61. John Ball, *Of Faith*, p. 368.
62. John Ball, *Covenant of Grace*, pp. 132, 133.
63. Thomas Taylor, *Regula Vitae*, pp. 1, 2.
64. *Seven Treatises*, Preface.
65. Edward Elton, *Treatises*: "Complaint of a Sanctifyed Sinner", p. 53, cf. p. 29.
66. Vavasor Powell, *Christ and Moses*, p. 255; cf. the anonymous work, *Covenant of Grace, not Absolute*, 1692, p. 34.
67. Edward Elton, *Treatises*: "Complaint of a Sanctifyed Sinner", p. 205.
68. James Durham, *Law Unsealed*, pp. 10, 16.
69. I Timothy i. 9.
70. *An Examination*, pp. 13, 14, 17. Cf. Thomas Taylor, *Regula Vitae*, p. 161; Calvin, *Inst*. II. vii. 10 where he explains this of the *usus politicus*.
71. Jeremiah Burroughs, *Gospel-Conversation*, p. 79.
72. Thomas Manton, *Mark*, 1678, in *Works*, II. 228; Richard Greenham, *Of Quenching the Spirit*, in *Works*, p. 54; Anthony Burgess, *Vindiciae Legis*, p. 4; *Justification*, Part II., p. 21.

> Gospel-motives vary not the nature of duties: as a Master may command the same duties to his sonne and his servant, upon different grounds. . . . Let none thinke that Law-curses, looseth us from all Law-obedience; or that Christ hath cryed downe the tenne Commandements; and that Gospel-liberty is a dispensation for Law-loosenesse. . . . Grace is active, dutifull in acting . . . solicitous in doing, as if there were not a Gospel; free, fearlesse bold; as if there were not a cursing Law, tender of the honour of the Law-giver, and of Gospel-glory due to him who justifies the ungodly.[73]

Thus, although the voluntary and loving obedience of the believer does not come from the fears and curses of the Law, it does nevertheless derive "from the binding and obliging authority of the Lawgiver."[74] In the *Triumph of Faith* he exclaims

> The way that cryeth down duties and sanctification, is not the way of grace; grace is an innocent thing, and will not take men off from duties, grace destroyeth not obedience; Christ has made faith a friend to the Law.[75]

This view is supported by Thomas Blake who maintains that

> It can be no part of our Christian freedome to be from under the Sovereignty of heaven. . . . God in the dayes of the Gospel keeps up the power and authority of his Law; the Obligation of it is still in force to binde the consciences of beleevers.[76]

He refers to the opinion of some that the Law "bindes the unregenerate part of man, but not the regenerate part", and answers this by drawing attention to Paul's words about delighting in the Law of God "after the inward man."[77] He understands these words to mean "so far as regenerate", and so asks, "How could he delight in it as a Law, and not be subject to it?" His question compels him to add, significantly, "It seemes these think only wicked ones to be bound, or rather wickednesse to be obliged; It will shortly be a marke of unregeneration . . . to be subject to it."[78] It is unthinkable that the believer should be regarded as "freed from the lawe, in respect of the obedience thereto"[79] for, as Samuel Bolton so succinctly puts it, "the law sends us to the Gospel, that we may be justified, and the

73. *Survey*, Part II. pp. 8, 29.
74. Samuel Rutherford, op. cit., Part II. p. 68.
75. Samuel Rutherford, *Triumph of Faith*, p. 121.
76. Thomas Blake, *Covenant of God*, p. 48.
77. Romans vii. 22.
78. Thomas Blake, *Covenant of God*, p. 57.
79. Andrew Willet, *Hexapla: Romanes*, p. 317.

Gospel sends us to the law againe to enquire what is our dutie being justified."[80]

Far from there being any reduction in the obligations resting on the believer, the facts are opposite, for "as Christ came to raise the comfort of the creature to the highest, so also the duty of the creature to the highest",[81] and "in the Christian religion all moral duties are advanced and heightened to their greatest perfection."[82] The Westminster Divines made an addition to an earlier draft of Chapter XIX, paragraph 6 of the *Confession of Faith*, and particularly instructed that the words "and bound" should be added after the word "directed" in the statement that the Law of God not only informs believers of their duty but "directs and binds them to walk accordingly."[83]

(iii) *The holy fear of God*

> We are not to consult whether the will of God is to be obeyed or no, for such a consultation cannot be free from impietie: but wee are to enquire onely to this end, that wee may understand what is the will of God.[84]

This dread of "impietie", and the realization of their relation to the holy Law of God, engendered that godly fear within the Puritans which has ever been regarded as one of their outstanding characteristics. William Perkins teaches that among the sanctified affections "is the feare of God, a most excellent and wonderfull grace of God",[85] and Richard Rogers, likewise, speaks of "fearing most of all to offend God."[86] There are two kinds of fear—a fear of holy diligence and a slavish fear—and the believer should have "the first kinde of fear" about "a duty commanded by God",[87] and this must "awe us, and hold us under a sense of our duty" to Him.[88]

The Puritans invested the concept of obligation with moral grandeur by means of the theological context in which they presented it. They lived in an awareness of the commanding authority of God, and this gave glory and dignity to all their actions. The Antinomian minimizing of this—although with the intention of magnifying grace—tended to obscure the Divine perfections and thus to destroy the glory of God.

80. *True Bounds*, p. 98.
81. Thomas Manton, *Ephesians*, 1678, in *Works*, II. 400.
82. Thomas Manton, *James*, in *Works*, IV. 122.
83. A. F. Mitchell and J. Struthers, *Minutes*, p. 272.
84. William Ames, *Conscience*, Book IV. p. 25.
85. *A Treatise*, 1588, in *Works*, p. 443.
86. *Seven Treatises*, p. 316.
87. Anthony Burgess, *Spiritual Refining*, "Of Sinne", p. 125.
88. Thomas Manton, *Hundred and Nineteenth Psalm*, I. 6.

C. UNALTERED DEMANDS OF THE LAW

The corollary of the continuance of moral obligation is the undiminished requirement of the Law.

(i) *No licence to sin*

The Law is a free rule, but "we may not live as we list."[89] The Christian enjoys a freedom from the bondage of evil and is ushered into a "Freedome in good things",[90] but he must observe a right use of this liberty.[91] Believers need the Law as a rule because of the reality of their freedom,[92] for true freedom is freedom to do right. Forgiveness does not "open a doore of libertie to make men more loose."[93]

> I am perswaded more souls drop down to Hell in our dayes under the abuse of Gospel Light, than ever did in the gross darkness of Popery. . . . Oh how many have we now adaies, who think they walk cleerly in the midst of Gospel Light, magnifying and exalting free Grace, triumphing in their Christian liberty, looking upon others as kept in bondage . . . and yet . . . make a mock of sin, being conceitedly set at liberty, but really sin and Satans bondslaves.[94]

"Christian liberty is not contrary to that subjection, which we owe either unto God or man", because "we are freed from sinne, but not from that duty, which is contrary unto sinne."[95]

> It will prove no good reason, that because an heire in minority is under tutours and rods, therefore hee may being come to yeares live as hee list, and become a lawlesse man: or that because the law as given by Moses to the Church of the Jewes is in some circumstances altered, therefore it must bee in the whole substance of it abolished.[96]

The liberty of the Christian man is not a freedom from the obedience of the Law, but from the disobedience of it;[97] for "to be free from obedience, is to be servants of sin."[98] An imagined "Liberty to Sin",

89. William Perkins, *Galatians*, p. 320.
90. William Perkins, op. cit., p. 357.
91. William Perkins, op. cit., p. 372.
92. William Perkins, op. cit., 293, 383.
93. John Preston, *New Covenant*, p. 115.
94. John Yates, To the Reader, in Jeremiah Burroughs, *Evil of Evils*.
95. William Ames, *Epistles of Peter*, 1641, p. 59.
96. Thomas Taylor, *Regula Vitae*, p. 30.
97. Thomas Taylor, *Regula Vitae*, p. 165.
98. Thomas Taylor, op. cit., p. 213; Thomas Manton, *Lord's Praye* in *Works*, I. 131.

says Walter Marshal, is "the worst of Slavery";[99] it "would not be freedom, but bondage."[100]

> Didst thou know the Tenor of the Covenant of Grace and Mercy, the Strictness of the Gospel, and Severity of Mercy it self against sin; thou wouldst see, There were an impossibility of having one sin forgiven, as long as one sin is unforsaken.[101]

"Damnation will befall such men as make Gods grace a stirrup for to help them up into the saddle of sin",[102] but, fundamentally, there can be no abuse of grace: though there may be of the doctrine.[103] John Sedgwick finds it hard to believe that anyone should think that the "granting of a Pardon" to a rebel should "give him a dispensation to practice Rebellion more freely",[104] and, using another metaphor, Thomas Blake writes, "Though the Law (the former husband) be dead to a beleever, yet a beleever is no widow, much lesse an harlot; for he is married to Christ, and is under the Law of Christ, which is love."[105]

At their 611th Session, 27 March, 1646, the discussion of the Westminster Divines on "Liberty of Conscience" produced the following Minute.

> None may practice any sin, or cherish any lust, or oppose any lawful power, or the lawful exercise of it, whether it be civil or ecclesiastical, upon pretence of Christian liberty—the liberty which is of Christ's procuring, and the powers which are of God's ordaining, not being opposite, or intended by God to destroy, but mutually to uphold and preserve one another.[106]

This subsequently found place in the *Confession of Faith*, with the added words that such as do practise sin in this manner "do thereby destroy the end of Christian liberty."[107]

(ii) *Universal obedience*

The Puritans never surrendered their conviction that the Law demands perfect obedience. This is what they meant by speaking so

99. *Sanctification*, p. 148.
100. Samuel Bolton, *True Bounds*, pp. 45, 46; cf. Ezekiel Hopkins, *Conscience*, 1701, in *Works*, p. 734.
101. Samuel Bolton, *Sin*, p. 37.
102. Vavasor Powell, *Christ and Moses*, p. 179.
103. Robert Traill, *Justification Vindicated*, in *Works*, I. p. 275; cf. Walter Cradock, *Gospel-Holinesse*, "Priviledge and Practice of the Saints", pp. 298, 299.
104. John Sedgwick, *Antinomianisme Anatomized*, pp. 37, 38.
105. *Covenant of God*, pp. 54, 55. Cf. Chapter IV for another view of the "husband" in Romans vii, but this does not destroy the truth which Thomas Blake is establishing.
106. A. F. Mitchell and J. Struthers, *Minutes*, p. 213.
107. Op. cit., XX. 3.

often of "universal" or "entire Obedience".[108] "Universal" obedience is not merely obedience rendered by everybody and everywhere, but obedience given to all the parts of the Law without exception,[109] for "whosoever shall keep the whole law, and yet offend in one point, he is guilty of all".[110] The laws of the Decalogue are absolute, and they set out a righteousness that is "full and complet."[111]

"The Gospel demands that we should keep the whole Law",[112] and "in a very strict, and spirituall manner",[113] so that "it is altogether bootlesse, for men to thinke of entring into Covenant with God, if they be not resolved to obey in all things",[114] for "the Law . . . doth not remit at all of . . . exactnesse of obedience."[115]

> The Holiness aimed at, consisteth in Conformity to the whole Moral Law, to which we are naturally obliged, if there had never been any Gospel, or any such Duty as believing in Christ for Salvation.[116]

"The rigor of the Law is abated" for the believer, but not in such a way "that the Law, as the Law, requireth lesse of him then absolutely perfect obedience."[117]

> The Gospel abateth nothing of the height of perfection, in commanding whatever the law commandeth in the same perfection; for tis as holy, pure, and spirituall in commanding . . . as the Law is.[118]

Christ came to "restore our nature unto such a perfection of righteousnesse, as the exactnesse of Gods Law doth require",[119] and through His Spirit the godly are humbled and subdued by "the spirituall exactnesse of the Law."[120] Ezekiel Hopkins makes the observation, "I much doubt, whether if God did not command us to do more than we can, we should do as much as we do",[121] and it is

108. E.g. John Ball, *Grounds of Christian Religion*, p. 196.
109. Cf. Thomas Manton, *James*, in *Works*, IV. 213; *Hundred and Nineteenth Psalm*, I. 330; William Strong, *The Two Covenants*, p. 52.
110. James ii. 10.
111. John Dod and Robert Cleaver, *Ten Commaundements*, p. 3. Cf. Isaac Chauncy, "If the Law require of me a small Matter or a great, it abates not one jot or tittle of what it requires, and my performing that is perfect obedience to the said Law. If the King's Law require one shilling Poll-Tax of me, eleven pence three Farthings, half farthing will not pay my due, nor be accepted." *Rejoynder*, p. 31.
112. John Preston, *New Covenant*, p. 216.
113. Vavasor Powell, *Christ and Moses*, p. 167.
114. John Ball, *Covenant of Grace*, p. 21.
115. Jeremiah Burroughs, *Saints Treasury*, p. 93.
116. Walter Marshal, *Sanctification*, p. 144.
117. Samuel Rutherford, *Survey*, Part I. p. 317.
118. Samuel Rutherford, *Survey*, Part II. p. 8.
119. Thomas Wilson, *Romanes*, p. 247.
120. Anthony Burgess, *Spiritual Refining*, "Of Sinne", pp. 119, 120.
121. *John*, in *Works*, p. 243.

in the spirit of this remark that John Owen declares that "a universal respect to all God's commandments is the only preservative from shame."[122]

Some discussion took place among the Puritans about the relation between the requirement of the Covenant and what it accepts. Thomas Blake says that, after thinking about it for "more then twenty years", he must conclude that "the Covenant requires no more then it accepts."[123] But it is hard to believe that he is right in this conclusion, and it is possible that he is confusing the things which belong to the sinner's entry into the covenant-relation with those which are expected of him once he is within it. It is undoubtedly to the sinner's entry into the covenant-relation that Thomas Blake refers when he speaks about the abundant grace of "the termes" upon which the sinner is freed "from the sentence" of the Law, but in addition to these terms of entry (sometimes called antecedent conditions) there are the duties of the covenant-life itself (sometimes called consequent conditions). Because of the gracious terms of entry, "no breach of Covenant" is caused by the believer's sins, but this does not alter the fact that they constitute "a transgression of the Law" of the covenant-relation itself. It is therefore untrue to say that "the Covenant requires no more then it accepts."

It is possible, however, that Thomas Blake means differently from what he says, because in the next few lines he speaks of "our inherent righteousnesse, which in reference to its rule labours under many imperfections."[124] What is "its rule" but that which is within the Covenant itself and confessedly requires more than it accepts? "God in Gospel-condescensions will have this rule eyed, with a single and upright heart universally eyed, and observed both in our returnes from sin, and in our application to God in new obedience."[125] This is the rule, he says, to which the believer must make a "sincere endeavour to conform". The "sincere endeavour", however, does not define what "the covenant requires", but merely indicates what God in His mercy will accept, and leaves the preceptive part of the Covenant of Grace identical with "the Moral Law". The Gospel "requireth perfection as well as the Law doth."[126] William Strong helps forward the explanation by saying,

> It is true, that perfect obedience . . . is required of us, as well as of Adam . . . but yet in the Covenant of Grace it is not required as the righteousness of the Covenant.[127]

122. *Indwelling Sin*, in *Works*, VI. 186.
123. *Covenant of God*, pp. 108, 109.
124. *Covenant of God*, p. 111.
125. Op. cit., p. 112.
126. Samuel Rutherford, *Survey*, Part II. p. 8.
127. *The Two Covenants*, p. 139.

Richard Baxter differs from the normal Puritan view by regarding the moral Law as informative only. He describes it as Christ's instrument "for direction to his Subjects", but that Christ "hath made it a proper part of his Gospel, not only as a Directory . . . but also as a Command: I am not yet convinced."[128] Most of the Puritans repudiated any suggestion of lowered requirements or change in the Law, and argued that what God in His grace will accept through the merits of Christ is one thing, but what His Law lays down as a requirement is another.

D. OBEDIENCE TO LAW AS LAW

The continuance of moral obligation in men implies, not only that the substance of the Law is to be understood as permanent, but also its law-form. The meaning of this for believers is that they will do what is right, not merely because it conforms to their renewed ideas, but because it is commanded. Whatever good action the believer performs, he "must doe it as his command",[129] for "Gods will is his Reason."[130] This is because "a law is a commanding thing" and "doth not barely notify";[131] it is "a binding rule, a rule with a strong obligation",[132] without which the Law is not the Law.

The Puritans frequently distinguished the "matter" from the "manner" of the Law, but stressed that obedience to the Law must be rendered "both in respect of the matter, and also the manner" of it;[133] it must be performed "because he willeth and commands it."[134] The Puritan pages are full of such exhortations. "Do not therefore this or that, because this will agree with thy ends . . . but do it because God hath required it.[135] "Whatsoever thou doest, doe it, because God commandeth thee."[136]

> The Substance and Matter of Obedience may be good, while the Circumstance and Manner is nought: . . . We must not only do *Bonum*, that which is good; but we must do it *Bene*, Well. God

128. *Aphorismes*, pp. 156–8; John Crandon answers Richard Baxter in a sarcastic passage in *Aphorisms Exorized*, Part I. pp. 214, 215.
129. John Preston, *Breastplate of Faith and Love*, "Of Love", p. 153.
130. Richard Baxter, *Directions for Weak Christians*, "Confirmed Christian", 1669, p. 58.
131. Thomas Jacomb, *Romans*, p. 109.
132. Thomas Manton, *Hundred and Nineteenth Psalm*, III. 172.
133. John Downame, *Guide to Godlynesse*, p. 15.
134. Anthony Burgess, *Spiritual Refining*, "Of Grace and Assurance", p. 70.
135. Anthony Burgess, op. cit., p. 70; cf. "Of Sinne", p. 77; Thomas Manton, *Ephesians*, in *Works*, II. 399.
136. Richard Greenham, *Of Good Workes*, in *Works*, p. 450; Thomas Taylor, *Progresse of Saints*, pp. 252, 254.

> delights to be served (as one saith) rather with Adverbs, then with Nouns or Verbs.[137]

It must be made manifest "not only that you do obey, but that you love the Commandement that you do obey",[138] because "you will labour, not only to obey God in the matter, but also in the manner of the command. . . . Our obedience must be grounded . . . upon a command."[139] It is possible that "hypocrites may perform the same Works for the matter, with true Saints; but they are defective in the manner of performance, wherein the excellency of the Work doth chiefly consist."[140]

This stress on the form of the Law as well as its matter led the Puritans to call for a complete abandonment of the believer to the authority of the commandment as such, and they affirmed it to be one of the marks of true believers that they perform, or refrain from, an action "when they see that it is the commaundement of him who loveth them most dearely."[141] Richard Sibbes says, "Our obedience must be . . . because he commands us",[142] for a "good conscience respects God and his command."[143] In *The Marrow, Evangelista* tells *Neophytus*

> You will do that which the Lord commandeth only because He commandeth it, and to the end that you may please Him; and you will forbear what He forbids only because He forbids it, to the end you may not displease Him. . . . The mind and will of Christ . . . is not only the rule of a believer's obedience, but also the reason of it, . . . so that he doth not only do that which is Christ's will, but he doth it because it is His will.[144]

Obedience, therefore, is to be given not merely on the basis of its congruity with reason, but ultimately on the authority of God.[145] It is to be rendered, not because of an inclination to do so, but solely because the Law of God requires it.[146] True obedience is "absolute" and can "admit of no discourse of reason", but whatever the appear-

137. Francis Roberts, *God's Covenants*, p. 452.
138. Jeremiah Burroughs, *Gospel-Conversation*, p. 40.
139. Thomas Brooks, *Cabinet of Jewels*, 1669, in *Works*, III. 340, 341; cf. *Heaven on Earth*, 1654, in *Works*, II. 472; *Apples of Gold*, 1657, in *Works*, I. 271; *Glory of Christianity*, in *Works*, IV. 146; Stephen Charnock, *Necessity of Regeneration*, 1683, in *Works*, III. 79.
140. Walter Marshal, *Sanctification*, p. 212.
141. Richard Rogers, *Seven Treatises*, Preface, cf. p. 79.
142. *Meditations*, 1638, in *Works*, VII. 207; cf. Thomas Manton, *Hundred and Nineteenth Psalm*, I. 36.
143. Richard Sibbes, *Demand of a Good Conscience*, 1640, in *Works*, VII. 486.
144. Op. cit., pp. 195, 212.
145. Anthony Burgess, *Vindiciae Legis*, p. 64; cf. John Ball, *Of Faith*, p. 67.
146. Samuel Bolton, *True Bounds*, p. 197.

ance of loss or gain "we are to doe the things that he injoyneth."[147] All is performed "in reference to God, and not for by-respects"[148] and

> Though our services may . . . meet with many discouragements and prejudices to us, yet so that by them God may receive glory, and I may expresse my obediential respect to him; here is winde enough to fill my sailes; I dare not do it, because God forbids; I will do it because God commands. . . . This is simplicity of obedience.[149]

Paul Baynes remarks that it is the Christian's "first vertue" when "wee love, desire, and doe any thing, especially because God commandeth and for that end."[150] Anything less than obedience because commanded is not holiness.[151] John Ball opens his treatise on the *Power of Godliness* in a similar manner by saying that conformity to the Divine will "is not to be reputed godliness, except man therein hath reall reference unto God."[152] "Many are damned for misdoing their good works, because they did them not in obedience to God,"[153] and Francis Roberts remarks epigrammatically, "Mis-Obedience offends God as well as Disobedience."[154] Some may do what they are told, but not because they are told; they "may have an eye to the command, when yet they obey not for the sake of the command", and there are those who obey "out of conscience so commanding, but not out of conscience of the command."[155]

The requirement, therefore, remains and the *Confession of Faith*, which describes the enabling grace of God, draws attention to the fact that what the believer does "freely and cheerfully" is at the same time that which "the law requireth to be done."[156]

To determine that Law is to be obeyed because it is Law is of primary importance, not only for a right understanding of Puritan "practical divinity", but for the establishing of an adequate Biblical doctrine of sanctification. The insistence on this truth carries the subject into the very heart of the believer and into the citadel of his will. Only the heart that can say, "I delight to do thy will, O my God",[157] can be adjudged to be truly converted and godly.[158]

147. John Downame, *Guide to Godlynesse*, p. 113.
148. Obadiah Sedgwick, *Anatomy*, 1660, p. 182.
149. Obadiah Sedgwick, op. cit., p. 213.
150. *Directions*, 1618, p. 131.
151. John Owen, *Holy Spirit*, in *Works*, III. 605.
152. Op. cit., p. 2 (unnumbered).
153. Richard Sibbes, *Christian Work*, 1639, in *Works*, V. 7.
154. *God's Covenants*, p. 716.
155. Thomas Goodwin, *Work of the Holy Ghost*, in *Works*, VI. 302.
156. Op. cit., XIX. 7.
157. Psalm xl. 8.
158. Further discussion of this Puritan conviction is to be found in the Conclusion.

E. LAW "IN THE HANDS OF CHRIST"

Because of easily-recognizable differences between the relation of men to the Law before and after faith, it became customary to speak of the believer as related to the Law "in the hands of Christ".[159] This phrase stood for the double notion of identity and difference: the identity was in the Law, and the difference was in the administration.

(i) *Christ as Lawgiver*

> Christ giveth not himselfe to any upon that condition, onely to save him, but we must take him as a Lord too, to be subject to him, to obey him, and to square our actions according to his will in everything. For . . . he will be a Saviour to none but those to whom he is a Master.[160]

In His "Regall Office" Christ is appointed "to be the Law-giver to the Church",[161] for, asks John Sedgwick, "Is not Christ as well a King and Lord as a Priest?"[162] John Barret "cannot but wonder any should question, whether the Gospel have the Nature of a Law",[163] and William Strong says that the "yoke"[164] which Christ invites men to take upon them when they come to Him

> is the obedience which in the Gospel the Lord requires, and that is nothing else but the obedience of the Law, for though Christ hath fulfilled it, yet it lies upon us still as a duty. . . . The Gospel requires obedience as well as the Law, and there is a Law of Christ to be kept, and there is a yoak of Christ to be born, (sic) and Christ that hath abolished the Law as a Covenant and a Curse, has established the Law as a rule of Gospel obedience.[165]

He who takes Jesus Christ as his Saviour, takes Him "*ipso facto*, as his Lord and as his Master."[166] Richard Baxter's "political" views of salvation find plenty of room for expression here, and leaving aside his opinion that the Gospel is another kind of Law, it is possible to agree with him that those who deny that the Gospel is a Law "do deny all our Christianity at once: For Christ is not Christ, if he be not

159. A. R. Vidler, *Christ's Strange Work*, p. 50 finds this thought first expressed by Origen, "it is Jesus who reads it to us".
160. John Preston, *Breastplate of Faith and Love*, "Of Faith", p. 42.
161. Nicholas Byfield, *Patterne*, p. 294.
162. *Antinomianisme Anatomized*, p. 34.
163. *Treatise of the Covenants*, p. 121.
164. Matthew xi. 30.
165. *The Two Covenants*, pp. 104, 158.
166. Thomas Goodwin, *Justifying Faith*, in *Works*, VIII. 325.

the King of the Church; nor is he King if he be not a Lawgiver; nor doth he Rule and Judge, if he have no Law."[167] The Puritans were unanimous in speaking of "the Law of the Covenant of Grace."[168] They recognized that "by the Law of Creation man oweth all Obedience to God", but contended that this obligation to obedience was "confirmed by Christ, and in the hand of Christ."[169]

(ii) "*In the law to Christ*"

The Puritan view of the relation of believers to the Law of God is well expressed by Thomas Taylor, who argues that the regenerate are never *sine lege*, nor are they *sub lege* in respect of justification, but they are nevertheless *in lege*, that is, within the compass of the Law for instruction, for subjection, and in so far as it is written within their hearts.[170] Anthony Burgess, too, compares the expressions, "of the law", "without the law", "under the law" and "in the law", and affirms that in 1 Corinthians ix. 21 the apostle "calleth himselfe excellently, ἔννομος τῷ χριστῷ";[171] and when Francis Roberts grapples with this expression of the apostle, he writes, "No Christian believer is said to be ὑπὸ νόμον under the Law, nor is he ἄνομος, without Law to God; but he is ἔννομος in the Law, or within the Law to Christ".[172] The same interpretation is given also by Thomas Manton in his commentary on *James*:

> The Gospel is a law. . . . So that they that are in Christ are not without a law, not ἄνομοι, but ἔννομοι. So the apostle, I Cor. ix. 21, "I am not without the law, but under the law to Christ"; that is, under the rule and direction of the moral law.[173]

There is no doubt that the Puritans rightly grasped Paul's meaning here. ἔννομος is the positive way of stating what was negatively expressed by the phrase μὴ ὢν ἄνομος, but because of the ambiguity of ἔννομος, aggravated by the unfortunate A.V. mis-translation, it is

167. Richard Baxter, *End of Doctrinal Controversies*, p. 149.
168. John Howe, *Blessedness of the Righteous*, 1668, in *Works*, II. 21–22.
169. John Barret, *Treatise of the Covenants*, pp. 21, 22.
170. *Regula Vitae*, pp. 31, 32.
171. *Vindiciae Legis*, p. 226. Χριστῷ is the Stephens' text, but most MSS have Χριστοῦ. This does not materially affect the meaning, and G. G. Findlay renders the expression "though I am not out-of-law in respect of God, but in-law (ἔννομος) in respect of Christ." (The Expositor's Greek Testament, edited W. Robertson Nicoll, II. 854). Alford regards θεοῦ and Χριστοῦ as genitives of dependence, and paraphrases the expression "a subject-of-the-law of Christ." He considers that the words are inserted rather to put before the reader the true position of a Christian with regard to God's Law revealed by Christ, than merely with an apologetic view to keep his own character from suffering by the interpretation of ἀνομία. *The Greek Testament*, Fifth Edition, 1865, II. 548.
172. Francis Roberts, *God's Covenants*, p. 729; on 1 Corinthians ix. 21.
173. *James*, in *Works*, IV. 163.

better to state the concept in its negative form and understand Paul to mean that he and other believers are "not outside" God's Law.[174]

(iii) *An abused concept*

The concept of the Law "in the hands of Christ" is open to misunderstanding, and it is because of the Antinomian readiness to employ it with a meaning that robs the Law of its commanding authority that Anthony Burgess is cautious in the use of it.[175] Against any such devaluation of the Law, he maintains that in the hands of Christ it is no less "law" than it was in the hands of Moses, for

> disobedience to it is still a sin in the beleever. . . . As for their evasion, it is a sin against the Law as in the hand of Christ, and so against the love of Christ, and no otherwayes, this cannot hold; for then there should be no sinnes, but sinnes of unkindnesse, or unthankfulnesse.[176]

John Barret attacks the author of *The Marrow*, but it seems also that he does not fully understand him, and regards it "intollerable" to oppose "the Moral Law, as in the hand of God-Creator to the same Law as in the hand of Christ."[177] Although the historical fact of *The Marrow* controversy suggests that many at that time thought that the author was an Antinomian, the perspective of later years acquits him of such a charge. In his dialogue, the author of *The Marrow* makes *Evangelista* say

> Wherefore, neighbour Neophitus, sith that you are now in Christ, beware that you receive not the Ten Commandments at the hands of God out of Christ, nor yet at the hands of Moses, but only at the hands of Christ; so shall you be sure to receive them as the law of Christ.[178]

He means by these words that the Law must be received by the believer only as part of the Covenant of Grace of which Christ is the Mediator. *Evangelista* thus replies to the legalism of *Nomologista*, not by throwing himself into the arms of the Antinomians, but by saying that the Ten Commandments "since Christ's coming in the flesh . . . are to be a rule of life to believing Jews and believing Gentiles unto the end of the world, not as they are delivered by Moses, but as they are delivered by Christ."[179] The mistaken pleasure of *Antinomista* at this is corrected by *Evangelista*, who points out not only that the Ten Commandments may most truly be called "the

174. Cf. a good discussion in F. Godet, 1 *Corinthians*, 1893, vol. II. pp. 38, 39.
175. *Vindiciae Legis*, p. 167.
176. Op. cit., pp. 221, 222.
177. *Treatise of the Covenants*, pp. 17, 22.
178. Op. cit., pp. 145, 146.
179. Op. cit., p. 147.

law of Christ", because Christ and the apostles employ them freely,[180] but that any release from those commandments which Christ brings is "only in the case of justification."[181] The author of *The Marrow* would undoubtedly agree with John Barret when he says,

> But I should think that believers as they are creatures, are bound to obey God in all things, and that Christ came not to take off the obligation to duty and obedience, but to take off the obligation to wrath and punishment.[182]

Simon Ford insists on the preaching of the Law to believers, but says

> Yet I must tell you, I would have the Law preached as it is in the hands of Christ, i.e. not as casting men under an irrecoverable condemnation for every offence, not as exacting rigorously every punctilio of a duty, under pain of being rejected by God, not as requiring obedience as a condition of a covenant of works to salvation.[183]

This is all that the author of *The Marrow* contends for, and is in agreement with most of the Puritans. Simon Ford, however, goes on to say that he thinks there is danger in the phrase "in the hands of Christ" when "it is grounded on a principle of Socinianisme."[184]

Provided the pitfalls of Antinomianism on the one side and of Neonomianism on the other be avoided, the conception of the Law "in the hands of Christ" is unexceptionable. It implies no change in the demands of the Law, nor in the obligation of the believer to recognize its binding authority, but signifies a different administration of it, with a different and deeper motive than is found outside of the experience of Christ. Robert Traill expresses this well when he says that, so far as the sanctification of believers is concerned, "the rule of their direction therein, is the holy spotless law of God in Christ's hand."[185]

F. THREATENINGS AND PROMISES OF REWARD

"The tamed horse needeth a spur, as well as the unbroken colt."[186] This is how Anthony Burgess picturesquely states the Puritan belief in the spiritual purpose of threatenings and promises, and he adds that although there is nothing servile in the obedience

180. Op. cit., p. 148.
181. Op. cit., p. 150.
182. *Treatise of the Covenants*, p. 24.
183. *Spirit of Bondage and Adoption*, pp. 34, 35.
184. Ibid. It is something of a Socinian understanding of the phrase that underlies Richard Baxter's views about the new Law of Christ. See chapter VI.
185. *Justification Vindicated*, in *Works*, I. 256.
186. *Vindiciae Legis*, p. 14.

of the believer, yet in so far as "he hath much flesh and corruption in him", he needs "so many sharpe goads" to provoke him "in the waies of piety."[187] "The tartnesse of the threatning makes us best tast the sweetnesse of the promise: Sowre and sweet make the best sauce."[188] The moral Law is still applicable to the believer in "its Minatory part", for "the carnall and unregenerate part of the godly, needs this whip"; but it also still applies to the believer in "its Promissory part", so that the godly may have an "eye to the recompense of reward."[189]

(i) *Threatenings*

One of the questions proposed for discussion by Samuel Bolton in *True Bounds*, is "Whether the freemen of Christ, may not sinne themselves into bondage again",[190] and he answers it in the affirmative, teaching that the believer can bring himself into bondage *by* sin, but not into the bondage *of* sin.[191] Vavasor Powell states categorically:

> There bee threatnings that doe belong to the Covenant of grace (or the Gospel) and these threatnings concerne those Beleevers that are under it; but yet they are not such threatnings as are the threatnings of the Law, viz. threatnings of damnation.[192]

The existence of sanctions, however, does not make the Gospel a law of works,[193] for such threatenings as are made to believers are evangelical in purpose. "The righteous ought to be awed with divine threatnings", because they are the "means appointed and blessed by God, to prevent their total Apostacy", and although to act only from fear "is the property of a slavish spirit", yet "to cast off all fear is the property of a vain, secure, and wanton spirit."[194]

As is to be expected, the Antinomians repudiated the idea of threatenings and scoffed at those who resorted to "the whippings of the law."[195]

(ii) *Promises of reward*

"The promises of the Gospell are not made to the worke, but to the worker", says William Perkins,[196] and by means of this distinction

187. Anthony Burgess, op. cit., p. 219.
188. John Ball, *Of Faith*, p. 422.
189. John Sedgwick, *Antinomianisme Anatomized*, p. 11.
190. Op. cit., To the Christian Reader.
191. Cf. op. cit., p. 226.
192. *Christ and Moses*, pp. 171, 172; cf. William Strong, *The Two Covenants*, p. 164; Thomas Brooks, *Precious Remedies*, 1652, in *Works*, I. 61.
193. John Owen, *Justification*, in *Works*, V. 160.
194. John Barret, *Treatise of the Covenants*, pp. 53, 55, 56.
195. John Eaton, *Honey-combe*, pp. 136, 137.
196. *Galatians*, p. 274.

he endeavours both to avert the danger of a return to legal concepts of merit and at the same time to provide place for God's love of complacency towards His obedient child. "If we have respect to all the Commandements, and labour faithfully to keepe them . . . then shall wee constantly enjoy all those blessings and graces, which God hath promised to his righteous servants."[197] It is "expedient to look to the prize",[198] and "to have an eie to the reward", although "this ought not bee our chief respect."[199] When Samuel Bolton teaches that it "may consist with our Christian freedome, to do duties with a respect to the recompense of reward",[200] he adds, "yet must wee not obey that we may have this promise: but rather having this promise, we must be quickened to obey."[201] Walter Marshal is bold enough to say that in this respect there is such a thing as "an holy Self-love."[202] To dismiss all love of reward as "mercenary love",[203] is unjustifiable, for there is nothing unspiritual about hoping for a reward that God has promised.

> If it were so, that men were not to obey with any respect to what God hath promised them . . . How great a part of Scripture is given to us in vain. . . . Shall we think that God hath made so many promises in vain. That those great and precious promises in Scripture are but Cyphers, and stand for nothing?[204]

It is therefore "not to be doubted but that the faithfull may encourage themselves in their well doing, by looking unto the reward set before them",[205] for "whatsoever God propounds as a motive to Duty, and whatsoever God promiseth as an encouragement or reward, on that the soul may most lawfully fix the eye."[206]

Richard Baxter is at home in this aspect of the Law of God in the believer's life. His contention that justification is perfected by the believer's own good works lends itself completely to the idea of rewards, but in this he goes far beyond the orthodox Puritans. He holds that the believer's acceptance at the judgment is according to his works.[207] "To deny the rewarding act, is to deny God's Law", for the believer's good works "have a moral Aptitude for that

197. John Dod and Robert Cleaver, *Ten Commaundements*, p. 374.
198. Richard Sibbes, *Philippians*, 1639, in *Works*, V. 111.
199. George Downame, *Justification*, p. 641.
200. *True Bounds*, To the Christian Reader.
201. Op. cit., p. 270.
202. Walter Marshal, *Sanctification*, pp. 31, 34.
203. John Barret, *Treatise of the Covenants*, p. 27.
204. Ibid.
205. Andrew Willet, *Hexapla: Romanes*, p. 137; cf. Richard Rogers, *Seven Treatises*, Preface; Samuel Rutherford, *Survey*, Part II. p. 9.
206. Obadiah Sedgwick, *Anatomy*, pp. 245, 246; cf. Thomas Blake, *Covenant of God*, p. 21.
207. *Aphorismes*, p. 317.

Reward." This moral aptitude is "pleasing to God" and is called "Worthiness." He remarks that "the ancient Christians did use the word Merit without any scruple", but the word has been brought into distaste by Popery. All the orthodox (who avoid the term merit) "confess the Rewardableness of our Obedience", and this is what "the ancient Christians meant by Merit."[208]

Most of the Antinomians were unable to accept the doctrine of rewards. Tobias Crisp warned his hearers that they should not look "that that Duty should bring any thing",[209] but Robert Towne did not mind speaking of the reward as of "meer grace" and "reckoned to the worker being in Christ."[210]

(iii) *Rewards of grace*

Penalty and reward spring from the same root, but their reasons are different. The penalty is by due, but the reward is by bounty.[211]

> We doe not all that is commanded but come short of our duty, and that which we doe is unperfect, and defective in respect of manner and measure; and therefore in justice deserveth punishment, rather than reward: and consequently the reward, when it is given, is to bee ascribed to Gods undeserved mercie and not to our merit.[212]

The reward is bestowed "for the faithfulnesse of the promiser, not for the desert of the worke",[213] and thus it is that "the Lord will richly cf his free grace reward these workes with glory and happinesse in his Kingdome", although "the strength of our title stand upon Gods free gift."[214]

The general Puritan position on the use of the Law in this way is summarized in the words of the *Confession of Faith:*

> The threatenings of it serve to shew what even their sins deserve, and what afflictions in this life they may expect for them, although freed from the curse thereof threatened in the Law. The promises of it, in like manner, shew them God's approbation of obedience, and what blessings they may expect upon the performance thereof.[215]

208. Richard Baxter, *End of Doctrinal Controversies.* pp. 291–4; cf. *Catholick Theologie*, Book II. pp. 226, 227.
209. *Christ Alone Exalted*, in *Works*, I. 73.
210. *Assertion of Grace*, p. 95.
211. Nehemiah Cox, *Of The Covenants*, p. 25.
212. George Downame, *Justification*, p. 470.
213. Thomas Taylor, *Regula Vitae*, p. 87.
214. John Downame, *Guide to Godlynesse*, p. 415; cf. Richard Baxter, *Aphorismes*, p. 137.
215. Op. cit., XIX. 6.

G. CHASTISEMENT

It was the belief of the Puritans that the believer's disobedience to the Law of God received Divine chastisement.

(i) *Antinomian denial of chastisement*

In spite of the care with which the Puritans defined their position, they were opposed in this by the Antinomians. John Eaton, for example, argues that the doctrine of chastisement puts things back to the schoolmaster stage, destroys true sanctification, and degenerates into legal preaching.[216] John Saltmarsh denies that God can be provoked to wrath by His children, and asks, "Can he love and not love?" He contends that the word "anger" cannot be used of God in relation to His children except as an allegory.[217] Tobias Crisp, however, writes with more caution[218] and even concedes that the curses of the law are salutary to the believer.[219]

These denials of the relation of chastisement to the sins of believers are based on the general Antinomian assumption that there are no such sins in God's eyes. When the Antinomians are confronted with the Biblical facts of the Divine chastisement of believers on this account, they deflect the force of this evidence by affirming that (*a*) such chastisements were confined to Old Covenant believers,[220] or (*b*) they applied to New Covenant believers before they were converted,[221] or (*c*) in the New Covenant instances it was a "mixed"[222] company of believers and unbelievers to whom the warnings were given, and therefore the chastisements were related only to the unbelievers in the mixed community.

(ii) *Chastisement related to sin*

The Puritans maintained that "God doth not afflict any but where there is sinne in the subject."[223] God's indignation against "the sins

216. *Honey-combe*, pp. 142–7.
217. *Reasons*, "Shadows Flying Away", p. 11; cf. *Sparkles of Glory*, p. 193.
218. *Christ Alone Exalted*, in *Works*, I. 18, 28–30.
219. Op. cit., IV. 92–93.
220. John Eaton, *Honey-combe*, pp. 99, 117, 121. Note the replies to this opinion in Anthony Burgess, *Justification*, Part I. pp. 27, 36, 46, 49, *Vindiciae Legis*, p. 216; Henry Burton, *Law and Gospel Reconciled*, p. 68, and Stephen Geree, *Plaine Confutation*, p. 20.
221. John Eaton, *Honey-combe*, p. 123.
222. John Eaton, op. cit., pp. 92, 93, 122, 133; Robert Towne, *Assertion of Grace*, p. 111. John Crandon, *Aphorisms Exorized*, Part I. p. 40 and Isaac Chauncy, *Neonomianism Unmask'd*, Part II. p. 68, both seem influenced by this view. Replies are found in Anthony Burgess, *Justification*, Part I. p. 34, and in the anonymous *Crispianism Unmask'd*, p. 43.
223. Anthony Burgess *Justification*, Part I. p. 30; William Ames, *Conscience*, Book II. p. 46.

even of his owne people" many times "enforces him" to raise up "adversaries" against them,[224] and when new sins break forth God cannot fail to "take notice of them."[225] The chastisement of God is the expression of His displeasure at sin, and His children "may contract a kinde of guiltiness unto them, so that they make their Father angry."[226] Although Christ has made satisfaction for all the believer's sins, it does not follow "that God therefore cannot . . . be angry with any of those, for whose sins Christ hath satisfied."[227]

(iii) *No vindicatory element in chastisement*

Thomas Goodwin distinguishes between wrath and anger in God, and says "not God's wrath, but an anger arising from love, is it that chastiseth us."[228] There are no "satisfactory" punishments,[229] for "the corrections of God's children, they come not from vindictive justice."[230] The Father sees sin in His children, but He does not see it "as a judge to punish."[231]

To the objection that, in his teaching about chastisement, he is confounding Gospel and Law, Anthony Burgess replies, "The Gospel and the Law are to be mingled in all spiritual administrations, but for different ends," but the affliction of believers for their sins does not make their crosses legal.[232] The justified believer who falls into sin does not lose his justification, but is put in "a state of suspension from all the effects of Gods grace in Justification. . . . He is under sequestration, though not ejection."[233] The believer's "wilfull oversights and defaults" provoke the Heavenly Father's "paternall indignation" against them,[234] but the afflictions thus experienced must not be received "under the law", and the child of God must know that even in God's hiding of His face He loves the believer

224. Robert Bolton, *Afflicted Consciences*, p. 96.
225. Thomas Goodwin, *Christ Set Forth*, in *Works*, IV. 65; cf. *Relapsing*, in *Works*, III. 413.
226. John Preston, *Breastplate of Faith and Love*, "Of Faith", p. 179; cf. Stephen Geree, *Plaine Confutation*, p. 11. John Ball, *Of Faith*, pp. 65, 105; *The Marrow*, p. 348; Thomas Edwards, *Gangraena*, p. 25.
227. Thomas Gataker, *Shadows without Substance*, p. 61. Cf. Thomas Watson, *Body of Divinity*, p. 174.
228. *Mediator*, in *Works*, V. 189.
229. Thomas Taylor, *Regula Vitae*, p. 101.
230. Richard Sibbes, *Judgment's Reason*, 1629, in *Works*, IV. 107; cf. Vavasor Powell, *Christ and Moses*, pp. 173, 175; Thomas Goodwin, *Child of Light*, in *Works*, III. 293, 294.
231. Henry Burton, *Law and Gospel Reconciled*, p. 15; cf. Edward Elton, *Gods Holy Minde*, "Prayer", pp. 87, 88; Samuel Rutherford, *Triumph of Faith*, pp. 23, 28. See the opposite view in Richard Baxter, *Aphorismes*, pp. 68, 69; *End of Doctrinal Controversies*, p. 255; *Confession*, p. 121.
232. *Justification*, Part I. p. 43.
233. Anthony Burgess, op. cit., Part I. p. 262.
234. Thomas Gataker, *Shadows without Substance*, p. 61. Cf. Henry Scudder, *Daily Walke*, p. 556.

still.[235] There is "a wide difference between a child *under* wrath, and a child *of* wrath."[236] God sends afflictions to His children "that by them, as the body by physicke, they may be purged from their sinfull drosse and feare him."[237] True believers receive whatever God sends, and "they murmure not against him, neither refuse to be chastised of him, but are thankfull."[238]

The continuance of the believer's moral obligation to fulfil the Law is thus one of the most established of the Puritan convictions, and to omit this from any appraisal of Puritan theology is to fail to do justice to the principles upon which the Puritans worked.

235. Walter Cradock, *Divine Drops Distilled*, p. 159.
236. Thomas Goodwin, *Child of Light*, in *Works*, III. 314.
237. Richard Rogers, *Seven Treatises*, p. 540.
238. Richard Rogers, op. cit., p. 542.

Chapter VI

CHRISTIAN LAW-KEEPING

Synopsis

A. LAW AS A RULE

(i) *Insufficiency of the inclination of the heart*
(ii) *Need for an objective standard*
(iii) *The way to salvation*

B. NEONOMIANISM

(i) *Views of Richard Baxter*
(ii) *Justification by evangelical works*
(iii) *Puritan rejection of Neonomianism*

C. EVIDENTIAL VALUE OF GOOD WORKS

(i) *Justification to be evidenced by sanctification*
(ii) *The believer's evidences to himself*
(iii) *Antinomian teaching about assurance*

D. IMPERFECT WORKS

(i) *Spiritual infirmity*
(ii) *The covering of the imperfections*
(iii) *Evangelical perfection*

E. EVANGELICAL OBEDIENCE

(i) *The Law established*
(ii) *The acceptability of good works*
(iii) *Activity in obedience*

Chapter VI

CHRISTIAN LAW-KEEPING

THERE has always been a tendency among the spiritually immature to "fall from grace"[1] and to seek to be "justified by the law".[2] In the minds of some, the possibility of this kind of legalism has inhibited them from the advocacy of Christian Law-keeping. But if it be true that the Christian is still duty-bound to do the will of God, then there can be no alternative to the keeping of God's Law, for "He that hath my commandments, and keepeth them, he it is that loveth me".[3]

The Puritans firmly believed that faith must express itself in obedience, and this chapter exhibits their convictions in this respect. The chapter begins by observing two opposite tendencies, the Antinomian reliance on the promptings of Christian inclination, and the Neonomian excess of emphasis on obedience to the Law. The Puritan doctrine of the evidential value of good works is next examined, together with the Antinomian denial of this. It is then shown that there is an evangelical obedience to be performed by believers which in spite of its imperfections, is acceptable to God.

A. LAW AS A RULE

(i) *Insufficiency of the inclination of the heart*

The Antinomians had a great distaste for the use of the Law as a rule of life and held that the only rule for the believer was the impulse of the Spirit within him through the inclination of his own heart. The contrast between the Puritan view and the Antinomian is well expressed by the retort against *Formalist* and *Hypocrisy* which John Bunyan puts into the mouth of Christian: "I walk by the Rule of my Master, you walk by the rude working of your fancies".[4] No small measure of contempt is discernible in Richard Byfield's reference to

> this notional, high-flown, conceited age wherein nothing is esteemed, but that which goes under the name of Mysterious, of a more spiritual dispensation, and above Scriptural.[5]

1. Galatians v. 4.
2. Galatians v. 4.
3. John xiv. 21.
4. *Pilgrim's Progress*, p. 40.
5. *Gospels Glory*, The Epistle Dedicatory.

James Durham writes similarly of those in whom "there is a great itching after some new and meer notional and a loathing of old and more solid and substantial things in Religion", and

> who someway disdain and account it below them to stay a while and talk with Moses at the foot of Mount Sinai, as if they could *per saltum*, or by one Falcon-flight come at the top of Mount Sion, and there converse with and make use of Jesus Christ.[6]

He rejects such proud subjectivism and affirms that "Obligation is not from our Vow, but from the Law."[7] Thomas Taylor rebukes the advocates of a "new Divinity" who say that the Christian "must not live by any rules, but by a wilde and spatious pretence of immediate, and enthusiasticall direction",[8] and affirms that

> To say, wee obey God by the spirit without a law or a commandement, is a meere non-sence: for is any obedience without a law? . . . What can bee more ridiculous than for a subject to professe obedience to his Prince, but yet hee will not bee under any law?[9]

Writing against the same "Antinomians" in 1646, Anthony Burgess says it is nothing but "falshood and arrogancy" for some to say "they are above Ordinances",[10] and when they put forward the judgment of their own hearts in the place of the Law, "this were to have the Sun follow the Clock".[11] Law in the heart does not render written Law needless. "The outward letter is a good book in the hand of the Spirit, to teach and guide believers what to doe, and how to doe."[12] "Our own desires and inclinations are not our rule",[13] and are insufficient as a guide to godliness.

> There must be also another Law written in Tables, and to be read by the eye, to be heard by the ear: Else how shall it be known to the rest of the Congregation, whether this man doth not swerve from the Law written in the heart, yea or not: Nay how shall the believer himself be sure that he doth not swerve from the right way wherein he ought to walk? . . . The Spirit, I grant, is the Justified mans Guide and Teacher: . . . But he teacheth them . . . by the Law and Testimony.[14]

6. *Law Unsealed*, To the Christian Reader.
7. Op. cit., p. 92.
8. *Regula Vitae*, pp. 139, 141. On his title page he describes those against whom he writes as "the pestiferous Sect of Libertines, Antinomians, and sonnes of Belial".
9. Op. cit., 183, cf. pp. 225–9.
10. *Spiritual Refining*, "Of Grace and Assurance", p. 563.
11. Op. cit., p. 363.
12. Vavasor Powell, *Christ and Moses*, p. 227.
13. Thomas Manton, *Hundred and Nineteenth Psalm*, I. 6.
14. Thomas Bedford, *An Examination*, pp. 15, 16.

"An outward authority" is needed "to quicken the Soul unto that unto which though by Grace it hath an inward affection, yet by reason of the powerful relliques of Corruption, that inward affection is not strong enough".[15] Thomas Bedford makes the important distinction that "To walk by Love, is the Duty of a Christian, not the Definition".[16]

The danger of being governed merely by the inclinations, however spiritual they may be, is pointed out by Samuel Rutherford, who says,

> If the Law in the heart be the onely Rule that obligeth a Christian, it must oblige as it stirreth and moveth us, then when it stirres or works not, it is no Rule; and if so, in all the sinnes committed by Christians, be they never so heynous, the Christian sinnes not; for he goes against no Law, nor any obliging Commandement.[17]

That is a true faith which, trusting no longer in the works of the Law and resting in the imputed righteousness of Christ, "doth notwithstanding looke upon the Morall Law of God as a rule of Christian conversation, and sanctification, acknowledging the conformity thereunto as a duty which God requireth of every true beleever".[18]

(ii) *Need for an objective standard*

In his famous work, *Seven Treatises,* Richard Rogers proceeds on the assumption of an objective standard and direction for the Christian life. He recognizes that some, "having given themselves such libertie in their lives, will thinke it strange that every day care should be had over their hearts and waies", but insists nevertheless that Christian life is "not at adventure, as every man thinks best, before he have learned how to goe about it, but to be directed therein by some certaine rules in the word of God, without which, he shall faile exceedingly, whosoever he be".[19]

The Law, therefore, is to be regarded as "so very necessary to all men in common, and to every Regenerate and unregenerate man in particular",[20] because it defines duty in such a way "that none are left to an Arbitrariness therein, but that all are tyed to a Rule".[21] The Law is that "perpetuall rule of Holinesse and Obedience whereby Man should walke and glorifie God",[22] and constitutes "an holy boundary"[23] that serves as a rule of safety. The guidance of the

15. Thomas Bedford, op. cit., p. 22.
16. Op. cit., p. 23.
17. *Survey*, Part I., p. 225.
18. Henry Burton, *Law and Gospel Reconciled*, p. 23.
19. Op. cit., pp. 295, 297; cf. pp. 311, 314.
20. James Durham, *Law Unsealed*, To the Christian Reader.
21. James Durham, op. cit., p. 184.
22. William Pemble, *Vindiciae Fidei*, p. 142.
23. Francis Roberts, *God's Covenants*, p. 681.

Spirit, which it is the privilege of believers to receive, "shuts them not from the guidance of the Moral Law",[24] for without the newly-written Law believers are "but Alphabetarians in Knowledge".[25]

"Such as are regenerate" find that one remedy against the assaults of sin is "to oppose the lawe . . . against the rebellion and loosenesse of the flesh . . . and to imbrace and keepe all his commaundements".[26] This keeps the conscience alert "so as it shal still accuse when occasion serveth; for the preventing of many dangerous sinnes which like wild beasts would make havocke of the soule".[27] It strengthens the believer to resist sin when he sees that "Gods Law runnes so straight against it".[28] The Law articulates the command in its forbidding and so "discovers the rebellion of the heart",[29] but the absence of the operations of the Law leaves men in ignorant presumption about themselves.[30]

> For if we know not the limits of Sin and Duty, what is required of us, and what is forbidden, it cannot be supposed, but that in this corrupted State of our Natures, we shall unavoidably run into many hainous Miscarriages. . . . That we might be informed what we ought to do, and what to avoid, it hath pleased God . . . to prescribe us Laws for the regulating of our Actions.[31]

God's covenant with Abraham required that he should be upright,[32] and the Mosaic Law is but an amplification of that rule, being given as "a rule of direction to them that be in Covenant,"[33] so that they

> might not thinke that God by making a gracious Promise, had utterly nullified the Law, and that now Men might live as they list; but that they might know these bounds prescribed them of God, within which compasse they were to keep themselves.[34]

"Jewrie" was thus "a little schoole set up in a corner of the world"[35] to teach God's people how they must walk well-pleasing to Him.

It was the custom in many Puritan homes to display large sheets, which were frequently headed, "Rules for Self-Examination", and

24. Francis Roberts, op. cit., p. 732.
25. Francis Roberts, op. cit., p. 1407.
26. William Perkins, *Golden Chaine*, in *Works*, pp. 96, 97.
27. William Perkins, *Of Conscience*, in *Works*, p. 659.
28. Thomas Taylor, *Progresse of Saints*, p. 79; cf. Thomas Brooks, *Precious Remedies*, in *Works*, I. 55.
29. Edward Elton, *Treatises*: "Complaint of a Sanctifyed Sinner", pp. 74, 75; cf. Thomas Manton, *James*, in *Works*, IV. 210, 217.
30. Edward Elton, op. cit., p. 88.
31. Ezekiel Hopkins, *Ten Commandments*, in *Works*, p. 53; cf. p. 59.
32. John Preston, *New Covenant*, p. 38; Francis Roberts, *God's Covenants*, p. 436.
33. John Ball, *Covenant of Grace*, p. 71; cf. *The Marrow*, 61–67.
34. William Pemble, *Vindiciae Fidei*, p. 142.
35. William Perkins, *Galatians*, p. 313.

described as "Necessary to be set up in all Men's Houses, for the Spiritual Benefit of their Families". In just such a sheet Thomas Taylor gives the following instruction: "Before you take in hand any thing, counsel with God's word if it be lawful".[36] Edward Reynolds illustrates this by saying that the Law is "added to the Gospell, as the Rule is to the hand of the workeman".[37] So clear are the instructions of the Law that

> it would guide aright every step which thou makest in the way which is called Holy, and is of that latitude for prohibition of sinne, and leading to purity and exact pleasing of God: That though we may see an end of all perfection, yet it is exceeding broad.[38]

It is "the royal Law to guide into all well-doing",[39] and "must be observed of all that will leade a godly life".[40]

> You cannot write without looking on your coppie, the best Saint cannot write one line without viewing and looking on his coppie for every letter. . . . Eyther eye Jesus Christ, and his example . . . or secondly, think of the rules of Jesus Christ. . . . When any case comes, follow not your lusts . . . but consider what is your rule, you walke by another rule.[41]

The true believer will keep himself continually under the test of these high demands, and will examine himself "by the commandements of the Law, but specially by the tenth, which ransacketh the heart to the very quick".[42] In this self-searching "it is very meete and convenient, that we passe through all the commandements of the morall law, laying them as most absolute rules to our hearts and lives".[43] Lest the believer should become falsely satisfied with his attainments, he must "compare, and examine, and measure himselfe, his wayes, and workes, by the Law of God; and hee shall there finde much matter of humiliation."[44] "This worke of humiliation" in the believer is effected "by the ministery of the law",[45] so that being

36. *Christian Practice*, 1688.
37. *Three Treatises*: "Sinfulnesse of Sinne", p. 388.
38. Robert Bolton, *Comfortable Walking*, p. 342.
39. Richard Byfield, *Gospels Glory*, p. 34. Cf. Paul Baynes, *Directions*, pp. 65, 71–83; *Ephesians*, p. 268; Thomas Watson, *A Body of Divinity*, pp. 22, 26; Samuel Slater: *The Two Covenants*, 1644, (pages unnumbered).
40. John Downame, *Guide to Godlynesse*, p. 94.
41. Walter Cradock, *Gospel-Holinesse*, "Priviledge and Practice of the Saints", pp. 242, 243. In this view of the use of the Law, the Puritans were close followers of Calvin, cf. *Inst.* II. vii. 13, 15.
42. William Perkins, *A Treatise*, in *Works*, p. 433.
43. William Perkins, *Two Treatises*, in *Works*, p. 543.
44. Robert Bolton, *Three-fold Treatise*, "Saints Guide", p. 140; cf. Richard Greenham, *Of Conscience*, in *Works*, p. 275.
45. George Downame, *Covenant of Grace*, p. 83.

sensitive to that Law, he will "make Conscience of small things, and never call anie sin little".[46] Christ died "not to blot out the sense of sin, but rather to quicken a Godly sense thereof",[47] and thus to strengthen holiness, for, says William Woodward, "where there is a golden Candlestick, there will be need of Snuffers, or clearer convictions of sin and righteousness".[48] Edward Reynolds alludes to this salutary ministry of the Law in the life of the believer and neatly says, "the same reason that compels men to come in, is requisite also to keepe them in."[49]

The Puritans wrote much on what they—echoing the Scripture phrase[50]—called "circumspect walking". John Preston entitles one of his sermons "Exact Walking", and teaches that "it is required of a Christian that hee walke with God exactly in all things".[51] This obedience must be exact even in the least things, "for there must be preciseness in keeping Gods Commandements".[52] "Every Christian man must walke warily. . . . The word ἀκριβῶς signifies, an accurate, and a strict walking".[53] It is the same word as used in Acts xxii. 3 where "Paul professeth he was brought up, κατὰ ἀκρίβειαν τοῦ . . . νόμου, 'according to the exact manner of the Law'."[54]

Exact walking requires the believer to exercise great care in learning his duty.

> For how can a man acknowledge the breach of that Law which he knoweth not? Or how can he serve God in the endeavour of the performance of it, unlesse he understand his Masters will?[55]

Ignorance does not absolve from responsibility, because

> whether we know Gods lawes or know them not, they still bind us. And we are bound not onely to doe them, but when we know them not, we are further bound not to be ignorant of them, but to seeke to know them.[56]

Care, first to know, and then to do the exact will of God lay at the

46. Jeremiah Burroughs, *Evil of Evils*, p. 449; John Owen, *Indwelling Sin*, in *Works*, VI. 197 f.
47. Samuel Rutherford, *Covenant of Life*, p. 221.
48. *Lord our Righteousness*, p. 59.
49. *Three Treatises*: "Sinfulnesse of Sinne", p. 380.
50. "Walk circumspectly", Ephesians, v. 15.
51. *Sermons*, "Exact Walking", 1631, p. 104; cf. Henry Scudder, *Daily Walke*, p. 7.
52. John Ball, *Power of Godliness*, p. 65; cf. Samuel Rutherford, *Survey*, Part II. p. 1 and the title of a sermon by Anthony Burgess, "A Plea for strictness in Religion", in *Spiritual Refining*, "Of Grace and Assurance", pp. 637, 642.
53. Thomas Taylor, *Circumspect Walking*, p. 3.
54. Thomas Taylor, op. cit., p. 4.
55. James Ussher, *Body of Divinitie*, p. 205.
56. William Perkins, *Of Conscience*, in *Works*, p. 622.

basis of Puritanism which, says R. B. Perry, "springs from the very core of the personal conscience",[57] and the large number of Puritan works on casuistry gives impressive evidence of the sensitivity of the Puritans in this respect.

Richard Baxter defends the need for a Law,[58] and his particular views are studied below, but his opinion of Law-keeping for justification detracts from the value of his evidence on the present subject.

There is a semblance of orthodoxy in Tobias Crisp when he says, "Let that Mouth be for ever stoped, that . . . shall be a means to discourage People from walking in the Commandments of God blameless",[59] and in his description of those commandments as the "way that God hath chalked out unto us",[60] but he confines his advocacy of the Law to "the matter of Obedience."[61] This same limitation of reference must likewise be understood when Robert Towne writes, "Let the Law then be still in full force and authoritie, and its very usefull to a Christian; I know none that teach otherwise",[62] and also when John Saltmarsh is willing to say that the Law tells the believer he sins.[63]

This use of the Law, both for instruction in righteousness and in heart-searching, produced in the Puritans those sterling qualities of character for which they have become renowned. They have sometimes been adversely criticized for their self-scrutiny in this way, but, as Edward Dowden says, "in a time of careless living and declining morals, the error of too scrupulous self-superintendence is not the most grievous error".[64]

(iii) *The way to salvation*

Obedience to the Law was often referred to by the Puritans as the way to salvation, an expression which was wholesome when understood correctly, but which, because of its ambiguity, occasioned much controversy.

There was no doubt among the Puritans that Christ alone was "the way",[65] but as practical theologians they were concerned to give guidance to spiritual pilgrims who desired to walk in Him.[66] Their ministry was to give directions for walking in the way, and by a

57. *Puritanism and Democracy*, p. 627.
58. See *Catholick Theologie*, Book I. Part 2, p. 42 f; and Book II. p. 243.
59. *Christ Alone Exalted*, in *Works*, I. 136.
60. Op. cit., I. 215; the phrase is also found in John Preston, *New Covenant*, p. 191.
61. Op. cit., IV. 93.
62. *Assertion of Grace*, p. 145; cf. p. 37.
63. *Free-Grace*, p. 128.
64. *Puritan and Anglican*, p. 20.
65. John xiv. 6.
66. Colossians ii. 6.

figure of speech the walking was spoken of as the way. The believer's obedience to the commandments of God was thus the-way-of-the-way, that is the way of life which was demanded by being in Christ. Stephen Geree supports this interpretation of the Puritan use of the term when he argues that Christ and good works are both the way, the latter being contained in the former.[67]

With this careful understanding of the words they were using, the majority of the Puritans spoke freely of obedience to the Law as the way to salvation. "Gods Commandements . . . are sayd to be the way; because they are the rules we ought to walke by. . . . This is the way, this is the path";[68] they serve "to teach us how to walke when wee are come to him",[69] and are thus "the high-way unto the kingdome",[70] and "Saints look upon Duties . . . as Bridges to give them a passage to God".[71] "Works" are a way to heaven, in the sense that a man's actions are spoken of as his "ways",[72] for "without observation in some measure to all the Commandments of God, we cannot enter into the kingdome of heaven".[73]

The Puritans were not unaware of the possibility of being misunderstood in a legalistic sense, and this made some of them uneasy about speaking of obedience in this manner. The author of *The Marrow* endeavours to preserve the Gospel against legalism by insisting on the difference between "Do this and live" and "Live and do this".[74] He does not like to speak of good works as "the way", but prefers to say that they are the "believer's walking in the way".[75] This is nothing more than a hesitation on the part of the author, and it is a gross misrepresentation of his views to regard them as Antinomian on this account.

As is to be expected, the Antinomians found difficulty in this kind of expression. Tobias Crisp interjects a disparaging reference to it when he says, "It is a received conceit among many persons, that our obedience is the way to Heaven",[76] and he reveals his characteristic fear of legalism by adding, "All this Sanctification of life . . . is the business of a person that he hath to do in his Way, Christ; but it is not the Way it self to Heaven".[77] Robert Towne rejects the use of the

67. *Plaine Confutation*, pp. 50, 51, 60.
68. John Preston, *New Covenant*, pp. 190, 191. James Durham speaks rather picturesquely of the two tables of the Law as "the two legs that Piety in practice walketh upon". *Law Unsealed*, p. 183.
69. John Dod and Robert Cleaver, *Catechism*, p. 4.
70. James Ussher, *Body of Divinitie*, p. 202.
71. Isaac Ambrose, *Prima, Media, & Ultima*, "The Middle Things", p. 33.
72. Anthony Burgess, *Vindiciae Legis*, p. 33.
73. John Ball, *Covenant of Grace*, p. 69.
74. Op. cit., p. 145.
75. Op. cit., p. 168.
76. *Christ Alone Exalted*, in *Works*, I. 45, 46.
77. Op. cit., I. 46.

word "way" to express this, and argues that in such a phrase as "the way to London" the word is used in a different sense from that in such a phrase as the "way of London", namely, the manner of life of the citizens.[78]

The Puritans, however, took pains to guard against misapprehension, and George Downame acknowledges that obedience "is not required unto justification and salvation as the condition"; and adds, "but the ability of performing obedience is the grace of the New Testament . . . and therefore our new obedience is required, as the fruit of our redemption, and as the way wherein wee being justified are to walke towards our glorification".[79] He deals with the legalistic misuse of the concept of the necessity of good works by showing that not all necessity is causal.

> The Asse and her colt were needfull for Christ going to Jerusalem, Shooes or bootes are needfull for him that travaileth. And such is the relation of the way to the journies end. Hee therefore that would goe to heaven, had need to goe the way which leadeth to it, that is, the way of good workes, which God hath prepared for us to walke in them.[80]

The good works of believers are necessary as a "consequent condition" of their justification,[81] but they involve no merit.

> A godly life, though it doe not merit everlasting happinesse . . . yet it is the way that leadeth us thereunto, in which, whoso travaile, shall at the end of their journey surely attaine to eternall blessednesse.[82]

Christian duty is thus "a way, not to the right of salvation, but to the actuall possession of it".[83]

B. NEONOMIANISM

That the Puritans held the doctrine of justification by faith does not need any proof, and it is no part of the present work to expound that doctrine. But some attention must be given to it in view of its close relation to their doctrine of the Law and the opinions of those

78. Robert Towne, *Assertion of Grace*, pp. 14, 87.
79. *Justification*, p. 443; cf. *Covenant of Grace*, p. 28.
80. Op. cit., p. 481.
81. Francis Roberts, *God's Covenants*, p. 788; cf. pp. 795, 1367; William Allen, *The Covenants*, pp. 56, 57; Richard Baxter, *Catholick Theologie*, Book I. Part 3, p. 100; John Flavel, *Vindiciae Legis & Foederis*, p. 35; John Barret, *Treatise of the Covenants*, p. 322; the *Confession of Faith*, XIX. 2.
82. John Downame, *Guide to Godlynesse*, p. 4.
83. Samuel Rutherford, *Triumph of Faith*, p. 131; cf. David Clarkson, *Justification*, in *Works*, I. 277, 297.

who attempted to introduce a doctrine of justification by obedience to a new Law.

Controversy here moved away from the Antinomians and centred in the views of those whom their opponents called Neonomians.[84] So intense was the feeling on this subject that Robert Traill says of "Mr Burgess and Mr Rutherford" that "if these godly and sound divines were on the present stage, they would be as ready to draw their pens against two books lately printed against Dr Crisp, as ever they were to write against the Doctor's book".[85] In the outbreak of the Crispian, or rather Neonomian, controversy at the end of the century, Isaac Chauncy was willing to represent himself in the dialogues of *Neonomianism Unmask'd*, under the description "Antinomian", understanding Antinomianism to be "a denial of the Justification of a sinner by our own works of the law."[86]

(i) *Views of Richard Baxter*

The chief apostle of Neonomianism was Richard Baxter, who put much stress on the distinction between God's "Preceptive Will" and God's "Will of purpose",[87] and used it to make room for a changing of the Law. On the assumption that the Law of God is of this rectoral and changeable kind, Richard Baxter evolves the following scheme of laws: (1) the Law of Nature, before man fell, and (2) the Law of Grace after the Fall. The Law of Nature is variously described by him as the Law of Creation, the Law of Innocency and the Covenant of Works, and he divides the Law of Grace into (*a*) the Law of lapsed Nature, (*b*) the Law of redeemed Nature, and (*c*) the "new law", or "law of Christ". He looks upon (*b*) and (*c*) as the first and second editions respectively of the "law of faith".[88]

Richard Baxter acknowledges that the Law of Innocency was "perfectly fulfilled" by Christ, who in this way put Himself in a position to be man's Saviour, but he denies that believers are justified solely on this ground.[89] The concept of the "Law of Grace" is introduced by Richard Baxter in order to provide for the adjustment of relations between God and fallen man, and its difference from the Law of Innocency lies in the two-fold fact of (*a*) the possibility of pardon, and (*b*) the relaxation of penalty. The possibility of pardon depends on faith and repentance, and the relaxation of penalty

84. Cf. a useful discussion in James Buchanan, *Justification*, pp. 176, 177, 183, 202, 203, 211.
85. *Justification Vindicated*, in *Works*, I. 261, 262.
86. Isaac Chauncy, *Fresh Antidote*, p. 3.
87. *Aphorismes*, p. 1; cf. *Confession*, p. 290.
88. The New Covenant is "the Law of Grace in the Second Edition", the first being that given to Adam immediately after the Fall. *Catholick Theologie*, Book I. Part 2, p. 42.
89. *End of Doctrinal Controversies*, pp. 243, 244.

depends partly on the death of Christ[90] and partly on the flexibility of Law. "When Threatnings are meerly parts of the Law, and not also predictions . . . of Gods purpose thereabouts, then they may be dispensed with without any breach of Truth".[91]

This new "Law of Grace" is universal in its scope: it was given to the entire race at the time of the Fall, it rests upon the universal redemption of mankind, and contains "positive Additions" to the Covenant of Innocency.[92]

> God brought all Mankind in Adam under a Law and Covenant of Grace . . . And this Law made to Mankind in Adam and Noahr was never repealed to the World, but perfected by a perfecte, Edition to those that have the Gospel.[93]

Because fallen man is unable to keep the first Law, "some alteration in the obligation" became necessary in order to bring the Divine requirements down to the level of what fallen man is "naturally capable of performing".[94] It is by this "Law of Grace" that sinners are at the last to be judged, for "it is not the same Law which condemneth us and justifieth us".[95] The result of all this is that righteousness is no longer eternal and unchangeable, but becomes merely relative.[96]

(ii) *Justification by evangelical works*

On the principles expounded by Richard Baxter, the ultimate justification of the believer is achieved by a combination of the merit of Christ and the believer's own good works in obedience to the new Law. He says there are two forms of righteousness: one is in freedom from penalty, and the other is in action. The believer receives only the former in Christ, but must achieve the other for himself.[97]

> To affirm therefore that our Evangelical or New Covenant-Righteousness is in Christ, and not in ourselves, or performed by Christ, and not by ourselves, is . . . a monstrous piece of Antinomian doctrine.[98]

90. He maintains that the death of Christ must not on any account be thought of as the bearing of the very same punishment which the sinner would have borne, but only such punishment as makes it consistent with God's rectoral purposes. *Catholick Theologie*, Book I. Part 2, pp. 38, 39. See above, pp. 141 f.
91. Richard Baxter, *Aphorismes*, p. 38.
92. Richard Baxter, *Confession*, p. 107; *End of Doctrinal Controversies*, pp. 131, 132.
93. Richard Baxter, *End of Doctrinal Controversies*, pp. 193, 194.
94. Richard Baxter, *Catholick Theologie*, Book I. Part 2, p. 29, and *End of Doctrinal Controversies*, p. 151. See Chapter IV.
95. *Catholick Theologie*, Book I. Part 2, p. 62; *End of Doctrinal Controversies*, pp. 151, 152, 154.
96. *End of Doctrinal Controversies*, p. 240.
97. *Aphorismes*, pp. 98–101.
98. Op. cit., p. 111; cf. Appendix, p. 76 ff.

There is no justification for the sinner "who hath not some ground in himself of personal and particular right and claim thereto":[99] he must have "a legal title" under the terms of the new Law.[100]

In all these opinions, however, Richard Baxter has no desire to do dishonour to the work of Christ. He acknowledges that the death of Christ is the sole ground of God's acceptance of the believer's good works, and it is for this reason that he insists that the believer's works must be understood to justify him evangelically, and not in any legalistic manner.[101] He contends that obedience to Christ's Law must never be misrepresented as "our own Righteousness",[102] because its acceptance by God is solely on the ground of "Christs Righteousness" as "the meritorious cause".[103] In view of his mixture of grace and works, it is possible that Richard Baxter deserves the retort which Isaac Chauncy makes to Daniel Williams, "I grant you deny Merit; . . . but this I tell you, it signifies not much to deny a Name to a thing whose Nature requires that Name if it be named aright".[104]

(iii) *Puritan rejection of Neonomianism*

The Puritans concur with Richard Baxter in the necessity for "Law-keeping" by the believer, but they reject his Neonomianism. They answer by saying,

> Call to minde that Christ is made unto thee holines, not as a new Moses to follow, but as a Messias to beleeve in, as the author and finisher of thy holines.[105]

They consider that "it is frivolous . . . to conceive the Gospel a new Law",[106] and they hold that Christ's new Commandment is none other than the old.[107] In so far as the commandment of Christ is "new", it may be so described, says Samuel Slater, "in regard of the principles, in the strength of which it is performed" and "in regard of the motives whereby it is urged.[108] Unmitigated censure of Richard

99. Richard Baxter, *Aphorismes*, p. 92.
100. Op. cit., pp. 95, 96, 102–108, 118, 119, 122, 123, 184, 196, 204, 230, 290, 312, 332; *Justification*, pp. 69–255, 259; *Catholick Theologie*, Book I. Part 2, pp. 68, 72; *Scripture Gospel Defended*, "Breviate of Justification", pp. 44, 46; *End of Doctrinal Controversies*, pp. 253, 290.
101. *Catholick Theologie*, Book I. Part 2, p. 23.
102. Op. cit., Book I. Part 3, p. 100.
103. *Catholick Theologie*, Book II. p. 252; cf. *End of Doctrinal Controversies*, p. 249.
104. *Rejoynder*, p. 6.
105. Richard Greenham, *Grave Counsels*, in *Works*, p. 32.
106. Thomas Taylor, *Regula Vitae*, p. 186; cf. James Ussher, *Body of Divinitie*, p. 203.
107. Francis Roberts, *God's Covenants*, pp. 721, 1365; cf. Anthony Burgess, *Vindiciae Legis*, pp. 184–92.
108. *The Two Covenants* (pages unnumbered).

Baxter is found in Thomas Edwards, who cannot tolerate his unfounded assertions about a "new Law" for justification of sinners.

> Do but observe the Apostle, Rom. 5. 19, who speaking of the Disobedience of one, and the Obedience of another, mentions not in the least any two distinct Laws . . . whence that by a Disobedience unto one of them many were made Sinners, and that by an Obedience to another of them, or some peculiar mediatorial Law, a remote meritorious Righteousness must come forth to make many righteous by a third Law; or that a former Law was vacated by Obedience to a middle Law, and all to bring in Justification by a third Law. . . . It is an Antinomianism of the worst sort, and most derogatory unto the Law of God, which affirms it to be divested of its Power, to oblige us unto perfect Obedience. . . . There is no Medium.[109]

To advocate justification by imperfect works of evangelical righteousness is to make "the starres shine when the Sunne is in its full lustre",[110] for "that cannot be a Condition of Justification which it self needeth Justification".[111] "Let the Law of Moses", therefore, "keep its own place, and be the rule of our sanctification; but in our justification, it hath no room at all.[112]

Both the appeal and the weakness of Neonomianism lie in its endeavour to cut the knot rather than patiently untie it. Throughout the centuries of Christian thought, it has been recognized by the wisest and deepest thinkers that the right holding together of the requirements of the Law and the liberty of the Spirit is one of the harder tasks in theology.[113] In this aspect of his thought Richard Baxter follows the same theological pattern as he does in his acceptance of Amyraldian ideas on the plan of salvation: his solution of the problem is too easy. As with Amyraldianism, so with Neonomianism, there is a philosophical attractiveness about it, but it is not easy to find support for it in Scripture. Neonomianism fastens on the occurrence of the word "law" in the New Testament, and then proceeds to identify "law" and "gospel" without sufficient reason. After this, it is not a long step to a legalistic concept of salvation by human effort.

109. *Baxterianism Barefac'd*, The Introduction, vii. and p. 73. By "Medium" he means middle path.
110. Anthony Burgess, *Justification*, Part II. p. 232.
111. Anthony Burgess, ibid.
112. Robert Traill, *Galatians*, in *Works*, IV. 200; *Justification Vindicated*, in *Works*, I. 293.
113. Cf. Luther, *Galatians*, p. 24.

C. EVIDENTIAL VALUE OF GOOD WORKS

Although the believer's good works have no justifying efficacy, they are not without their value as evidence of justification.

(i) *Justification to be evidenced by sanctification*

It was the common dictum of the Puritans that godly life was the evidence of faith. "It is vaine to thinke we have faith without a new life",[114] because good works are "The Markes of a Righteous Man".[115] It is consistently expressed throughout the Puritan writings, that "our new obedience or practice of good works is the fruite and end of our redemption."[116] By walking in perfection Abraham showed that he was God's,[117] for "when a Man beleeves, workes will follow".[118] "A disposition to good workes is necessary to justification, being the qualification of an active and lively faith",[119] and they "testifie or give proofe that faith is lively."[120] The assurance of "no condemnation"[121] is given not merely to those "who believe", but "to those who walk not after the flesh, but after the Spirit."[122] Good works are the "Signs" of grace,[123] for "as the Sun can never be without light; so neither can this righteousnesse be without true holinesse."[124]

> Tho' we are not saved by good Works as procuring Causes, yet we are saved to good Works as Fruits and Effects of Saving Grace, which God hath prepared that we should walk in them, Eph. 2. 10.[125]

"The garments of Christs righteousness must not be made a cloak for sin",[126] and Christians must "prove their Mystical Union with Christ by their Moral Union."[127] Robert Traill says with keen insight, "When the law is written in the heart, it is copied out in the life."[128]

114. Richard Rogers, *Seven Treatises*, p. 78.
115. Richard Greenham, Title of a sermon, in *Works*, p. 148.
116. George Downame, *Covenant of Grace*, p. 67; cf. *Justification*, pp. 78, 79, 331, 372, 373.
117. John Preston, *New Covenant*, p. 4.
118. John Preston, *New Covenant*, p. 363; cf. *Breastplate of Faith and Love*, "Of Love", p. 212; William Ames, *Marrow of Sacred Divinity*, p. 200.
119. John Ball, *Covenant of Grace*, p. 20; William Allen, *The Covenants*, pp. 52, 136; Richard Allen, *Antidote against Heresy*, pp. 77, 78.
120. John Ball, *Covenant of Grace*, p. 73.
121. Romans viii. 1.
122. Cf. Richard Byfield, *Gospels Glory*, p. 10.
123. Anthony Burgess, *Spiritual Refining*, "Of Grace and Assurance", p. 43; cf. pp. 61–66, 304, 386.
124. Anthony Burgess, *Justification*, Part II. p. 122a; cf. Question 29 of *The A, B, C, or Catechisme for Yong Children*, quoted by A. F. Mitchell, *Catechisms*, p. 272.
125. Walter Marshal, *Sanctification*, p. 148.
126. William Woodward, *Lord our Righteousness*, p. 76.
127. Thomas Gouge, *Principles of Christian Religion*, p. 110.
128. *Justification Vindicated*, in *Works*, I. 278.

> You may know there is life by the beating of the pulses: a living faith will be active, and bewray itself in some gracious effects. . . . New obedience is an inseparable companion of justification.[129]

(ii) *The believer's evidences to himself*

Good works have meaning to the believer as a testimony within himself. Without an upright heart, says Richard Greenham, "Wee cannot assure our selves to be justified and sanctified in Christ Jesus",[130] and so he urges, "Make your election sure by good workes, 2 Pet. 1. 10 as by a signe consequent, not as by a cause antecedent".[131]

> No man can have assurance, that he is justified, unlesse he be in some measure sanctified. . . . Dost thou . . . endeavour to keepe a good conscience and to walke uprightly before God; then it is certaine, that thou art justified.[132]

Among the provisions of the Lord for His people against an evil day are "a sincere respect to all Gods Commandements, a carefull performance of all spirituall Duties", and "a conscionable partaking of all Gods Ordinances".[133] Therefore, says Richard Sibbes,

> Labour to grow in faith and obedience, that we may read our evidence clearly; that it be not overgrown with the dust of the world.[134]

Works of evangelical obedience have the power to "justifie faith to a mans own conscience",[135] but the Christian is to beware of "forcing" himself to obedience to the commandments in order to produce "evidence" to himself.[136] It would be fair to say that the Antinomian objection to the evidential value of the believer's works—to be noticed below—is largely directed against this "forcing". Nevertheless, "a constant delight in the law of God"[137] is one of those evidences

129. Thomas Manton, *James*, in *Works*, IV. 237, 264; Thomas Watson, *A Body of Divinity*, pp. 90, 108, 159, 171; John Owen, *Justification*, in *Works*, V. 73; David Clarkson, *Justification*, in *Works*, I. 277; *Truths Victory*, p. 132; Obadiah Grew, *Sinner's Justification*, pp. 113, 188, 211 and the summary in the *Confession of Faith*, XVI. 2. E. Brunner maintains that the view of "good works" as proofs of election does not go back to Calvin, but belongs to "Reformed thinkers after Calvin", *Divine Imperative*, p. 594.
130. *Notes of Salvation*, in *Works*, 202.
131. *Good Workes*, in *Works*, 451. Cf. Richard Rogers, *Seven Treatises*, p. 205.
132. George Downame, *Covenant of Grace*, pp. 35, 38.
133. Robert Bolton, *Afflicted Consciences*, pp. 44, 45.
134. *Precious Promises*, in *Works*, IV. 138.
135. John Sedgwick, *Antinomianisme Anatomized*, p. 24.
136. *The Marrow*, p. 205.
137. Thomas Taylor, *Progresse of Saints*, p. 13.

without which "we cannot solidly perswade our selves that we are actually and effectually Christs New-Covenant-people".[138] The believer must look for the "fruits of the Spirit" in his life, because "though the Spirit testifie immediately, yet it submits the trial of his own testimony to his works."[139] The evidence of sanctification is less exposed to the questionings of "a mans own cavilling heart" than the "immediate" testimony of the Spirit, and so the believer should direct his attention to the former as well as to the latter, because "this is certain, the more holinesse, the more assurance".[140] Thomas Goodwin charmingly says that the believer's graces and duties are the "daughters of faith", who "may in time of need indeed nourish their mother".[141] "Faith and obedience once proved to be true and genuine, are good evidences of our interest in Christ",[142] "for our Fruit will shew upon what Root we grow".[143] Robert Traill uses another metaphor and says, "The evidences of a Christian are not his charters for heaven, (the covenant of grace contains them); but they are as light, by which a Christian reads his charters."[144]

(iii) *Antinomian teaching about assurance*

The Antinomians denied the evidential value of good works and regarded "all notes and signes of a Christians estate" as "legall and unlawfull".[145] The believer must therefore obtain his assurance from the testimony of the Spirit who "giveth such full and cleare evidence" of his good estate, that he has "no need to be tried by the fruits of sanctification".[146]

John Saltmarsh says that Paul's phrase, "such were some of you" in 1 Corinthians "is not a method of personal assurance, but merely an expression to describe the outward state of the Church. It is a false basis of spiritual comfort and an occasion of distress".[147] Tobias Crisp likewise affirms that "Inherent Qualifications are doubtful Evidences for Heaven",[148] and although he acknowledges that the Christian walks by the rule of the commandments for his conversa-

138. Francis Roberts, *God's Covenants*, p. 725.
139. Simon Ford, *Spirit of Bondage and Adoption*, p. 223.
140. Simon Ford, op. cit., p. 233, 234, 320; cf. Thomas Gouge, *Principles of Christian Religion*, p. 116; Thomas Wilson, *Romanes*, p. 253; Thomas Brooks, *Precious Remedies*, in *Works*, I. 79; Isaac Ambrose, *Prima, Media, & Ultima*, "The Middle Things", pp. 11, 12
141. Thomas Goodwin, *Christ Set Forth*, in *Works*, IV. 13.
142. Thomas Cole, *Faith*, 1689, p. 44.
143. *Crispianism Unmask'd*, p. 56.
144. *Throne of Grace*, 1696, in *Works*, I. 228; cf. *Justification Vindicated*, in *Works*, I. 255, 278, and *Galatians*, in *Works*, IV. 162.
145. Thomas Edwards, *Gangraena*, p. 24.
146. Thomas Welde, *Rise, reigne, and ruine*, p. 14.
147. John Saltmarsh, *Free-Grace*, p. 55.
148. *Christ Alone Exalted*, in *Works*, II. p. 444.

tion, he denies that he "walks by such a rule for his Peace".[149] Robert Towne reverses the normal way of expressing the subject of evidences and declares that the believer must first have assurance about his faith before ever he can hope to find any from his works.

> I must first know that I have faith . . . else all such signs will leave me uncertain. . . . For, as this Argument holdeth not, Here is light, therefore the Sun is up: for all light is not from the Sun; the Moon, and the Candle have proper lights also: so all that we call graces . . . come not from faith, nor are not only found to be in him, who is in a justified estate, and therefore cannot convincingly argue such an estate.[150]

In his *Conference*, Henry Denne tells the "sick man" that "workes indeed are an evidence of Faith among men. . . . But Faith is an evidence of our works in the Court of Conscience, and judgement of certeinty". He explains that sorrow for sin, zeal, and love to God's people are but tokens "whereby we know one another to be the children of God".[151]

The utmost that the Antinomians would concede about the believer's good works was that they supplied evidence only "to manward". They argued that (*a*) God does not need any evidence, for the believer is accepted as clothed with the wedding garment of Christ's righteousness; (*b*) the believer is not in a position to interpret the evidence, because he can be so easily deceived; and therefore, (*c*) good works are of evidential value only to others. "Wee cleanse, and mortifie, and purifie ourselves only Declaratively to the sight of men", and the Holy Spirit "enables us by walking holily and righteously, to avoyd and purifie out of our own sight, sense, and feeling, and out of the sight of other men, that sin which the wedding-garment hath purified and abolished before, out of the sight of God".[152] The phrase "declaratively to manward" occurs with monotonous frequency in the *Honey-combe*,[153] and, on James ii. 14, John Eaton makes the comment,

> He saith not, shew God thy faith by thy works, nor shew thy selfe thy faith by thy works; but shew me, that am thy Christian minister . . . or thy Christian neighbours.[154]

The Antinomian motive was the praiseworthy one of desiring to exclude all "confidence in the flesh" and at the same time to comfort

149. Op. cit., II. 465; cf. John Gill on these passages, in Tobias Crisp, *Works*, (ed. Gill) II. 82, 97, 110.
150. *Re-assertion*, pp. 26, 27; cf. John Eaton, *Honey-combe*, p. 115.
151. Op. cit., pp. 8–14.
152. John Eaton, *Honey-combe*, pp. 164, 165; cf. 30, 91, 307, 308.
153. Cf. *Abraham's Steps of Faith*, p. 192; *Dangerous Dead Faith*, p. 160.
154. John Eaton, *Dangerous Dead Faith*, pp. 162, 163.

the trembling believer against the fears arising from "a legalistic pre-occupation with sins".[155] A rigid morality sometimes results in "anxious introversion" and it was the Antinomian attempt to avoid this "troubled mind" complex which led eventually to Quakerism.[156]

The orthodox Puritans followed a middle course between Neonomianism on the one side and Antinomianism on the other. They had the support of Calvin in their views both against Antinomianism[157] and against Neonomianism.[158] Subsequently, however, the Neonomianism of Richard Baxter gained ascendancy and became part of the teaching of Methodism.[159]

Considerable sympathy can be extended to the Antinomian distrust of the evidence of good works, but although assurance may not be built on this ground alone, it is, nevertheless, necessary to insist that the evidence of good works shall at least be regarded as a *sine qua non*. It would not appear to be an over-simplification to say that this is fundamentally all that the Puritans were concerned to maintain. The truth is that without good works there is no evidence of new life, but that with this external evidence there must be also the witnessing of the Spirit of God "with our spirit, that we are the children of God".[160] Assurance is something deeper than the collecting of evidence, and this is the important spiritual reality to which the Antinomians direct attention.

D. IMPERFECT WORKS

It was the view of the Puritans that though the demands of the Law were not diminished in the least, yet, for Christ's sake, "God will accept of our imperfect obedience, if it be sincere".[161]

(i) *Spiritual infirmity*

The Puritans were keenly aware that the requirements of God's Law still called for a perfection which the believer could not reach,[162] and, therefore, that his best works fell far short of legal perfection.

> The matter of our sanctification is . . . a righteousnesse which is but begun in us, and that new obedience, which though it be sincere and unfained, is with great infirmity performed by us.[163]

155. J. I. Packer, op. cit., p. 405.
156. G. F. Nuttall, "Law and Liberty in Puritanism", *Congregational Quarterly*, XXIX. 1. p. 26.
157. *Inst.*, II. vii. 4–12.
158. *Inst.*, II. viii. 7.
159. Cf. J. Fletcher, *Check to Antinomianism* in *Works*, I. 202, 239, 293–320, 356–8; II. 31, 32, 417, 439, 442, 453, 466.
160. Romans viii. 16.
161. William Perkins, *Of Conscience*, in *Works*, 646.
162. John Crandon, *Aphorisms Exorized*, Part I. p. 209; and Anthony Burgess, *Vindiciae Legis*, p. 218.
163. George Downame, *Justification*, p. 77.

The utmost that believers do is "imperfect",[164] and "the most holy faile alwaies in their best duties".[165] Their obedience is "weak",[166] and is but a "measure of obedience".[167] The godly fulfil all the commands of God in the main substance, but their deeds are defective on account of the "stubs and reliques" of original corruption.[168] "Sin hath so lamed and crippled us, that we shall never perfectly recover our legs while we live; but shall go lame to our graves."[169]

(ii) *The covering of the imperfections*

Such is the compassion of God that "our unperfect obedience is accepted of God in Christ".[170] It is "for his sake" alone[171] and "through Christ his intercession",[172] that the believer's works are "accepted through grace".[173] It would be folly, however, says Jeremiah Burroughs, to think that God's mercy is "added" in order to "eke out what we are wanting in for our justification",[174] for God does not look upon the obedience of believers as merely theirs, but sees it as "his owne worke in them".[175] The studied words of the *Confession of Faith* state the Puritan conviction unambiguously.

> Yet notwithstanding, the persons of believers being accepted through Christ, their good works also are accepted in him; not as though they were in this life wholly unblameable and unreproveable in God's sight; but that he, looking upon them in his Son, is pleased to accept and reward that which is sincere, although accompanied with many weaknesses and imperfections.[176]

164. John Ball, *Covenant of Grace*, p. 135; Anthony Burgess, *Spiritual Refining*, "Of Grace and Assurance", pp. 62, 63; Edward Elton, *Treatises*: "Complaint of a Sanctifyed Sinner", p. 176; *Treatises*: "Triumph of a True Christian", pp. 32, 51; *The Marrow*, pp. 342–5; Richard Baxter, *Catholick Theologie*, Book I. Part 2, p. 5; Francis Roberts, *God's Covenants*, p. 874.
165. John Ball, *Catechism*, p. 36, cf. *Grounds of Christian Religion*, p. 237.
166. John Ball, *Of Faith*, p. 368.
167. Edward Elton, *Treatises*: "Triumph of a True Christian", p. 33.
168. Anthony Burgess, *Spiritual Refining*, "Of Grace and Assurance", pp. 638, 639; John Downame, *Guide to Godlynesse*, p. 78.
169. Thomas Gouge, *Principles of Christian Religion*, p. 228.
170. George Downame, *Justification*, p. 495; James Durham, *Law Unsealed*, p. 3; Anthony Burgess, *Vindiciae Legis*, p. 218; William Ames, *Marrow of Sacred Divinity*, p. 196; *Conscience*, Book III. pp. 61, 62; John Dod and Robert Cleaver, *Ten Commaundements*, p. 374; Tobias Crisp, *Christ Alone Exalted*, in *Works*, IV. 94.
171. John Barret, *Treatise of the Covenants*, p. 77.
172. Ezekiel Rogers, *Chief Grounds*, quoted in A. F. Mitchell, *Catechisms*, p. 62.
173. John Ball, *Power of Godliness*, p. 63.
174. Jeremiah Burroughs, *Saints Treasury*, p. 44.
175. Thomas Taylor, *Regula Vitae*, p. 11.
176. Op. cit., XVI. 6. A. F. Mitchell and J. Struthers in *Minutes*, p. 278, give an earlier form of this paragraph in which any ambiguity in the word "they" is removed by the phrase "their works".

The mistake must not be made of confusing God's acceptance of the believer's sincere obedience with the Antinomian idea of "all our works, vocations, affaires and businesses" being "made perfectly holy and righteous",[177] for the sin in these things can only be condemned.[178] "Whatever is of self, flesh, unbelief (that is, hay and stubble)—that he consumes, wastes, takes away"; but in the time of reckoning and reward "the saints' good works", being of the Spirit, "shall meet them one day with a changed countenance, that they shall scarce know them."[179]

(iii) *Evangelical perfection*

Thomas Blake acknowledges the mercy of God who condescends "through rich grace to crowne weak obedience", and then adds the striking sentence, "in this sense our imperfection hath its perfectnesse."[180] This "perfectnesse" led to the concept of "evangelical perfection", the constitutive quality of which is sincerity.[181]

Evangelical perfection, says Thomas Gouge, is the "sincere desire" and "earnest endeavour" to obey, "with godly sorrow and grief of heart for our failings" and "trusting upon Christ for acceptance of our imperfect performances".[182] There may be much failure,

> yet if God can spy out but the least good thing in thee, he will take notice of that, and cast away all the evil: if God sees but anything of his own spirit in thee, he will be sure to take notice of that. If there be but one dust of Gold . . . God will not loose it, but will finde it out. . . . If there be but a will, a desire in thee, God accepts that will for the deed.[183]

The "perfection" of the child of God in this life is "a perfection of parts", not "of degrees"[184] and although not sinless it is "blamelesse".[185] The Puritans recognized a kind of perfection of the way, and although no believer can reach "an absolute unspottednes", yet "to that perfection which the Scripture taketh for soundnes, trueth, and sinceritie of heart, which is voide of carelesse remisnes, wee may come."[186]

177. John Eaton, *Honey-combe*, p. 321. See above, pp. 97, 98.
178. See above, pp. 97, 98.
179. John Owen, *Communion with God*, in *Works*, II. 171.
180. *Covenant of God*, p. 111.
181. Cf. John Ball, *Covenant of Grace*, pp. 134, 135.
182. *Principles of Christian Religion*, p. 228; cf. Thomas Watson, *A Body of Divinity*, p. 110; John Calvin, *Inst.*, II. vii. 4; III. xix. 5.
183. Jeremiah Burroughs, *Saints Treasury*, pp. 101, 102. It is a little strange to find Henry Denne using this last sentence in *Conference*, p. 6.
184. Williams Perkins, *Galatians*, p. 271; cf. John Preston, *New Covenant*, pp. 215, 216.
185. Anthony Burgess, *Spiritual Refining*, "Of Grace and Assurance", p. 64.
186. Richard Greenham, *Sweete Comfort*, in *Works*, p. 134.

God will passe by the imperfections which he espieth in the best service of his Children, when once he seeth their hearts to be intire and perfect towards him. . . . The Widowes Mite was little in worth, had not her good heart raised its price.[187]

The acceptability of sincerity is taught by Richard Sibbes,[188] Edward Elton,[189] John Preston,[190] Thomas Goodwin,[191] Francis Roberts,[192] William Perkins[193] and a great many others. Richard Baxter, however, goes beyond most of the Puritans, and affirms that sincerity is perfection, "not as it is accepted instead of perfection, but as it is truly so."[194]

Sincerity reveals itself in a number of ways and is described as "without hypocrisie", "soundnes", "simplicitie", "singlenesse of heart",[195] "integrity",[196] and as "loving God above all; or as the chiefe Good".[197] The believer's new obedience "is not to bee measured by the perfect performance, but by the sincere and upright desire and purpose of the heart. For this uprightnesse goeth under the name of perfection".[198]

The chief feature of sincerity is that of the general direction of the believer's desire and purpose.

A man hath a pure heart, though there be corruption there, when . . . the very streame of the heart is pure, and holy: . . . There is somthing in a pure heart that opposeth sinne, and opposeth temptation; there is some *non ultra* in the heart of a godly man: Sinne gets the advantage over his eyes, and over his hand, and over his tongue; but there is a baracado in his heart that it can goe no farther.[199]

This direction of spiritual desire is seen in the fixity of "uniforme constant obedience".[200] John Preston says, "we are not to be judged by a few actions, and a few paces, but by the constant tenor of our life",[201] and he gives the following illustration of what is often the

187. John Ball, *Power of Godliness*, pp. 41, 42.
188. *Bruised Reed*, in *Works*, I. 69.
189. *Treatises*: "Complaint of a Sanctifyed Sinner", p. 176.
190. *New Covenant*, pp. 236, 241–4, 345.
191. *Ephesians*, 1681, in *Works*, I. 81.
192. *God's Covenants*, pp. 176, 475 f., 888 f.
193. *Reformed Catholike*, in *Works*, 719.
194. *Aphorismes*, p. 133.
195. John Preston, *New Covenant*, pp. 2, 223–5.
196. Francis Roberts, *God's Covenants*, p. 489.
197. Richard Baxter, *Aphorismes*, p. 286.
198. George Downame, *Justification*, p. 235; cf. John Downame, *Guide to Godlynesse*, p. 405; Henry Scudder, *Daily Walke*, pp. 319, 320.
199. Walter Cradock, *Gospel-Holinesse*, p. 52; Thomas Taylor, *RegulaVitae*, p. 130.
200. John Ball, *Of Faith*, p. 367.
201. *New Covenant*, p. 210.

experience of the believer. "As if a man be sailing into France, a tempest driveth him into Spaine, so the Saints face is towards heaven but a suddaine passion may drive them another way."[202]

E. EVANGELICAL OBEDIENCE

(i) *The Law established*

The obedience of the believer, that is to say, "the righteousnesse by which wee are sanctified, is prescribed in the Law",[203] and so "we establish the law".[204]

> In that legall perfection which God requireth: this godly life is an absolute conformitie of all our actions . . . unto the will of God . . . as it is revealed . . . in the Decalogue.[205]

The believer gives himself to that love for God which is "the keeping and fulfilling of all the Commandements of God",[206] in a "new obedience".[207] "Evangelical Grace directs a man to no other obedience than that of which the Law is the Rule",[208] and bestows on believers a "new and inchoat obedience to the Law, which is a kinde of fulfilling it".[209] Although from certain points of view this obedience may be called "new", it must be understood that

> The righteousnesse of the Law, and of the Gospell, are not two severall kindes of righteousnesse; but the same in regard of the matter and substance thereof.[210]

In his great work on *Justification by Faith,* John Owen takes particular care to point out that the alleged distinction between personal righteousness "of the law" and personal righteousness "evangelical" cannot be sustained, for "that righteousness which is evangelical in respect of its efficient cause . . . is legal in respect of the formal reason of it and our obligation unto it".[211] What John Goodwin affirms about Christ's obedience may be said with equal truth about the evangelical obedience of the believer. With special reference to Christ he argues that "The greatnesse or holinesse of the person working

202. John Preston, *Law out lawed*, p. 6.
203. George Downame, *Justification*, p. 78; cf. Thomas Taylor, *Progresse of Saints*, p. 192; James Ussher, *Body of Divinitie*, p. 203.
204. Romans iii. 31.
205. John Downame, *Guide to Godlynesse*, p. 5, cf. p. 205.
206. William Ames, *Marrow of Sacred Divinity*, p. 234.
207. Robert Bolton, *Three-fold Treatise*, "Saints Guide", p. 67; John Ball, *Of Faith*, pp. 41, 42.
208. Edward Reynolds, *Three Treatises*: "Sinfulnesse of Sinne", p. 388; cf. Robert Traill, *Justification Vindicated*, in *Works*, I. 287.
209. Thomas Taylor, *Regula Vitae*, p. 11; cf. 171; *The Marrow*, p. 175.
210. William Pemble, *Vindiciae Fidei*, p. 3.
211. Op. cit., in *Works*, V. 158.

according to the Law, doth not alter or change the nature or property of the works, but they are the works of the Law, whosoever doeth them, Christs being Christ, doth not make the Law, not to be the Law."[212] By the same reasoning, the obedience of the regenerate man is still obedience to Law, whatever change may have taken place in his ability and motive. The Law does not cease to be the Law now that the Christian has come to love it. Thomas Goodwin boldly affirms that the Law is "the original copy of all the grace which the saints have", and that "all grace is but the copy of the law",[213] and thus Christian obedience is truly a "righteousness of the Law".[214]

Believers "still keep the Law",[215] and this is important in the eyes of the Lawgiver, for it is not

> all one to the Law, whether the debt of obedience, or the debt of punishment were paid; for certainly its the debt of obedience the Law doth principally aim at, and when the debt of punishment is paid, the debt of obedience is not thereby abrogated.[216]

"Our doing his Commandments tends to the full accomplishment of his design of reconciling God and us, and so of making us happy. . . . If we . . . keep his Commandments, then he has the end of his Mediatorial undertaking, which is the reconciling God to us and us to God."[217] Sanctification, therefore, is "that Practice and Manner of Life, which we call Holiness . . . and which God requireth of us in the Law;"[218] it is the "Performance of the Law" [219] Positive Law in so far as it is still applicable under the Gospel—is no less established by evangelical obedience than moral Law, for the majesty of God is involved in both.

(ii) *The acceptability of good works*

The believer "must get good works" after he has been justified,[220] because "this Righteousness in the Saints pleaseth God".[221]

> This holy frame of a compleat and active will . . . is a most sweet

212. *Imputatio Fidei*, p. 71.
213. *Mediator*, in *Works*, V. 85, 86.
214. Thomas Goodwin, op. cit., p. 354.
215. Anthony Burgess, *Vindiciae Legis*, p. 210.
216. Anthony Burgess, *Justification*, Part II. p. 451; cf. William Strong, *The Two Covenants*, p. 54.
217. William Allen, *Christians Justification*, pp. 266, 267.
218. Walter Marshal, *Sanctification*, pp. 1, 2.
219. Walter Marshal, op. cit., pp. 236, 237.
220. Walter Cradock, *Gospel-Holinesse*, "Priviledge and Practice of the Saints", p. 231.
221. Obadiah Grew, *Sinner's Justification*, pp. 59–61; Andrew Willet, *Hexapla: Romanes*, p. 143.

> smelling sacrifice, and mounts into the most gracious acceptance of God in Christ.[222]

Paul Baynes says that "we honour and glorifie God in, by, and with our graces".[223] Although the believer's good works are, from one point of view, nothing but "filthy rags",[224] yet in so far as they are evidence of sanctification "they are jewels and ornaments".[225] They are "such as our Gracious Merciful God will certainly delight in, and be pleas'd with, during our State of Imperfection."[226]

The Antinomians denied the acceptability of the believer's obedience and declared that "all the workes of the regenerate are sinne",[227] and Thomas Welde reports them as saying, "If I be holy I am never the better accepted of God".[228] John Saltmarsh rejects the idea that "God loves us for his own graces in us",[229] and so does John Eaton, who adds that "all our righteousnesse, even of sanctification, is as foule, stained, filthy rags".[230] Tobias Crisp likewise teaches that the believer's "own blameless works" are but "loss and Dung",[231] and to offer them to God is "to throw dirt anew in the face of God".[232]

The Divine acceptance of the believer's good works constitutes something of a paradox to which both the Puritans and the Antinomians endeavoured to be true, namely, that the believer's works are both unacceptable and acceptable, their acceptability being solely due to the merits of Christ. At the basis of the Antinomian objection to the believer's works was their recurring confusion of justification and sanctification, with the result that they thought of sanctification in terms of imputation. They were right in recognizing Christ as the source and power of the believer's sanctification, but mistaken in their view of the method by which the grace of Christ was made real to the believer. They were unable to distinguish between legal categories which belonged to justification and experimental categories which belonged to sanctification, and so applied the method of imputation to both.

The Puritans never tired of explaining that

> There is a Righteousnesse imputed, and there is a Righteousnesse

222. Obadiah Sedgwick, *Anatomy*, p. 221, cf. 250.
223. *Ephesians*, p. 266.
224. Richard Sibbes, *Church's Complaint*, in *Works*, VI. 191, 192.
225. Richard Sibbes, *Philippians*, in *Works*, V. 85.
226. Walter Marshal, *Sanctification*, p. 3.
227. Such a saying is repudiated by Andrew Willet, *Hexapla: Romanes*, p. 136.
228. Thomas Welde, *Rise, reigne, and ruine*, p. 18.
229. *Reasons*, "Shadows flying away", p. 12.
230. *Dangerous Dead Faith*, p. 81; John Eaton, *Honey-combe*, pp. 322, 323; cf. Thomas Edwards, *Gangraena*, p. 24; Thomas Welde, *Rise, reigne, and ruine*, p. 3.
231. *Christ Alone Exalted*, in *Works*, II. 227.
232. Op. cit., II. 322.

imparted; the one inherent in Christ, and imputed to us; the other imparted by Christ, and inherent in us.[233]

This imparted righteousness is called "the Righteousnesse of God", not because the believer has nothing to do with it, but because "it is conformable to the Law of God".[234] It consists

> in the inherent holinesse of Mans whole person, when such gratious Qualities are fixed and planted in every faculty of soule and Body: as doe dispose and incline the Motions of both onely unto that which is conformable to the Righteousnesse of the Law.[235]

It is, therefore, "Unsavoury" to say "If Christ be my Sanctification, what neede I looke to any thing in my selfe, to evidence my justification?"[236]

There is nothing of surprise in finding that Richard Baxter opposes the Antinomians here, and, although the context and object of his reasoning cannot be upheld, what he has to say on this is pertinent.

> I abhor the opinion, that Christ's Righteousness given us, is all without us, and none within us, when Christ dwelleth in us; as if 600 Texts of Scripture were all false, that speak of the necessity of an inherent and active Righteousness.[237]

(iii) *Activity in obedience*

The Antinomians believed that no spiritual good in the believer could bear any relation to his will and action. They held that anything truly commendable in the believer had to be regarded as the direct work of the Holy Spirit, in the doing of which the believer himself took no part at all. Further, given the premise of sanctification by imputation, the conclusion of the believer's passivity became inescapable.

> Some say there is a sanctification in us; but wherein doth it consist? Not in any habitual holiness, or graces in us, but in the immediate actings of Christ in us; and so the Lord makes his music without any strings, and reveals things to us without eyes, and makes us live without any power of life. And so after justification they put a Christian in such an estate of sanctification as that he is . . . like a weathercock which hath not power at all to move, but as the wind blows it, good or bad.[238]

233. Thomas Gataker, *Christian Mans Care*, 1624, p. 24; cf. *Truths Victory*, pp. 88, 89.
234. Thomas Gataker, op. cit., pp. 27, 33.
235. William Pemble, *Vindiciae Fidei*, p. 66.
236. Thomas Welde, *Rise, reigne, and ruine*, p. 20.
237. *Scripture Gospel Defended*, "Defence of Christ and Free Grace", To the Reader.
238. Thomas Shepard, *Parable of the Ten Virgins*, 1660, *Works*, II. 332.

It was the Antinomian belief that "in the conversion of a sinner . . . the faculties of the soule . . . in things partaining to God, are destroyed and made to cease", and "in stead of them, the Holy Ghost doth come and take place, and doth all the works".[239] John Eaton says that by the power of his imputation God

> doth so truly cloath us both within and without with this his Sons doing and fulfilling of the Law perfectly, that we also continue in all things to doe them in the sight of God, not inherently and actively, by our own doing, but because his Sonnes perfect doing all things is objectively and passively so truly in us, that we are made perfectly holy.[240]

It is something of a question how believers can "doe" something not "actively", but this does not deter Robert Towne from saying that "as their obedience is the work of the Spirit in them; so its passive to them",[241] and he asks, "But what is caused and accomplished by Christ simply and alone, . . . must that be sought and laboured for by the Ministerie and urging of the Law?"[242] The grotesqueness of the thorough Antinomian position is exposed by Isaac Ambrose.

> Might we still lie in our Ivory Beds, under no Law, under no Obligation of doing, no danger of sinning, no broken bones, no terrors, no sense of sorrow for sin, no progress in personal Repentance, Mortification, Sanctification, no care of watchful walking to perfect holiness in the fear of God, no abstaining from worldly lusts, no strictness of Conversation, but only believe that Christ hath suffered, and Christ hath done all Duties for us, Repented for us, Mortified lusts for us, walked strictly and holily for us, this were an easie work indeed.[243]

The common Puritan view is that the believer's sanctification in the eyes of God is both active and progressive. "In the duties of sanctification wee are also agents, who being acted by the holy Ghost, doe cooperate with him."[244] Gospel righteousness is that which "you must perform yourselves" and it must be "your own personal and inherent obedience."[245] The believer "must not be

239. Thomas Welde, *Rise, reigne, and ruine*, p. 1.
240. *Honey-combe*, p. 288.
241. Robert Towne, *Assertion of Grace*, p. 23; cf. pp. 47 ff.
242. Op. cit., p. 119.
243. *Prima, Media, & Ultima*, "The Middle Things", To the Reader.
244. George Downame, *Justification*, p. 79; Richard Greenham, *Of Good Works*, in *Works*, p. 450.
245. Thomas Jacomb, *Romans*, p. 370.

lazie and luskish,[246] idle and slothfull; but exceeding industrious, painfull, and diligent."[247] Walter Marshal makes the comment

> That though all Holiness be effectually attained by the life of Faith in Christ, yet the use of any Means appointed in the Word for attaining and promoting Holiness is not hereby made void, but rather established. This is needful to be observed against the Pride and Ignorance of some carnal Gospellers, who being puft up with a Conceit of their feigned Faith, imagine themselves to be in such a state of Perfection, that they are above all Ordinances, except singing Halelujahs.[248]

It is a "counterfeit Faith" when a man thinks he has it "but yet hee finds no life, no motion . . . no worke proceeding from his Faith. . . . For, if it be a right Faith, it will worke."[249] It was a Puritan maxim that "so much working as you find in any man, so much faith there is."[250] Anthony Burgess emphasizes the believer's own activity in sanctification when he draws attention to the word "ye" in "ye through the Spirit"[251] and says it denotes

> that we also are to work and act . . . and not as some do now dangerously maintain, give up all, expecting the operation of the Spirit only.[252]

The Puritans pointed out that one of the dangers of inactivity was that "he that endeavours not to be better, will by little and little grow worse,"[253] and they regularly reminded their hearers that there were not only "*Credenda*", but also "*Agenda*, things to be done",[254] for justification by faith gives no slight to good works.[255] "Supernatural graces" must be exercised "in holy walking".[256] It is no contradiction of this when Andrew Willet says, "It is grace onely that worketh, the nature of man is wrought upon."[257] He does not deny the activity of the believing man, but simply rejects the synergistic principle by which "the lawe of nature is made a joynt worker with grace."[258] It is not the unregenerate man who is active in good works, but the

246. "luskish" is an obsolete word meaning "lazy".
247. John Downame, *Guide to Godlynesse*, p. 23.
248. *Sanctification*, p. 274.
249. John Preston, *New Covenant*, p. 391.
250. John Preston, *Breastplate of Faith and Love*, "Of Faith", p. 176.
251. Romans viii. 13.
252. *Justification*, Part I. p. 63; Thomas Taylor, *Progresse of Saints*, p. 191.
253. Robert Bolton, *Three-fold Treatise*, "Saints Guide", p. 40; cf. "Selfe-enriching Examination", p. 53.
254. Thomas Goodwin, *Ephesians*, in *Works*, I. p. 132.
255. Thomas Goodwin, *Justifying Faith*, in *Works*, VIII. p. 476.
256. Thomas Brooks, *Glory of Christianity*, in *Works*, IV. p. 46.
257. *Hexapla: Romanes*, p. 140.
258. Andrew Willet, ibid.

spiritually-renewed man, and these good works are to be defined as "the graces of Gods Spirit in us, and the actions flowing from them."[259]

The false conclusions to which the principle of entire passivity in holiness must lead is well expressed by Samuel Rutherford when he calls upon believers to a life of activity in the things of God. "If we by Grace were no agents in these, but meer Patients, and Christ and the holy Ghost the onely immediate agents", then in the doing of what is forbidden in the Law, "we should not sin, all these wicked acts were to be imputed to the Grace of Christ and the holy Ghost, which is blasphemy."[260] Richard Baxter rightly says that it is an excessive view of grace that lifts the expression of it out of the moral realm,[261] and he warns his readers to "take heed of those Preachers that stifle practice",[262] because "the Spirit worketh not on man as a dead thing, which hath no principle of activity in it self."[263]

The concurrence of the Divine and human in the realm of spiritual activity is another of the paradoxes of Christian experience. It receives classic expression in the words of the New Testament itself. "Work out your own salvation with fear and trembling. For it is God which worketh in you both to will and to do of his good pleasure."[264] Thomas Watson says on these words, "As the teacher guides the child's hand, and helps him to form his letters, so that it is not so much the child's writing as the master's, so our obedience is not so much our working as the Spirit's co-working."[265] The truth of sanctification is found in both the passive and the active aspects of it, and Puritans and Antinomians alike do their best, each in their own way, to conserve the element of the truth which they regard as important.

There is thus a kind of passive-activity or active-passivity in the believer's acts of godliness, and the paradox appears sharply in Walter Cradock who, with an understanding of both aspects, says, "Consider . . . in all the good works that you do, how wonderful passive you are in the doing of them."[266] The truth enunciated by Walter Cradock is confirmed by such a different writer as Samuel Rutherford.

> Gospel-obedience . . . hath lesse of the nature of obedience, then that of Adam. . . . We are more (as it were) patients, in obeying Gospel-Commands, not that we are meer patients, as Libertines teach, for grace makes us willing, . . . and so in Gospel-obedience

259. Anthony Burgess, *Vindiciae Legis*, p. 39.
260. *Triumph of Faith*, pp. 276, 277; cf. *Survey*, Part II. pp. 58, 65.
261. *Catholick Theologie*, Book I. Part 1, p. 41.
262. *Poor Man's Family Book*, 1674, p. 335.
263. *Life of Faith*, p. 226.
264. Philippians ii. 12–13.
265. *A Body of Divinity*, p. 90.
266. *Divine Drops Distilled*, p. 172 f. Not to be understood in the Antinomian sense.

> we offer more of the Lords own, and lesse of our own, because he both commands, and gives us grace to obey.[267]

There are times when an intellectual problem resolves itself in the realm of the experimental, and John Downame points the way to just such a practical synthesis when he writes,

> If we respect our owne strength, it will plainely appeare to be utterly impossible to goe forward in the course of godlinesse . . . whereas contrariwise, if wee renounce our selves, and our owne strength, and by a lively fayth rest upon the power and promises of God, for the beginning, continuing and perfecting of this worke, then neede we not to be discouraged by our wants and weaknesses, from undertaking or proceeding in it.[268]

The Antinomian disinclination to activity was plainly an excrescence on Puritanism proper, and produced fanatical extremists whom John Fletcher aptly calls "Laodicean loiterers",[269] but, at the same time, among those who stood at the other extreme there was the danger of an activism that bordered on Socinianism. The Puritans endeavoured to walk a middle path, but, as John Eusden says, being indwelt by the Spirit of God they "could do no other than lead an activist life."[270]

The Puritan insistence upon Christian Law-keeping preserved their piety from evaporating into sentiment and fostered that moral virility which must ever be the mark of the redeemed and restored sinner.

267. *Covenant of Life*, pp. 198, 199.
268. John Downame, *Guide to Godlynesse*, p. 50.
269. *Third Check*, in *Works*, I. p. 391.
270. *Puritans, Lawyers, and Politics*, p. 22.

Chapter VII

PERFECT FREEDOM

Synopsis

A. LAW IN THE HEART
- (i) *The original Law*
- (ii) *Spiritual acceptance of the Law*
- (iii) *A "Correspondency"*

B. THE ANTITHESIS OF LEGALISM
- (i) *No irksome servility*
- (ii) *No legalistic morality*

C. EVANGELICAL ABILITY
- (i) *The new life*
- (ii) *The forgiveness of sins*
- (iii) *The indwelling of Christ*
- (iv) *The work of the Holy Spirit*

D. LOVE FOR THE LAW
- (i) *Made "friends"*
- (ii) *Spontaneous obedience*

E. LIBERTY IN THE LAW
- (i) *Antinomian denial of liberty in the Law*
- (ii) *No infringement of liberty by commandment*

Chapter VII

PERFECT FREEDOM

IN a sermon on the believer's freedom in Christ, Jeremiah Burroughs says he intends to give his hearers a view of "the bondage that we are all in, under the law" and to reveal "wherein the liberty of the Gospell doth consist." He then adds, "These two things (brethren) have in them the chiefe doctrine of divinity, and except you be well instructed and setled in these two, you cannot know aright any point of religion."[1] This chapter inquires into the Puritan doctrine of Christian liberty, and begins by observing the attention given by the Puritans to the terms of the New Covenant, which state God's promise to write His Law within the hearts of His people. The Puritan conception of this as outworked in enabling grace is next exhibited, together with the transformed attitude to Law which such grace brings. The chapter then shows how widely the believer's new relation to the Law differs from the harsh features of legalism and concludes with an exposition of the Puritan doctrine of the "law of liberty".

A. LAW IN THE HEART

The Puritans held fast to the promise of the "new covenant" given by God through Jeremiah, "I will put my law in their inward parts, and write it in their hearts; and will be their God, and they shall be my people."[2] In accordance with the teaching of Hebrews,[3] they believed that this promise was fulfilled in the Gospel.

(i) *The original Law*

The inscription wrought within the heart of the regenerate is truly to be called a writing of "the Law". The result of the Divine action is not merely the purging of the volitions, but the giving of a specific direction to them in the form of an awareness and acceptance of the Law of God. "The heart of the righteous" becomes "a rich . . . storehouse, wherein the Law of God is safely laid up."[4] "The Law of God written, and the Law of their hearts is all one in substance":[5] it is the very same Law, "my Law", not another of a different or easier

1. *Saints Treasury*, p. 90.
2. Jeremiah xxxi. 33; cf. Ezekiel xxxvi. 26, 27.
3. Hebrews viii. 7–13.
4. John Ball, *Power of Godliness*, p. 63.
5. Edward Elton, *Treatises*: "Complaint of a Sanctifyed Sinner", p. 205.

kind.[6] The Law of God which was "at first inbred and natural unto man" and subsequently written "in tables of stone" is "turned to an internal law again" as God "implants it on the heart as it was at first."[7] The fact of identity between the original Law and the newly-written Law is in John Flavel's mind when he speaks of God's action as a reviving of the knowledge of the Law in the heart of man and a trimming of the lamp of reason.[8]

(ii) *Spiritual acceptance of the Law*

From the terms of the New Covenant promise it is clear that a distinction must be made between the way the Law was written in man's heart at the creation, and the manner of that special inscribing promised in Jeremiah. The former is the inwritten Law in the knowledge of it: the latter is the inwritten Law in the power of it and relates to God's saving act of grace.[9]

Francis Roberts devotes twenty-nine pages to the exposition of these Old Testament passages in terms of Christian experience,[10] and William Ames understands them to refer to the grace of God as "it applies our will to fulfill the Will of God" and "makes the will ready to commit the command of God to execution", bringing about "a conformity betwixt the Will of God and ours" in such a way that obedience becomes holiness.[11] The experience of the Law of God written in the heart is one of the "meanes of knowing whether we be in the Covenant"[12] and this is because, as Tobias Crisp concurs, the Law in the heart is a "consequence" of grace, not an "antecedence."[13] On the psalmist's prayer, "Grant me thy law",[14] Thomas Manton remarks, "David had the book of the law already, . . . but he understandeth it not of the law written in a book, but of the law written upon his heart".[15] Indeed, "what is holiness", asks Thomas Goodwin, "but the law of God written in the heart, the real living law?"[16]

(iii) *A "Correspondency"*

The Puritans held together the two truths of (*a*) the identity of the Law under the two covenants and (*b*) the work of the Holy Spirit in the heart by saying that for believers the promise means "there shall

6. Francis Roberts, *God's Covenants*, p. 1365, who observes that Calvin draws attention to this.
7. John Owen, *Indwelling Sin*, in *Works*, VI. 165, 166.
8. John Flavel, *Personal Reformation*, p. 3; and see above pp. 52 ff.
9. Anthony Burgess, *Vindiciae Legis*, p. 60.
10. *God's Covenants*, pp. 1369–98.
11. William Ames, *Marrow of Sacred Divinity*, pp. 191, 192.
12. John Preston, *New Covenant*, p. 426.
13. Tobias Crisp, *Christ Alone Exalted*, in *Works*, I. 81, 82.
14. Psalm cxix. 29.
15. *Hundred and Nineteenth Psalm*, I. 265.
16. *Unregenerate Man's Guiltiness*, in *Works*, X. 57.

be a Law within them, answerable and conform to the Law without them."[17] "Before this writing, there was an universal Contrariety: but since, theres an universal Correspondency, betwixt Gods Laws and their Hearts. Now theres a Spiritual Law within, called The Law of the Mind, answering in every point to the Literal Law without."[18] "The law of the minde" is that "obedience and conformitie, which the mind regenerate hath with the law of God."[19]

> The heart within echoes and answers to the commandments without. . . . An obedient soul is like a crystal glass with a light in the midst, which shines forth through every part thereof. So that royal law that is written upon his heart shines forth into every parcel of his life; his outward works do echo to a law within.[20]

In this work of the Holy Spirit there is "a form of grace introduced into the soul, that suits with every point of the law",[21] because where

> Christ doth rule the heart, his Lawes have a marvellous sutablenesse with the spirit of that man: his Law is written in the heart, there is a powerful and answerable inclination stamped in the heart which gives way to the command.[22]

Man "can never look upon the law as the perfect law of liberty, until his nature answers the law, and it is written in his heart."[23]

> Adam had the Law written in his heart, not only a Law without, but inward dispositions conformable to it within: and when man had blotted it out, God wrote it in tables of stone; but now he will put it into the hearts of men, so that they shall have an inward principle answerable to the Law-rule without, and whatever he does require in the Law, something within shall answer to it, but this Law is put in by the hand of God.[24]

B. THE ANTITHESIS OF LEGALISM

Christian experience in keeping the Law of God is the antithesis of legalism: it has in it neither irksome servility nor legalistic morality.

17. Francis Roberts, *God's Covenants*, p. 167.
18. Francis Roberts, op. cit., p. 1378.
19. Andrew Willet, *Hexapla: Romanes*, p. 331, on Romans vii. 22, 23.
20. Thomas Brooks, *Heaven on Earth*, in *Works*, II. 469.
21. Thomas Manton, *Hundred and Nineteenth Psalm*, I. 49.
22. Obadiah Sedgwick, *Anatomy*, p. 140.
23. William Strong, *The Two Covenants*, p. 57.
24. William Strong, op. cit., p. 103. It has been observed in an earlier chapter that William Strong thinks that the writing referred to in Romans ii. 15 is not the original act of creation but a first act of recovering grace, "not the dross of the old Adam, but the foundation of the new". (ibid.).

(i) *No irksome servility*

Walter Cradock told his hearers that a test of their true humbling before God could be seen in "the carriage" of their souls, "in respect of the injunctions, or commands of God that are layd upon" them. "The nature and property of a heart truly humbled by seeing of God in Jesus Christ is this: to be willing to obey God in any thing that God layes upon him."[25] That is not godly life "which counteth it preciseness to be abridged of any libertie that he hath been wont to use",[26] and such as speak like this are but "carnall Professours"[27] who weary of the Law. In his defence of the *Morality of the Fourth Commandement*, William Twisse cannot see how the observance of the Sabbath "as a morall and perpetuall duty, should seeme distastfull to any"[28] and considers it a mark of unregeneracy to say, "When will the Sabbath be gone?"[29] Jeremiah Burroughs writes of the servile spirit revealed in

> the Speech of one that cried out, Oh that God had never made the seventh Commandement: He had an inlightened conscience, but a filthy heart; but conscience now stood in his way, he hates therefore the Command that forbid that sin.[30]

This is slavish Law-keeping in the "oldnesse of the letter", it is "the idle, fruitlesse, and bare knowledge of the Law in externall Discipline, that reigns in an unrenewed man."[31] William Strong deprecates the "legal spirit" of those who keep the commandment, "performing it as a task, and are glad it is over."[32] He contends that the Law was never made for the godly "as the only principle upon which they should act",[33] and that the "coaction" of the Law has ceased for the believer, that is to say, he is not under the Law "forcibly compelling."[34] He gives tests for true inwardness of obedience, in contrast to legalism, and says, "If you are led by the spirit you are not under the Law; that is, not under the Law as a slave under a Tyrant, . . . but you have a spirit of Sonship."[35] The change, however, is in the manner of doing, not in the Law itself.

25. *Gospel-Holinesse*, pp. 116, 117.
26. Richard Rogers, *Seven Treatises*, p. 205.
27. Robert Bolton, *Afflicted Consciences*, p. 322.
28. Op. cit., p. 235.
29. William Twisse, op. cit., p. 243.
30. *Evil of Evils*, p. 524.
31. Samuel Rutherford, *Covenant of Life*, p. 213.
32. *The Two Covenants*, p. 28; cf. Thomas Watson, *A Body of Divinity*, pp. 164, 165, 169.
33. Note the force of "only": it is this which makes it legalism. Cf. Thomas Goodwin, *Gospel Holiness*, 1703, in *Works*, VII. 215; *Work of the Holy Ghost*, in *Works*, VI. 302; and Jeremiah Burroughs, *Saints Treasury*, p. 101.
34. *The Two Covenants*, pp. 37, 50. "Coaction" is an obsolete word standing for the exercise of force in compulsion or restraint.
35. William Strong, *The Two Covenants*, p. 84.

The Puritans insisted again and again that it was far from the purpose of the Law to keep servile, or to exact rigour;[36] and taught that the believer has been liberated from the doing of duty as a task or in the manner of a slave.[37] The believer is moved by a deep reverence for God, without any trace of a servile spirit, or of being driven to obedience "with terrours."[38] He keeps the Law, not "Legally" but "Evangelically",[39] and finds nothing irksome in any of the commandments. Thomas Goodwin, as a true pastor, expresses a warning to the excessively scrupulous about the way in which an active conscience still tries to "keep a man under the law" and teaches that the work of God in the soul is to "subdue conscience unto faith."[40]

The liberty of the Gospel takes all baseness and servility out of Law-keeping. Believers "are not servants, but sonnes."[41] For the metaphor of sonship, John Preston substitutes that of marriage.

> You must respect him as a Wife doth her Husband, not as a servant doth a hard Master: you must not looke on his Commandements as a hard Taske, whereof you could willingly be excused, but as one that hath his heart inflamed to walk in them: as a loving Wife, that needs not to be bidden[42] to doe this, or that; but if the doing of it may advantage her Husband, it wil be a greater grief to her to let it lye undone, then labour to doe it. . . . They that be humble, that have their hearts wounded with the sense of sinne, are willing to take him on his owne tearmes; to keepe his Commandements, and not thinke them grievous. . . . Therefore, be not thou shie in taking of him, for you have free libertie.[43]

The expression of covenanted grace in the preface to the Decalogue "serveth to teach us to keepe the law spiritually, because it is spirituall".[44] For a good man, the Law is not made "as a Bar, but as a defence; not to restrain but to secure them."[45] "Obedience is no dull service, no dead piece of worke, but the way to blessedness and the crowne of glory."[46] It is not servitude but friendship,[47] and will be

36. Francis Roberts, *God's Covenants*, p. 708; cf. Thomas Manton, *James*, in *Works*, IV. 228.
37. Samuel Bolton, *True Bounds*, p. 209; John Owen, *Holy Spirit*, in *Works*, III. 606, 607.
38. John Preston, *New Covenant*, p. 431.
39. John Preston, *Sermons*, "Exact Walking", p. 111.
40. *Ephesians*, in *Works*, II. 347.
41. William Perkins, *Galatians*, pp. 311 f.; cf. John Preston, *New Covenant* pp. 321, 322.
42. I.e., servilely.
43. John Preston, *Breastplate of Faith and Love*, "Of Faith", pp. 20, 27.
44. John Dod and Robert Cleaver, *Ten Commaundements*, p. 8.
45. Anonymous author, *Liberty of Conscience*, p. 3, on I Timothy i. 9.
46. John Ball, *Of Faith*, p. 385; cf. John Sedgwick, *Antinomianisme Anatomized*, p. 10.
47. Ezekiel Hopkins, *Practical Christianity*, 1701, in *Works*, p. 677.

rendered "without repining, fretting, grudging at any Duty, as if it were a grievous Yoke and Burden."[48] The child of God offers the response of a new heart, and not "a violent and constrained obedience, as doe the divels",[49] therefore, says Richard Baxter in his autobiography,

> I advise all Men to take heed of placing Religion too much in Fears, and Tears, and Scruples; or in any other kind of Sorrow, but such as tendeth to raise us to a high Estimation of Christ, and to the magnifying of Grace.[50]

(ii) *No legalistic morality*

The Puritans had a great fear of what they called "morality", by which they meant a mere legalism in the doing of good works for no other reason than that they were expected to do so. Outward conformity of this kind, without any true delight in the commandment or love for the Lawgiver is the kind of Law-keeping that Robert Bolton has in mind when he describes the unregenerate man's efforts in virtue as bringing him only to the "manhood of a meere morall Puritane."[51] Zealous conformity to Law is not sanctification, says the Antinomian Robert Towne,[52] and all the Puritans say the same.

Believers are committed to an obedience which is not "meerly Legal";[53] it is neither "a mere scrupulosity",[54] nor is it a performance of the Law in an external manner.[55] "It may fall out that a mans religious duties be the stage upon which all a mans lusts do eminently act, as the Pharisees who did all things to be seen of men."[56] One may keep many commandments, yet not exalt God.[57] "The great Characteristical difference betwixt morality and piety", says John Ball, "lyeth in this particular, that the one determineth in man, and the other relateth unto God."[58] This same contrast between "morality and piety" is drawn by George Downame who says that "the meere civill honest man" does not perform duties "in obedience to God, or

48. Walter Marshal, *Sanctification*, p. 2.
49. Richard Greenham, *Divine Aphorismes*, in *Works*, p. 491.
o. *Reliquiae Baxterianae*, Part III. pp. 85, 86.
51. *Afflicted Consciences*, p. 70. See discussion above in Chapter I.
52. *Assertion of Grace*, p. 4. Paul Hobson is against this "pharisaicall boldnesse" of mere "externall conformity to the Law", *Practicall Divinity*, 1646, p. 20.
53. Jeremiah Burroughs, *Gospel-Conversation*, pp. 41, 42.
54. Anthony Burgess, *Spiritual Refining*, "Of Sinne", p. 337.
55. Andrew Willet, *Hexapla: Romanes*, p. 318.
56. Anthony Burgess, *Spiritual Refining*, "Of Grace and Assurance", p. 16.
57. John Preston, *New Covenant*, p. 283.
58. *Power of Godliness*, p. 2 (unnumbered) cf. John Sedgwick, *Antinomianisme Anatomized*, p. 42; Henry Burton, *Law and Gospel Reconciled*, p. 32; and James Durham, *Law Unsealed*, p. 185.

for Gods sake."[59] The outward acts of religion may be punctiliously performed, yet the heart may still be under the dominion of sin, "as a man may be a Traitor, while he yet doth seeme to do something of the service to a Prince",[60] for "though a man were a morall Saint . . . yet without the inward power of grace . . . hee is but a spectacle of commiseration."[61]

> 1. We call not these good Works that are extorted by the terrours of the Law: as a captive keepeth the high way, because his Keeper leadeth him in an iron chaine. Nor 2. these which flow from the sole authority of God as Lawgiver. Or 3. which issue from meere morall principles, without saving grace: but these we call good works in an Evangelicall sense, that not onely are done from the authority of the Law-giver, but also from a mediatory and Evangelike obligation, from the sweet attractions and drawing coards of the secrets of Christs love.[62]

John Owen says that careful distinction must be made between "law-works" and Gospel holiness,[63] and by this statement he directs attention to the fact that the "practice of moral virtue" may easily fall short of holiness.[64]

> Though this holiness be legal, in respect of the materials and pattern of it, the law of God, yet it is not legal in respect of the subject or state of the person that hath it begun, or in respect of the tenure of the covenant, or of the virtue efficient that wrought it.[65]

As the believer will not be a "libertine" in his practice so will he not be a "legalist", for his obedience will run in another channel. The works of love "which are the end of the commandment, must flow from a good spring, from a gracious Principle, or a Principle of Grace", and therefore, no works which do not proceed from such a gracious principle can be understood truly to fulfil the Law, but "were call'd by some of the godly learned Antients 'shining sins'."[66]

Distinguishing the regenerate man's delight in God's Law from external "morality", Thomas Edwards writes,

> Morality is not this new Creature Change. . . . We cannot speak too much against it, it being a soft Pillow from whence many slide insensibly into Destruction. How many upon this account

59. *Covenant of Grace*, p. 62.
60. Obadiah Sedgwick, *Anatomy*, p. 139.
61. Robert Bolton, *True Happinesse*, pp. 67, 141.
62. Samuel Rutherford, *Survey*, Part II. pp. 36, 37.
63. *Holy Spirit*, in *Works*, III. 374, 376.
64. Op. cit., p. 524; cf. John Owen, *Justification*, in *Works*, V. 363–71.
65. Thomas Goodwin, *Work of the Holy Ghost*, in *Works*, VI. 391; Thomas Manton, *Hundred and Nineteenth Psalm*, I. 15.
66. Joseph Caryl, *Nature of Love*, pp. 16, 25.

> think themselves new Creatures, who are yet deeply under the Image of Satan; and tho they have blown off some dust from the Law of Nature, yet never had a Syllable of the Law of Grace writ in their Hearts? . . . Water heated to the highest pitch is but Water still; and Morality in the greatest elevation of it, is but refined Flesh; an old Nature in an higher form. . . . Moral Virtue colours the Skin, renewing Grace enlivens the Heart. . . . 'Tis an Habit, a Law writ in the Heart; not a transient Pang, or a sudden Affection; . . . but a new Creature, a divine Frame spreading it self over every Faculty: . . . a serious Humility, a constant Grief under the Remainder of Corruption yet unextirpated; a perpetual Recourse to God, and Delight in him through Jesus Christ.[67]

The pastoral spirit of William Strong compels him to express his anxiety that "men have been prest to duty without a through discovery of a mans Union with Christ as the ground of his assistance and acceptance . . . and so men have been put upon duties in a Moral or Legal way."[68] This is the inevitable result of a Pelagian or humanistic attitude to Law-keeping, and John Owen expresses the conviction that "the separation of the Duties of the Law from the Grace of the Gospel . . . will quickly issue in a pretence of Morality, set up in opposition unto true Evangelical Obedience."[69]

It was the Puritan view that nothing could be more barren than this legalistic morality. In this they shared the concern of the Antinomians and were opposed to all the nomistic tendencies of their day.[70]

C. EVANGELICAL ABILITY

There is an identity and a difference between man's first reception of the Law and the second. The difference is in the supernatural grace which enables the believer to fulfil the Law. This evangelical ability is generally described by the Puritans in a four-fold manner.

(i) *The new life*

"There can be no vitall actions brought forth, unlesse a principle of life be first begotten within."[71] Francis Roberts remarks that the

67. *Baxterianism Barefac'd*, pp. 153–8. (There is great confusion in the page enumeration here, and the above quotations are found in the second occurrence of these page numbers, following the first occurrence of p. 184, which is also repeated.)
68. *The Two Covenants*, p. 109.
69. John Owen, To the Christian Reader in James Durham, *Law Unsealed*; cf. Edward Elton, *Treatises*: "Complaint of a Sanctifyed Sinner", p. 63.
70. The Puritans were supported by the best of the Caroline moral theologians, as H. R. McAdoo points out in *Caroline Moral Theology*, pp. 16, 17, 46.
71. William Ames, *Marrow of Sacred Divinity*, p. 4; cf. Stephen Charnock, *Necessity of Regeneration*, in *Works*, III. 30, 34; Walter Marshal, *Sanctification*, p. 82.

Covenant of Works and the Covenant of Faith are similar in that in both a response is required of man: (*a*) Adam had the ability for this by the Law written naturally in his heart, (*b*) believers have the Law written supernaturally.[72] The principles of obedience in the regenerate "do in reality differ from those in Adam",[73] because they arise from inward knowledge, approval, propensity, affection and ability.[74] Believers are made good in order that they may do good;[75] as God's "workmanship" they then perform good works.[76] The Holy Spirit "will quicken us in the life of grace",[77] because "we must first by him be made righteous, before wee can doe the workes of righteousnesse; wee must first become good trees, before we can yeeld good fruits."[78] This is what is meant by the repeatedly-emphasized and much controverted statement that the believer works not "for life", but "from life."[79]

The believer is able to keep the Law of God because of the power that comes to him by God's enabling grace. Faith is a necessary prerequisite to spiritual obedience, and Christians must believe "that they shall receive grace from God to bring foorth fruites of amendment of life" and that "God will make them able to obey his will."[80] "Faith obtaines grace, by which the Law is fulfilled";[81] it is "the first wheele in the clock that moveth all the rest."[82] Jeremiah Burroughs quaintly remarks that saints have "as it were a pipe layd into that Cistern that hath all fulness"[83] and explains this elsewhere by saying, "The Gospel . . . brings the spirit of power and life along with it; there goes a vertue together with the commands of the Gospel to strengthen the soul to obedience."[84] The grace of God is sufficient to enable the believer to keep the Law and to fix it in the heart,[85] and it is for this reason that the godly pray for quickening and inclining grace in order to do the things commanded.[86] God's Covenant, says John Preston, "is to keepe thy heart in his feare",[87] and to give all needful strength to walk in the way of His command-

72. *God's Covenants*, pp. 174, 175.
73. Thomas Goodwin, *Of the Creatures*, in *Works*, VII. 47.
74. Stephen Charnock, *Nature of Regeneration*, 1683, in *Works*, III. 118–24.
75. Anthony Burgess, *Spiritual Refining*, "Of Grace and Assurance", p. 303.
76. Anthony Burgess, op. cit., p. 538.
77. John Downame, *Guide to Godlynesse*, p. 7.
78. John Downame, op. cit., p. 10; cf. p. 40.
79. Cf. Walter Marshal, *Sanctification*, p. 256.
80. Richard Rogers, *Seven Treatises*, pp. 80, 82.
81. Thomas Taylor, *Regula Vitae*, p. 52, quoting Augustine.
82. John Ball, *Of Faith*, p. 44; cf. p. 376.
83. *Gospel-Conversation*, p. 45.
84. Jeremiah Burroughs, *Saints Treasury*, p. 103.
85. Anthony Burgess, *Spiritual Refining*, "Of Grace and Assurance", p. 63.
86. Anthony Burgess, op. cit., p. 550.
87. *New Covenant*, p. 91.

ments.[88] Evidence to this effect can be quoted almost indefinitely.[89]

In the New Covenant, empowering grace is associated with the command.[90] There is life in the Word. "You may shew me much that I ought to do", says Robert Towne, pleading against the use of the Law, "but what is this, if you cannot sweetly incline, and freely enlarge my heart hereunto?"[91] The Puritans gave the answer, "With Gods Word of command there usually goeth forth a secret energy and vertue from him; enabling us to do what he commandeth."[92] So close is the relation between regeneration and sanctification that "if you have no regard to make the law of Christ your rule by endeavouring to do what is required in the Ten Commandments and to avoid what is there forbidden, it is a very evil sign."[93]

(ii) *The forgiveness of sins*

The Puritans did not leave their teaching about enabling grace in the form of a merely general statement. They traced it to the new motives springing from the awareness of the forgiveness of sins and taught that sanctification arose from justification.[94] They frequently drew attention to the Prologue to the Ten Commandments as providing the sufficient motive for the keeping of them. John Dod and Robert Cleaver, in their famous work on the Decalogue, say that God "encourageth us by this, That he is our God, and gives us these commandements for our own benefit, and because he loves us. . . . If ever wee will obey God in soundnes, then we must know him to be our God."[95] Obedience is not to "God abstractly considered", says James Durham, "but to God as our God."[96] The experience of God's saving mercy impels to obedience.

> Thy justification tells thee, that Christ dwells in thee by faith, and that thy heart is built up to be an habitation of God by the Spirit.[97]

Although Henry Burton refutes the conclusions of the Antinomians, their tenet which he quotes serves to demonstrate the living power of

88. John Preston, op. cit., p. 193.
89. Cf. Thomas Goodwin, *Ephesians*, in *Works*, II. 318; Ezekiel Hopkins, *Practical Christianity*, in *Works*, 678; Francis Roberts, *God's Covenants*, p. 867; Thomas Brooks, *Heaven on Earth*, in *Works*, II. 470; Thomas Blake, *Covenant of God*, p. 15; Constantine Jessop, *Nature of the Covenant of Grace*, 1655, p. 3; Richard Baxter, *Aphorismes*, p. 115.
90. John Owen, *Holy Spirit*, in *Works*, III. 617.
91. *Assertion of Grace*, p. 39.
92. Thomas Gouge, *Principles of Christian Religion*, p. 228.
93. *The Marrow*, p. 157.
94. John Preston, *New Covenant*, p. 350.
95. John Dod and Robert Cleaver, *Ten Commaundements*, p. 17.
96. *Law Unsealed*, p. 16.
97. Thomas Taylor, *Progresse of Saints*, p. 225.

personal faith in Christ, namely, that faith "infallibly inflames the heart with true love, making the true beleever to breake off his former corrupt conversation."[98] Richard Sibbes considers that "obedience from a broken heart is the best sacrifice."[99] Obedience springs from justification,[100] and it is by virtue of the imputed active obedience of Christ that "we are enabled by him dayly to dye unto sinne, and more and more to live unto righteousnesse of life."[101] Faith emancipates the soul for works, because "liberty from justification by the Law, doth not destroy, but increase and stir up the obligation of, and obedience to the Law."[102] "We must be reconciled to God, and justified by the Remission of our Sins, and Imputation of Righteousness, before any sincere Obedience to the Law, that we may be enabled for the Practice of it."[103]

At this place in the discussion of Christian experience the Antinomians come into their own. John Eaton writes of "Gods pardon or forgiveness . . . the joyfull faith whereof sanctifieth us, and makes us . . . to walk to the glory of God in the spirituall meaning of all Gods tenne Commandements zealously."[104] "The lessening of the glory of our justification extinguisheth the vigour of our sanctification; both hindering our joy, lessening our love, and quenching our zeale. . . . Obedience is not worth a butten, except it be willing and cheerfull for joy of Free Justification, and then it is true sanctification indeed".[105] The knowledge of justification leads the believer to a sincere hating of sin,[106] and it is the peace and joy of justification which "encreaseth and enflameth the heart" to obedience.[107] Because the believer is justified, he is constrained "to break off from, and to mortifie all sinne, and ungodly conversation; and to walke freely, cheerfully, sincerely, and zealously in all Gods will and commandements . . . which is true sanctification."[108]

Tobias Crisp repels the objection that licentiousness must arise from free justification by showing that grace is an effectual power in the heart.[109] He holds that the knowledge of Christ "oyls the Wheels of our Spirits, and puts them into a nimble frame",[110] in other words, justification gives strength and motive to sanctification. Henry

98. *Law and Gospel Reconciled*, p. 18.
99. *Bowels Opened*, 1639, in *Works*, II. 12.
100. Samuel Bolton, *True Bounds*, p. 96.
101. James Ussher, *Body of Divinitie*, p. 175.
102. John Sedgwick, *Antinomianisme Anatomized*, p. 26.
103. Walter Marshal, *Sanctification*, p. 22.
104. John Eaton, *Honey-combe*, p. 7.
105. John Eaton, op. cit., pp. 142, 145.
106. John Eaton, op. cit., p. 457.
107. John Eaton, *Dangerous Dead Faith*, p. 78.
108. John Eaton, op. cit., pp. 156, 157.
109. *Christ Alone Exalted*, in *Works*, I. 21.
110. Tobias Crisp, op. cit., I. 47.

Denne, similarly, exclaims "we call heaven and earth to record, whether the Gospel do not draw us unto an holy obedience, with as forcible . . . and effectuall cords, than any doctrine whatsoever."[111]

(iii) *The indwelling of Christ*

The power for keeping the Law is Christ Himself, who is the life of every believer.

> There is the fulnesse of Christ conveyed into the soul: so that our sanctification is not only from him meritoriously, but efficiently, yea, and in a kinde materially too, for . . . through our union with him there is a kinde of flowing of sanctification from him into us, as the principle of our life. . . . From him as from a fountaine, sanctification flowes into the souls of the Saints: there sanctification comes not so much from their strugling, and endeavours, and vowes, and resolutions, as it comes flowing to them from . . . their union with him.[112]

This, of course, is the view of the Antinomians as well as of the Puritans, and there is no greater truth about the Christian life than this. John Saltmarsh says that the "power wherein wee are perfectly mortified, is our union with Christ",[113] and in this view he is supported by his fellow-Antinomian, Henry Denne, who writes, "Christ entring into the soule, shall drive out whatsoever is prophane, and draw up the soule by the cords of love unto new obedience."[114]

The moral Law is fulfilled by Christ in a two-fold way, "partly in himselfe by perfect obedience thereunto, and making satisfaction for our disobedience; and partly in us, by giving us more power to performe obedience thereunto through faith in him."[115] This is brought about by "the work of Godis Spirit by the Word, putting in us the lif of Christ",[116] for "Christ coming into the believer, breaks down sinnes dominion, and sets up his own government in the soul, the authority of the Law-giver, the spiritualnesse of the Law."[117] Edward Elton interprets the "law of the spirit of life"[118] as meaning the power of the life of Christ in the believer,[119] and he works out the implication of the marriage relation used by Paul in Romans vii to say that the believer's good works are "child-bearing" to Christ by

111. *Man of Sin Discovered*, p. 5.
112. Jeremiah Burroughs, *Saints Treasury*, p. 46.
113. *Free-Grace*, p. 67.
114. *Grace, Mercy, and Peace*, "Mans Reconciliation to God", 1640, p. 21.
115. William Twisse, *Morality of the Fourth Commandment*, p. 216.
116. Samuel Rutherford, *Catechisme*, Cap. 19, quoted by A. F. Mitchell, *Catechisms*, p. 201.
117. Richard Byfield, *Gospels Glory*, p. 131.
118. Romans viii. 2.
119. *Treatises*: "Triumph of a True Christian", p. 20.

His life in us.[120] John Crandon writes an Epistle Dedicatory to *Aphorisms Exorized* in which he says,

> I hold not forth a maimed Christ to the people, but Christ with all his benefits, in particular to Sanctification no lesse then to Justification. If it be Antinomianism so to reduce all to Christ, and derive all from him, I must undergo the worlds condemnation for Christ's sake.[121]

As justification follows from the "Merit" of the "Death and Life of Christ", so sanctification follows from its "Efficacy".[122] This is the doctrine of the "mystical union" of Christ and believers and is contained within the important Pauline phrase "in Christ."

Walter Marshal entitles his work *The Gospel Mystery of Sanctification,* because this "great Mystery" lies at its root.

> As we are justified by a Righteousness wrought out in Christ, and imputed to us, so we are sanctified by such an holy Frame and Qualifications, as are first wrought out, and compleated in Christ for us, and then imparted to us: And as our natural Corruption was produced originally in the first Adam, and propagated from him to us; so our new Nature and Holiness is first produced in Christ, and derived from him to us, or as it were propagated. . . . Another great Mystery in the Way of Sanctification, is the glorious Manner of our Fellowship with Christ in receiving an holy Frame of Heart from him; it is by our being in Christ, and having Christ himself in us; and that not merely by his universal Presence as he is God, but by such a close Union as that we are one Spirit, and one Flesh with him, which is a Privilege peculiar to those that are truly sanctified. I may well call this a mystical Union, because the Apostle calleth it a great Mystery.[123]

(iv) *The work of the Holy Spirit*

The renewing of the spiritual powers of the believer is effected by the Holy Spirit Himself.[124] "The Spirit works in us a principle of spiritual life. . . . From this Fountain springs all those habits of Spiritual grace, which are severally distinguished by the names of Faith, Hope, Love", and "from these habits of grace abiding in us,

120. Edward Elton, *Treatises*: "Complaint of a Sanctifyed Sinner", p. 36.
121. Op. cit., the epithet "Antinomian" is such a relative term, that Richard Baxter used it of almost all the Puritans who did not echo his Neonomianism.
122. Thomas Edwards, *Baxterianism Barefac'd*, p. 143.
123. Walter Marshal, *Sanctification*, pp. 42–44.
124. Francis Roberts, *God's Covenants*, pp. 1129, 1347; Thomas Taylor, *Regula Vitae*, p. 11.

ordinarily proceed Spiritual motions and operations according to those habits."[125] The obedience of the Christian follows from holy principles of understanding, which are within the heart.[126] The Covenant of Grace is "accompanied with the law of the spirit," but this "law of the Spirit" is said by the apostle to be "the law of the Spirit of life in Christ Jesus",[127] because "it works from the spirit of Christ, and conforms us to the life of Christ as our original pattern."[128] True sanctification is thus "a holie walking in the creature according to the law flowing from that inward principle of puritie stirred up and blowne upon by the Spirit of God",[129] or as brought about "by a secret and yet sacred blast of the Spirit of God breaking in and blowing where he listeth."[130] Samuel Slater says that the difference between Law-obedience and Gospel-obedience is that the former is attempted by natural abilities, but the latter is performed in the "strength of a renewing Spirit".[131]

D. LOVE FOR THE LAW

It is impossible to read the Psalms and other devotional literature of the Bible without observing the great delight of the saints in the will and Law of God. The Puritans perceived this and saw the connection between it and the regenerating work of the Holy Spirit within the heart of the believer. They recognized that it was this inward work of the Holy Spirit which accounted for the believer's new relation to the Law.

(i) *Made "friends"*

It is part of the reconciling work of Christ that believers are made "friends" with the Law,[132] for "after Christ hes maid agreement betwixt us and the law, we delight to walk in it for the love of Christ."[133]

Love is "joyned with a care to obey the commandements",[134] and "in the hearts of believers is the principle ground, motive, and agent that puts them a doing."[135] The Gospel calls for obedience "in such a sweet and loving way that it would make any heart in the world in

125. Isaac Ambrose, *Prima, Media, & Ultima*, "The Middle Things", pp. 10, 11.
126. Thomas Goodwin, *Gospel Holiness*, in *Works*, VII. 139.
127. Romans viii. 2.
128. Thomas Manton, *Hundred and Nineteenth Psalm*, I. 301.
129. Thomas Wyllie, quoted by A. F. Mitchell, *Catechisms*, p. 259.
130. William Strong, *The Two Covenants*, p. 102.
131. *The Two Covenants* (pages unnumbered).
132. Samuel Rutherford, *Triumph of Faith*, p. 102.
133. Samuel Rutherford, *Catechisme*, quoted by A. F. Mitchell, *Catechisms*, p. 226.
134. Richard Greenham *Grave Counsels*, in *Works*, p. 36.
135. Vavasor Powell, *Christ and Moses*, p. 226; cf. Joseph Caryl, *Nature of Love*, p. 10.

love with it, it drawes by the cords of love."[136] The Puritan writers almost vie with one another in extolling the power of love in the keeping of the commandments. John Preston writes,

> Love makes me to do it in that manner as a man that is compelled. . . . So it hath the same effect that compulsion hath, though there be nothing more different from compulsion than love. . . . It is such a change as drawes one to serve the Lord out of an inward attractive, . . . so that there is no other spurre, no other attractive, but the amiablenesse of the object.[137]

Love, in turn, is to be measured by obedience, "for indeed love cannot be otherwise judged of than in obeying. . . . Therefore so much diligence in keeping his commands, so much love."[138]

Believers are "more willing and desirous to do what the Lord commands" than before,[139] and with the gift of faith there comes a "loathing of sin and love to the law."[140] "The doing of Gods Commandements doth follow the Circumcision of the heart".[141] The Christian finds that obedience to the Law of God is "sweeter"[142] than in his unregenerate days, because a changed heart makes the ways of God easy;[143] and, therefore, although the child of God finds some of the commandments difficult, through the weakness of the flesh, "yet he resolveth, and striveth to do what he can, and is much displeased and grieved, if he do not as he should."[144]

One of the blessed effects of grace in the heart is the destruction of the power of the Law in its provocation to sin. This implies no change in the Law, but arises from the new attitude of the believer towards it. A sweet ease of soul comes with the writing of the Law within the heart, in that it is not able any longer to provoke to sin.[145] "Our Saviour hath delivered us . . . from the irritation of the lawe, in regard whereof especially it is called the strength of sinne", and being made dead to sin, "we are mortified to the lawe, and the lawe to us in respect of this irritation accidentally caused by our corruption."[146] A caution is expressed by William Strong to the effect that

136. Jeremiah Burroughs, *Saints Treasury*, p. 102.
137. John Preston, *Breastplate of Faith and Love*, "Of Love", p. 29; cf. *Breastplate of Faith and Love*, "Of Faith", p. 180.
138. John Preston, *Breastplate of Faith and Love*, "Of Love", p. 200.
139. *The Marrow*, p. 160.
140. Op. cit., p. 177. Joseph Caryl's Recommendation, 1648, of Part II of *The Marrow* says that "The Commandments of God are Marrow to the Saints".
141. Paul Baynes, *Ephesians*, p. 265.
142. Thomas Goodwin, *Gospel Holiness*, in *Works*, VII. 213.
143. John Preston, *New Covenant*, p. 119.
144. Isaac Ambrose, *Prima, Media, & Ultima*, "The First Things", pp. 44, 45; cf. John Dod and Robert Cleaver, *Ten Commaundements*, p. 1.
145. Anthony Burgess, *Vindiciae Legis*, p. 219.
146. George Downame, *Covenant of Grace*, pp. 49, 50, 51.

"so far as there are remainders of sin in the Saints, they are lyable to an Irritation . . . but yet in a far different manner from that which is in unregenerate men."[147]

(ii) *Spontaneous obedience*

Love for God and His Law produces a new naturalness in obedience that amounts almost to spontaneity.

> When a mans nature is changed, it must needs be active: for that which is naturall to a man, hee doth without unevennesse . . . he doth it constantly, where there are naturall principles of actions, the actions flow like water from a spring: . . . a man doth it with facility and with desire; it is his meat and drink to doe the will of God.[148]

"You have the grace of sanctification to change your hearts, and enable you to every good word and worke, so that you delight in the Law."[149] "Faith makes the soule active . . . to run in the way of Gods Commandements . . . and . . . cannot run too fast."[150] Richard Sibbes says that a son does duties "out of nature" and like "water out of a spring": they are not forced, but they have "a blessed freedom to all duties, an enlargement of heart to duties. God's people are a voluntary people."[151] He uses the same imagery in *Meditations*, "Good duties come from unsound Christians as fire out of the flint; but they flow from the child of God, as water out of a spring."[152] The believer discovers that "the Law of God is his Element";[153] Christian obedience becomes natural, and is like "fruit brought forth."[154] It is "cordial and hearty",[155] being "pleasant",[156] "delightful"[157] and "sweetest liberty."[158] "Love makes Law easy",[159] and "is . . . the spring of sound obedience to Gods Law."[160] It constrains the child

147. *The Two Covenants*, p. 38.
148. John Preston, *Breastplate of Faith and Love*, "Of Love", pp. 216, 217.
149. John Preston, *Law out lawed*, p. 1.
150. George Hughes, *Dry Rod Blooming*, p. 103; cf. Jeremiah Burroughs, *Gospel-Conversation*, p. 50; Richard Allen, *Antidote against Heresy*, p. 85.
151. *Excellency of the Gospel*, in *Works*, IV. 221, 231.
152. Richard Sibbes, *Meditations*, in *Works*, VII. p. 190.
153. Francis Roberts, *God's Covenants*, p. 1381; cf. p. 795.
154. Thomas Goodwin, *Gospel Holiness*, in *Works*, VII. 162, 170 f.
155. Thomas Brooks, *Heaven on Earth*, in *Works*, II. 468; cf. *Glory of Christianity*, in *Works*, IV. 147; Ezekiel Hopkins, *Lord's Prayer*, 1692, in *Works*, p. 285.
156. John Owen, *Holy Spirit*, in *Works*, III. 621.
157. John Owen, *Gospel Vindicated*, in *Works*, XII. 566; cf. Isaac Ambrose, *Prima, Media, & Ultima*, "The Middle Things", p. 32; Thomas Manton, *Hundred and Nineteenth Psalm*, I. 313; William Strong, *The Two Covenants*, p. 52.
158. Samuel Rutherford, *Survey*, Part II. p. 122.
159. Samuel Bolton, *True Bounds*, p. 53; cf. p. 93; cf. Walter Cradock, *Gospel-Holinesse*, pp. 67–68.
160. John Sedgwick, *Antinomianisme Anatomized*, p. 24.

of God to a joyous and free keeping of the commandments in the "sweet necessity of the new nature."[161]

> The easinesse . . . and lightnesse of the Law of God is not in the proportion of it to our strength: but in the grace of our Lord Jesus Christ, and the Love of God together with the Communication of the Holy Spirit: which is with all those that love the Law of God.[162]

Through grace the soul is "prepared unto every good worke",[163] and "the dueties both of piety towards God, and charity to our brethren", are "performed with willing mindes and cheerfull hearts."[164] Knowledge with affection makes for understanding in spiritual duties,[165] and the believer finds that they are no more "a tiresome task", but rather that "the yoak of Christ is easie to him, and his burthen light."[166]

> You have such lively fixed intentions of God, that you can perceive that you do all, even common things, of purpose for his pleasure, will and glory; and that the love of God doth carry you about from duty to duty, and constrain you to it.[167]

Obadiah Sedgwick has a wise comment on this spontaneity of the believer's obedience and relates it to the realities of the changes of mood which sometimes characterize the believer's experience.

> Cheerfulness or uncheerfulness in the performance of duties, are not infallible symptoms either way. By Cheerfulness I mean the liberty or freedom of the spirits; and by uncheerfulness the sadness, heaviness or dulness of them. . . . There is a difference twixt Affections in Duties, and Cheerfulness in Duties; as much difference as twixt life and lively-hood,[168] twixt burning and flaming. A brand may be red hot, and burn to purpose, and yet not flame at all: so a man may bring living affections to his services, he may present them, and offer them out of the dearest love to God, and truest respect to his honour, who yet may not feel any such sparkling and flaming inlargements of his spirits in the times of disgrace of such services.[169]

In no aspect of their religious life have the Puritans been more maligned or misunderstood than in this. It has become popular to

161. Stephen Charnock, *Nature of Regeneration*, in *Works*, III. 111.
162. William Ames, *Marrow of Sacred Divinity*, p. 338.
163. Richard Rogers, *Seven Treatises*, p. 503, on 2 Timothy ii. 21.
164. George Downame, *Covenant of Grace*, pp. 114, 115.
165. Richard Baxter, *Christian Directory*, p. 307.
166. Richard Baxter, *Directions for Weak Christians*, "Confirmed Christian", p. 60.
167. Richard Baxter, *Directions for Weak Christians*, 1669, p. 112.
168. I.e. liveliness.
169. *Anatomy*, p. 243.

describe Puritan sainthood as "sombre and gloomy",[170] and there is no doubt that heart-searching and devout desire for the mortification of sin imparted a seriousness and gravity to life, but these qualities are not to be identified with gloom. The Puritans found, as the Psalmist did, that in keeping of the commandments of God "there is great reward."[171]

Such spontaneity makes it appear that believers are a law to themselves, and this is what many of the Puritans say, but not in the Antinomian manner.

> Hee that is got from under the Law is now a Law to himselfe, that is, he willingly submitteth himselfe to the rule and obedience of the Law: the way to escape the yoake and coaction of the Law is to become a free and cheerfull observer of the Law.[172]

In these words Thomas Taylor carefully shows in what way the phrase "Law to himselfe" is to be understood. Those who are led by the Spirit are not under the Law "as if they needed thereby to bee forced to obedience, but they are, as it were, a law unto themselves, willingly performing obedience to that which the law prescribeth."[173] They respond to the Law "as if there were no law."[174]

> In this new obedience, the Spirit so oyleth the wheeles of free-will as obedience, in its kinde, is as free, con-naturall, delightfull, being sweetned with the love of God, as if there were not an awing Law, but a sweetly alluring and heart-drawing free love, so that the beleever obeyes with an Angell-like obedience; then the Spirit seemes to exhaust all the commanding awsomenesse of the Law, and supplyes the Lawes imperious power with the strength and power of love; if we suppose there had been no Law commanding Christ absolute obedience, yet if we suppose a meer directing light, without any compelling, to shew him what is good and agreeable to Gods commanding will, so did Christ obey perfectly from a principle of love, and so doth the justified beleever give obedience, though imperfect, yet sincere to what is Gods will.[175]

In *Saints Treasury* Jeremiah Burroughs describes his sermon on John viii. 36 as "holding forth . . . The Naturall Mans bondage to the Law, and the Christians liberty by the Gospel",[176] and in the course

170. H. G. Wood, Article "Puritanism", 1918, *ERE*, p. 513.
171. Psalm xix. 11.
172. Thomas Taylor, *Regula Vitae*, p. 14.
173. George Downame, *Justification*, p. 524.
174. William Perkins, *Galatians*, p. 293; cf. Edward Elton, *Treatises*: "Complaint of a Sanctifyed Sinner", p. 205.
175. Samuel Rutherford, *Survey*, Part I. p. 318; cf. *Covenant of Life*, p. 62.
176. Jeremiah Burroughs, *Saints Treasury*, p. 87, and title page.

of the sermon he says that as God is now "thy husband", the rigour of the Law is not the same.

> Being delivered from the bondage of the law, this is now thy liberty, that thou art made a law to thyself. I meane thus: there is nothing now required of thee but it is written in thy own heart: God writes his law in the tables of stone: and all that is required of thee in obedience to it, is written in thy heart: so that thou doest not now so much yield obedience to the law; because of the condemning power of it, and punishment due unto it, as from a principle of love to it: For we must know, that we are not set free by Christ from obedience to the law, we are bound to obey the law still; but here is the difference, we are not servile to the law, we keep it freely: thou keepest the law now, by being a law to thyself, and having all that God requires of thee in his law written in thy heart, by the law of sanctity that he hath given thee.[177]

G. F. Nuttall makes the observation that

> Outwardly, the first Quakers were . . . at one with the earlier Puritans in observing, as Baxter admits, "a Life of extream Austerity." But inwardly, the spring is different. . . . Inwardly . . . the early Quakers walked at liberty, as those for whom the law was no longer law, because they loved it.[178]

In view of the evidence brought forward in the preceding paragraphs it might, perhaps, be not wrong to ask whether the inward spring really was so "different" and to suggest that the spiritually-minded Puritan and the devout Quaker were much closer to each other than the contrast between the legalistic caricature[179] of the Puritan and the wild extravagances of the Ranters might seem to suggest.[180]

The Antinomians agreed with the Puritans on the power of love to sanctify the heart, and Henry Denne adequately represents them when he asks, "What motive to obedience so strong as love? . . . What greater feare then that which proceedeth from love? . . . What greater aggravation of sinne, then to sin against love?"[181]

> A believer walketh according to the rule of the Law; yet it is not by vertue from the Law regulating him, but from another power

177. Op. cit., pp. 100, 101.
178. "Law and Liberty in Puritanism", *Congregational Quarterly*, XXIX, 1, pp. 27, 28.
179. It cannot be denied that there were some legalistically-minded Puritans whose ways justified the Quaker recoil.
180. The *Memoirs*, 1715, of Thomas Halyburton give the experimental illustration of this great Puritan truth; cf. pp. 75–7, 158–62.
181. Henry Denne, *Grace, Mercy, and Peace*, "Gods Reconciliation to Man", 1640, p. 52.

> within, renewing and disposing the heart thereunto. He is like the honest Traveller, who keepeth the high way freely of his own accord, and taketh pleasure in so doing.[182]

When Tobias Crisp expounds John viii. 36, he says, "To be called a Libertine, is the gloriousest Title under Heaven; take a Libertine for one that is truly free by Christ."[183] This may not be the wisest of language, but if correctly understood it is not out of harmony with the Puritan view. John Eaton uses an extravagant expression when he writes, "Christ living in me, I am now dead to the Law, that is He abolisheth the law to me",[184] but a charitable construction of his words leaves no mistake about the idea of freedom which he wishes to convey.

E. LIBERTY IN THE LAW

> Believers are freed from the Law in its condemnation,
>
> but from the Commandement, as a rule of life, we are not freed, but contrariwise enclined and disposed, by his free spirit, to the willing obedience thereof. Thus to the regenerate the Law becometh as it were Gospell, even a law of libertie.[185]

The liberty of the Christian man is thus a liberty "in the Law" carrying with it subjection to authority and obedience to command. Law is still Law, and the discernment of this truth is crucial to the entire Antinomian controversy.

"Law" is a constant factor in the life of godliness. When Thomas Goodwin comments on Romans viii. 4, he asks why "the Spirit of life in Christ Jesus" is called a "law". He finds one of the reasons in Psalm xl. 8, where "the inherent holiness of Christ's nature is called a law", from which he says it may be inferred that "His delight to do God's will flowed from the writing of the law in his heart."[186] He means that as the Law was in Christ, so it is in the believer.[187] In a similar manner Richard Sibbes understands "the law of the Spirit of life",[188] to be "the commanding power of the Spirit of Christ, that commands as a law in the hearts of God's people."[189] Edward Elton explains the apostle's phrase "the law of my mind"[190] as a figurative expression for the commanding aspect of

182. Robert Towne, *Re-assertion*, p. 139.
183. *Christ Alone Exalted*, in *Works*, I. 114.
184. *Honey-combe*, p. 443.
185. Samuel Crooke, *True Blessednesse*, p. 85.
186. *Mediator*, in *Works*, V. 350.
187. Cf. Thomas Goodwin, *Ephesians*, in *Works*, I. 134.
188. Romans viii. 2.
189. *Excellency of the Gospel*, in *Works*, IV. 222.
190. Romans vii. 23.

sanctifying grace, showing at the same time how truly integrated it is with the mind of the apostle.[191] Although the conduct of believers is characterized by the willing sweetness of love, it is "not as if the Law were not a rule to them",[192] for it is the privilege of believers always to be "subject to the head."[193]

(i) *Antinomian denial of liberty in the Law*

In their deep-seated antipathy to the Law, the Antinomians denied that the commandment of the Law and the liberty of grace can exist together.

John Eaton contends that if commandments are put before the believer

> Wee confound the Old Testament with the new: we bring back the full grown heir to Schoole again to be whipped of his School-master, contrary to the expresse doctrine and direction of the holy Ghost, saying, that after faith is come, wee are no longer under a School-master, Gal. 3. 25. And if wee doe not pull off the wedding-garment over the Brides head; yet wee bring forth rods to whip the Queen, standing at the right hand of the King, in the Vesture of the gold of Ophir, Psalm 45. 9. We doe hinder true Sanctification; and either with legall threats or rewards doe cause but a constrained hireling sanctitie, which is hypocriticall legall holinesse, or else doe cause people to run, though more cautiously, yet the faster, into the iniquities and sinnes so vehemently with legall terrors forbidden.[194]

He declares that Law destroys the filial motive and makes sanctification servile, and not from "loving inclination."[195] In *Dangerous Dead Faith* he complains against "legal arguments" for "a preposterous sanctification, repentance, mortification, . . . holy and righteous walking, universall obedience to all Gods commandements," with "hope of rewards" and "feare of punishments", which are "legally extorted, so much the more under termes and titles of the Gospell,"[196] and he holds the "blind zeale of the good workes of the Law to be meer superstitious hypocrisie."[197]

Robert Towne, with his customary inability to follow the straight course of an argument, concedes that the moral Law instructs the

191. *Treatises*: "Complaint of a Sanctifyed Sinner", p. 194.
192. Anthony Burgess, *Spiritual Refining*, "Of Grace and Assurance", p. 239.
193. Thomas Brooks, *Heaven on Earth*, in *Works*, II. 427.
194. *Honey-combe*, pp. 114, 115.
195. Op. cit., p. 143.
196. John Eaton, op. cit., pp. 27–29.
197. Op. cit., p. 48.

believer, but rejects the idea of commandment as inconsistent with his personal liberty.

> It cannot be said, that my spirit doth that voluntarily, which the command of the Law bindeth and forceth unto; its one thing for a man at his own free libertie to keep the Kings high way of the Law; and another to be kept in by pales and ditches.[198]

(ii) *No infringement of liberty by commandment*

Any suggestion that liberty implies no Law or that Law implies bondage is answered by the Puritans in the spirit of the psalmist who said, "I will walk at liberty: for I seek thy precepts."[199] The liberty of the Christian man suffers no limitation on account of the commandment. There is nothing inconsistent in the doing of a work by commandment and the doing of it freely. An action can be the expression of obedience and also of desire: and the one does not destroy the other. Samuel Bolton asks, "Whether this may consist with our Christian freedom, to be tyed to do dutie because God hath commanded". He answers,

> It is no infringement to our Liberty in Christ to be tyed to the performance of dutie: It was the great end of our freedom and redemption that we might serve him. . . . He hath redeemed us from a slavish spirit in service, to a son-like; from a spirit of bondage, to a spirit of liberty.[200]

John Sedgwick remarks that it is sometimes "a trouble to Christians, that they are not more obedient to the Law, but it never troubled them that they have been obedient to it."[201]

> The Spirits joy, and the power of the Law to command, are so farre from opposing one the other, that the Spirit gives testimony of Gods abode in no other but such as confesse and yeeld to this power.[202]

So little does Samuel Rutherford think that there is any incongruity between the doing of an action by commandment and the performance of it by love, that he even says, "Law-threatning (when Faith assureth the conscience, of freedome from the wrath to come) and love-perswading are most consistent."[203] The "obliging rule, and govern-

198. Robert Towne, *Assertion of Grace*, p. 137.
199. Psalm cxix. 45.
200. *True Bounds*, pp. 195, 196.
201. *Antinomianisme Anatomized*, p. 33.
202. Thomas Blake, *Covenant of God*, p. 54.
203. *Survey*, Part II. p. 13.

ment of the Law" is in no way "contrary to the sweet cords of Gospel-love, by which the Spirit kindly draweth, and gently leadeth the Saints in the way of Sanctification."[204] These two things, he says, are joined together in Christ, "and jarre not as contraries."[205] "Grace and condemnation are opposite, but not Grace and the commanding power of the Law."[206] The doing of good works "from the principle of the love of Christ constraining us", and "from the Law commanding, or directing us", he says, "are no way contrary, the Regenerate from both Principles are to walke in love and holinesse as Christ did; the Law directing is not abolished by Grace, or by love to Christ."[207] "The Law of God, honeyed with the love of Christ, hath a Majestie and power to keep from sin."[208] He clinches his argument by means of a comparison with the relation between human freedom and Divine sovereignty.

> Looke how wee say the willing free obedience of men consisteth well with the necessity of Gods absolute decree, so sweet delightfull freenesse of a Gospel-spirit led by God, does well consist with the necessity of an obliging and strongly commanding Law, though the sting of the cursing, and threatning be removed.[209]

The New Covenant writing of the Law within the believer's heart, creates "a connaturalnesse to the wayes of his Commandements",[210] by which the believer discovers within himself a "great pronenesse and aptnesse . . . and willingnesse to keepe the Law."[211] God "sets a new Byas upon the soule" so that good works are not done as of necessity or as a task.[212] The experience of God's saving grace fastens "the power and authority of the Law" upon the believer "together with a disposition to obedience upon the heart, so that the heart shall be no more contrary to it, but sweetly concurring with it."[213] By reason of this, the believer "does duty from an ingenuous and free spirit" and not by "legal principles",[214] and is like the willing slave with a bored ear,[215] whose obedience is not merely by command, but from love.[216] William Perkins seems to invite the commandment of the Law and declares, "The more we are bound to obedience, the

204. Samuel Rutherford, op. cit., Part II. p. 68.
205. Ibid.
206. Samuel Rutherford, *Triumph of Faith*, p. 105.
207. Op. cit., p. 104.
208. Op. cit., p. 122.
209. Samuel Rutherford, *Survey*, Part I. p. 319. "Looke how" means "just as".
210. John Preston, *New Covenant*, p. 119.
211. John Preston, op. cit., pp. 430, 431.
212. John Preston, op. cit., p. 432.
213. John Sedgwick, *Antinomianisme Anatomized*, pp. 17, 18.
214. William Strong, *The Two Covenants*, p. 57.
215. Thomas Goodwin, *Mediator*, in *Works*, V. 145.
216. Thomas Goodwin, op. cit., p. 221.

freer we are: because the service of God is not bondage, but perfect libertie."[217]

The Law is kept "evangelically", in a spiritual way and by "Gospel motives",[218] all of which terms are congruous with the true nature of Law, and "Legal duties" are done "in a Gospel manner."[219]

> The precepts of Grace are so sublime, and spiritual, that they must be understood spiritually. . . . That is the reason why a man under Grace is brought into fuller obedience to a freer service then a man under the Law.[220]

There is a real liberty in duty, says Thomas Manton, for "why should we account that a bondage which is part of our happiness?"[221] "The law in the hands of Christ is a law of liberty",[222] and although the believer's "warrant is the command" his "poise and weight should be love."[223] John Owen draws many strands of argument together when he equates the "law of the mind" with the "law of grace" and these, in turn, with the "law of God."[224]

One of the frequent illustrations used by the Puritans is the comparison with the angels whose subjection to Law is their very liberty.[225] Anthony Burgess quotes the Antinomian saying that "a Beleever is carried by love, he needs no law", and refutes it by means of the examples of the angels, of Adam, of the mother of Moses, and of Christ Himself. He argues that "if it was not a commandement" that was laid upon Christ, it would not be possible to speak of the "obedience of Christ", and infers from this that "to doe a thing out of obedience to a command, because a command, doth not inferre want of love."[226] The author of *The Marrow* suggests that obedience to the Law of Christ is "the middle path" of truth between Legalism and Antinomianism.[227] He maintains that the believer does good works without "compulsion", that is to say, not being slavishly driven to do them by threat or fear. The binding authority of the Law is not destroyed, even when the believer does right "freely of his own accord."[228]

217. *Galatians*, p. 357.
218. Francis Roberts, *God's Covenants*, pp. 716, 719, 721.
219. James Durham, *Law Unsealed*, pp. 4, 10.
220. Walter Cradock, *Divine Drops Distilled*, p. 162.
221. *Lord's Prayer*, in *Works*, I. 131.
222. Thomas Manton, *James*, in *Works*, IV. 219; cf. 164, 165; *Hundred and Nineteenth Psalm*, I. 445.
223. Thomas Manton, op. cit., 166.
224. *Indwelling Sin*, in *Works*, VI. 195.
225. Cf. William Perkins, *Galatians*, p. 319; Samuel Rutherford, *Triumph of Faith*, p. 289, and Edward Elton, *Treatises*: "Complaint of a Sanctifyed Sinner", p. 21.
226. *Vindiciae Legis*, pp. 13, 14.
227. Op. cit., To the Reader, p. 9.
228. *The Marrow*, p. 164.

The Puritans believed that the highest spirituality was to be seen in a life that rejoices to be commanded. They held that, far from involving the believer in legalistic bondage, it gave expression to his desire to please God, from which, as a subjective motive such an obedient life sprang. The spiritual man has such "a true love and liking of the Law of God"[229] that "absence of a delight is a sign of unspirituality."[230] John Preston holds it to be one of the tokens of perfection in a believer "that the principall motive, that which sets him aworke upon all occasions, is some Commandement from God."[231] So true is this, that not until a believer is deeply spiritual is he able to "perform his Christian duties aright."[232]

In their 699th session on 4 September, 1646, the Westminster Divines recorded that, it is no "evidence that a man is under the law, and not under grace, when he refrains from evil and doeth good, because the law encourageth to the one and deters from the other", but, rather, it is one of the highest expressions of spirituality, and anything short of this kind of obedience is carnal.[233]

The Puritans needed to defend their position on two sides. On the one hand, they found that the Law was being so abused that sanctification was reduced to morality, or even legalism; and on the other, they met with fellow-Puritans whose attitude to the Law was such as to make it "void" and to dissolve sanctification into emotionalism. Their considered definition is found in the *Confession of Faith*, "The liberty which Christ hath purchased for believers under the gospel, consists in . . . their yielding obedience unto him, not out of slavish fear, but a child-like love, and willing mind."[234] The authors of the *Confession of Faith* indicate that this liberty was "common also to believers under the law", but under the Gospel there are "fuller communications of the free Spirit of God, than believers under the law did ordinarily partake of."[235]

The spiritual freedom for which the Puritans contended, and in which so many of them lived, was the great reality of their salvation in Christ. It was at the same time fully consistent with their acknowledgment of the sovereignty of the Law of God.

229. Edward Elton, *Treatises*: "Complaint of a Sanctifyed Sinner", p. 157.
230. Edward Elton, op. cit., p. 189; cf. Thomas Wilson, *Romanes*, p. 234.
231. *New Covenant*, pp. 290–94; cf. *Breastplate of Faith and Love*, "Of Love", p. 113.
232. *The Marrow*, p. 169.
233. Quoted by A. F. Mitchell and J. Struthers, *Minutes*, p. 274; cf. *Confession of Faith*, XIX. 6.
234. Op. cit., XX. 1.
235. Ibid.

Conclusion

THE PURITAN DOCTRINE: AN ASSESSMENT IN THE LIGHT OF RECENT CRITICAL STUDIES

Synopsis

Summary of the Puritan doctrine

A. ITS BIBLICAL METHOD

B. ITS ETHICAL PRINCIPLES

(i) *Legalism*
(ii) *Antinomianism*

C. ITS THEOLOGICAL FOUNDATION

D. ITS SOTERIOLOGICAL INTEREST

The Grace of Law

Conclusion

THE PURITAN DOCTRINE: AN ASSESSMENT IN THE LIGHT OF RECENT CRITICAL STUDIES

IN a great many places the present writer's own convictions are so clearly expressed by the Puritans that this concluding chapter wears something of the character of an *Apologia pro Puritanis* and takes the form of a presentation of their views in the context of present-day thinking. It begins with a summary of the material that has been surveyed in the preceding chapters, and then, after a brief glance at the evidence of the re-awakened interest in the subject of the Law of God, attention is drawn to the method of Biblical interpretation which underlies the Puritan doctrine—a method to which, in one of its aspects, modern scholarship is again turning. This is followed by an examination of the ethical principles accepted by the Puritans and it is shown that they were neither Legalists nor Antinomians. The next section brings under review the essentially theological aspect of the Puritan concern for the moral Law, with its theocentric interpretation of life; and the chapter is concluded by an exposition of the soteriological interest which lies at the heart of the Puritan teaching.

Summary of the Puritan doctrine

The material presented in the preceding chapters may be summarized as follows. The Law is the Law of God and is the expression of the Divine majesty. It is based on the Creator-creature relation, for "He that said what we should Be, to him it certainly belongeth to say what we should Do."[1] The Creator exercises His authority over man consistently with the rational and moral nature with which He has endowed him, and expresses His sovereignty in the form of Law. In obedience to this Law man may both glorify his Maker and find his own proper blessedness. Sin is the breaking of the Law of God and is to be estimated not merely by the intrinsic wrongness of the action but "by the offence it containeth against Gods majestie."[2] The entry of sin into the world brought a dimming of man's knowledge of God's Law and, more significantly still, a complete inability

1. John Barret. See above, p. 48.
2. William Perkins. See above, p. 48.

to fulfil it. One of the uses of the Law in a sinful world is to restrain sin, but on account of man's corrupted nature it frequently has the opposite effect of provoking it. Supremely, and in spite of this "accidentall"[3] contradiction, the function of the Law of God in relation to sin is to condemn it and to convict the sinner. It is by means of the Law that the Holy Spirit creates in the sinner an awareness of the bondage into which he has been brought by sin and so prepares him for the freedom of the Gospel. The relation of Law to sin makes it impossible to think of the imperfections of the believer as anything other than sin, and the Antinomian opinion that God sees no sin in the believer is to be rejected. Further, the sin which man sees in himself, which is brought to his notice by the Law of God, and which must not be explained away as mere infirmity, is to be acknowledged and confessed, for "when we do that which is . . . forbidden by God, this is more than an Infirmity; . . . 'tis not a weak action, but a wicked one".[4] The function of the Law of God in relation to sin has a place in the saving purpose of God. In the historical unfolding of the Divine plan of salvation, the Law is given to man a second time, through the ministry of Moses, but this formal promulgation of the Law was not made until God had first declared His purpose of grace. The Law was thus designed by God, not to provide the sinner with a means of self-justification, but to be a means of grace. Any legalistic attitude to Law-keeping, therefore, is utterly incompatible with the Divine purpose in the giving of the Law and is itself an offence against the Law. If there is any contrariety between the Law and the Gospel, it is "not in themselves, but in the ignorance, pride and hardnesse of heart of them, who . . . did pervert the right end of the Law."[5] The Covenant of Grace began to be revealed in the Garden of Eden at the moment of man's fall, and it is one and the same throughout both the old and the new dispensations. This continuity of grace requires that the Bible shall be expounded as one book, and, therefore, "a proof out of the old Testament is as much Gospel if rightly applied, as any in the New-Testament."[6] The saving purpose of the Law has found its fulfilment in Christ who, by His work of redemption, has become "the end of the law for righteousness to every one that believeth".[7] This relation between the work of Christ and the Law of God, however, does not mean the abrogation of the Law. Given to man at his creation, the Law lies at the basis of all God's relations with him, but is itself to be distinguished from them. For this reason the concepts of "law" and "covenant" are not to be confounded.

3. Samuel Rutherford. See above, p. 81.
4. Thomas Cole. See above, p. 103.
5. John Ball. See above, p. 131.
6. Richard Byfield. See above, p. 121.
7. Romans x. 4.

God's covenants may change, but the same constant Law is to be honoured throughout. That there should be any abrogation of the Law on account of the Fall is inconceivable. "We are no more discharged of our duties, because we have no strength to doe it: then a debter is quitted of his Bands because he wants money to make payment."[8] It is likewise unthinkable that the Law should be abrogated by grace, for "when God became a Saviour to the Elect of mankind, he did not cease to be a Sovereign."[9] This being so, the continuance of moral obligation follows as a necessary corollary, and, far from being reduced by God's grace, the obligation to obey the Law of God is increased. Furthermore, the Law is to be obeyed, not merely by the performance of the things laid down by it, but by the doing of them because they are so laid down. "Our obedience must be . . . because he commands us",[10] and no amount of doing of what is commanded is "to be reputed godliness, except man therein hath reall reference unto God."[11] Believers are still "in the law to Christ",[12] and their obedience or disobedience to the Law provides the basis of God's approval or disapproval of them as His children. Obedience to Law, however, does not mean that the believer is justified by his evangelical works. The Neonomian doctrine of justification by obedience of this kind is but a refined form of legalism and is contrary both to the glory of Christ and the grace of the Gospel. Nevertheless, the believer should be able to give evidence of his justification, and this is to be found in his good works, for without these he is not fulfilling the purpose of his salvation. Neonomianism on the one hand and Antinomianism on the other must be equally firmly rejected. The obedience of the believer establishes the Law in respect of its Divine purpose, for it is not "all one to the Law, whether the debt of obedience, or the debt of punishment were paid";[13] and despite the imperfections which mar even his best obedience, this is acceptable to God through the merits of Christ. There is no loss of spiritual liberty in Law-keeping. The obedience of the Christian man is the result of the Law in the heart and is the very antithesis of legalism. By the effectual working of the Holy Spirit the believer is emancipated from the tyranny of sin and made truly free for the keeping of the Law. He has become "friends"[14] with the Law in such a way that in keeping the commandments he finds his widest liberty.

These Puritan convictions, couched in seventeenth-century

8. William Pemble. See above, p. 152.
9. Thomas Blake. See above, p. 156.
10. Richard Sibbes. See above, p. 182.
11. John Ball. See above, p. 183.
12. I Corinthians ix. 21.
13. Anthony Burgess. See above, p. 217.
14. Samuel Rutherford. See above, p. 238.

language as they were, and formulated in the theological patterns of their day, are remarkably relevant to modern thinking. It is significant, for example, that the World Council of Churches decided that the third of its Ecumenical Biblical Studies held at Treysa (Germany) in August 1950, should be directed to an examination of *The Biblical Doctrine of Justice and Law*,[15] and they described their studies as an attempt to contribute to the solution of "one of the most pressing modern problems".[16] Previous to the World Council Study Group at Treysa, a similar but less formal conference was held, extending over several years, at St Deiniol's Library, Hawarden. The results of this conference were published in a booklet entitled, *Natural Law, a Christian Reconsideration*.[17] Contemporary with this earlier conference there appeared an outstanding, though small, book on the subject by A. R. Vidler, bearing the title, *Christ's Strange Work*, a volume which was chosen as the Bishop of London's Lent Book for 1944. The renewed interest in the study of the Law of God is also reflected in the considerable number of books which have appeared in recent times.[18]

One important result of these studies has been the emancipation of the concept of natural Law from its captivity to the empirical sciences[19] and its reinstatement within the realm of moral studies. Such a reinstatement, however, opens up questions that have been long silenced, and makes it necessary once again to endeavour to press behind ethical phenomena to their source in God the Creator.[20] This, in turn, provokes the further inquiry into the relation of natural Law to revealed Law, and, in particular, to the Law of the Ten Commandments. Questions of this kind thus carry the inquiry directly into the area of thought occupied by the Puritans and justify a renewed study of their writings.

A critical assessment of the Puritan doctrine may be made from

15. This is the title of the 200-page report edited by H. H. Schrey, H. H. Walz and W. A. Whitehouse.
16. Op. cit., Preface.
17. Edited by A. R. Vidler and W. A. Whitehouse, 1946.
18. Noteworthy among these are *The Ten Commandments in the 20th century*, J. Drewett, 1941; *The Catholic Conception of the Law of Nature*, J. Dalby, 1943; *Justice and the Social Order*, E. Brunner, Eng. trans. 1945; *Natural Law in the Bible*, and *Gospel and Law*, C. H. Dodd, 1946 and 1950; *The New Testament Basis of Moral Theology*, F. D. Coggan, 1948; *The Ten Words*, S. Myers, 1956, written "to re-assert the unchanging worth of this part of the Biblical revelation as the Great Charter of human well-being"; *The Revelation of Law in Scripture*, P. Fairbairn, reprinted in 1957; *The Ten Commandments and Modern Man*, H. G. G. Herklots, 1958; *The Theological Foundation of Law*, J. Ellul, 1946, Eng. trans. 1961; *Creation and Law*, G. Wingren, Eng. trans., 1961; and *Law and Gospel*, W. Andersen, 1961.

See A. R. Vidler and W. A. Whitehouse, *Natural Law*, p. 15.

But see W. G. Maclagan, *The Theological Frontier of Ethics*, 1961.

four points of view: its Biblical method; its ethical principles; its theological foundation; and its soteriological interest.

A. ITS BIBLICAL METHOD

It would be tedious and unnecessary to attempt to give Scripture proof for the *minutiae* of Puritan doctrine, partly because the Puritans do this themselves, and partly because any passages of disputed meaning have been discussed already in their appropriate place. There is no little significance, however, in the principles of interpretation by which the Puritan exegesis was governed, and these are worthy of examination.

The Puritans regarded the Bible as a whole and taught the fundamental unity of the Old and New Testaments. It is true, as many have pointed out, that some of their detailed expositions suffered from a defect in historical perspective and were based upon a kind of mathematical unity rather than a teleological one. It is also true that proof-texts were frequently cited by them as if every verse of Scripture were of universal validity irrespective of considerations of time and place. But these familiar criticisms of the expository methods of the Puritans leave their main principle of Biblical unity unaffected. Governed by this principle, they were able to give full value to the concept of fulfilment, and, being perfectly at home with what W. J. Phythian-Adams calls the principle of "homology",[21] they found no difficulty in understanding the New Testament statements which spoke of the blessings of the second Covenant in terms of the first.

This conviction about the Bible put the Puritans in a strong theological position, and they convincingly developed the doctrinal implications of their view.[22]

They worked out the conception of Biblical unity in a number of important theological directions. Of these, one of the most significant was that of the unity of the covenants,[23] and from this truth two others emerged as corollaries. They were not unaware of the difference between the covenants, and taught that underlying this diversity of administration there was the unity of grace. What were known in Scripture as the old and new covenants were in reality the first and second dispensations of the one Covenant of Grace. Absence of sufficient attention to the differences of administration in the two dispensations led the Puritans into a difference of judgment among themselves about the doctrine of the Church and Sacraments, but

21. *The Way of At-one-ment*, 1944, p. 11.
22. Cf. J. I. Packer, "The Puritans as Interpreters of Scripture", in *A Goodly Heritage*, 1958, pp. 18–26.
23. See above, Chapter III.

their clear understanding of the principle of grace that bound the dispensations into a unity provided them with strong foundations for the construction of their doctrinal system. Two important corollaries followed upon the unity of the covenants, the first of which was the unity of the covenant people. The Puritans saw the people of God—God's elect—as one holy community throughout both the dispensations of the Covenant of Grace. The second corollary was the perpetual validity of the moral Law, with all the theological implications of this which the Puritans expounded.

During the nineteenth century, and in the early part of the twentieth, the prevailing method of Biblical interpretation tended to be analytical in style. There were some exceptions to this, and appreciation of the theological unity of the Old and New Testaments is found in such Old Testament scholars as E. W. Hengstenberg,[24] J. H. Kurtz,[25] G. F. Oehler,[26] H. Schultz,[27] A. B. Davidson,[28] and others.[29] The two Testaments were kept widely apart, and the individual books were studied almost as isolated productions. The analysis was carried even farther by some scholars and penetrated to the dividing up of the books themselves. But this analytical habit of the past hundred years has steadily given place to a method which seeks again to interpret the Bible in its wholeness and to stress the essential unity that underlies all the parts of Divine revelation.[30] It is now one of the generally agreed principles that "the two testaments are to be interpreted in relation to one another".[31] This recovered concept of the unity of the Bible, however, is not a mere return to a static view of revelation, nor does it throw away the valuable insights gained by a historical approach to the Scripture.[32] It conserves the gains of recent

24. *Christology of the Old Testament*, 1829, Eng. trans. 1858; *History of the Kingdom of God under the Old Testament*, 1869, Eng. trans. 1871, especially I. 10–21.
25. *History of the Old Covenant*, 1853, Eng. trans. 1859, pp. 1–16.
26. *Theology of the Old Testament*, 1873, Eng. trans. 1892, I. 37–67.
27. *Old Testament Theology*, 1892, Eng. trans. 1909, I. 51–60.
28. *The Theology of the Old Testament*, pp. 1–11.
29. See the survey made by J. C. J. Waite, *The Activity of the Holy Spirit within the Old Testament Period*, 1961, pp. 4–8.
30. Cf. A. Richardson, *Preface to Bible Study*, 1943, pp. 63–74; A. R. Vidler, *Christ's Strange Work*, pp. 1, 5, 58; W. J. Phythian-Adams, *The Way of At-one-ment*, pp. 9–26; R. V. G. Tasker, *The Old Testament in the New Testament*, 1946, pp. 9–13; W. Vischer, *The Witness of the Old Testament to Christ*, 1936, Eng. trans. 1949; pp. 7–34; H. H. Rowley, *The Unity of the Bible*, 1953, pp. 1–29; H. H. Schrey, H. H. Walz, W. A. Whitehouse, *The Biblical Doctrine of Justice and Law*, pp. 46, 47; G. Wingren, *Creation and Law*, pp. 7, 9, 15, 17, 28, 29, 84n, 128; E. Jacob, *Theology of the Old Testament*, 1955, Eng. trans. 1958, pp. 11–26; Th. G. Vriezen, *An Outline of Old Testament Theology*, 1949, Eng. trans. 1958, pp. 2–126; G. A. F. Knight, *A Christian Theology of the Old Testament*, 1959. Apart from the striking title, see also pp. 7–11, 349–58.
31. J. D. Wood, *The Interpretation of the Bible*, 1958, p. 169.
32. Cf. A. G. Hebert, *The Throne of David*, 1941, p. 32.

Biblical study, but at the same time it retrieves the losses and recovers the message of the Bible as a theological whole.[33] That there have been serious losses during some of the periods of Old Testament study there can be no doubt. The excessive analysis undertaken by some schools of thought, and the "dispensationalism" of others,[34] have led not only to a general fragmentation of Christian doctrine, but more particularly to the depreciation of the Law of God and the denial of its place in Christian life.

A healthier theological situation is now being restored, however, and the thinking of the present day reveals an approximation to each other of the hermeneutical principles of the seventeenth century and the twentieth. This new circumstance provides the Puritans and the moderns with a meeting place for mutual understanding, and calls for a respectful attitude to the theological views of the Puritans.

B. ITS ETHICAL PRINCIPLES

"What is the chief end of man?" This is the first question which the Puritans put to their young catechumens, and the answer to it determines the ethical principles of Puritanism. "Man's chief end is to glorify God, and to enjoy him for ever."[35] This immediately disqualifies such concepts of ethics as hedonism, self-realization and other similar naturalistic theories. The Puritans did not regard man as an end in himself, and rejected all views of the moral life that detracted from the majesty of the Law of God. Their conception of the moral life was far removed from that which sees it merely as "a harmonious development of natural powers guided by the idea of happiness": instead, it was a conception that saw it to be "a life of discipline and subordination to an authoritative law."[36]

With the passing of the centuries, the Puritan doctrine has become increasingly neglected, and modern trends in ethical thought reveal a drift towards a point of view totally different from that of authoritative command. T. C. Hall speaks of the "sense of inner compulsion" which is everywhere "becoming the regulative principle of human society, displacing in the moral man outward law, and giving the sense of new freedom."[37]

(i) *Legalism*

One of the most fashionable misrepresentations of Puritanism has been to identify it with legalism—a term which is seldom used

33. It is for this reason that J. D. Wood calls it a "theological interpretation", op. cit., p. 166.
34. Cf. O. T. Allis, *Prophecy and the Church*, 1945, pp. 16–54.
35. *Shorter Catechism*, Q.1.
36. N. Wilde, Article "Moral Law", *ERE*, VIII. p. 833.
37. T. C. Hall, Article "Moral Obligation", *ERE*, VIII. p. 835.

accurately. The Oxford Dictionary defines its theological meaning as "adherence to the Law as opposed to the Gospel; the doctrine of justification by works, or teaching which savours of it." The Puritans sometimes described this attitude of mind as being "of the Works of the Law". Thomas Bedford uses this phrase and asks the question:

> But what is it to be of the Works of the Law? Is it to take directions from the Law for our ways and walking? Is it to yield obedience to the Law? No: It is to seek Justification and Salvation by the merits of works done in obedience to the Law.[38]

The essence of the current controversy about the alleged legalism of the Puritans is found in this distinction which Thomas Bedford draws and which so many modern writers seem not to perceive.

A perusal of recent books on Christian ethics reveals no little evidence of an inability to distinguish between Law and legalism, between what is "legal" and what is "legalistic". Why must obedience always be deprecated as "blind"?[39] Why must T. W. Manson speak of "cast-iron Law" when describing the Law of the Old Testament?[40] Why must the phrase "Law and Legalism"[41] meet the reader everywhere he turns, as if Law could not exist without legalism? Christ undoubtedly "undermined legalism", as S. Cave affirms,[42] but He did not thereby undermine the Law. This author seems to think that to use such a phrase as "a legal conception of God"[43] is sufficient to silence all further argument, but the expression needs definition before it can be effectually employed. It is easy enough to become indignant about "the tyranny of legalism"[44] and to proclaim Paul's "radical breach with legalism",[45] about which nobody disagrees, but what support does this give to the opinion that the Law is no longer a valid expression of man's relation to God?[46] It requires a great amount of reading of alien ideas into Paul's words to believe that he ever thought of the Law as among the "antagonists" of man and "severed from God".[47] This is an outstanding example of the contemporary confusion between the concepts of law and legalism.[48] "Legalism" is an "antagonist" and a "tyrant", but not Law. J. Fletcher makes a pungent remark exposing this superficial identifica-

38. *An Examination*, p. 13.
39. Cf. W. Lillie, *The Law of Christ*, p. 25.
40. *Ethics and the Gospel*, 1960, p. 66. In this expression he is not merely alluding to the pharisaical abuse of the Law but reflects back on the law itself.
41. S. Cave, *The Gospel of St. Paul*, 1928, p. 132.
42. *The Doctrines of the Christian Faith*, 1931, p. 66n.
43. Op. cit., p. 75.
44. Op. cit., p. 131.
45. Op. cit., p. 133.
46. Op. cit., p. 129.
47. Cf. *The Gospel of St. Paul*, p. 130, The "hypostasization" seems to be overdone.
48. Cf. J. S. Stewart, *A Man in Christ*, 1935, pp. 113, 291, 292.

tion of "legal" and "legalistic" when he says, "Pharisees are no more truly legal than antinomians are truly evangelical."[49]

Once "legalism" is distinguished from "law", it can be seen for what it really is. It is the abuse of the Law as a means of obtaining a meritorious standing before God; it is the use of the Law "as pharisaically conceived",[50] and an employment of it in its outward form without regard to its inward demands.[51] That the natural man has an inclination to legalism no one can doubt. He "is always prone to conceive his relation to God in terms of law" and to "turn his obedience into a yoke of bondage".[52] He thinks that the Law can "be tamed and used as a means to self-justification",[53] and, having adopted a legalistic attitude, he defends himself in it by an appeal to the negative form of the Decalogue.[54]

The temptation to take a legalistic view of life is an ever-present danger and may not be ignored in any assessment of the present situation within the Christian Church. It is impossible, however, to charge the Puritans with legalism. Such a way of thinking does not enter at all into their system of doctrine, and it was as firmly deprecated by the Puritans in the seventeenth century as by other writers in the twentieth. Any criticism of Puritanism which is based upon its alleged "legalism" must, therefore, be dismissed as uninformed. The "legalism" of Puritanism is a "bogey" constructed by prejudiced imagination from the popular caricature of the God-fearing Puritan and from ignorance of what he taught.[55] The words of E. Brunner, "We are not Antinomians because we do not wish to be legalists",[56] could be equally well reversed and put into the lips of the Puritans who would say, "We are not legalists because we do not wish to be Antinomians."

The Puritans were not legalists.

49. *Second Check*, in *Works*, I. 338.
50. A. B. Bruce, *St Paul's Conception of Christianity*, 1894, p. 300; cf. 296–298.
51. P. Fairbairn, *Law in Scripture*, pp. 370–76; cf. G. S. Hendry, *The Westminster Confession for Today*, p. 139; C. A. A. Scott, *Christianity according to St. Paul*, p. 38 f.; A. R. Vidler, *Christ's Strange Work*, p. 39; J. S. Stewart, *A Man in Christ*, pp. 84, 85, 88.
52. C. A. A. Scott, op. cit., pp. 41, 45.
53. H. H. Schrey, H. H. Walz, W. A. Whitehouse, *The Biblical Doctrine of Justice and Law*, p. 89.
54. L. H. Marshall, *The Challenge of New Testament Ethics*, 1946, p. 44; cf. p. 73.
55. J. Marlowe, who says, "Ultimately, the Puritan has only remained a Christian to the extent of his abandonment of Puritanism", *The Puritan Tradition in English Life*, 1956, p. 140, produces a bibliography at the end of his book in which not one single Puritan work is named! Similarly, C. F. Simcox, in an otherwise constructive book on *Living the Ten Commandments*, falls into the same snare when treating of the Sabbath. The only way he seems able to express his own views is to flay the Puritans and to group them with the Pharisees, but, again, not with a shred of evidence. Op. cit., 1957, pp. 56–66.
56. *Divine Imperative*, p. 138.

(ii) *Antinomianism*

The reason why Puritanism is decried by many modern writers is that they themselves are Antinomians in some sort. W. Haller shrewdly remarks, "Perhaps the desire of later generations to escape from Puritanism has been at least in part a desire to do business with less hindrance from a scheme of life so insistent upon keeping the individual forever in mind of his moral responsibilities."[57] The arguments presented by the Antinomians today are much the same as those presented by John Eaton, John Saltmarsh and Robert Towne in theirs, and it is assumed that Law and love are so contradictory that where one is the other cannot be. M. Burrows, for example, considers that "the Christian is free from the law precisely because he is ruled by the spirit of love and therefore needs no law."[58] The general Antinomian opinion of the present day is that Law is superfluous to the good, and so the moral imperatives of Jesus are not to be thought of as "laws".[59] Love, therefore, is thought to take the place of Law in Christian life, and it is the opinion of many that "if we really try to love our neighbour, we shall automatically keep all the Commandments."[60]

This exaltation of love as the comprehensive ethical standard is usually supported by the contention that the Gospel contains inspiring principles of conduct, but no laws or rules. The Christian life is thus considered to be an "adventurous quest",[61] or an "ethical achievement",[62] both of which descriptions seem to merit E. Brunner's caustic criticism of them as "antinomian Vitalism".[63] T. W. Manson holds that Jesus gave principles, not laws: and that what Jesus offers in His ethical teaching is "not a set of rules of conduct, but a number of illustrations of the way in which a transformed character will express itself in conduct."[64] Others regard the ethical teaching of Jesus as no more than the announcement of a mere "practical possibility."[65] R. Niebuhr expresses a completely Antinomian sentiment when he says that "Orthodox Christianity . . . cannot come to

57. *Rise of Puritanism*, p. 119. See the forceful article by R. W. Dale, "The Old Antinomianism and the New", *Congregational Review*, 1887, I. pp. 11–18.
58. *An Outline of Biblical Theology*, 1946, p. 160.
59. L. H. Marshall, *The Challenge of New Testament Ethics*, p. 101; cf. H. A. A. Kennedy, *The Theology of the Epistles*, 1919, p. 241.
60. J. Drewett, *The Ten Commandments in the 20th Century*, p. 12.
61. W. Lillie, *The Law of Christ*, p. 18.
62. L. H. Marshall, *The Challenge of New Testament Ethics*, p. 69.
63. *Divine Imperative*, p. 74. It should be observed, however, that in this comment he is attacking not so much the "Antinomianism" as the "Vitalism", for he himself is as Antinomian as those whom he criticises. Cf. the judgment of R. A. Gessert in "The Integrity of Faith", *SJT*, XIII. pp. 254, 255; and N. H. G. Robinson, *Christ and Conscience*, pp: 22, 23, 72, 88, 102.
64. *The Teaching of Jesus*, 1931, p. 301; cf. L. H. Marshall, op. cit., p. 99; Olaf Moe, Article, "Commandment", 1915, *DAC*, I. 233.
65. H. H. Schrey, H. H. Walz, W. A. Whitehouse, op. cit., p. 102

the aid of modern man . . . because its morality is expressed in dogmatic and authoritarian moral codes."[66]

Support for the view that the "Law" of God now continues as an inward "principle" is derived in part from the fact that νόμος also means principle, but whether this meaning can be established in the New Testament is open to doubt. C. H. Dodd,[67] recognizes some element of the authoritative in "the law of Christ", and he demonstrates this in *ΕΝΝΟΜΟΣ ΧΡΙΣΤΟΥ*,[68] but his conclusion seems to be in favour of the idea of a potent spiritual principle to which Christ's example gives the direction and quality.[69]

All these were old and familiar arguments to the Puritans, and the main body of this thesis has shown how they dealt with them. The Puritans saw that Antinomianism—in all its guises—was as dangerous as legalism, and so they stood for the continuance of the Law and the obligation of the Christian believer to keep it.

The Puritans were not Antinomians.

A. R. Vidler remarks that "The Church on earth has always, as it were, to walk on the razor edge between legalism and antinomianism, between taking the Law too seriously and not taking it seriously enough. It is not surprising that every Church tends to err in one direction or the other".[70] The Puritans walked this middle path and rendered a service to the Christian doctrine of sanctification which cannot be over-estimated. They rejected Antinomianism as firmly as they repudiated Legalism, and their exposition of evangelical Law-keeping remains today as a bulwark against the naturalistic Antinomianism of liberalism, the dispensationalist Antinomianism of certain schools of orthodoxy, the evangelical Antinomianism of holiness movements, and the supernatural Antinomianism of neo-orthodoxy. In all this resistance against Antinomianism the Puritans contended, in the words of an immediately post-Puritan Scottish preacher, Ralph Erskine, that

> When once the fiery Law of God
> Has chas'd me to the Gospel road;
> Then back unto the holy law
> Most kindly Gospel-grace will draw.[71]

66. *An Interpretation of Christian Ethics*, 1956, p. 14.
67. Other writers, also, such as W. Lillie, C. A. A. Scott, and L. H. Marshall.
68. In *Studia Paulina*, pp. 96–110.
69. *Gospel and Law*, 1950, pp. 71–73. C. E. Simcox makes an endeavour to draw the principle of love into proximity to the Commandment of God by saying, "If we love God rightly, we may do as we please; and we shall be pleased to do only that which is pleasing in His sight," *Living the Ten Commandments*, p. 23; but even this does not come up fully to the level of living under Divine authority. Law must be subsumed under love but not submerged by it.
70. *Christ's Strange Work*, p. 53.
71. *Gospel Sonnets* 1720 in *Works*, X. 270.

C. ITS THEOLOGICAL FOUNDATION

The Puritans emphasized the God-relatedness of human life and the moral obligations resulting from man's creation by God. They held that the obligation to obey derived from the creature-Creator relation, and that the right to command arose from the Creator-creature relation. On this ground, therefore, they maintained that the obligation to obedience and the right to command remained undiminished either by the Fall or through the intervention of grace.

This truth has recently been ably discussed by G. Wingren in *Creation and Law*, and he expounds what is distinctively the Puritan position in this respect as opposed to that of neo-orthodoxy. The Puritans related man's obligation under Law to his creatureliness, and, as G. Wingren would put it, they thought within the framework, "Law and Gospel", rather than "Gospel and Law."[72] The arguments of this Swedish scholar were anticipated by a few years in the discussions reported in *The Biblical Doctrine of Justice and Law*. The question then raised was: "Is the foundation of Christian ethics, and therefore of the Christian doctrine of law, to be found in the biblical message of the Lordship of Christ, as Karl Barth and others maintain? Or is it rather to be sought in the biblical doctrine of God's work as Creator and Preserver of his world through the law? Lutheran theologians such as Nygren and Aulén maintained this second position in opposition to Barth's Christological one."[73] This protest against the neo-orthodox formula "Gospel and Law" is not a denial that in the history of redemption the Covenant of Grace ante-dated the Sinaitic Law, but it draws attention to the priority of man's creature relation to God over his "new-creature" relation. There cannot be any fundamental difference between "natural" and "Christian" ethics. "Indeed", says G. Wingren, "to raise this question means that we have failed to think of God as the One who acts in the universe and whose dealings with humanity will culminate in His Judgment of the whole world on the last day."[74] It is still the "old commandment" that lies upon the Christian believer, for "when the Gospel is proclaimed together with the Law in preaching, the hearer resumes an obedience to a demand which he has continually defied."[75] It is by His Law and its accompanying sanctions that "*God continues to be God* and to rule His Creation",[76] and "any attempt to

72. "If, with Barth, we change law and Gospel into 'Gospel and law'—in that order—something of the Bible's own content disappears." G. Wingren, *The Living Word*, 1949, p. 148n. Cf. *Creation and Law*, p. 66.
73. Op. cit., pp. 38, 39.
74. *Creation and Law*, p. 57.
75. G. Wingren, op. cit., p. 61.
76. Op. cit., p. 66 (italics his).

eliminate God's dealings with the world through the Law will come into conflict with scripture itself, which assumes this very fact."[77]

The Puritans identified this Creation-Law with the Decalogue and based their teaching not on any undefined demand remaining vaguely in man's fallen nature, but on the plain terms of the revealed Law of God given by the hand of Moses.[78] G. Wingren affirms that it was "*their correspondence to the natural law*" which constituted the positive value of certain of the Old Testament commandments, for "if we reject the concept of a natural law, then the Law of the Old Testament becomes an insoluble problem. The problem of the multitude of Old Testament regulations can be simplified only by starting with the concept of an unrecognized demand which is operative in human life itself and experienced by all men."[79] The "unrecognized demand", or the Law of conscience as it has more customarily been called, reveals itself to be at one with the Mosaic, and this is the generally-understood meaning of Paul's words in Romans ii. 13–15.[80]

It is noticeable in some recent works that there is a return to a more theological view of ethics. C. J. Barker, for example, writes: "No ethics that are not religious can be finally satisfying. . . . They cannot give the final ground of their own precepts, nor answer the questions to which they inevitably give rise."[81] The commandments "are addressed by a personal Being to personal beings", says A. R. Vidler,[82] and God's will confronts men "as a demand."[83] This is a recognition

77. Op. cit., p. 67.
78. It is repeatedly remarked by writers on the Law of God that *tôrâh* is not to be identified with commanding law, but that it stands for the Covenant instructions given by God to His people. In his examination of the Greek words for law, C. H. Dodd gives his opinion that *tôrâh* is so closely represented by *νόμος* that it is almost identical with it. He points out that διδαχή is never used to stand for *tôrâh*, and although in one sense *νόμος* is a misleading translation of *tôrâh* it sheds light on what *tôrâh* became for Hellenistic Judaism. *The Bible and the Greeks*, 1935, p. 33; cf. pp. 25–41. It may be added that perhaps the association was even closer, and in its forms of *mitsvâh*, *chôq* and *mishpât* the *tôrâh* truly was *νόμος*. T. W. Manson reiterates the inadequacy of the translation of the word *tôrâh* by "law" but says that one aspect of God's sufficiency to His people as their king "consists in his being the final authority on matters of right and wrong" and that this authoritative direction is embodied in the *tôrâh*. He contends that although "the idea that underlies the word *Torah* is not primarily the formulation of a series of categorical commands and prohibitions", this may be accepted as "part of its meaning." *Ethics and the Gospel*, pp. 28, 29. The impression gained from many of the discussions of *tôrâh* and *νόμος* is that the concessions made to the customary idea of Law are sufficiently great to regard the theological difference of the words as negligible. The Puritans understood the difference between *tôrâh* and *νόμος* well enough (see chapter III) but did not consider that it detracted from their arguments in the slightest degree.
79. *Creation and Law*, p. 124.
80. Cf. Chapter I, above, and P. Fairbairn, *Law in Scripture*, pp. 405–408.
81. *The Way of Life*, 1946, p. 13.
82. *Christ's Strange Work*, p. 7.
83. Op. cit., p. 24.

that the dimly-perceived "I ought" of natural morality is not displaced by the revelation of God, but is overshadowed by the "Thou shalt" of the Divine imperative.[84] A. L. Williams, who considers "the law of Christ" to be not a series of commands, but subjection to a Person, remarks nevertheless that "of course, in one sense, moral obligation to a Person is the highest Law of all."[85] T. W. Manson likewise points out that in the Old Testament "the last ground of moral obligation is the command of God."[86] He goes on to show that the Jews revered the Law in this manner, and that by the use of the term *kawwānāh* they indicated "the doing of God's commandments just because they are his commandments and with a view to pleasing him."[87] To this extent there was more reverence in the heart of the devout Jew than in the antinomian type of Christian. In opposition to the subjectivism of humanistic ethics, C. H. Dodd writes, "Paul certainly did not mean to say that there is no law for the Christian except his own 'inner light'. . . . It is, indeed, difficult to maintain, in face of the New Testament, the once-popular view that Christianity is a 'religion of the spirit' in a sense which contrasts it with 'religions of authority'. Its basic postulate is the Kingdom of God; and a kingdom implies authority. . . . Clearly, then, it would be a mistake to think that the difference between the 'administration of the written word' and the 'administration of the spirit' is precisely that between objective and subjective ethical standards, or between authority and freedom. . . . The law of the new covenant . . . is aboriginal. It is the law of our creation, and its field of application is as wide as the creation itself."[88] All the while that a subjective or humanistic standard is accepted, there will be inadequate conceptions of the exceeding sinfulness of sin. T. W. Manson expresses this when he writes: "It is this ethic of self-realization which leads to the explicit or implied corollary that wrong-doing is most harmful to the wrong-doer. So

84. Cf. N. H. G. Robinson, *Christ and Conscience*, p. 76. Cf. R. W. Dale who writes, "What conscience requires is the strong support of a Supreme Personal Will, enforcing righteousness; and where the teaching of the Lord Jesus Christ and of the apostles is frankly received this support is given. Men are not left to order their life according to an ideal law, the ideal law is expressed and asserted in the Will of the Personal God; and to keep the law men have to obey Him." "The Old Antinomianism and the New", op. cit., p. 16.
85. *Galatians*, 1910, p. 131.
86. *Ethics and the Gospel*, p. 19; cf. H. Schultz, *Old Testament Theology*, I. 214; W. S. Bruce, *The Ethics of the Old Testament*, 1909, pp. 24, 25.
87. Op. cit., p. 43. G. F. Moore, in *Judaism in the First Centuries of the Christian Era*, 1927, Vol. II. p. 223, says that the principle of *kawwānāh* may be concisely formulated as "Commandments demand intention". On the principle of *kawwānāh*, "the mere doing of a thing that is commanded in the law is not the fulfilment of the commandment; to make it such it is necessary that in the act a man should have in mind that it is a commandment and mean to fulfil it for that reason."
88. *Gospel and Law*, pp. 70, 71, 79.

we get in many quarters a general attitude that forgets the wrongs done to the victims of crime . . . in concern for the psychological health of the criminal and enthusiasm for reforming him. The Prodigal does not say, 'I am the victim of a psychological upset'; he says, 'I have sinned *against heaven* (i.e. God) and in thy sight' (Luke 15. 21)".[89]

All this recent work gives welcome support to the Puritan view of the Law of God and shows, once more, how valid a conception it is. In "An Inquiry into the Meaning of Law in the Thought of John Calvin", R. A. Gessert points out that Calvin observes the implications for Law of such concepts as *aequitas* and *jus* but is then driven to remark, "One does not have to read far in Calvin, however, to discover that it is finally *legislator* (Lawgiver) that gives law its character as law".[90] The concern of the Puritans for moral Law was thus the direct descendant of the thought of the great reformer, and their conception of it was theological through and through.

D. ITS SOTERIOLOGICAL INTEREST

The Puritans were not mere revivers of Law but, as evangelists and pastors, their advocacy of it was soteriological. They recognized that the Law was the standard by which God would judge the world and condemn the ungodly, but they also perceived its saving use as it slew men's self-confidence, revealed their guilt and pollution, and drove them to Christ. They found their way through the paradox of the Law in its simultaneous condemnation of sin and provocation to it, and they discovered that only by obedience to the Law was the believer truly free from it. They learned that the grace that led them from Law-keeping for justification led them to Law-keeping in sanctification. They were occupied with obedience to the Law as the way of the believing man and with the fulfilment of the Law as the end for which he was saved. The Law of God thus connoted for the Puritan nothing but blessedness and delight: it belonged to the doctrine of salvation.

In their belief in the soteriological purpose of the Law the Puritans are in harmony with later Biblical scholarship. This is clearly expressed by such Old Testament scholars as O. F. Oehler,[91] H. Schultz,[92] A. B. Davidson,[93] W. S. Bruce[94] and others. T. W. Manson refers

89. *Ethics and the Gospel*, p. 64 (italics his).
90. "The Integrity of Faith", in *SJT*, XIII. p. 248, with reference to Calvin, *Inst.* II. viii. 6.
91. *Theology of the Old Testament*, I. 254 f.; 266.
92. *Old Testament Theology*, II. 36–39.
93. *The Theology of the Old Testament*, pp. 280, 281.
94. *The Ethics of the Old Testament*, pp. 26–27.

to the contexts of grace in which the Decalogue is set, both in Exodus and in Deuteronomy, and says that "this setting of God's requirements in the framework of God's gifts is a phenomenon that constantly recurs in the Bible."[95] St Paul's views are well argued by A. B. Bruce in his chapter on "The Law" in *St Paul's conception of Christianity*,[96] and H. A. A. Kennedy rather naively says that "the apostle by the sheer force of his spiritual sensibility anticipates the discovery of modern investigation that legalism was not the essential foundation of Old Testament religion."[97] C. Hodge speaks of the "evangelical character which unquestionably belongs to the Mosaic covenant."[98] G. Wingren refers to the "sharpening" of the demands of the Law by Jesus, which "is the reverse side of grace and forgiveness"[99] and contends that "the law, in exercising its function, is not at strife with the *kerygma* but in its service."[100] It is thus the function of the Law "to fix upon us the bondage of a salutary despair"[101] and so to serve the ends of grace. This is what the Puritans meant by the "Spirit of bondage",[102] and their belief in this respect was perfectly expressed by the later hymn-writer, Joseph Hart, when he wrote:

> What comfort can a Saviour bring
> To those who never felt their woe?
> A sinner is a sacred thing,
> The Holy Ghost hath made him so.[103]

The soteriological significance of the Law, however, is not limited to its power of conviction of sin, but manifests itself in the redeemed life of sanctification. The believer's life is a life in the Law, and he thereby renders to God the homage of obedient love.[104]

In the theological confusion of the seventeenth century, the Puritans found themselves opposing the Antinomians on the one hand and the Neonomians on the other. Both these parties, however. were moved by the same praiseworthy desire to state the Christian doctrine of sanctification in a way that would preserve it from abuse. The

95. *Ethics and the Gospel*, p. 20.
96. See pp. 295, 303, 305; cf. J. S. Stewart, *A Man in Christ*, p. 115.
97. *The Theology of the Epistles*, p. 45.
98. *Systematic Theology*, II. 375; see also E. F. Kevan, *The Law of God in Christian Experience*, 1955, pp. 45–61.
99. *Creation and Law*, p. 43; cf. 59n.
100. *The Living Word*, p. 139.
101. A. R. Vidler, *Christ's Strange Work*, p. 42.
102. See above, chapter II.
103. Joseph Hart (1712–68) was minister at the Independent Chapel, Jewin Street, London. Julian says that "at one time his hymns were widely used, especially by Calvinistic Nonconformists".
104. Cf. a valuable introductory chapter in R. W. Dale, *The Ten Commandments*, 1872, pp. 1–20 and an equally important chapter "On Obeying Christ" in his volume, *Laws of Christ for Common Life*, 1911, pp. 273–88.

former desired to secure it against legalism and the latter against libertinism. The Puritans resisted both these extremes and expounded the truth of sanctification in terms of the paradox of active-passivity, or a working out in active godliness of that which had been worked in by the renewing and enabling grace of God.[105] They taught that in the work of sanctification the believer was neither self-indulgently-passive nor self-sufficiently-active.

The Puritans held that Christian liberty freed the believer, not *from* the Law, but *for* the Law;[106] so that although he is no longer "under" the Law, he is, nevertheless, still "in" the Law.[107] This, they taught, was freedom itself.[108] The Puritans believed that this freedom in the Law—a freedom dependent on the Law—was effected by the Holy Spirit who applied the saving merits of Christ's death to the believer and then wrote the Law within his heart. Love for the Law thus gave power to keep it.

An unawareness of the gracious ability of the Holy Spirit within the believer has led many to a state of spiritual despair. Walter Marshal says,

> Many that are seriously devout, take a great deal of Pains to mortifie their corrupted Nature, and beget an holy Frame of Heart in themselves, by striving earnestly to master their sinful Lusts, and by pressing vehemently upon their Hearts many Motives to Godliness, labouring importunately to squeeze good Qualifications out of them, as Oyl out of a Flint. They account that tho' they be justified by a Righteousness wrought out by Christ, yet they must be sanctified by a Holiness wrought out by themselves. And tho' out of Humility they are willing to call it infused Grace, yet they think they must get the Infusion of it by the same manner of working, as if it were wholly acquired by their Endeavours.[109]

The Puritan doctrine, therefore, takes note of the gracious ability that God gives[110] and looks for the manifestation of that grace in the liberty of obedience which is the true life and heritage of the Christian.

105. This is not in the least to be identified with the scholastic conception of a materialistic infusion of grace.
106. A. S. P. Woodhouse, *Puritanism and Liberty*, Introduction, pp. 67, 68.
107. There is no fundamental opposition between Law and Gospel. What theoretical opposition there appears to be, says R. A. Gessert, arises from the fact that "we apprehend them under the distortions of existence", "The Integrity of Faith", *SJT*, p. 259.
108. Cf. Calvin, *Inst.* III. xix. 1.
109. *Sanctification*, pp. 42–43. What is said here in deprecation of "Holiness wrought out by themselves" is no denial of the believer's true activity in salvation, but is to be understood in the light of the later expression, "wholly acquired".
110. See a stimulating discussion on the paradox of ability and inability in W. P. Du Bose, *The Gospel according to Saint Paul*, 1907, p. 190.

The Law is "of unspeakable use", says John Wesley, "in deriving strength from our Head into His living members, whereby He empowers them to do what His law commands; and . . . in confirming our hope of whatsoever it commands and we have not yet attained."[111]

It is possible that in the doctrine of gracious ability there may be some bridge of thought between the concept of an outward authoritative Law and the sense of liberty which every obedient believer experiences. It has been shown above[112] that the Puritans taught a spontaneity in Law-keeping, so that the works of the Law come from the believer as fruit from a tree.[113] The Puritans would readily have concurred with Karl Barth that to the regenerate the Law is no longer "external and heteronomous law"[114] and with P. T. Forsyth who, in 1905, wrote, "Theonomy is not heteronomy. He, our law, becomes also our life".[115] For the true child of God there is no such alternative as duty or devotion: he is devoted to duty, and in this he is saved.

The Grace of Law

As a summary of what has been presented in this treatise it is appropriate to assert that the Puritans taught the exquisite doctrine of the Grace of Law. They took it into their lives and were ennobled by it. That it brought a seriousness into life no one can deny, but it was a seriousness with a glory. J. Marlowe cynically remarks, "Ultimately the Puritan was faced with the alternatives of apostacy, hypocrisy or sainthood".[116] He was possibly nearer the truth than he knew, but the imperishable glory of the Puritans is that most of them chose to be saints.

111. *Christian Theology*, p. 176.
112. Chapter VII.
113. Galatians v. 22, 23.
114. *Romans*, p. 297.
115. Article, "The Evangelical Churches and the Higher Criticism", *The Contemporary Review*, LXXXVIII, 1905, p. 578.
116. *The Puritan Tradition in English Life*, p. 135.

SELECT BIBLIOGRAPHY

I. PRIMARY SOURCES

The bracketed note following an entry, or after a series of titles, indicates the edition used, where the date of this is later than that of the work as originally published.

A, B, C, or A Catechisme for Yong Children appoynted by act of the Church and Councell of Scotland, 1641 (Printed in A. F. Mitchell, *Catechisms of the Second Reformation*, 1886).

ADAMS, Thomas: *The Fatal Banquet: Breaking up of the Faith*, London, 1614.

The Sacrifice of Thankfulness, London, 1616.

(The above pieces are quoted from *The Works of Thomas Adams*, ed. T. Smith, Edinburgh, 1861).

AIRAY, Henry: *Lectures upon the whole Epistle of St Paul to the Philippians*, London, 1618.

ALLEN, Richard: *An Antidote against Heresy*, London, 1648.

ALLEN, William: *A Discourse on the Nature, Ends and Difference of the two Covenants*, London, 1673. This work was published anonymously.

The Christians Justification stated, London, 1678.

AMBROSE, Isaac: *Prima, Media, & Ultima: The First, Middle, and Last Things; in Three Treatises*, London, 1650 (1654, 1657).

AMES, William: *Conscience, with the Power and Cases thereof*, London, 1639 (1643).

An Analyticall Exposition of both the Epistles of the Apostle Peter, London, 1641.

The Marrow of Sacred Divinity, Drawne out of the holy Scriptures, and ... brought into Method, London, 1641 (1643).

AQUINAS, Thomas: *Summa Theologica*, "Treatise on Law", Eng. trans., Dominican Fathers, London, 1911–1925.

BABINGTON, Gervase: *A very fruitfull Exposition of the Commaundements*, London, 1583.

BALL, John: *A Short Catechism Contayning the Principles of Religion*, London, 1642 (1653).

A Treatise of the Covenant of Grace: wherein The graduall breakings out of Gospel-grace from Adam to Christ are clearly discovered, London, 1645.

A Short Treatise Containing all the Principal Grounds of Christian Religion, London, 1629 (1670).

A Treatise of Faith, London, 1630 (1637).

The Power of Godliness, both doctrinally, and practically handled, London, 1657.

BARRET, John: *Good Will towards Men, or a Treatise of the Covenants*, Nottingham, 1675. "To the Reader", is signed by J. B., known to be John Barret.

BAXTER, Richard: *Aphorismes of Justification, with their Explication annexed*, London, 1649.

A Call to the Unconverted to Turn and Live, Kederminster, 1658.

Catholick Theologie: Plain, Pure, Peaceable: for Pacification of the Dogmatical Word-Warriours, London, 1675.

A Christian Directory, or, A Summ of Practical Theologie, and Cases of Conscience, London, 1673.

Directions and Perswasions to a Sound Conversion, Kederminster, 1658.

Directions for Weak distempered Christians, to Grow up to a confirmed State of Grace and *The Character of a Sound, Confirmed Christian*, London, 1669.

An End of Doctrinal Controversies Which have Lately Troubled the Churches by Reconciling Explication, without much Disputing, London, 1691.

Of Justification: Four Disputations Clearing and amicably Defending the Truth, London, 1658.

The Life of Faith, London, 1670.

An Apology for the Nonconformists Ministry, London, 1681.

The Poor Man's Family Book, London, 1674.

Reliquiae Baxterianae: or, Mr. Richard Baxter's Narrative of the most Memorable Passages of his Life and Times, ed. M. Sylvester, London, 1696.

Richard Baxter's Apology against the Modest Exceptions of Mr. T. Blake ... and an Admonition of Mr W. Eyre of Salisbury, London, 1654.

Rich: Baxter's Confesssion (sic) of his Faith, Especially concerning the Interest of Repentance and sincere Obedience to Christ, in our Justification & Salvation, London, 1655.

The Scripture Gospel Defended, London, 1690.

Universal Redemption of Mankind, by the Lord Jesus Christ, London, 1694.

The Unreasonableness of Infidelity, London, 1655.

BAYNES, Paul: *Briefe Directions unto a godly Life*, London, 1618.

An Entire Commentary upon the Whole Epistle of the Apostle Paul to the Ephesians, London, 1643.

BEDFORD, Thomas: *An Examination of the chief Points of Antinomianism, Collected out of some Lectures lately preached*, London, 1646.

BLAKE, Thomas: *Vindiciae Foederis, or a Treatise of the Covenant of God entered with man-kinde, in the several Kindes and Degrees of it*, London, 1653.

BOLTON, Robert: *Instructions for a Right Comforting Afflicted Consciences*, London, 1631 (1640).

Two Sermons Preached at Northampton at two several Assises there, London, 1635 (1639).

Some Generall Directions for a Comfortable Walking with God, London, 1625.

Helpes to Humiliation, Oxford, 1631 (1640).
A Three-fold Treatise: Containing the Saints Sure and Perpetuall Guide. Selfe-enriching Examination. Soule-fatting Fasting, London, 1634.
A Discourse about the State of True Happinesse, London, 1611 (1612).

BOLTON, Samuel: *Ἁμαρτωλὸς ἁμαρτία, or the Sinfulness of Sin: held forth in a sermon preached ... at Margarets Westminster*, London, 1646 (1657).
The True Bounds of Christian Freedome, London, 1645 (1656).

BROOKS, Thomas: *Apples of Gold for Young Men and Women*, and, *A Crown of Glory for Old Men and Women*, London, 1657.
A Cabinet of Choice Jewels, London, 1669.
The Crown and Glory of Christianity, London, 1662.
The Golden Key to Open Hidden Treasures, London, 1675.
Heaven on Earth, London, 1654.
Paradise Opened, London, 1675.
(The above pieces are quoted from *The Works of Thomas Brooks*, ed. A. B. Grosart, Edinburgh, 1866, 1867).

BUNYAN, John: *Grace Abounding to the Chief of Sinners*, London, 1666 (1688).
The Pilgrim's Progress from This World, to That which is to come, London, 1678.

BURGESS, Anthony: *The True Doctrine of Justification*, London, 1648, 1654 (1655, 1654).
Spiritual Refining: Part I, A Treatise of Grace and Assurance. Part II, A Treatise of Sinne, London, 1652, 1654.
Vindiciae Legis, London, 1646.

BURROUGHS, Jeremiah: *A Treatise of the Evil of Evils, or the Exceeding Sinfulness of Sin*, London, 1654.
Gospel-Conversation, London, 1648.
The Saints Treasury, London, 1654.

BURTON, Henry: *The Law and the Gospell reconciled. A Treatise shewing the perpetuall use of the Morall Law under the Gospell to beleevers*, London, 1631.

BYFIELD, Nicholas: *The Principles, or The Patterne of wholsome words*, London, 1618 (1636).

BYFIELD, Richard: *The Gospels Glory, without prejudice to the Law*, London, 1659.
The Doctrine of the Sabbath Vindicated, London, 1631.
Temple Defilers Defiled, London, 1645.

CALVIN, John: *Institutes of the Christian Religion*, 1559 (Eng. trans., J. Allen, 1813, reprinted Philadelphia, 1936).
Commentary on the Epistle to the Romans, 1539 (Eng. trans., J. Owen, 1849, reprinted Grand Rapids, 1947).

CARYL, Joseph: *The Nature and Principles of Love, As the End of the Commandment*, London, 1673.

CHARNOCK, Stephen: *Discourse on the existence and attributes of God*, London, 1682.
A Discourse of Conviction of Sin, London, 1684.
A Discourse of the Efficient of Regeneration, London, 1683.
Man's Enmity to God, London, 1699.
A Discourse of the Nature of Regeneration, London, 1683.
The Necessity of Regeneration, London, 1683.
(The above pieces are quoted from *The Works of Stephen Charnock*, ed. T. Smith, Edinburgh, 1864–6).

CHAUNCY, Isaac: *Alexipharmacon. A Fresh Antidote against Neonomian Bane and Poyson to the Protestant Religion*, London, 1700.
Neonomianism Unmask'd. Or the Ancient Gospel pleaded, Against the Other, called A New Law or Gospel, London, 1692, 1693.
A Rejoynder to Mr Daniel Williams His Reply to the First Part of Neomianism (sic) Unmaskt, London, 1693.

CLARKSON, David: *Of Faith*, London, 1696.
Justification by the Righteousness of Christ, London, 1675.
The Lord Rules over all, London, 1696.
Of Repentance, London, 1696.
(The above pieces are quoted from *The Works of David Clarkson*, ed. T. Smith, Edinburgh, 1864, 1865).

CLEAVER, Robert: (with John Dod) *A Plaine and familiar Exposition of the Ten Commaundements*, London, 1603, (1604).

COLE, Thomas: *A Discourse of Regeneration, Faith and Repentance*, London, 1689.

The Confession of Faith: agreed upon by the Assembly of Divines at Westminster, London, 1647.

Covenant of Grace, not Absolute, but Conditional, Modestly Asserted, London, 1692.

COX, Nehemiah: *A Discourse of the Covenants that God made with Men before the Law*, London, 1681.

CRADOCK, Walter: *Divine Drops Distilled*, London, 1650.
Gospel-Holinesse, or The saving sight of God, London, 1651.
Gospel-Libertie, London, 1648.

CRANDON, John: *Mr Baxters Aphorisms exorized and Anthorized*, London, 1654.

CRISP, Tobias: *Christ Alone Exalted*, London, 1643 (ed. S. Crisp, 1690).

Crispianism Unmask'd: or, a Discovery of the several Erroneous Assertions ... in Dr Crisp's Sermons, London, 1693. Attributed to John Edwards.

CROOKE, Samuel: *The Guide unto True Blessednesse*, London, 1613 (1614).

CULVERWEL, Nathanael: *An Elegant and Learned Discourse of the Light of Nature*, London, 1652 (1654).

Declaration against the Antinomians and their Doctrine of Liberty, London, 1644.

DENNE, Henry: *A Conference Between a Sick Man, and a Minister*, London, 1643.

Grace, Mercy, and Peace, containing 1. *Gods Reconciliation to Man.* 2. *Mans Reconciliation to God*, London, 1640.

Antichrist unmasked in two Treatises ... The Second, The Man of Sinne discovered in Doctrine, London, 1645.

DENT, Arthur: *The Plaine Mans Path-way to Heaven*, London, 1601.

DICKSON, David: see *Truths Victory over Error.*

Discourse concerning Puritans, London, 1641. Ambiguously attributed in *Wing* to John Ley and to Henry Parker.

DOD, John (with Robert Cleaver): *A Plaine and familiar Exposition of the Ten Commaundements*, London, 1603 (1604).

DOWNAME, George: *The Christian's Freedom*, Oxford, 1635.

The Covenant of Grace, Dublin, 1631.

An Abstract of the Duties Commanded ... in the Law of God, London, 1620 (1635).

A Treatise of Justification, London, 1633.

DOWNAME, John: *A Guide to Godlynesse, Or a Treatise of a Christian Life shewing the duties wherein it consisteth*, London, 1622.

DURHAM, James: *The Law Unsealed: Or, A Practical Exposition of the Ten Commandments*, Edinburgh, 1676 (1703).

EATON, John: *The Discovery of the most dangerous Dead Faith* and *Abrahams Steps of Faith*, London, 1642.

The Honey-combe of Free Justification by Christ Alone, London, 1642.

EDWARDS, John: *A Free Discourse concerning Truth and Error*, London, 1701.

EDWARDS, Thomas (1599–1647): *Gangraena: or a Catalogue and Discovery of many of the Errours, Heresies, Blasphemies and pernicious Practices of the Sectaries of this time*, London, 1646.

EDWARDS, Thomas (1649–1700): *Baxterianism Barefac'd Drawn from literal Transcript of Mr Baxter's*, London, 1699.

A Short Review of ... Crispianism unmask'd, London, 1693.

ELTON, Edward: *Gods Holy Minde Touching Matters Morall: ... also Christs holy Minde touching Prayer*, London, 1625 (1647, 1648).

Three Excellent and Pious Treatises, viz. 1. *The Complaint of a Sanctifyed Sinner.* 2. *The Triumph of A true Christian.* 3. *The Great Mystery of Godlinesse Opened*, London, 1618, 1623, 1653 (1653).

EYRE, William: *Vindiciae Justificationis Gratuitae: ... The Free Justification of a Sinner*, London, 1654.

F., E.: *The Marrow of Modern Divinity*, London, 1645 (ed. C. G. M'Crie, 1902).

FIRMIN, Giles: *The Real Christian, Or a Treatise of Effectual Calling*, London, 1670.

FLAVEL, John: *Πλανηλογία, A Succinct and Seasonable Discourse of the Occasions, ... and Remedies of Mental Errors*, London, 1691.

The Method of Grace, in the Holy Spirit's applying to the souls of men the eternal redemption contrived by the Father, and accomplished by the Son, London, 1681 (1731).

The Reasonableness of Personal Reformation and the Necessity of Conversion, London, 1691.

Vindiciae Legis & Foederis, London, 1690.

FORD, Simon: *The Spirit of Bondage and Adoption*, London, 1655.

GATAKER, Thomas: *An Antidote against errour concerning Justification*, London, 1670.

Antinomianism Discovered and Confuted, London, 1652.

The Christian Mans Care, London, 1624.

God's Eye on his Israel, London, 1645.

A Mistake or Misconstruction removed, London, 1646.

Shadows without substance, London, 1646.

GEREE, John: *The Character of an old English Puritane, or Non-Conformist*, London, 1646.

GEREE, Stephen: *A Plaine Confutation of Diverse dangerous positions in ... Dr Crispe's 14 Sermons entitled Christ alone Exalted*, London, 1644.

GILLESPIE, George: *Wholsome Severity reconciled with Christian Liberty*, London, 1645.

GOODWIN, John: *Imputatio Fidei. Or A Treatise of Justification*, London, 1642.

GOODWIN, Thomas: *Aggravation of Sin*, London, 1637.

A Child of Light walking in Darkness, London, 1636.

Christ Set Forth, London, 1642.

The Trial of a Christian's Growth, London, 1641.

Of the Creatures, and the Condition of their State by Creation, London, 1682.

Exposition of Ephesians, London, 1681.

A Discourse of the Glory of the Gospel, London, 1703.

Of Gospel Holiness in the Heart and Life, London, 1703.

The Heart of Christ in Heaven to Sinners on Earth, London, 1642.

The Objects and Acts of Justifying Faith, London, 1697.

Of Christ the Mediator, London, 1692.

Reconciliation of all the People of God ... by Christ's Death, London, 1703.

The Folly of Relapsing after Peace Spoken, London, 1641.

An Unregenerate Man's Guiltiness before God, London, 1692.

The Work of the Holy Ghost in our Salvation, London, 1703.

(The above pieces are quoted from *The Works of Thomas Goodwin*, ed. J. C. Miller, Edinburgh, 1861–1865).

GOODWIN, Thomas (the Younger): *A Discourse of the True Nature of the Gospel: demonstrating That it is no New Law*, London, 1695.

GOUGE, Thomas: *The Principles of Christian Religion explained to the capacity of the meanest*, London, 1645.

GRAILE, John: *A Modest Vindication of the Doctrine of Conditions in the Covenant of Grace*, London, 1655.

GREENHAM, Richard: *Of Conscience*, London, 1599.
Divine Aphorismes, London, 1599.
Faith, Justification, and Feeling, London, 1599.
Of good workes and our obedience to the word, London, 1599.
Grave Counsels, London, 1599.
The Markes of a Righteous Man, London, 1599.
Notes of Salvation, London, 1599.
Of Quenching the Spirit, London, 1599.
A Treatise of the Sabboth, London, 1599.
A Short Catechisme, London, 1599.
A sweete comfort for an afflicted Conscience, London, 1599.
(The above pieces are quoted from *The Workes of the Reverend and Faithfull Servant of Jesus Christ, M. Richard Greenham*, ed. H(enry) H(olland), London, 1601).

GREW, Obadiah: *A Sinner's Justification*, London, 1670.

HINDE, William: *The Office and Use of the Morall Law of God in the dayes of the Gospell*, London, 1622.

HOBSON, Paul: *Practicall Divinity*, London, 1646.

HOOKER, Richard: *Of the Laws of Ecclesiastical Polity*, Oxford, 1592–1597 (ed. Keble, 1865).

HOOKER, Thomas: *The Soules Preparation for Christ*, London, 1632.

HOPKINS, Ezekiel: *A Discourse of the Nature, Corruption and Renewing of the Conscience*, London, 1701.
Sermon on Galatians III. 10, London, 1701.
Sermon on John VII. 19, London, 1701.
A Practical Exposition on the Lord's Prayer, London, 1692.
The Great Duty of Mortification, London, 1701.
Practical Christianity, London, 1701.
Exposition of the Ten Commandments, London, 1692.
True Happiness, London, 1701.

HOWE, John: *The Blessedness of the Righteous, discoursed from Psalm xvii. 15*, London, 1668.
Delighting in God, London, 1674.
The Living Temple, London, 1675.
Man's Creation, in an Holy but Mutable State, London, 1660.
(The above pieces are quoted from *The Works of John Howe*, ed. J. P. Hewlett, London, 1848).

HUGHES, George: *A Dry Rod Blooming, and fruit bearing; or a Treatise on the Pain, Gain, and Use of Chastenings*, London, 1644.

JACOMB, Thomas: *Severall Sermons Preach'd on the whole eighth chapter of the Epistle to the Romans*, London, 1672.

JESSOP, Constantine: "Concerning the Nature of the Covenant of Grace ... clearing Dr Twisse from Antinomianism". Preface to John Graile, *Conditions in the Covenant of Grace*, London, 1655.

LANCASTER, Robert: Preface to Tobias Crisp, *Christ alone Exalted*, London, 1690.
Vindiciae Evangelii: Or, a Vindication of the Gospel, with the Establishment of the Law, London, 1694.

The Larger Catechism, agreed upon by the Assembly of Divines at Westminster, London, 1647.

LEY, John: see *Discourse concerning Puritans.*

Liberty of Conscience ... Proved to be The Just Right, ... of True Natural, and Christian Religion, London, 1681.

LIGHTFOOTE, John: *Erubhin: or Miscellanies Christian and Judaicall and others*, London, 1629.

LUTHER, Martin: *A Commentary on St Paul's Epistle to the Galatians*, 1535 (Eng. trans., P. S. Watson, London, 1953).

MANTON, Thomas: *Sermon on Ephesians II. 10*, London, 1678.
The Epistle of James, London, 1651.
A Practical Exposition of the Lord's Prayer, London, 1684.
Sermon on Mark IX. 49, London, 1678.
Sermon on Psalm XXXII. 1, 2, London, 1678.
Sermons on the Second Chapter of the Second Epistle to the Thessalonians, London, 1679.
(The above pieces are quoted from *The Works of Thomas Manton*, ed. T. Smith, London, 1870, 1871).
The Hundred and Nineteenth Psalm, London, 1681–1701 (ed. W. Bates, 1845).

MARSHAL, Walter: *Gospel Mystery of Sanctification*, London, 1692 (1714).

OWEN, John: *Of Communion with God*, Oxford, 1657.
A Treatise of the Dominion of Sin and Grace, London, 1688.
Gospel Grounds and Evidences of the Faith of God's Elect, London, 1695.
Vindiciae Evangelicae: or the Mystery of the Gospel vindicated, Oxford, 1655.
Πνευματολογία, or, a discourse concerning the Holy Spirit, London, 1674.
The Nature, Power, Deceit, and Prevalency of the Remainders of Indwelling Sin in Believers, London, 1668.
The Doctrine of Justification by Faith, through the imputation of the Righteousness of Christ, London, 1677.
Of the Mortification of Sin in Believers, Oxford, 1656.
The Principles of the Doctrine of Christ, London, 1645.
(The above pieces are quoted from *The Works of John Owen*, ed. W. H. Goold, London, 1850–3).

PAGITT, Ephraim: *Heresiography: or, a description of the Heretickes and Sectaries of these latter times*, London, 1645.

PARKER, Henry: see *Discourse concerning Puritans.*

PEMBLE, William: *Vindiciae Fidei, or A Treatise of Justification by Faith*, Oxford, 1625.

Vindiciae Gratiae, or A plea for Grace, London, 1627.

PERKINS, William: *A Discourse of Conscience*, Cambridge, 1596.

The Creede, Cambridge, 1595.

The Foundation of Christian Religion, gathered into sixe Principles, London, 1590.

A Golden Chaine, or the Description of Theologie, containing the Order of the Causes of Salvation and Damnation according to Gods Word, London, 1591.

Reformed Catholike, Cambridge, 1598.

A Treatise tending unto a declaration, whether a man be in the estate of damnation, or in the estate of grace, London, 1588.

Two Treatises: 1. Of the nature and practice of Repentance. 2. Of the combat of the flesh and spirit, Cambridge, 1593.

(The above pieces are quoted from the edition of *The Works of William Perkins* published in 1603, after his death, by J. Legat of Cambridge). *A Commentarie, or Exposition upon the Five First Chapters of the Epistle to the Galatians*, Cambridge, 1604.

POWELL, Vavasor: *Christ and Moses Excellency: or, Sin and Sinai's Glory: being a triplex treatise, distinguishing and explaining the two Covenants, or the Gospel and the Law*, London, 1650.

PRESTON, John: *The Breast-Plate of Faith and Love*, London, 1630 (1651).

The Law out lawed, or, The Charter of the Gospell, Edinburgh, 1631.

The New Covenant, or the Saints Portion, London, 1629.

Sermons: Exact Walking, London, 1631.

Sermons: New Life, London, 1631.

REYNOLDS, Edward: *Three Treatises of The Vanity of the Creature. The Sinfulnesse of Sinne. The Life of Christ*, London, 1631 (1634).

ROBERTS, Francis: *Of God's Covenants ... The Mysterie and Marrow of the Bible: viz. Gods-Covenants with man*, London, 1657.

ROGERS, Ezekiel: *The Chiefe Grounds of Christian Religion set down by way of catechising*, London, 1642.

ROGERS, John: *The Doctrine of Faith*, London, 1627 (1629).

ROGERS, Richard: *Seven treatises containing such direction as is gathered out of the Holie Scriptures, leading and guiding to true happiness*, London, 1603.

ROLLE, Samuel: *Justification Justified*, London, 1674.

Rules for Self-Examination, London, 1686.

RUTHERFORD, Samuel: *Ane Catachisme containing the Soume of Christian Religion*, (A. F. Mitchell, *Catechisms*, 1886).

The Covenant of Life Opened: Or, a Treatise of the Covenant of Grace, Edinburgh, 1655.

A Survey of the Spirituall Antichrist, Part I and Part II, London, 1648.

The Tryal and Triumph of Faith, London, 1645.

SALTMARSH, John: *Free-Grace: or, the Flowings of Christs Blood freely to Sinners*, London, 1645 (1649).

Reasons for Unitie, Peace, and Love. With an Answer (Called Shadows flying away) to a Book of Mr. Gataker ... intituled, A Mistake, London, 1646.

Sparkles of Glory, or, Some Beams of the Morning Star, London, 1647.

SCUDDER, Henry: *The Christians Daily Walke in holy Securitie and Peace*, London, 1628 (1635).

SEDGWICK, John: *Antinomianisme Anatomized. Or, A Glasse for the Lawless: Who deny the Ruling use of the Morall Law unto Christians under the Gospel*, London, 1643.

SEDGWICK, Obadiah: *The Anatomy of Secret Sins*, London, 1660.

SHEPARD, Thomas: *The Parable of the Ten Virgins*, London, 1660.

The Shorter Catechism, agreed upon by the Assembly of Divines at Westminster, London, 1648.

SIBBES, Richard: *Bowels Opened, or a discovery of the ... Communion betwixt Christ and the Church*, London, 1639.

The Bruised Reed and Smoking Flax, London, 1630.

The Christian Work, London, 1639.

The Church's Complaint and Confidence, London, 1639.

The Demand of a Good Conscience, London, 1640.

The Excellency of the Gospel above the Law, London, 1639.

The Faithful Covenanter, London, 1640.

The Hidden Life, London, 1639.

Judgment's Reason, London, 1629.

Divine Meditations and Holy Contemplations, London, 1638.

Exposition of Philippians III, London, 1639.

Yea and Amen: Or, Precious Promises, London, 1638.

Spiritual Jubilee, London, 1638.

The Witness of Salvation, London, 1629.

(The above pieces are quoted from *The Works of Richard Sibbes*, ed. A. B. Grosart, Edinburgh, 1862–4).

SINCLAIR, George: see *Truths Victory over Error*.

SLATER, Samuel: *The Two Covenants from Sinai and Sion, drawn up Catechetically, and plainly*, London, 1644.

STRONG, William: *A discourse of the two covenants: Wherein the nature, differences, and effects of the covenant of works and of grace are ... discussed*, London, 1678.

TAYLOR, Thomas: *A threefold Alphabet of Rules concerning Christian Practice*, London, 1688.
Circumspect Walking: Describing the severall Rules, as so many severall Steps in the way of Wisedome, London, 1631.
The Principles of Christian Practice, London, 1635.
The Progresse of Saints to Full Holinesse, London, 1630.
Regula Vitae, The Rule of the Law under the Gospel, London, 1631 (1635).

TEMPLE, Thomas: "To the Reader", in Simon Ford, *The Spirit of Bondage and Adoption*, London, 1655.

TOWNE, Robert: *The Assertion of Grace*, London, 1644.
A Re-Assertion of Grace, London, 1654.

TRAILL, Robert: *Six Sermons on Important Subjects from Galatians II. 21*, London, 1696.
A Vindication of the Protestant Doctrine concerning Justification ... from the unjust charge of Antinomianism, London, 1692.
On the Lord's Prayer from John XVII. 24, London, 1705.
Sermons concerning the Throne of Grace, London, 1696.
(The above pieces are quoted from *The Works of Robert Traill*, Edinburgh, 1810).

Truths Victory over Error, Edinburgh, 1684. *Wing* attributes this to David Dickson, but it is also attributed to George Sinclair.

TWISSE, William: *A briefe Catecheticall Exposition of Christian Doctrine*, London, 1632 (1645).
Of the Morality of the Fourth Commandement, as still in force to binde Christians, London, 1641.

USSHER, James: *A Body of Divinitie*, London, 1645 (1653).

VENNING, Ralph: *Sin the plague of plagues: or, sinful sin the worst of evils*, London, 1669.

WATSON, Thomas: *A Body of Divinity*, London, 1692 (1958).

WELDE, Thomas: *A Short Story of the Rise, reigne, and ruine of the Antinomians*, London, 1644.

WILLET, Andrew: *Hexapla: That is, A Six-Fold Commentarie upon the most Divine Epistle of the Holy Apostle St. Paul to the Romanes*, London, 1611.

WILLIAMS, Daniel: *A Defence of Gospel Truth, being a Reply to Mr Chauncy*, London, 1693.
Gospel-Truth stated and vindicated: wherein some of Dr Crisp's opinions are considered; and the opposite truths are plainly stated and Confirmed, London, 1692.

WILSON, Thomas: *A Commentarie upon the ... Romanes*, London, 1614 (1653).

WOODBRIDGE, Benjamin: *The Method of Grace in the Justification of Sinners being a Reply to a book ... by Mr W. Eyre*, London, 1656.

WOODWARD, William: *The Lord our Righteousness*, London, 1696.

WYLLIE, Thomas: *Catechism* (A. F. Mitchell, *Catechisms*, 1886).

YATES, John: "To the Reader", in Jeremiah Burroughs, *Evil of Evils*, London, 1654.

II. SECONDARY SOURCES

A. GENERAL WORKS OF REFERENCE

DICTIONARY OF THE APOSTOLIC CHURCH, ed. J. Hastings, Edinburgh, 1915–18 (*DAC*).

DICTIONARY OF DOCTRINAL AND HISTORICAL THEOLOGY, ed. J. H. Blunt, London, 1871 (*DDHT*).

DICTIONARY OF NATIONAL BIOGRAPHY, ed. L. Stephen and S. Lee, London, 1937–8 (*DNB*).

ENCYCLOPAEDIA OF RELIGION AND ETHICS, ed. J. Hastings, London, 1908–26 (*ERE*).

THE NEW SCHAFF-HERZOG ENCYCLOPAEDIA OF RELIGIOUS KNOWLEDGE, ed. S. M. Jackson, London, 1908–12 (*S-H: ERK*).

PROTESTANT DICTIONARY, ed. C. S. S. Carter and G. E. A. Weeks, London, 1933 (*PD*).

B. SELECT WORKS

ALEXANDER, A. B. D: *Christianity and Ethics*, London, 1914.

ALFORD, H: *The Greek Testament*, vol. II, London, 1865.

ALLIS, O. T: *Prophecy and the Church*, Philadelphia, 1945.

ANDERSEN, W: *Law and Gospel*, London, 1961.

ANDERSON, J. N. D: *Law and Grace*, London, 1954.

Articles of Religion, London, 1571.

AULÉN, G: *Church, Law and Society*, Eng. trans., New York, 1948.

BARKER, A: *Milton and the Puritan Dilemma*, Toronto, 1942.

BARKER, C. J: *The Way of Life*, London, 1946.

BARRETT, C. K: *A Commentary on the Epistle to the Romans*, London, 1957.

BARTH, K: *God, Grace and Gospel*, "Gospel and Law", Eng. trans., Edinburgh, 1959.

The Epistle to the Romans, Eng. trans., Oxford, 1933.

BEET, A: *St Paul's Epistle to the Romans*, London, 1887.

BENGEL, J. A: *Gnomon of the New Testament*, vol. III. Eng. trans., Edinburgh, 1857.

BERKHOF, L: *Reformed Dogmatics*, Grand Rapids, 1941.

BLANSHARD, B: *Reason and Goodness*, London, 1961.

BOSTON, T: *A General Account of my Life*, London, 1730 (ed. G. D. Low, 1908).
The Marrow of Modern Divinity, Edinburgh, 1818.

BRANSCOMB, B. H: *Jesus and the Law of Moses*, New York, 1930.

BRIGGS, C. A: *History of the Study of Theology*, London, 1916.

BROOK, B: *The Lives of the Puritans*, London, 1813.

BRUCE, A. B: *St Paul's Conception of Christianity*, Edinburgh, 1894.

BRUCE, W. S: *The Ethics of the Old Testament*, Edinburgh, 1909.

BRUNNER, E: *The Divine Imperative*, Eng. trans., London, 1937.
Justice and the Social Order, Eng. trans., London, 1945.
The Mediator, Eng. trans., London, 1934.

BUCHANAN, J: *The Doctrine of Justification*, Edinburgh, 1867 (1954).

BURKITT, W: *Expository Notes ... on the New Testament*, Vol. II, London, 1700.

BURROWS, M: *An Outline of Biblical Theology*, Philadelphia, 1946.

BUSHNELL, H: *Forgiveness and Law*, London, 1874.

CALAMY, E: *An Historical Account of my own Life*, ed J. T. Rutt, London, 1829.
The Nonconformist's Memorial, 1774 (ed. S. Palmer, 1802).

CAMERON, T: *The Kindly Laws of the Old Testament*, London, 1945.

CARRUTHERS, S. W: *The Everyday Work of the Westminster Assembly*, Philadelphia, 1943.

CAVE, S: *The Christian Way*, London, 1949.
The Doctrines of the Christian Faith, London, 1931.
The Gospel of St Paul, London, 1928.

CHARLES, R. H: *The Decalogue*, Edinburgh, 1923.

COGGAN, F. D: *The New Testament Basis of Moral Theology*, London, 1948.

CRAGG, C. R: *Puritanism in the Period of the Great Persecution, 1660–1688*, Cambridge, 1957.

DAKIN, A: *Calvinism*, London, 1940.

DALBY, J: *The Catholic Conception of the Law of Nature*, London, 1943.

DALE, R. W: *Laws of Christ for Common Life*, London, 1911.
The Ten Commandments, London, 1872.

DARK, S: *The Passing of the Puritan*, London, 1946.

DAVIDSON, A. B: *The Theology of the Old Testament*, Edinburgh, 1904 (1925).

DAVIES, H: *The Worship of the English Puritans*, London, 1948.

DENNEY, J: *The Expositor's Greek Testament*, ed. W. Robertson Nicoll, London, 1917 (Eerdmans edn.).

DEWAR, L: *An Outline of New Testament Ethics*, London, 1949.

DEWAR, L. (with Hudson): *Christian Morals*, London, 1945.

DICKIE, E. P: *The Obedience of a Christian Man*, London, 1944.

DIGGLE, J. W: *The Foundations of Duty*, London, 1913.

DODD, C. H: *The Bible and the Greeks*, London, 1935.
Gospel and Law, Cambridge, 1950.
Natural Law in the Bible, London, 1946.
The Epistle of Paul to the Romans, London, 1932.

DORNER, I. A: *History of Protestant Theology*, Eng. trans., Edinburgh, 1871.

DOWDEN, E: *Puritan and Anglican*, London, 1900.

DREWETT, J: *The Ten Commandments in the 20th Century*, London, 1941.

DU BOSE, W. P: *The Gospel according to St Paul*, London, 1907.

ELLUL, J: *The Theological Foundation of Law*, 1946, Eng. trans., London, 1961.

D'ENTRÈVES, A. P: *Natural Law: An introduction to legal Philosophy*, London, 1951.

ERSKINE, R: *Works*, Glasgow, 1720 (ed. 1778).

EUSDEN, J. D: *Puritans, Lawyers, and Politics in Early Seventeenth Century England*, New Haven, 1958.

FAIRBAIRN, P: *The Revelation of Law in Scripture*, Edinburgh, 1868 (reprinted 1957).

FINDLAY, G. G: *The Expositor's Greek Testament*, ed. W. Robertson Nicoll, London, 1917 (Eerdmans edn.).

FISHER, G. P: *History of Christian Doctrine*, Edinburgh, 1896 (1927).

FLETCHER, J: *Works*, London, 1771–5 (ed. 1844).

FORBES, J: *The Epistle to the Romans*, London, 1868.

FOX, George: *Journal*, London, 1694 (1902).

FOX, George, and NAILOR, James: *A Word from the Lord*, London, 1654.

FULLER, T: *Church History of Britain*, London, 1655 (ed. 1842).
The History of the Worthies of England, London, 1662 (ed. P. A. Nuttall, 1840).

GARVIE, A. E: *The Epistle of Paul the Apostle to the Romans, Century Bible*, London, 1910.

GIFFORD, E. H: *The Epistle of St Paul to the Romans*, London, 1886.

GILL, J: *The Complete Works of Tobias Crisp*, London, 1832.

GREEN, P: *The Problem of Right Conduct*, London, 1931.

GREGORY, J: *Puritanism in the Old World and in the New*, London, 1895.

GODET, F: *Commentary on St Paul's Epistle to the Romans*, Eng. trans., Edinburgh, 1892.

GORE, C: *Dominant Ideas and Corrective Principles*, London, 1918.

HAGENBACH, K. R: *A History of Christian Doctrines*, Eng. trans., Edinburgh, 1880.

HALDANE, R: *The Epistle to the Romans*, London, 1835.

HALLER, W: *The Rise of Puritanism*, New York, 1938.

HALYBURTON, T: *Memoirs of the Life of the Reverend Mr Thomas Halyburton*, Edinburgh, 1715.

HARRISON, A. W: *Liberal Puritanism*, London, 1935.

HEADLAM, A. C: See Sanday.

HEBERT, A. G: *The Throne of David*, London, 1941.

HENDRY, G. S: *The Westminster Confession for Today*, London, 1960.

HENGSTENBERG, E. W: *Christology of the Old Testament*, 1829, Eng. trans., Edinburgh, 1858.
History of the Kingdom of God under the Old Testament, 1869, Eng. trans., Edinburgh, 1871.

HENRY, C. F. H: *Christian Personal Ethics*, Grand Rapids, 1957.

HENSON, H. H: *Studies in English Religion in the Seventeenth Century*, London, 1903.

HEPPE, H: *Reformed Dogmatics*, 1861, Eng. trans., London, 1950.

HERKLOTS, H. G. G.: *The Ten Commandments and Modern Man*, London, 1958.

HEYWOOD, O: *His Autobiography, Diaries, Anecdote and Event Books*, ed. J. H. Turner, Brighouse, 1882–5.

HILDEBRANDT, F: *Melanchthon: Alien or Ally?* Cambridge, 1946.

HILL, C: *Puritanism and Revolution*, London, 1958.

HODGE, A. A: *The Confession of Faith*, New York, 1869 (1958).
Outlines of Theology, London, 1880.

HODGE, C: *Commentary on the Epistle to the Romans*, New York, 1864 (1875).
Systematic Theology, New York, 1871 (1946).

HUDSON, C. E: See Dewar.

HUEHNS, G: *Antinomianism in English History*, London, 1951.

HUNTER, A. M: *The Teaching of Calvin*, London, 1950.

JACOB, E: *Theology of the Old Testament*, 1955, Eng. trans., London, 1958.

JAMES, W: *The Varieties of Religious Experience*, London, 1902 (1929).

JOHNSON, T. H: (with Miller) *The Puritans*, New York, 1938.

JONES, R. M: *Spiritual Reformers in the 16th & 17th Centuries*, London, 1928.

Journal of the House of Commons, London, 1643.

JOWETT, B: *The Epistle to the Romans*, London, 1859.

KEBLE, J: See Hooker, Richard.

KENNEDY, H. A. A: *The Theology of the Epistles*, London, 1919.

KERR, H. T: *A Compend of Luther's Theology*, Philadelphia, 1943.

KEVAN, E. F: *The Evangelical Doctrine of Law*, London, 1955.
The Law of God in Christian Experience, London, 1955.

KIRK, K. E: *The Threshold of Ethics*, London, 1933.

KNAPPEN, M. M: *Tudor Puritanism*, Chicago, 1939.

KNIGHT, G. A. F: *A Christian Theology of the Old Testament*, London, 1959.

KRAMM, H. H: *The Theology of Martin Luther*, London, 1947.

KURTZ, J. H: *History of the Old Covenant*, 1853, Eng. trans., Edinburgh, 1859.

LEWIS, E: *The Puritans and the Seventh of Romans*, London, 1955.

LILLIE, W: *The Law of Christ*, London, 1956.
Studies in New Testament Ethics, Edinburgh, 1961.

LUTHARDT, C. E: *History of Christian Ethics: Part I. Before the Reformation*, Eng. trans., Edinburgh, 1889.

LYON, T: *Religious Liberty in England, 1603–1639*, Cambridge, 1937.

MACLAGAN, W. G: *The Theological Frontier of Ethics*, London, 1961.

MACLEOD, J: *Scottish Theology*, Edinburgh, 1943.

MACMILLAN, Lord: *Law and other Things*, Cambridge, 1938.

MANSON, T. W: *Ethics and the Gospel*, London, 1960.
The Teaching of Jesus, London, 1931.

MARLOWE, J: *The Puritan Tradition in English Life*, London, 1956.

MARSDEN, J. B: *History of the Early Puritans*, London, 1850.
History of the Later Puritans, London, 1852.

MARSHALL, L. H: *The Challenge of New Testament Ethics*, London, 1946.

MATTHEWS, A. G: *Calamy Revised*, Oxford, 1934.

MCADOO, H. R: *The Structure of Caroline Moral Theology*, London, 1949.

M'COSH, J: *Introduction to Charnock's Works*, Edinburgh, 1864.

MEYER, H. A. W: *Commentary on the New Testament, Romans*, Vol. II, Edinburgh, 1874.

MICKLEM, N: *The Theology of Law*, London, 1943.

MILLER, P: *The New England Mind: The Seventeenth Century*, New York, 1939.

MILLER, P. (with Johnson): *The Puritans*, New York, 1938.

MITCHELL, A. F: *Catechisms of the Second Reformation*, London, 1886.
The Westminster Assembly, London, 1883.
The Westminster Confession of Faith, London, 1867.

MITCHELL, A. F: (with Struthers) *Minutes of the Sessions of the Westminster Assembly of Divines*, Edinburgh, 1874.

MOFFATT, J: *A New Translation of the Bible*, London, 1913.

MOORE, G. F: *Judaism in the First Centuries of the Christian Era*, Cambridge, Mass., 1927 (1958).

MORGAN, G. C: *The Ten Commandments*, London, 1901.

MORTIMER, R. C: *The Elements of Moral Theology*, London, 1947.

MOSSE, G. L: *The Holy Pretence*, Oxford, 1957.

MURRAY, J: *Principles of Conduct*, London, 1957.
The Epistle to the Romans, Grand Rapids, 1959.

MYERS, S: *The Ten Words*, London, 1956.

NAILOR, James: see Fox, George.

NEAL, D: *The History of the Puritans*, London, 1731 (1822).

New English Bible, Oxford and Cambridge, 1961.

NIEBUHR, R: *Christian Realism and Political Problems*, London, 1954.
An Interpretation of Christian Ethics, New York, 1956.

NUTTALL, G. F: *The Holy Spirit in Puritan Faith and Experience*, Oxford, 1946.
Visible Saints, Oxford, 1957.
The Welsh Saints, Cardiff, 1957.

NYGREN, A: *Romans*, Eng. trans., London, 1952.

OEHLER, G. F: *Theology of the Old Testament*, 1873, Eng. trans., Edinburgh, 1892.

PENN, W: "Preface" to *Journal* of George Fox, London, 1694 (1902).

PERRY, R. B: *Puritanism and Democracy*, New York, 1944.

PHYTHIAN-ADAMS, W. J: *The Way of At-one-ment*, London, 1944.

POWICKE, F. J: *The Cambridge Platonists*, London, 1926.

RAMSEY, P: *Basic Christian Ethics*, New York, 1950.

RASHDALL, H: *Conscience and Christ*, London, 1916.

RICHARDSON, A: *Preface to Bible Study*, London, 1943.

ROBERTSON, A. T: *Word Pictures in the New Testament*, New York, 1930.

ROBINSON, N. H. G: *Christ and Conscience*, London, 1956.

ROSS, W. D: *The Right and the Good*, Oxford, 1930.

ROWLEY, H. H: *The Unity of the Bible*, London, 1953.

RUPP, G: *The Righteousness of God*, London, 1953.

SANDAY, W: (with Headlam) *The Epistle to the Romans, International Critical Commentary*, Edinburgh, 1895 (1930).

SANGSTER, W. E: *The Path to Perfection*, London, 1943.

SCHENK, W: *The Concern for Social Justice in the Puritan Revolution*, London, 1948.

SCHNEIDER, H. W: *The Puritan Mind*, London, 1931.

SCHREY, H. H: (with Walz and Whitehouse) *The Biblical Doctrine of Justice and Law*, London, 1955.

SCHULTZ, H: *Old Testament Theology*, 1892, Eng. trans., Edinburgh, 1909.

SCOTT, C. A. A: *Christianity according to St Paul*, Cambridge, 1927.
New Testament Ethics, Cambridge, 1942.

SIMCOX, C. E: *Living the Ten Commandments*, London, 1957.

SNAITH, N. H: *The Distinctive Ideas of the Old Testament*, London, 1944.

STEVENS, G. B: *The Pauline Theology*, London, 1892.
The Theology of the New Testament, Edinburgh, 1899.

STEWART, J. S: *A Man in Christ*, London, 1936.

STOUGHTON, J: *History of Religion in England*, London, 1881.

STRONG, T. B: *Christian Ethics*, London, 1896.

STRUTHERS, J: (with Mitchell) *Minutes of the Sessions of the Westminster Assembly of Divines*, Edinburgh, 1874.

STUART, M: *Epistle to the Romans*, London, 1865.

TASKER, R. V. G: *The Old Testament in the New Testament*, London, 1946.

TEMPLE, W: *Christianity and Social Order*, London, 1942.

THOMAS, W. H. G: *The Principles of Theology*, London, 1930.

TULLOCH, J: *Rational Theology and Christian Philosophy in England in the 17th century*, Edinburgh, 1874.

VIDLER, A. R: *Christ's Strange Work*, London, 1944.

VIDLER, A. R: (with Whitehouse) *Natural Law*, London, 1946.

VISCHER, W: *The Witness of the Old Testament to Christ*, 1936, Eng. trans., London, 1949.

VOS, G: *Biblical Theology*, Grand Rapids, 1948.

VRIEZEN, Th. C: *An Outline of Old Testament Theology*, 1949, Eng. trans., Oxford, 1958.

WAITE, J. C. J: *The Activity of the Holy Spirit within the Old Testament Period*, London, 1961.

WAKEFIELD, G. S: *Puritan Devotion*, London, 1957.

WALZ, H. H: See Schrey.

WARFIELD, B. B: "Introductory Note", in Abraham Kuyper, *The Work of the Holy Spirit*, Grand Rapids, 1946.

WESLEY, J: *Christian Theology*, ed. Thornley Smith, London, 1872.
Explanatory Notes on the New Testament, 1754, ed. C. H. Kelly, London, 1869.

WHALE, J. S: *The Protestant Tradition*, Cambridge, 1955.

WHITEHOUSE, W. A: See Schrey; See Vidler.

WHITING, C. E: *Studies in English Puritanism from the Restoration to Revolution, 1660–88*, London, 1931.

WHYTE, A: *A Commentary on the Shorter Catechism*, Edinburgh, 1883 (1949).

WILLIAMS, A. L: *The Epistle of Paul the Apostle to the Galatians, Cambridge Greek Teastament*, Cambridge, 1910.

WILSON, D: *The Lord's Day*, London, 1827 (reprinted London, 1956).

WINGREN, G: *Creation and Law*, 1958, Eng. trans., Edinburgh, 1961.
The Living Word, 1949, Eng. trans., London, 1960.

WOOD, A: *Athonae Oxonienses*, London, 1691 (ed. P. Bliss, London, 1817).

WOOD, J. D: *The Interpretation of the Bible*, London, 1958.

WOOD, T: *English Casuistical Divinity during the 17th Century*, London, 1952.

WOODHOUSE, A. S. P: *Puritanism and Liberty*, London, 1938 (1951).

C. ARTICLES

BLUNT, J. H: "Antinomianism", *DDHT*.

BROWN, W. A: "Covenant Theology", *ERE* IV.

DALE, R. W: "The Old Antinomianism and the New", *The Congregational Review*, I, London, 1887.

DODD, C. H: *ΕΝΝΟΜΟΣ ΧΡΙΣΤΟΥ*, *Studia Paulina*, ed. J. N. Sevenster and W. C. van Unnik, Haarlem, 1953.

DREWETT, A. J: "Natural Law, in Medieval Catholicism, in Luther and in Calvin", *The Churchman*, LXIX. 3, London, 1955.

FORSYTH, P. T: "The Evangelical Churches and the Higher Criticism", *The Contemporary Review*, LXXXVIII, London, 1905.

GESSERT, R. A: "The Integrity of Faith, An Inquiry into the Meaning of Law in the Thought of John Calvin", *Scottish Journal of Theology*, XIII. 3, Edinburgh, 1960.

HALL, T. C: "Moral Obligation", *ERE*, VIII.

MCINTYRE, D. M: "First Strictures on 'The Marrow of Modern Divinity'", *Evangelical Quarterly*, X. 1, London, 1938.

MILLER, P: "The Marrow of Puritan Divinity", *Publications of the Colonial Society of Massachusetts*, XXXII, Boston, 1935.

MOE, O: "Commandment", *DAC*, I.

NEWMAN, A. H: "Antinomianism and Antinomian Controversies", *S–H: ERK* I.

NUTTALL, G. F: "Law and Liberty in Puritanism", *The Congregational Quarterly*, XXIX, 1, London, 1951.

ORR, J: "Calvinism", *ERE*, III.

PACKER, J. I: "The Puritans as Interpreters of Scripture", *A Goodly Heritage*, London, 1958.

POWICKE, F. J: "Puritanism", *P D*.

STERRETT, J. M: "Antinomianism", *ERE*, I.

TORRANCE, T. F: "Justification: Its Radical Nature and Place in Reformed Doctrine and Life", *Scottish Journal of Theology*, XIII. 3, Edinburgh, 1960.

WILDE, N: "Moral Law", *ERE*, VIII.

WILES, M. F: "St Paul's Conception of Law", *The Churchman*, LXIX, 3, 4, London, 1955.

WOOD, H. G: "Puritanism", *ERE*, X.

D. UNPUBLISHED THESIS

PACKER, J. I: "The Redemption and Restoration of Man in the Thought of Richard Baxter". Thesis for Oxford, D.Phil, 1954 (quoted by permission of the writer).

INDICES

(The page numbers in italics represent secondary references only)

I. AUTHORS AND WORKS

II. TEXTS